LIEUT.-GENERAL SIR FREDERICK SLEIGH ROBERTS, V.C., G.C.B., C.I.E.

MAJOR-GENERAL
SIR FREDERICK S. ROBERTS,

BART., V.C., G.C.B., C.I.E., R.A.

A MEMOIR.

BY

CHARLES RATHBONE LOW, I.N., F.R.G.S.,

AUTHOR OF THE "HISTORY OF THE INDIAN NAVY,"
"MEMOIR OF LORD WOLSELEY,"
"HISTORY OF MARITIME DISCOVERY,"
ETC., ETC.

LONDON:
W. H. ALLEN & CO., 13, WATERLOO PLACE,
PALL MALL, S.W.

1883.

PREFACE.

—o—

THE practice of writing a memoir * of a living public man scarcely stands in need of defence, since it has become of such common practice. Within recent years, the careers of Lord Beaconsfield and Mr. Gladstone, Lord Wolseley and Mr. Bright, have been given to the public during their lifetime; and the only question that arises, when considering the advisability of such a publication,—conceding the necessity of abstaining from publishing matter that would violate any confidences, or unduly cause pain to the living or the representatives of the dead,—would appear to have reference to the public demand in each particular instance.

Such a question as applied to Sir Frederick Roberts must be unhesitatingly given in the affirmative. The military achievements of the gallant officer are great and undeniable, "as a mountain open, palpable." They have received the unstinted acknowledgments not only of all classes of his countrymen, but of the highest professional authorities of the Continent. Count Von Moltke and the German generals expressed their unbounded admiration of the great march from Cabul to Candahar; and the heroic Skobeleff, whose untimely death was such a crushing blow to the army he adorned, as well as to the cause of Panslavism, though the peace of Europe was the gainer by his

---

* It should be stated that this memoir was completed early in 1882, but circumstances delayed its publication. It has been compiled from the Blue Books and official despatches, and from personal reminiscences supplied in conversation and by correspondence with Sir Frederick Roberts, who himself revised the entire work, chapter by chapter.

removal from the scene—was enthusiastic in praise of the military genius displayed by Roberts throughout the two years he was the central figure of the war in Afghanistan. And here we may note a remarkable resemblance in the character and method of these two distinguished soldiers. Both were gifted with impetuous valour, complete knowledge of their profession, a quick intelligence in seizing the features of ground, and adapting the measures at their disposal to the end sought to be attained; an unfailing skill in their tactical combinations, a perfect yet calm self-reliance, and a faculty for inspiring confidence in others.

Roberts's dispositions for the capture of the Peiwar Kotul were most masterly, and his rapid march on Cabul with only 8,000 men, his skill in forcing the enemy's position at Charasia, and his seizure of Cabul were brilliant feats of arms worthy the best days of British prowess. On the abdication of Yakoob Khan he was, for a time, the *de facto* ruler of Afghanistan. His word was law, and he might have said :—

"Hoc sic jubeo; sit pro ratione voluntas."

Severe measures were necessary with the wretches who had murdered a British Envoy, a personage who, in the East as in every clime, is invested with a special sanctity; but no Afghan suffered the extreme penalty who had not been implicated in that deed of shame. An unworthy attempt was made to impute blood-thirstiness to Sir Frederick Roberts, but to those who are conversant with his character, such a charge will scarcely demand refutation. In his humanity and gentleness of character, our hero resembles the "Happy Warrior" sketched by Wordsworth :—

> "He who, though thus endued as with a sense
> And faculty for storm and turbulence,
> Is yet a soul whose master-bias leans
> To homefelt pleasures and to gentle scenes."

Sir Frederick Roberts displayed in a remarkable degree the

self-reliance to which we have referred, during the memorable events that occurred at Cabul in December, 1879, when the cantonment of Sherpur was invested by no less than 100,000 or 120,000 armed men. At no time was there any change in the serenity of manner for which the General was distinguished, and which infused a like confidence in his small force beleaguered in the depth of winter by foes outnumbering them twenty-fold.

Since the death of the great Ameer, Dost Mahomed Khan, the political condition of Afghanistan bore a striking analogy to that of England during the Wars of the Roses. As the rival Houses of York and Lancaster contended for the crown, dividing the nobles and the country into two factions, so Afzul Khan and Shere Ali, the sons of the Dost, and their sons, Abdul Rahman and Yakoob Khan, bathed the country in the blood of their adherents. As in England during the 15th century, so in Afghanistan during the 19th, "uneasy lies the head that wears a crown;" and in the see-saw from the throne to the dungeon, the epigram might be applied to the rival claimants for the perilous honour of ruling the turbulent races of Afghanistan:—

> "Treason does never prosper; what's the reason?
> Why, when it prospers, none dare call it treason."

With the removal of Yakoob Khan to India, and the appearance of pretenders in the person of his younger brother, Ayoob Khan, and other claimants for the throne, the task before Sir Frederick Roberts became more difficult, but with the assistance of his political officer, Major Hastings, and afterwards of Mr. (now Sir) Lepel Griffin, he initiated the negotiations with Abdul Rahman, which have resulted so favourably for the peace of Afghanistan. Sir Frederick Roberts's final achievement, the forced march from Cabul to Candahar with 10,000 soldiers and 8,000 non-combatants, and his brilliant victory over Ayoob Khan on the day following his arrival under the walls of the capital of Western Afghanistan, are now historic, and have earned for him a prominent place in that illustrious band of soldiers who have acquired for this country her Eastern Empire.

The roll of England's victories—chequered at distant intervals by reverses—beginning at Cressy, has been prolonged to Candahar and Tel-el-Kebir. Not even the annals of Rome can show such a record of victory, achieved over races the most savage and warlike, assisted by the forces of Nature when arrayed in her most austere and rugged mood. In climes where the eagles of her great prototype never penetrated, the standards of Britain have been planted, and countries having to her people only a legendary existence—West Africa, the land of Prester John, and China—have been subjugated by her arms or compelled to sign an ignominious peace.

England has watered her horses on the banks of the classic Nile and Euphrates, and her legions have driven her hereditary foe, the Gaul, from America and India, and have triumphed alike over the Zulu in South Africa, the Afghan in Central Asia, and the Maori in New Zealand. Soldiers that could overcome the most renowned and martial races of four continents must be:—

> "Types of a race who shall to time unborn
> Their country leave unconquered as of yore."

But much, if not everything, depends upon leadership, and should a crisis arise in Europe or in any portion of our world-encompassing Empire, the eyes of the nation—as after the massacre of the Cavagnari Mission, the disaster at Maiwand, and in our ignominious struggle with the Boers—will instinctively turn to Sir Frederick Roberts as conspicuous among that small band of tried and capable officers to whom will be confided the defence of the honour and interests of the Mother country and her Colonies.

C. R. LOW.

Kensington, June, 1883.

CONTENTS.

—o—

CHAPTER I.

PAGE

Introduction—Some Account of Sir Frederick Roberts's Family—The Services of his Father, General Sir Abraham Roberts—His Early Life, and Career at Eton, Sandhurst, and Woolwich—Proceeds to India in the Bengal Artillery—Serves on his Father's Staff and on the Frontier at Peshawur—Outbreak of the Indian Mutiny . 1

CHAPTER II.

The Siege of Delhi—Roberts joins the Punjaub Movable Column—Proceeds to Delhi as Deputy-Assistant Quartermaster-General of Artillery—Lieutenant Roberts participates in the Action of the 9th July—Gallantry of his Friend, Lieutenant Hills—Roberts is wounded in the Fighting on the 14th July—Preparations for the Bombardment—Roberts serves in No. 2 Battery at Ludlow Castle—The Storm and Capture of Delhi—Sir James Brind's Reminiscences of Sir Frederick Roberts at Delhi . . 18

CHAPTER III.

Lieutenant Roberts takes the Field with Colonel Greathed's Movable Column—The Action at Bolundshur—Narrow Escape of Lieutenant Roberts—The Capture of Allyghur—Roberts is engaged in the Pursuit with 9th Lancers—The Surprise at Agra of the 10th of October—Roberts's share in the Severe Fighting and Pursuit—The March to Mynpoorie—Skirmish and Pursuit of the Rebels to the Ganges—Arrival at Cawnpore . . . 48

CHAPTER IV.

Departure of Lieutenant Roberts from Cawnpore with Brigadier Hope Grant's Column for the Relief of Lucknow—Narrow Escape of Roberts from Capture by the Rebels at Buntheera—March upon Lucknow—Roberts as Quartermaster-General of Sir Hope Grant's

Division—He leads the Army from the Alumbagh—Is sent by Sir Colin Campbell on a Special Mission to Alumbagh—Is associated with Captain Garnet Wolseley in the Capture of the 32nd Mess-house—The Return March to Cawnpore—The Battle of Cawnpore on the 6th of December—The Affair at Serai Ghât.   62

CHAPTER V.

Roberts gains the V.C. at Khodagunj—Occupation of Futtehgurh on the 2nd of January, 1858—A Day's Pig-sticking—The Army crosses into Oude—Arduous Nature of Roberts's Duties on the Staff—Storm of Meeangunj—Roberts's Humanity—The Siege of Lucknow—Operations Trans-Goomtee—The Action of Koo sie—Roberts is invalided and returns to England   76

CHAPTER VI.

Lieutenant Roberts returns to India—Is employed in Charge of the Viceroy's Camp—Lord Clyde's Letter to Lord Canning recommending Roberts—Promotion to a Brevet-Majority—On Tour with Sir Hugh Rose—Is ordered on Special Service to Umbeyla—Critical State of Affairs on the North-West Frontier in 1863—The Action of Laloo—The Capture of Umbeyla—The Burning of Mulkah—Major Roberts Compiles a Route Book for the Bengal Presidency—Returns to England on Sick Leave—On his return to India proceeds to Abyssinia with the Expedition under Sir Robert Napier—Major Roberts's Services in Abyssinia.   91

CHAPTER VII.

The Looshai Campaign—Description of the Country and Cause of the War—Colonel Roberts fits out the two Columns of the Expeditionary Force—He joins General Bourchier at Cachar—March of the Cachar Column—Arrival at Tipai Mookh—Attack on the Kholel Villages led by Colonel Roberts—Further Operations against the Looshais—Action of the 25th of January, 1872—Colonel Roberts Commands at the Capture of Taikoom—Arrival at Chumfai—Conclusion of Peace and Return of the Column to India—Roberts is appointed Quartermaster-General at Army Head-quarters—His Services in that Capacity—Lord Lytton and General Roberts—Roberts is nominated Commandant of the Punjaub Irregular Force and Special Commissioner on the Scinde-Punjaub Frontier   109

Contents. ix

CHAPTER VIII.

PAGE

The Afghan War—General Roberts is Appointed to the Command of the Kurram Field Force—Constitution of the Field Force—Brief Description of the Kurram Valley and its Inhabitants—The Advance from Thull into Afghan Territory—The Occupation of the Kurram Fort—The Operations of the 28th November—Reconnoissances and Preparations for the Attack on the Peiwar Kotul 132

CHAPTER IX.

The Midnight March up the Spingawi Ravine—Treachery in the Ranks—The Capture of the Spingawi Pass—Advance along the Ridge and Severe Fighting—General Roberts is Wounded—The Night Bivouac in the Mountains—Occupation of the Peiwar Kotal—Account of the Operations by an Officer of the Staff—General Roberts Reconnoitres the Shutargardan Pass . . . 149

CHAPTER X.

General Roberts returns to Kurram by the Sappri Defile—Attack by the Mangals on the Baggage Escort—Preparations for the Occupation of the Kurram Valley during the Winter—The Court-Martial on the Treacherous Soldiers of the 29th Punjaub N.I., and Roberts's General Order to the Force—Disposal of the Troops into Winter Quarters—Expedition into the Khost Valley—The March from Kurram to Hazir Pir, and thence into the Khost Valley—Occupation of the Fort of Matun—Action of the 7th January and Defeat of the Mangals—Reconnoissance by General Roberts of the Khost Valley 174

CHAPTER XI.

General Roberts makes a Tour of the Valley—Army Signalling in Khost—Durbar of the Headmen of the Khostiwals and Mangals—Evacuation of Matun and Return March to Hazir Pir—Preparations for the Advance on Cabul—Reconnoissance by General Roberts—Conclusion of the Treaty of Gundamuck—Arrival at Ali Kheyl of the Cavagnari Mission—General Roberts Returns to Simla 195

CHAPTER XII.

Massacre of the British Mission at Cabul—Receipt of the Intelligence by Sir Frederick Roberts at Simla—He Proceeds to take the Field—Arrival at Ali Kheyl—Preparations for the Advance on Cabul—Sir Frederick Roberts Moves across the Shutargardan Pass—He Experiences a Narrow Escape—Arrival at Kooshi—Interview with Yakoob Khan—Proclamations of Sir Frederick Roberts to the Army and the People of Cabul 218

CHAPTER XIII.

Advance on Cabul—Battle of Charasia—Sir Frederick Roberts arrives before the Capital—His Visit to the Scene of the Massacre of the British Mission—Occupation of the Bala Hissar—Proclamation of the 12th of October—The Punishment Meted out to Cabul 236

CHAPTER XIV.

The Cabul District after its Occupation by the British—Events at the Shutargardan Pass—The Explosion in the Bala Hissar—Occupation of the Sherpur Cantonment—Sir Frederick Roberts Reconnoitres the Passes towards Jugdulluck—Abandonment of the Shutargardan—The Expedition to Maidan—Unsettled State of the Country—Deportation of Yakoob Khan to India—A Review of the Situation in Northern Afghanistan before the Events of December 1879 256

CHAPTER XV.

The National Rising of December, 1879—The Plans of Sir Frederick Roberts to Check the Movement—The Cavalry Action of the 11th December—Critical Condition of Affairs at Sherpur and in Cabul—Prompt Action of Sir Frederick Roberts—Movements of Brigadier-Generals Macpherson and Baker—The Attempt to Capture the Takht-i-Shah on the 12th December—Severe fighting on the 13th December—Capture of Koh Asmai—Successful Counter-Attack by the Enemy—Heavy Losses Experienced by the British Force—Sir Frederick Roberts Determines to Concentrate in Sherpur—Retirement of the British Troops within the Cantonment 280

CHAPTER XVI.

The Situation at Sherpur and in Cabul—The City and Bala Hissar Seized by the Enemy—Their Movements against Sherpur—Sir Frederick Roberts places the Cantonment in a Condition of Defence—Colonel Hudson and the Garrison at Lutterbund—Desultory Fighting with the Enemy between the 14th and 21st December—The Attack of the 23rd December—Final Rout of the Afghans by Sir Frederick Roberts—Arrival of Brigadier-General Charles Gough with Reinforcements — The Future Government of Afghanistan — The Rival Pretenders to the Ameership—Sir Donald Steward succeeds to the Chief Command in North-Eastern Afghanistan 302

CHAPTER XVII.

Sir Frederick Roberts and the Negotiations with Abdul Rahman—Appointment of the Sirdar to the Ameership—Restless State of the Sirdars and People of Afghanistan—Arrival of Abdul Rahman at Cabul and Assumption of the Ameership—Sir Frederick Roberts's Views on the Kurram Valley Question—The Maiwand Disaster—Sir Frederick Roberts appointed to the Command of the Relieving Column—His Preparations for the March on Candahar—Dramatic Aspects of the Afghan War . 328

CHAPTER XVIII.

English Public Opinion on the Projected March through Afghanistan—Sir Frederick Roberts quits Cabul for Beni Hissar—Incidents of the Forced March to Ghuznee—Arrival at Ghuznee and Surrender of the Town and Citadel—The Forced March to Khelat-i-Ghilzye—Relief and Removal of the Garrison—Sir Frederick Roberts on the Line of March—The Advance on Candahar—Preparations for the Attack on Ayoob Khan's Position . 343

CHAPTER XIX.

Arrival of the Cabul-Candahar Force at Robat—Letter from General Phayre—Sir Frederick Roberts's State of Health—Arrival before Candahar—Reconnoissance of the 31st August—Preparations for the Attack—Dispositions of the Army—The Advance on the Pir Paimal Position—Storming of the Village of Gundi Mulla Sahibdad—Death of Colonel Brownlow—Capture of Pir Paimal—Brilliant Advance of Macpherson's and Baker's Brigades—Gallant Conduct of Major White—Incidents of the Fight—

Capture of the Enemy's Camp at Mazra—Losses of the British—Results of the Victory—Sir Frederick Roberts Resigns his Command in Afghanistan 362

CHAPTER XX.

Sir Frederick Roberts quits Afghanistan—The Question of the Retention of Candahar—Sir Frederick Roberts Arrives in England—His Reception by his Countrymen—Rewards Conferred on Sir Frederick Roberts—Precedents in the Case of Rewards for Military Services—His Speech at the Mansion House—Changes in Army Reform due to Sir Frederick Roberts's Criticisms—He is appointed to the Command of the Army sent to Coerce the Boers—Departure for and Return from South Africa—Sir Frederick Roberts attends the German Autumn Manœuvres—His Comments on the German Army and Military System—Sir Frederick Roberts is appointed Commander-in-Chief of the Madras Army—He leaves England for India—Conclusion . . 377

MEMOIR

OF

SIR FREDERICK ROBERTS.

CHAPTER I.

Introduction—Some Account of Sir Frederick Roberts's Family—The Services of his Father, General Sir Abraham Roberts—His Early Life, and Career at Eton, Sandhurst, and Woolwich—Proceeds to India in the Bengal Artillery—Serves on his Father's Staff and on the Frontier at Peshawur—Outbreak of the Indian Mutiny.

A MEMOIR of an officer, of whose principal achievement, the march from Cabul to Candahar, German military critics declare that it is the most brilliant performance of a British Army since Waterloo, and which a distinguished officer, who had served throughout Lord Strathnairn's victorious campaign in Central India, declared to us was, in his estimation, the finest exploit achieved by our arms since Sir Charles Napier's conquest of Scinde—the memoir of such a soldier cannot be without interest not only to men of his own cloth, but to the British public, which reads with avidity biographies of its military heroes.

Sir Frederick Roberts comes of a military stock, and was cradled, so to speak, amid arms and soldiers. His father, the late General Sir Abraham Roberts, G.C.B., lived to attain the age of ninety, and was the patriarch of Indian Generals. In his day he had achieved no mean renown; but though his name has been commemorated in military history as that of a gallant and capable soldier, it is by the achievements of his still more remarkable son that the name of Roberts will live in our history. There are yet surviving a few grizzled and aged warriors, who can bear witness that Brigadier Roberts, of the first Afghan War, was a good soldier and true, and more, was possessed of a sagacity and prescience, which, had it been found in those responsible for the political and military direction of affairs in Afghanistan, might have averted a terrible calamity.

The late Sir Abraham Roberts entered the Royal Army in July 1801, with the intention of making it his profession, but the Peace of Amiens in the following year, which caused great reductions, induced him, with many other officers, to join the Indian Service, which had then every prospect of active employment. On the 1st January, 1803, he was gazetted an Ensign in the Army of the Honourable East India Company, on the Bengal Establishment, and, in the following year, served under Lord Lake in his campaign against the Mahrattas. The young officer lived to see the boundaries of British India extended from Delhi and Ferozepore to the Khyber Pass, and was fated to take a prominent part in restoring to his throne that Shah Soojah, who, with his brother Zemaun Shah, at this time fluttered the Council Chamber at Calcutta with fears of an Afghan invasion. How vast were the changes, political, military, and social, he witnessed in India during the seventy years succeeding his arrival at Calcutta!

The poet Campbell writes of the motives that induced our forefathers to conquer India:—

> "Did Peace descend, to triumph and to save,
> When freeborn Britons cross'd the Indian wave?
> Ah, no! to more than Rome's ambition true,
> The nurse of Freedom gave it not to you."

It was the pursuit of commerce that brought us to India, and were we to own the truth, it is no high-flown sense of duty, but our own selfish purposes, and our national love of aggrandizement that keeps us there, and has induced us to lavish the best blood of England in fighting our way to supreme sovereignty over an empire vaster than that of Aurungzebe, and maintaining it against a military revolt that would have ousted from the country any other power but ours. However, as was said by Marshal McMahon on a memorable occasion :—"*J'y suis, et j'y reste.*"

In 1805, Lieutenant Roberts accompanied Lord Lake in the pursuit, across the Sutlej, of Holkar and Ameer Khan, and, in April, 1806, he joined the first battalion 13th Regiment Native Infantry, then on service in Bundelcund. While so employed he suffered severely from the prevailing sickness, caused by fatiguing duties and constant exposure, as, in the absence of cantonments, the army was under canvas during the hot winds and rains, and continually employed against Pindàrees and marauders.

Early in 1807, Lieutenant Roberts was appointed Adjutant of his regiment, being at the time the youngest officer on the establishment performing this duty. At the close of the year he acted as Major of Brigade to General Dickens's force at the sieges of Komona and Gunnowrie, in the Doab, where the troops suffered severely in killed and wounded. In 1810, he volunteered for Java, but his services were not accepted.

In May, 1814, Lieutenant Roberts was appointed to the department of Public Works, but, in November of that year, his regiment being warned for service in Nepaul, he obtained permission to rejoin it, and was present at the storm of Kullunga, where the gallant General Sir Rollo Gillespie fell. On the 27th December following, though only a subaltern, he commanded his regiment, which was actively engaged with the enemy at the Morle-ke-Tebee, close to the fort of Jetuk. The force, which was commanded by Major (afterwards General Sir) William Richards, received the high approbation of the Marquis of Hastings.* On the 2nd April, 1815, Roberts was Staff Officer

---

* The Adjutant-General wrote to General G. Martindale, commanding the column :—"The conduct of Major Richards and his detachment claims the unqualified approbation of the Commander-in-Chief; that officer successfully accomplished the main object for which he was detached, and maintained his position against superior numbers for an entire day, during which Major Richards afforded conspicuous proofs of his judgment, coolness and deliberate valour. His Excellency desires that his particular thanks and approbation be expressed to Major Richards for his conduct on the above arduous occasion, as well as to the whole of the officers and men who composed his detachment, and so ably supported him by their determined exertions of bravery, zeal, and discipline, and patient endurance of fatigue and privations."

to a Brigade under the command of Sir William Richards, which was successfully engaged at Birla-ke-Tebee, capturing the Nepaul chief, and completely routing the enemy, for which service he received the thanks of his Commanding Officer, and of the Governor-General, the Marquis of Hastings, who permitted him on the conclusion of the campaign, as a mark of favour, to return to his appointment in the Public Works Department.

On the 9th April, 1816, Lieutenant Roberts again joined his regiment, which was ordered by express from Moradabad to quell a rebellion at Bareilly, in Rohilcund, and made the march of fifty miles without a halt. While in Rohilcund he was placed in charge of the Famine Fund, and had the satisfaction of relieving many thousands of poor sufferers. He now again returned to his appointment in the Public Works Department, where his zeal and activity were proverbial.* Ever anxious to see active service, like his distinguished son, Captain Roberts, in 1824, volunteered for service in the Burmese War, and received the following reply from Colonel Marley, Military Secretary to the Commander-in-Chief, General Sir Edward Paget, G.C.B., dated 30th June, 1824 :—" With respect to yourself, there cannot be a doubt upon the subject, you fill a very responsible situation under Government, and it is in it your services will be most useful. Every one who is acquainted with you knows well, that if storming a stockade formed any part of your duty, you would go at it like an Irishman."

So valuable were the services in the Public Works Department, alluded to above, that, on the 2nd February, 1828, Lord

---

* Colonel Penson, the Superintendent of Public Works, writing to Mr. W. B. Bailey, Chief Secretary to Government, under date 30th May, 1817, submitting letters and bills from Lieutenant Roberts, says :—" The sum which has been saved on the estimate is considerable, and is highly creditable to Lieutenant Roberts. I have likewise the pleasure to submit several testimonials in behalf of Lieutenant Roberts, which show how great a favourite this gentleman is in both Civil and Military Departments, and when I consider how greatly an officer of his activity, practical knowledge, and integrity, is wanting to look after the valuable public property in the extensive district of Rohilkund, I hope they may ultimately lead to his fixture in that province. I lately had an opportunity of examining the addition to the jail at Mynporee while erecting under this gentleman's superintendence, and I think he may challenge all India to produce better work."

Amherst, the Governor-General, presented Major Roberts with a handsome piece of plate, with an inscription testifying to "the services rendered by him as head of his department."

On the 28th September, 1831, he was promoted to Lieutenant-Colonel, and, in the following year, was selected by Sir E. Barnes, Commander-in-Chief, to command the 1st Bengal Fusiliers, the only European regiment then on the Establishment; and the offer of the appointment was accompanied with handsome letters from the Adjutant and Quartermaster-Generals. Colonel Roberts worked up this fine regiment, then mustering considerably over 1,000 bayonets, to a high state of efficiency, and the General commanding the Dinapore Division wrote to him on 18th January, 1833 :—"What I said to the regiment this morning, was what I really felt, and had I the power of language, or a greater fluency of speech, a fair field was open to me to say more. My A.D.C., who has seen many reviews at home, declared he had not for years seen a better performance than the one your fine regiment treated us with this morning." At length, after an uninterrupted service of over thirty years in India, Colonel Roberts * quitted the country on his return home to arrange for the education of his children.

After a residence in England of two years, Colonel Roberts returned to India. In 1838 took place the Afghan War, and on the 1st November, Colonel Roberts was placed in command of the 4th Brigade of the Army of the Indus, composed of his own regiment and the 35th and 37th Bengal N.I. In February, 1839, he commanded in Upper Scinde, and at Bukker, on the Indus, had to superintend the crossing of the park, treasure, Commissariat stores, and baggage of the army, which was done

---

* When Colonel Roberts was about to return home from Cawnpore, General Sir James Sleigh, K.C.B., wrote to him, under date January 5th, 1834 :—"As you are about to embark for England, and the Lord knows when we may again meet, I am induced to send you these few lines to offer you a memento of my esteem and regard; and from your having been so considerable a time stationed at Cawnpore, while I had the honour of commanding successively the Station and Division, it may not be less gratifying to you than it is pleasing to myself to assure you how much that esteem was increased by the assiduity and attention invariably observed in your exertions to promote the good of the service, and to fulfil the important duties intrusted to your superintendence."

without loss. Brigadier Roberts commanded the 4th Brigade at the storming of Ghuznee on the 23rd July, 1839, and received the thanks of the Commander-in-Chief and Governor-General. Succeeding Sir Robert Sale, who was wounded, in command of the fortress, under the arrangements he made, Captain (the late Sir George) Macgregor secured the person of the commandant, Hyder Khan, a son of Dost Mahomed, with many of his followers, for which Sir John Keane personally thanked Brigadier Roberts.

On the termination of the campaign, the Brigadier was appointed to the command of the Shah's troops, and Lord Auckland promised him the chief command in Afghanistan. Brigadier Roberts was an outspoken officer, possessing great experience of Orientals, and he entirely disagreed with the course adopted by Sir William Macnaghten, the Envoy and Minister to the Court of our puppet, Shah Soojah, who, having passed his life in the secretariat, had no experience of governing a turbulent race, but took an optimist view of affairs in Afghanistan, and persisted in disregarding the warnings of his coadjutors and assistants, Burnes, Rawlinson, Macgregor, Nott, Roberts, and others. Macnaghten being all-powerful at Simla, carried everything with a high hand, and any one who displayed independence incurred his displeasure. Thus he counselled the recall from Candahar of General Nott, because of his blunt outspokenness and unconciliatory manners; but the Government had the good sense to retain this capable officer, who saved British honour in Southern Afghanistan.

Brigadier Roberts saw the true position of affairs, and, warned by the unsettled state of the country, and the several minor disasters that had occurred at outposts, was convinced of the urgent necessity of precautionary measures. Accordingly he recommended that the Bala Hissar and detached forts at Cabul should be strengthened and well armed with artillery; that in them all the treasure, with an ample supply of grain, should be lodged, and the troops quartered, so that a large force might be available for service in the field. He also remonstrated against the location of troops in remote or exposed situations where they could not be efficiently supported, and, above all, entreated that the force of Afghan levies might be very limited, until officers were better qualified, by more perfect knowledge of their language, customs, and feelings, to command them, and until, from observation and experience, some trustworthy judgment could be formed of their conduct, trustworthiness and utility. But his counsels were disregarded, and the levies raised under Maule, Hopkins, and other officers, eventually proved to be mutinous and utterly useless. Again, the military chest for the whole army was kept in the paymaster's quarters in the city, and Roberts pointed out the great danger of this practice, particularly as the force at Cabul was often very weak. While at Cabul, with the consent of the Envoy, he caused the treasure to be placed in the Bala Hissar, and at the same time stored therein a supply of grain. However, shortly after, at the request of the paymaster, but contrary to the wishes of Brigadier Roberts, the treasure was sent back to the city, and when, on the fatal 2nd November, 1841, the paymaster's house was attacked, the money fell into the hands of the insurgents, not only feeding the rebellion but leaving the British force without funds.

Thus it was that the most ordinary military precautions in an enemy's country were deemed superfluous by the ruling civil authority, and the steps Roberts had taken, and the measures he had recommended, were considered either unnecessary, or as indicative of an admission of weakness. After the crash, a high political officer, writing to Roberts on 14th February, 1842, bears witness to his sagacity :—" How satisfactory it must now be for you to have written those opinions to which you can refer as having been calculated to prevent much, if not all, of the sad disasters that have befallen the fine force you left here."

The Envoy—with whom privately Roberts was on the best of terms, for Sir William Macnaghten was an accomplished gentleman, and possessed a generous, noble nature—looked upon Roberts as an alarmist, and pitted his own ignorance of military affairs against the veteran soldier's experience of forty years. He accordingly vetoed Roberts's measures and thwarted his endeavours to provide for the coming storm. Lord Auckland, who had confidence in the Brigadier, supported him, and in the following letter, dated 6th July, 1840, administered something like a reprimand to his zealous, but injudicious representative:—"It may, however, I am directed to remark, be of advantage to both services, as well as to the public finances, if deference were upon many points paid to the opinion of Brigadier Roberts. . . . . . His Lordship in Council has a strong desire, in which he looks for your concurrence, to uphold the military position of Brigadier Roberts. Whenever the regular forces shall be withdrawn from Afghanistan, he will be your first military authority, and every British officer employed in that country should be led to look up to him. But for the reasons that have been given, his Lordship in Council, though he would be glad to know that he is frequently consulted by you and the Shah, would not have him directly interfere with the organization and internal management of the corps which are not attached to the Contingent. His Lordship can only express his approbation of the care which is exhibited by the Brigadier for the force committed to his charge, and he will be glad when circumstances will permit him to carry into effect his views for its discipline and comfort. His Lordship in Council can have no doubt that in the event of a Corps of Afghans being substituted for one of the Hindostanee corps of the Contingent, Brigadier Roberts will regularly attend to any instructions which he may receive from you upon those 'grave political considerations' which are attached to every measure bearing upon the national habits of Afghanistan." Fortified by this expression of confidence, Roberts continued to press his advice on the Envoy with a freedom justified by his responsibilities and the vast interests at stake: but all to no effect.

He writes of his action in the matter:—" We had ample means, if properly applied, for any emergency, for Lord Auckland had the force most liberally supplied with all requisites for attack or defence, and he was no doubt disappointed at receiving such different reports from the Envoy and myself, but as I was not permitted to use my own judgment in military matters, or to exercise a salutary control over the force I was supposed to command, and as I could not convince the ruling local authority that precaution was necessary, I, with great regret, wrote to Lord Auckland to say how distressed I was at all that had occurred, and stated that under existing circumstances I felt that I could not do justice to the very responsible situation I had the honour to hold."

On again writing in the same sense, Roberts was informed that his resignation was accepted, and, in 1841, Brigadier Anquetil, who perished in the passes during the disastrous retreat in January, 1842, was sent to relieve him, and so his connection with Afghanistan ceased.

In 1842, when a large force was concentrated at Ferozepore, Roberts was placed in command of the 4th Brigade of the Army of Reserve, and, in 1844, proceeded to England, thus missing the Gwalior Campaign and the Sutlej and Punjaub Campaigns. In 1851 Colonel Roberts returned to India, and was appointed to the command of the Lahore and Peshawur Divisions. On the murder of Colonel Mackeson, Political Agent at Peshawur, in 1853, Brigadier-General Roberts restored confidence by his prompt military arrangements. In December, 1853, he was compelled from very severe illness to resign his command, and finally returned to England, thus concluding an honourable and useful military career.

Attaining the rank of Major-General in 1854, ten years later he became a full General, and in 1862 was appointed Colonel of the 101st Regiment, formerly his old corps, the 1st Bengal Fusiliers, which boasts of so brilliant a record of service from Plassey to Lucknow, and which he had commanded at the time of the birth of the subject of this memoir. A Companion of the Bath of 1839, General Roberts received the K.C.B. on the 20th of March, 1865, and, finally, on the 8th of December, 1873, was decorated by Her Majesty at Windsor Castle with the Grand Cross of that Order. Within three weeks of receiving this honour, the aged soldier, who could speak of the "brave days of old" of Wellesley and Lake, sank to his rest, full of years and honours.

His widow, through the kindness of the Queen, resided, until her death last year, in Hampton Court Palace, and had the gratification, denied to her husband, of surviving to witness the achievements of her son on the fields where his father had earned distinction before him.

Our hero's earliest memories were connected with that most

debatable of all military subjects, the first Afghan War, in which the varying phases of success and failure became to his youthful mind an oft-told, but ever entrancing tale. As a boy at his father's table, the talk was—

> "Of sallies and retires; of trenches, tents;
> Of palisadoes, frontiers, parapets;
> Of basilisks, of cannon, culverin;
> Of prisoners' ransom, and of soldiers slain,
> And all the currents of a heady fight."

To him Afghanistan was a word conjuring up memories that quickened his pulse, and as, round the board of his venerable father, he heard discussions with old companions-in-arms of those dramatic scenes of war, of disgraceful capitulation, of seemingly hopeless imprisonment, and, finally, of glorious retrieval, the boy often longed for the time when he would embark on a military career in that distant land, our conquest of which forms one of the most remarkable episodes in the world's history. Of those veteran comrades of his father few indeed now survive, the most distinguished being Sir George Lawrence, Sir James Airey, Sir Vincent Eyre, Sir George Macgregor, and General Colin Mackenzie,*—who, though he did unsurpassed good service during the events at Cabul in 1841-42, alone remains undecorated. Such were the incidents, having a prominent place in the memories of childhood, that occupied the thoughts of young Roberts, and it is scarcely surprising that the future hero of Peiwar Kotul, Charasiah and Candahar, should have dreamed of emulating the career of his sire in the fields which witnessed some of the most painful and glorious events in our military annals.

Of the family of Sir Frederick Roberts, some particulars kindly placed at our disposal by Sir Albert W. Woods, Garter-King-at-Arms, will interest those of genealogical tendencies. The Roberts family have been settled for generations in County Waterford, Ireland. One John Roberts married Mary, daughter of Major Sautelle, one of the French Protestant refugees, who fought under William the Third, at the battle of the Boyne.

---

* Since this was written, nearly two years ago, the three last-named gallant officers have "gone over to the majority."

Genealogy of the Roberts Family.

Their son was the Rev. John Roberts, Magistrate of Passage, Co. Waterford, who married, on 23rd January, 1771, Anne, daughter of Rev. Abraham Sandys, of Dublin, and died in 1814, leaving, among other issue, Captain Sir Samuel Roberts, C.B., R.N., of Belmont, near Waterford; Captain Thomas Roberts, R.N.; and the father of the subject of this memoir, born at Waterford, on the 11th April, 1784.

The late Sir Abraham Roberts married, as his first wife, Frances Isabella, daughter of George Poyntz Ricketts, Bengal Civil Service, and by her had one son, Major-General George Ricketts Roberts, Bengal Army; and two daughters, Fanny Eliza, married Major Charles Grant, Bengal Horse Artillery (died in November, 1853); and Maria Isabella, married Lieutenant William Maconachie Wellwood. Sir Abraham married secondly, on the 2nd August, 1830, Isabella, daughter of Abraham Bunbury* of Kilfeacle, Co. Tipperary (formerly captain in the 62nd regiment) and widow of Major Hamilton George Maxwell, of Ardwell, by whom she had one son, Colonel Hamilton Maxwell, and one daughter, married to John Davis Sherston, Esq., of Evercreach, Somerset. Besides our hero, Frederick Sleigh† Roberts, the issue of this marriage was one daughter, Henrietta Mercer, who died unmarried on the 8th October, 1880. Sir Abraham Roberts died on the 28th December, 1873, in his 90th year, and was buried in the parish church of Clifton, where he had continued to reside after his return from India.‡

Sir Frederick Roberts was born at Cawnpore on the 30th September, 1832, and proceeded to England early in 1834 with his parents, who, on their return to India, two years later, left

---

* The Bunburys, who came over to England with the Conqueror, had not long been resident in Waterford.

† He received his second name of Sleigh from his godmother, widow of General Sir Francis Sleigh.

‡ The following is the heraldic description of the arms, crest, and supporters, conferred on Sir Frederick Roberts as G.C.B. :—Arms. Azure, three estoiles or, on a chief wavy of the last, an eastern crown gules.

Crest. A Lion rampant or, armed and langued gules, charged in the shoulder with an eastern crown of the last, and holding in the dexter paw a sword, the blade wavy argent, hilt and pommel gold.

Supporters—Dexter, a Highlander of the 92nd Regiment, sinister, a Ghoorka, both habited and holding in their exterior hands a rifle, all proper. Motto—*Virtute et valore.*

him at Clifton. During the succeeding eleven years the home of young Roberts was at Clifton, where he made many friends, who will recall the delicate, rather sickly boy whose buoyant spirits and indomitable nature even then gave promise of future eminence.

Frederick Roberts received the rudiments of his education at Miss Carpenter's, Long Ashton, between 1838–40, and for the following two years at Monsieur Desprez's, at Clifton. Between 1842–45 he was a pupil of Mr. Mills, at Hampton, and, in September of the latter year, was entered at Eton, where his tutor was the Rev. T. Eyre Young. He was in the fourth form at Eton, and gained a prize in mathematics, and recently we have seen how his old school claimed the honour of welcoming its distinguished *Alumnus*, to whom the boys presented a sword.

In July, 1846, young Roberts left Eton, and, in the following January, entered Sandhurst, of which Sir George Scovell was Governor, and General Taylor Lieutenant-Governor. At Sandhurst, where he remained until June, 1848, he gained a German prize and took up three out of the six steps required for a commission without purchase. At this time his father, who was on leave in England, procured him a nomination to Addiscombe, through the interest of General Caulfield.

There was, however, no vacancy at the Company's Military Seminary, and Roberts was entered temporarily as a pupil at Stoton's (now Brackenbury's) Preparatory Military Academy at Wimbledon, whence he proceeded to Addiscombe on the 1st February, 1850. Here his military education was conducted under the superintendence of General Stannus, and of his successor in the Governorship, Sir Frederick Abbott, who still survives to congratulate himself on his successful pupil.

At Addiscombe, where Roberts attained the rank of corporal, he remained for nearly two years, and, in the winter of 1851, came out ninth in a batch of between forty and fifty cadets who passed the qualifying examination. The six at the top of the list selected the corps of Engineers. The two next, to his great satisfaction, preferred the Bombay Artillery, and so Roberts was posted, according to his special wish, to the Bengal Artillery,—the chances of seeing service, and the field of distinction being greater during the present century in that Presidency than in those of Madras and Bombay.

Among Roberts's contemporaries, during the four terms he was at Addiscombe, were Major-General Sir James Hills, V.C., K.C.B., whose services at Delhi, in Abyssinia, and in Afghanistan, shed such lustre on the corps of which, like Roberts, he was a member; Captain Elliott Brownlow, of the Bengal Engineers, who was killed at Lucknow; Colonel Lambert, of the 1st Bengal Fusiliers; and Colonel Æneas Perkins, R.E., C.B., A.D.C., for whose services as Commanding Engineer, Roberts applied when he was first appointed to the command of the Koorum force, and who served under his old Addiscombe friend throughout the Afghan War. The two latter officers were, with Roberts, members of a party of six, who "chummed" together and had a fund in common which was placed at the disposal of the fortunate individual who got leave to London from Saturday to Monday.

While at Addiscombe, Roberts was in very indifferent health, and suffered so much from heart complaint, that at times he would have sherry by his bedside at night to revive him. However, his spirits never flagged, but rose superior to the ailments of a delicate body, so that he was always remarkable for his gaiety and cheeriness. Though small and far from robust, his figure was well knit and very wiry, and his personal appearance in his Addiscombe days is described as giving the impression of his being much older than he was, and he was then, as through life under the most discouraging circumstances, very particular in his dress.

On the 12th December, 1851, Roberts was gazetted a second Lieutenant in the Bengal Artillery, a branch of the Company's Service which has reared many eminent soldiers, as Horsford, D'Arcy Todd, Pollock, Henry Lawrence, Archdale Wilson, Harry Tombs, and others too numerous to mention. On the 20th February, 1852, Lieutenant Roberts sailed from Southampton in the Peninsular and Oriental Company's steamship *Ripon*, by the overland route, which, with its changes at Alexandria, Cairo, and Suez (and at Aden for the Bombay passengers), those who went out to India, "Consule Planco," will contrast unfavourably with the present through system of passage by the Canal. At Suez, Roberts took passage in the *Oriental*, which embarked a double complement of passengers, owing to a delay in the previous steamer. The heat in the Red Sea was very trying to the "griffins," who had left England in the depth of winter, and one of the number, a gallant officer, who has seen much hard service in Delhi and elsewhere, told us he had never forgotten Roberts remarking to some of them one day:—"I don't know how we shall ever be able to fight in India if it is as hot as this." The gallant youngster, however, learned to fight throughout the terrible heat of the days at Delhi, and recently we have seen how the fiery sun of Afghanistan was unable to quench his ardour for the rough school of war.

Among Roberts's fellow-passengers to Calcutta were Sir Barnes Peacock, Chief Justice of Bengal, who is still in harness as a Member of the Judicial Committee of the Privy Council, and that veteran officer, Sir John Gough, G.C.B., going out to resume his office of Quartermaster-General of Queen's troops. On his arrival in India, Roberts reported himself at Dum Dum, then the head-quarters of the Bengal Artillery, but, after a brief stay of four months, proceeded up-country to Peshawur, where his father was Brigadier-General in command of the Division. Here he served on his father's staff in the capacity of acting aide-de-camp, not having passed the languages, but, early in 1852, joined the 1st Peshawur Mountain Battery, commanded by Captain (now Major-General) Tom Brougham, who had the satisfaction of giving the first training in the duties of gunner to the hero of the second Afghan War. Lieutenant Roberts's activity and smartness in acquiring his duties procured him the coveted "jacket," and, at the end of 1854, he was posted to the 1st troop, 2nd Brigade, Bengal Horse Artillery,—that splendid service which drew from Lord Hardinge, no mean judge, the avowal that it was unequalled by any in the world. It was no mean distinction to serve in this troop, then commanded by Colonel Barr, an officer who had served with distinction in Afghanistan, and Roberts, by his zeal and efficiency as an artillery officer, kept up the prestige it had acquired.

Roberts's early service was uneventful. He was not so

fortunate as to be engaged in the war against Burmah, which took place in the year of his arrival in India, but though a valuable province was acquired as the result of the campaign, little honour accrued to our arms in the defeat of so unworthy a foe. Still it was disappointing to an eager soldier like Roberts, and a weary five years passed without his seeing a shot fired. To serve on the staff is in India, as in England, the ambition of the most capable officers of the army, and, on the 25th March, 1856, Roberts was appointed to officiate as Deputy-Assistant-Quartermaster-General of the Peshawur Division, an appointment he held, with a brief intermission, until the outbreak of the Mutiny in 1857. The question of the causes of the Mutiny have been discussed by so many writers that it may almost be said, *quot hominis tot sententiæ*. Many well qualified to speak have attributed that great convulsion—which rivalled the French Revolution in its horrors, and the magnitude of the political and social changes introduced by its agency—to our recent annexation of Oude, to the bad faith with which the Native Army was treated, and to our denial of the rights of adoption to the Hindoo chiefs; but these, whether taken singly or together, do not, in our opinion, account for the Indian Mutiny. The annexation was a measure for the good of the people of Oude, necessitated by the incredible misgovernment of its rulers, who had been warned since the time of Lord Wellesley of its imminence. The question of adoption had only a contingent interest for the Native rulers, and in no way concerned the Native Army; and as to the charge of bad faith, the Sepoys had been petted and spoiled until they entertained an overweening estimate of their importance—an idea likely to be renewed if the fuss made over the Indian Contingent for their recent services in Egypt is to be repeated on every occasion we have need of their services beyond the Indian frontier.

Rather may we attribute the Mutiny to the lax discipline of the Native Army, the small power entrusted to the European officers, which had been so whittled away that, by an order of Sir William Gomm (Commander-in-Chief in succession to Sir Charles Napier, in 1851), a Sepoy might appeal against the Commanding officer to a court-martial. In our opinion Sir

Richard Temple, whose experience of Indian questions is unsurpassed, hit the right nail on the head when, in his "Men and Events of my Time," he gives the following reason as a "sufficient and self-evident explanation" of the great Mutiny:—
"The short and plain truth is that the great Mutiny of 1857 arose because the British Government in India had for a long time maintained a Native Army much too large, and a British force much too small. The Government thus unwittingly placed itself in the power of the Sepoys. This, and this alone, was the main cause of that tremendous event. The Sepoys would never have revolted unless they had felt themselves able to do so with some chance of success."

Nothing is so certain in India as the unforeseen. When, early in 1857, the first symptoms of disaffection manifested themselves among our Sepoys, few even among the most sagacious anticipated the deluge of mutiny that was about to overwhelm the land. It was a time of fierce trial to every English-speaking individual in the peninsula. In view of the magnitude of the interests affected, the extent of the area over which warlike operations raged, and the dramatic nature of the scenes that enthralled the attention of the civilized world, well might the portents have been expected, anticipated by Cæsar's wife on the eve of the "Ides of March," so memorable in classic history:—

> "Fierce fiery warriors fight upon the clouds,
> In ranks, and squadrons, and right form of war,
> Which drizzled blood upon the Capitol;
> The noise of battle hurtled in the air,
> Horses did neigh, and dying men did groan."

But though mutterings of sedition were heard at Barrackpore and elsewhere, and portended disaster to those "who had ears to hear," and recalled the scenes before enacted there and at Vellore, yet no one dreamed of the storm that was about to burst over the land. Balls and pic-nics enlivened the dulness of the military stations as in former years, and all "went merry as a marriage bell" at Meerut, Jhansi, Futtehgurh, and Cawnpore—that name of horror to English ears—always one of the gayest of stations. The fair women, some newly arrived from England, looked forward with pleasing anticipations to winning the hearts of the gallant men, of which many were so soon to be stilled in death. And these brave men, whose names are imperishably recorded in the history of the events of '57, what recked they of the wrath to come? Did not a great master of their art enunciate for their guidance a philosophic truth that has nerved the hearts of many in the supreme moment of battle?

" Cowards die many times before their deaths,
The valiant never taste of death but once."

CHAPTER II.

The Siege of Delhi—Roberts joins the Punjaub Movable Column—Proceeds to Delhi as Deputy-Assistant Quartermaster-General of Artillery—Lieutenant Roberts participates in the Action of the 9th July—Gallantry of his Friend, Lieutenant Hills—Roberts is wounded in the Fighting on the 14th July—Preparations for the Bombardment—Roberts serves in No. 2 Battery at Ludlow Castle—The Storm and Capture of Delhi—Sir James Brind's Reminiscences of Sir Frederick Roberts at Delhi.

ON the 12th May, 1857, news of the mutiny at Meerut and the seizure of Delhi was received at Peshawur, where Lieutenant Roberts was officiating as Deputy-Assistant Quartermaster-General of the division then commanded by Major-General Reed. Before noon of the following day, a council of war to provide for the defence of the Peshawur valley and the Punjaub generally, was held at the General's quarters, at which was assembled a group of officers such as any country might be proud to number among her sons—Brigadier Sydney Cotton, commanding the Peshawur garrison; Lieutenant-Colonel Herbert Edwardes, Commissioner of the division; Lieutenant-Colonel Nicholson, Deputy Commissioner of Peshawur; and Brigadier Neville Chamberlain, commanding the Punjaub Frontier Force. It was a meeting fraught with mighty consequences, for on the counsels of the assembled officers rested, in a measure, the destinies not only of the Punjaub, but of the entire Peninsula. At Nicholson's suggestion it was decided that a Movable Column should be formed to operate upon any point menaced with danger.

General Reed, accompanied by Lieutenant Roberts as the officer representing the Quartermaster-General's department of his division, went to Rawul Pindee, whither he had been summoned by Sir John Lawrence, Chief Commissioner of the Punjaub, to concert measures for the safety of the border province of the Empire during the crisis which, that sagacious statesman recognized with prescient vision, had arrived. After conferring with Sir John Lawrence, General Reed submitted to the Commander-in-Chief by telegraph the names of Cotton, Edwardes, Nicholson, and Chamberlain for the command of the Movable Column formed on the 20th May, and General Anson telegraphed back his selection of the last-named officer for the responsible duty.

General Chamberlain appointed Lieutenant Roberts to be staff officer of the column, which they joined at Wuzeerabad on the Chenaub. It consisted of the following troops from Sealkote:—H.M.'s 52nd Light Infantry, Colonel Campbell; Major Michael Dawes' troop of Horse Artillery; Captain G. Bourchier's (No. 17) Field Battery; the 35th Native Infantry, Colonel Younghusband; and a wing of the 9th Cavalry. There were also attached Major Knatchbull's battery of Native Artillery, the 16th Irregular Cavalry, and wing of the 17th Cavalry. A difficulty now arose on a question that, in our Army, has so often proved a stumbling-block to military efficiency—the question of command as regulated by seniority. Colonel Campbell was senior to Neville Chamberlain, and declined to serve under his junior; but on referring the matter to Lahore, it was soon set at rest, Colonel Campbell being informed that he must either retire from the force or serve under his junior's command. Like a good soldier he selected the latter alternative, and, at a later date, arriving at Delhi with General Nicholson, did good service at the siege. As Colonel Herbert Edwardes wrote at the time:—" How common sense revenges itself upon defective systems when real dangers assail a State. Had there been no struggle for life or death when would Neville Chamberlain and John Nicholson, in the prime of their lives,[*] with all their faculties of doing and enduring, have attained the rank of brigadier-general? Why should we keep down in peace the men whom we must put up in war?"

The Movable Column marched from Wuzeerabad on the 28th May, and in a few days arrived at Lahore. The troops at Meean Meer, the military cantonment of Lahore, consisting of three regiments of infantry and one of cavalry, had already been dis-

---

[*] General Nicholson was at this time thirty-five, and General Chamberlain two years his senior. Edwardes himself was only thirty-eight.

armed by Brigadier Corbett, and it was now decided to dismount the 8th Cavalry, a notoriously disaffected corps, like most of the mounted regiments. The operation was successfully effected in the following manner. By a slight change in the usual marching order of the column, H.M.'s 52nd were placed in front, it having been previously intimated to the officer commanding that, while the left wing and the rest of the column halted at the civil station at Anarkullee, the right wing was to march on to Meean Meer, the encampment six miles farther on, and take up ground at the central picket. The wing arrived in the dim twilight, and drew up alongside the picket, which consisted of two companies of H.M.'s 81st Foot, four guns of the Horse Artillery, and Lieutenant Nicholson's * Irregular Cavalry. The 8th were then ordered out. Overawed by the proximity of so large a European force, and with Coke's unsympathising Punjaubees at their side, they sullenly obeyed the order to dismount.

General Chamberlain halted with the Movable Column at Lahore for a few days, during which two Sepoys of the 35th Native Infantry, the same regiment which had done such good service at Jellahabad under Sir Robert Sale, were tried for using seditious language and endeavouring to instigate their comrades to mutiny, and, being convicted, were, on the 9th of June, blown away from guns. On the previous evening intelligence had been received by telegraph of the mutiny of the 36th and 61st Native Infantry at Jullundhur, and, on the night of the execution, the Movable Column marched thither, and, on the following day, had covered the distance of thirty miles between Lahore and Umritsur.

Near the sacred city of the Sikhs is the important fortress of Govindghur, garrisoned at this time by a company of artillery, and a company of H.M.'s 81st Regiment. Here General Chamberlain received orders to join the Delhi Field Force, to take the place of Colonel Chester, the Adjutant-General, who had been killed at the action of Budlee-Kee-Serai, on the 9th June; and Colonel Denniss, second in command of the 52nd, took tempo-

---

* Lieutenant Charles Nicholson, who was a brother of General Nicholson, lost an arm at the storm of Delhi, and died some time later when on a visit to the grave of his brother, whose death affected his health.

rary command until the arrival of the Column at Jullundhur on the 21st of June. On the following day, Brigadier-General Nicholson assumed charge, to the great satisfaction of the entire force, and, on the 24th, proceeded to Phillour. Lieutenant Roberts continued on Nicholson's staff in charge of the quartermaster-general's department, and soon gained the entire confidence of his chief.

These two soldiers, whose exploits during crises in our Indian history have placed their names high in the temple of fame, had much in common. Both possessed that impetuous valour which refuses to be deterred by difficulties when an object has to be achieved, and yet both were gifted with that military insight which correctly gauges the means necessary to effect the end sought to be attained; inspired on the field of battle by the "*Gaudia certaminis*," the rapture of the strife, referred to by Attila in his address to his soldiers, these born leaders of men were never more self-possessed than at such a time. In short, Nicholson and Roberts were gifted with that spark of heavenly fire we call genius, whether possessed by the poet, painter, statesman, or soldier. Speaking of the military qualifications of the officers under whom he served during the Indian Mutiny, Roberts gives the palm incontestably to Nicholson, as not only the best, but indeed the only one who was possessed of that rarest of attributes.

From Jullundhur General Nicholson marched to Phillour, twenty-four miles distant, on the right bank of the Sutlej, in the direct line of the Grand Trunk Road, a place of such great strategical value, that Sir Charles Napier described it as the "key of the Punjaub." The safety of Phillour was of essential importance, as in the strong fort is a magazine, with munitions of war only inferior in importance to those stored at Ferozepore and at Delhi, now feeding the rebellion, owing to the same system of crass stupidity which cost us an army at Cabul—the system by which the very sinews of war are placed within the keeping of those who may be our enemies.

Some difficulty was experienced in crossing the Beas, which had risen; but Lieutenant Roberts effected the passage of the troops and stores with a success that elicited the commendation of his chief. On the morning of the 25th of June, on his arrival at Phillour, General Nicholson put into execution a step he had been for some time revolving in his mind. This was the disarming of the 33rd and 35th Regiments of Native Infantry, the arrangements for which were made by Lieutenant Roberts, and were carried out with complete success. When the General made his appearance on the camping-ground, there were no signs of preparation for any unusual occurrence. The Europeans and the guns were in advance, and so placed that when the suspected Sepoy regiments came up in succession to the camping-ground, they were completely at the mercy of their white comrades. These had their instructions, and were so disposed, many of the Europeans lying on the ground as if for rest, that the most suspicious could detect no symptom of the impending disarmament. As, however, the first of the Native regiments came up, the men were told to pile their arms by Nicholson, who, leaning over one of the guns, gave his orders as unconcernedly as though they were of the most ordinary character.

"If they bolt," he said to Captain Bourchier, of the artillery, "you follow as hard as you can ; the bridge will have been destroyed, and we shall have a Sobraon on a small scale."

But the Sepoy regiments, entrapped by the suddenness of the order, and scarcely knowing what they were doing, piled their arms at the word of command, and suffered them to be taken to the fort. This done, Nicholson addressed them, saying that desertion would be punished with death, and that they could not possibly escape, as the fords were watched. Eight men made the attempt, but were brought back, tried, and condemned.*

On the following day Lieutenant Roberts severed his connection with the Punjaub Movable Column. Hearing that artillery officers were urgently required at Delhi, he applied for permission to resign his appointment, and join the army there. General Nicholson at first would not give his consent, but Roberts urged his request so earnestly, that, at length, the gallant General, who could not but sympathize with the ardour of the young staff officer, whose ambition to be where blows were

---

* See "Eight Months' Campaign against the Bengal Sepoy Army," by Colonel G. Bourchier, C.B., Bengal Horse Artillery.

thickest, struck a responsive chord in his own breast, gave the required permission.

Quitting the column at Phillour, Lieutenant Roberts travelled in a mail cart with two officers—Lieutenant C. F. Packe, 4th Native Infantry (attached to the 4th Sikh Infantry during the siege), who was shot in the ankle and maimed for life the morning after their arrival at Delhi, and Captain W. G. Law, 10th Native Infantry (attached to the 1st Punjaub Infantry, known as Coke's Rifles, from their gallant leader), who was killed during the siege.

On arriving at Delhi, on Sunday, the 28th of June, Lieutenant Roberts was first appointed Deputy-Assistant Quartermaster-General to the cavalry brigade, but, at his own request, was transferred in the same capacity to the artillery. Within a few days of his arrival in the camp, beneath the historic "ridge" whereon the batteries of the immortal Delhi Field Force were placed, the army was strengthened by some small reinforcements, but at no time did it exceed 9,000 efficient combatants.

The siege, upon which the small British force, under the command of Sir Henry Barnard, entered in June, 1857, is, probably, unparalleled in modern times, for the besiegers were at times equally the besieged, and they were outnumbered as three to one, so that the labour and fighting were harassing in the extreme. Such an event as a regular siege undertaken during the monsoon months was unknown in our Indian history, and would have horrified such old campaigners as Lord Gough, being contrary to what honest Fluellen calls "the true and ancient prerogatifes and laws of the wars." It was a time when the stubborn character of the English blood was displayed at its best, and the men who know not when they are beaten clung with desperate tenacity to their lines and batteries, whilst continuous bodies of rebels poured into the city, flushed with murder and rapine, and bent on establishing the truth of the prophecy held out as a bait to them—that the English Raj, which was founded at Plassey on the 23rd of June, 1757, would come to an end on the hundredth anniversary of that event. It was a time of stern, arduous effort, when every man had to play his part, and the heroic in the nature of each found opportunities of display.

Delhi in 1857 was no place for poltroons or fops, such as the lord who excited the ire of the soldierly Percy :—

> "Neat, trimly dress'd,
> Fresh as a bridegroom ; and his chin, new reap'd,
> Show'd like a stubble-land at harvest time.
> * * * *
> As the soldiers bore dead bodies by,
> He called them untaught knaves, unmannerly,
> To bring a slovenly unhandsome corse
> Betwixt the wind and his nobility."

All eyes in India were centred on Delhi, the focus of rebellion, and it was universally recognized that upon the ability of the small British force, scarce stronger at times than a brigade, to bring the siege to a successful conclusion, depended our hold of the great Eastern dependency and the safety of every white man, woman, and child in the country. It was resolved, in spite of some more timid counsels in high places, to fight it out on that ridge, and, bull-dog like, to die, if needs be, before relinquishing their hold on the throat of rebellion.

While the effective strength of the besieging force, even with the addition of wings of H.M.'s 8th and 61st Regiments, only numbered 6,600 men, the rebels received constant reinforcements, and, on the 1st and 2nd July, the Rohilcund mutineers marched over the bridge of boats across the Jumna, in full view of the British troops on the ridge above the camp. They consisted of No. 15 Horse Battery, two 6-pounder guns, the 8th Irregular Cavalry, and the 18th, 28th, 29th, and 68th Native Infantry. The rebels continued to receive accessions of strength, and, during the month of June, there arrived the Jhansi troops, consisting of half No. 18 Light Field Battery, a wing 12th Native Infantry, and the 14th Irregular Cavalry; and the Neemuch Brigade, which included a troop of Native Horse Artillery, a wing 1st Light Cavalry, the 72nd Native Infantry, the 7th Regiment of the Gwalior Contingent, and the cavalry and infantry of the Kotah Contingent. At the lowest estimate, Lieutenant Norman, Assistant Adjutant-General of the Field Force, places the rebel strength in August at 30,000 men, exclusive of undisciplined men recruited from the city and rural population. Their supply of guns and ammunition was practically inexhaustible, owing to their possession of the magazine in Delhi, the British force being scarcely sufficient to invest one-third of the walls, and access to the left bank of the Jumna being secured to the rebels by the bridge of boats, which was protected by the fire of the guns at Selimgurh, and was fully 2,500 yards from the British batteries. A constant stream of supplies was poured into the city, the British commanders being content to be able to keep open their rear, and communicate with the Punjaub, whence all their supplies were derived. Had the large force of trained regular and irregular cavalry at the disposal of the rebel leaders been properly handled, it is certain that communications with Umballa and other points in the rear could not have been maintained, thus ensuring the raising of the siege and the temporary success of the rebellion until the arrival of reinforcements from England; but throughout the protracted operations known as the Mutiny, the rebellious Sepoys were destitute of any directing head or leader of capacity, and there being no plan of combined action, such advantages as they possessed were neglected.

Lieutenant Roberts had not been long in camp before his ardent spirit was gratified by participating in the almost daily conflicts in which the Field Force was engaged, either repelling an attack or taking the initiative. On the 30th June the rebels made an attack on the position on the extreme right, at Hindoo Rao's house, and Lieutenant Roberts witnessed some sharp fighting, lasting from 9 A.M. till 2 P.M., when the enemy were repulsed.

During the afternoon of the 3rd July, encouraged by the arrival of large reinforcements, a body of some 5,000 or 6,000 insurgents moved into the gardens and suburbs on the right of the British position, and pushed on rapidly from Alipore, one march in rear of the camp, compelling the squadron of 5th Punjaub Cavalry stationed there to fall back towards Rhye. The fire of the enemy's guns could be heard in camp, and at 2 A.M. on the 4th July, Major Coke was sent to intercept the rebels with a column, consisting of four guns of Captain Money's troop of Horse Artillery, and two guns of the native troop, Major Scott's Horse Battery, a squadron Carabineers, a squadron 9th Lancers, the Guide Cavalry, the wing H.M.'s 61st Regiment, and the 1st Punjaub Rifles. Roberts, in the capacity of staff officer, accompanied this column, which numbered in all about 300 cavalry, 800 infantry, and 12 guns, which were all that could be spared from the camp.

At one time grave fears were felt that the rebels might be pushing on to attack Kurnaul, or, at least, to intercept treasure on the road under native escort between that station and Delhi. About sunrise, however, it became known that they had re-crossed the canal near Alipore, and were returning towards Delhi along the high and dry ground running nearly parallel with the canal, and at a distance from it of a mile or more. Major Coke at once moved to take them in the flank, but had to proceed over a swampy cross-country road for a mile and a half to a bridge over the canal, and then had more than a mile of swampy fields to pass over. The Artillery came first into action, and were immediately answered by the insurgents' guns, which had been moved into a village when they perceived the British approach, their infantry and cavalry at the same time facing towards the advancing enemy. The infantry, however, save some posted in the village, soon commenced moving off again, their cavalry shortly did the same, and their artillery fire slackening, it was evident their guns also were being withdrawn. Major Coke again advanced his guns, though with much difficulty, owing to the nature of the ground, and, hurrying on the infantry and mounted men, the Guide Cavalry on the left were directed to push forward and get on the line of the enemy's retreat; owing, however, to the deep mud, little progress could be made, and the rebels carried off all their guns. However, all the plunder taken from Alipore was re-captured, together with some artillery waggons and ammunition.

On his return towards camp, Major Coke rested his infantry and some of his cavalry at the canal bank, and, while here, was attacked by some fresh troops from Delhi, including a body of 800 horse. The firing was sharp, and cavalry and artillery were sent from camp to Major Coke's support. The attack, however, had been virtually repulsed before these supports arrived, and all returned to camp, the Europeans having suffered much from the intense heat of the sun.

On the 5th of July, the Commander-in-Chief, Sir Henry

The Sortie of the 9th July.

Barnard, an officer much liked and respected, expired of cholera, after an illness of six hours, and General Reed, as senior officer in the camp, became Provisional Commander-in-Chief, being the third since the 23rd of May, when General Anson had died of that terrible Indian scourge.

On the 9th of July, a severe action was fought with the enemy, in which Lieutenant Roberts participated in the capacity of staff officer of the force engaged. During the morning the rebels, in great force, showed out of the city in the suburbs on the right, and about ten o'clock a body of horse, assisted by the treachery of the 9th Irregular Cavalry, made a determined raid into the British lines. On the right was a mound, on which was a battery of three 18-pounders, with an infantry picket, facing the Subzee Mundee suburb, and to the right again were stationed two Horse Artillery guns, with an escort of a troop of the 6th Dragoon Guards (Carabineers). Beyond these, at a position called the Fakir's Enclosure, was a native officer's picket of the 9th Irregulars, with two vedettes thrown forward. The folly of placing an inlet of the camp practically in the keeping of these horsemen, who had shown by their action at Budlee-Kee-Serai, on the 8th of June, that little confidence could be reposed in them, was soon made manifest. The rebel cavalry suddenly charged through the picket of Irregulars and dashed upon the two Horse Artillery guns of Major Tomb's troop, commanded by Lieutenant Hills.* The gallantry and self-sacrifice displayed by this officer should be chronicled here in a memoir of his old Addiscombe friend, whom he accompanied in his memorable advance on Cabul, after the massacre of the Cavagnari mission.

The Carabineers, only numbering thirty-two troopers, all young soldiers, turned and broke, with the exception of Lieutenant Stillman and two or three men. Lieutenant Hills, seeing the rebel horsemen advancing unopposed, and desirous of giving his gunners time to unlimber, took the desperate resolution of charging single-handed the head of the column. It was a self-sacrificing resolve, worthy to be compared with

---

* Now Major-General Sir James Hills, V.C., K.C.B.

that of the Curtius who sacrificed his life for the good of the Republic, and it was right gallantly carried out, and gained that young officer the coveted V.C., which was never more worthily bestowed. Charging with impetuosity, Hills cut down the first man he met with, slashed a second across the face with his sword, and turned to meet two other horsemen who had made at him. The horse of the young officer came into violent collision with the steeds of the sowars, and he was hurled to the ground; the fall probably saved his life, for both his enemies had made desperate cuts at him, which did not take effect, though one laid open his jacket just below the left arm. Hills lay for a moment stunned, and the sowars, thinking him killed, passed on; recovering himself, he regained his sword, which lay about ten yards off, and had just time to secure it before he found himself confronted with three "Pandies," two on horseback and the third on foot. The position was as desperate as can well be imagined, but Hills managed to engage them in detail. The first man he brought down from his horse by a sword-cut, and as the second charged him, lance in rest, he dexterously guarded the thrust, and, with a swinging blow, brought him also off his perch. The fellow had received a terrible gash across the head and face, but advanced upon young Hills, who, in a second encounter, despatched him by a sabre wound on the head. He had hardly disposed of this antagonist when the third and most formidable of the trio, a young and powerful man, was upon him. Hills was now exhausted, and moreover was almost suffocated by his cloak, which during the struggle had got tightly twisted round his throat. A cut he made at his adversary's head was parried, and the Pandy, running in, seized the hilt of Hills' sword and wrenched it out of his hand. Having nothing left but his fists, the young Englishman brought into play the "noble art" he had acquired at Addiscombe. "Punching the head" would, however, do little in the case of a man with a sword, and Hills fell in the struggle, and would have been despatched had not Major Tombs, at the critical moment, dropped his antagonist by a lucky "potshot" with his revolver at thirty yards.

But Hills' *penchant* for fighting was not yet satisfied. Returning after some time to secure the unlimbered gun which had been left behind, the two officers saw the man whom they thought killed making off with a pistol which Hills had hurled at one of his assailants during the recent *mêlée*. The young officer ran after him, and made a cut at him with his sword, which the Pandy cleverly avoided by springing on one side, at the same time inflicting a severe wound on Hills' head. The latter sprang to his feet, and cutting at his adversary, nearly severed his hand at the wrist. Major Tombs now arrived and despatched the plucky native by running him through the body. Both these gallant artillery officers received the Victoria Cross, and both acquired great subsequent distinction.*

Meanwhile, the rebel horsemen riding over and past the guns, followed the flying Dragoons in at the right of the camp, but, failing to induce a troop of native horse artillerymen to join them, were soon driven out by some troops hastily collected together by Captain Fagan, of the Artillery. During this episode the rebels maintained a heavy cannonade from the guns on the city walls and field-pieces in the open, while large bodies of the enemy, stationed in the enclosures and gardens of the suburbs, opened fire on the batteries and Subzee Mundee pickets. To dislodge these a column was formed, under the command of General Chamberlain, who was accompanied by Lieutenant Roberts. The force consisted of Major Scott's Horse Battery, the available men of the wings 8th and 61st Foot, and the 4th Sikh Infantry, in all about 700 infantry and six guns, reinforced *en route* by the head-quarters and two companies 60th Rifles, under Lieutenant-Colonel J. Jones, the infantry being commanded by Brigadier W. Jones, C.B. As this column, under constant and heavy showers of rain, swept up through the Subzee Mundee, Major Reid, commanding the Sirmoor Battalion, was instructed to move down from Hindoo Rao's picket on the ridge and co-operate with such infantry as could be spared from the main picket. The insurgents were cleared out of the dense vegetation of the gardens without difficulty, though at some of the serais they offered a very obstinate resistance, and were not dislodged without considerable

---

* Sir Harry Tombs, the very *beau ideal* of a soldier in character and personal appearance, died a few years ago of a painful malady.

loss. The success of the day, says Norman, "was greatly due to the admirable and steady practice of Major Scott's Battery, under a heavy fire, eleven men being put *hors de combat* out of its small complement." The British loss was one officer and forty men killed, and eight officers and 163 men wounded; that of the enemy being officially computed at 500.

This was the first severe action in which Roberts was engaged, and it so whetted his appetite for fighting that a few days later, when another "tamasha" came off, he was in the thick of it, and received a wound which was near putting a premature termination to his career.

The hardships of camp life were much increased by the torrents of rain which continued to deluge the British lines, while that terrible scourge, cholera, decimated the ranks of the brave little army; the wings of the 8th and 61st Regiments being the chief sufferers. Reports were received that the rebel chiefs, probably encouraged by the destruction of the cantonment at Agra by the Neemuch Brigade, had sworn to capture the British guns on the ridge, and smoke their hookahs in Hindoo Rao's house, the key of the position, which was held throughout the siege by Major Reid with the Sirmoor Battalion and two companies of the 60th Rifles. Accordingly, on the morning of the 14th July, they swarmed out in great force, and attacked the batteries on the right flank, and the fire for many hours from great guns and small-arms was continuous and very heavy.

As the batteries on the ridge failed to drive the rebels back, about four o'clock a column of attack was formed, under Brigadier Showers, who was accompanied by General Chamberlain, on whose staff Roberts served for the day. The column consisted of half of Major Turner's and Captain Money's troops of Horse Artillery, six guns; the 1st Bengal Fusiliers, under Major Jacob; Coke's Corps of Punjaubees, and Major Reid's Sirmoor Battalion; with some details of Guide Cavalry and Hodson's Horse. The action that ensued was not an unqualified success, for though the rebels lost heavily, our small army, in which every life was of consequence, also suffered severely.

The column marched through the Subzee Mundee, and drove

off the enemy, on whom they inflicted great loss, but, in the ardour of the pursuit, followed them up close under the walls of the city, when they got under the range of the heavy guns, which opened on them with grape. There was nothing to do but to retreat, when the rebels sallied out, but did not care to come to close quarters, and a charge of cavalry was effectively met by Hodson, who, wrote Greathed, in his letter describing the events of the day, "always turns up in moments of difficulty." The British loss was fifteen men killed and sixteen officers and 117 men wounded. Among the officers wounded were Brigadier-General Chamberlain, who had his arm shattered by a grape-shot when leading the troops with all the ardour that distinguished this *beau sabreur*.

Roberts, who was actively engaged on the staff, had a narrow escape of his life. As the force was retreating, a bullet lodged in his cap-pouch, and broke the skin of his back, making a severe bruise close to the spine, though had it not been for the cap-pouch he must have been killed. This article of accoutrement was a small native-made affair, less than three inches across, similar to what was worn by most officers in carrying revolver caps, and was always carried in front. By some means the pouch had worked round to the back, and was thus the means of saving the life of its wearer, who, on being struck, put his hand to the part affected, and could not at first make out what it was he had got there. For more than a month Lieutenant Roberts was not permitted to go on duty by the doctor, which was a great trial to him, though he visited the batteries, and could not be prevailed upon to keep quiet in his tent.

The enemy suffered severely on the 14th of July, their loss being estimated at 1,000, and, for hours, carts were seen conveying their dead into the city.

A change now again took place in the chief command. General Reed, who had been in ill-health since he joined the force on the 8th of June, and was daily growing feebler, resigned the command into the hands of Brigadier Archdale Wilson, commanding the Artillery, an officer who possessed the confidence of the army, having, in the actions of the 30th and 31st of May, on the Hindun, displayed considerable skill, and with 700 men defeated a rebel force seven times his strength. There were officers senior to Wilson in the camp, but the times were too grave for such considerations to have any weight. The only one of them having superior claims was General Chamberlain, who would have been selected with the unanimous approval of the camp had not the severe wound received on the 14th, incapacitated him from active service during the remainder of the siege, and even from continuing his duties as Adjutant-General, which were filled with conspicuous ability and success by Lieutenant (now General Sir) Henry Norman, of the 31st Native Infantry.

On the 18th of July, the last serious fighting took place in the Subzee Mundee, for, by this time, the Engineers had cleared away the walls, serais, and gardens for some distance round the posts held by the British pickets in that suburb, while the breastwork connecting them with the crest of the Hindoo Rao range was completed. The nearest post to the city, an old temple, called by the European soldiers the " Sammy House," some way down the slope of the ridge, and within 900 yards' grape range of the Moree Bastion, was greatly strengthened and cover provided for its garrison. On the ridge itself, additional captured field-guns were planted in favourable positions, thus greatly increasing the duties of the Bengal Artillery, an unsurpassed body of gunners; and had it not been for the aid of the newly-raised Sikh Artillery, and volunteers from European regiments, it would have been impossible to have worked the guns. In these congenial duties, Lieutenant Roberts, when time and opportunity offered, participated with the ardour which, it is said, induces actors, during their evenings of occasional leisure, to witness the performance of their brethren of the " sock and buskin."

On the 20th of July, a reconnoissance was made by a column, under Lieutenant-Colonel Seaton, C.B., 35th Native Infantry, a gallant and able officer, who had served under Sir Robert Sale throughout the siege of Jellalabad; and, three days later, a strong force was sent under Brigadier Showers to drive away the enemy, who, emerging from the Cashmere Gate, had occupied Ludlow Castle, and annoyed the pickets with the fire from some field-guns. The rebels were dispersed after some smart skirmishing; among the British officers wounded being Colonels Seaton and Drought, and Captain Money, commanding a troop of horse artillery, the command of which now devolved on Captain Blunt.

The enemy at this time displayed great boldness, and, on the night of the 1st of August, a strong body, with guns and mortars, which had marched out of Delhi on the preceding day with the intention of getting into the rear of the camp, on their return moved through the Kissengunj suburb, and attacked the position on the extreme right of the ridge, coming close up to the breastworks, as many as 127 bodies being counted in front of one to the right of the Sammy House. The rebels now turned their attention to annoying the British position at Metcalfe's picket on the extreme left, near the river, and in front of Ludlow Castle and the Khoodsee Bagh. At dawn of the 12th of August, a column proceeded to drive them out of their positions, under the command of Brigadier Showers, and was completely successful, though at considerable loss, among the severely wounded being those invaluable officers, Brigadier Showers and Major Coke, the commander of the 1st Punjaub Infantry, or Coke's Rifles.

Meanwhile Sir John Lawrence was straining every nerve to reinforce the Delhi Army, for, with characteristic sagacity, he recognized the fact that, on the early downfall of the headquarters of the rebellion, depended the safety of the Empire. Denuding his province of almost every soldier, he despatched Brigadier-General Nicholson to the assistance of General Wilson, with a brigade of all arms, including H.M.'s 52nd Regiment, 600 bayonets, the remaining wing of H.M.'s 61st Regiment, and Bourchier's Light Field Battery. Nicholson, posting on in advance of the column, arrived at the camp on the 8th of August, and dined that night at the head-quarters mess, Mr. Greathed* describing him as "a fine, imposing-

---

* The letters of Mr. Hervey Harris Greathed, Commissioner and Political Agent with the Delhi Field Force, who died on the 19th of September before the walls of Delhi, were republished by his widow, and form one of the most interesting records of that eventful struggle. He was one of three brothers who served throughout the siege of Delhi, the others being Colonel (the late General Sir) Edward Greathed, commanding H.M.'s 8th Regiment, and Lieutenant Wilberforce Greathed, of the Bengal Engineers, who was severely wounded at the assault on the 14th of September.

looking man, who never speaks if he can help it." Returning to rejoin his brigade, it marched into camp with drums beating and colours flying on the 13th of August. The advent of Nicholson was hailed with satisfaction by the entire camp, as he had a great reputation as a fighting general, like his friend Neville Chamberlain, but was credited with more caution; both had been trained in the Punjaub school, like other soldiers then before Delhi, the famous Hodson, and Coke, Daly, Probyn, Watson, and Roberts.

On the 25th August, Nicholson moved with a strong force, including 16 guns and 800 European infantry, to Nujufgurh, in which direction a large column of the enemy had marched with the intention of intercepting the siege train then moving up from Ferozepore under a weak escort. He asked Roberts to accompany him as staff officer, but on the latter applying to do so, the doctors refused permission as his wound was not sufficiently healed. It was a great disappointment to our hero. Nicholson was completely successful, and the rebels were defeated with the loss of thirteen out of eighteen guns they had taken with them.

On the day this action was fought, the 26th of August, the enemy turned out of Delhi in great force, under the belief, apparently, that the camp would be denuded of troops, but they were repulsed with severe loss.

On the 4th of September, the siege train arrived, and all the reinforcements expected having come in, the total strength of all arms, including Lascars and artillery drivers, was 8,748,* of whom the Europeans were: artillery 580, cavalry 443, infantry 2,292. This was exclusive of the men in hospital, 2,977, and sickness prevailed to such an alarming extent that some European regiments were mere skeletons, the 52nd Light Infantry, which arrived only three weeks before, 600 strong, having but 242 effectives.

The siege train consisted of forty heavy guns and howitzers, ten heavy and twelve light mortars, manned by some companies of artillerymen, and there were, in addition, four troops of

---

* These numbers are exclusive of the Cashmere Contingent, which was accompanied by Major (now Lieutenant-General) R. Lawrence, 2,200 men and four guns, and some few hundred men under the Rajah of Jheend.

Opening of the Breaching Batteries.

horse artillery (one, Major Tombs's, having only four guns), and two field batteries. The engineer force was small, only consisting of 120 trained sappers, but the officers who planned the attack, were unsurpassed in the knowledge of their profession, and included Colonel Baird Smith, chief engineer; Captain (now Sir) Alexander Taylor, director of the attack, on whom the actual responsibilities of the siege operations, properly so called, devolved owing to his superior being wounded; and a band of young officers, including Lieutenants Salkeld, Home, Maunsell, and Greathed, such as any corps might be proud to own. The park, under Lieutenant Brownlow, of the Bengal Engineers, had been assiduous in collecting material, and 10,000 fascines, an equal number of gabions, and 100,000 sand-bags had been prepared, with scaling-ladders and other necessaries.

The plan adopted by the General was to hold in check the enemy's batteries on the right, between the Moree Bastion and Cabul Gate, and to push the main attack on the left between the Cabul Gate and Water Bastions, close to the river, which protected the flank, and where there was better cover. The Moree, Cashmere, and Water Bastions were very strong, and the curtain walls connecting them were 24 feet in height, and protected by a ditch 16 feet deep and 20 feet wide, with an escarp 8 feet in height, revetted with stone, and a sloping glacis.

On the evening of the 7th of September, No. 1 Battery was traced within 700 yards of the Moree Bastion, and by the following morning it was armed. The battery was in two portions, the right, for five 18-pounders and one 8-inch howitzer, to silence the Bastion, and the left portion, for four 18-pounders, to hold the Cashmere Bastion partially in check. The officer in charge of this battery, forming the right attack, which succeeded in silencing the enemy's fire exposed to it, was Major (now General Sir) James Brind, a gallant and able officer, who commanded the foot artillery throughout the siege from the 26th June, and subsequently did excellent service under General Walpole and Sir Colin Campbell. Setting to work directly his guns were in position, Major Brind's practice soon made a visible impression on the Moree

Bastion. Mr. Greathed says in his letter of the 9th of September:—" Major Brind has got his sixteen guns at work, and was firing salvos at the Moree and Cashmere. The effect on the Moree, which is nearest, is very telling; every shot strikes home and sends up a column of dust, and the shells burst inside it."

The next battery established, known in its proper sequence as No. 2, is of especial interest as that in which Lieutenant Roberts served throughout the bombardment. No. 2 Battery was traced in the evening of the 8th of September, within 600 yards of the city walls, at the advanced position at Ludlow Castle, which, to their surprise, the rebels allowed the besiegers to seize without opposition. An Engineer officer— to whose perspicuous account of the siege operations, published in the *Lahore Chronicle,* under the *nom de plume* of "Felix," and to Lieutenant Norman's excellent official narrative, we are indebted for these details—expresses his opinion that this inertness was due to the belief of the enemy that the attack was to be on the right, where all the fighting had hitherto been and the old batteries were mostly located. Ludlow Castle and the Khoodsee Bagh were occupied with strong detachments, and formed the chief supports to the left attack. During the 9th, the rebels opened a sharp musketry fire on these positions from the jungles in front, and with shot and shell from the Water and Cashmere Bastions, but the work of completing the battery went on, and, during the nights of the 9th and 10th, it was completed and partially armed. No. 2 Battery was in two divisions, one to the left, armed with nine 24-pounders, under command of Major Campbell, whose fire was directed to breach the curtain between the Cashmere and Water Bastions, immediately to the left of the former, and to knock off the parapet to the right and left for some distance so as to give no cover for musketry. Lieutenant Roberts, having gained permission of General Wilson, attached himself to this portion of No. 2 Battery. His ardent spirit could not confine itself to watching the effects of the fire of our guns, while his services might be utilized in directing them. Like the fiery Hotspur:—

" His forward spirit
Would lift him where most trade of danger ranged."

The second portion of No. 2 Battery, placed 200 yards to the right, commanded by Major Kaye, consisted of seven 8-inch howitzers and two 18-pounders, and its duty was to co-operate with the first portion. During the afternoon of the 10th of September, the left section of Major Brind's Battery, consisting of four guns, under the immediate command of Major Kaye, met with an accident, to which we will refer here as Lieutenant Roberts was engaged. Sir James Brind writes to us :—" On the 10th of September the left section of my battery was destroyed by the enemy's fire, which would have been attended by disastrous consequences had we not succeeded in removing its guns and magazine into the shelter of the adjacent ravine before he perceived his advantage, and brought to bear upon the burning mass a greatly increased fire which caused some casualties. The work of this section of the battery had fortunately been effected, and as the guns were urgently required for the Ludlow Castle Battery, Major Johnson was directed to take them in charge. This energetic officer claimed my assistance in accomplishing a most difficult task under the cover of night. He was accompanied by Lieutenant Roberts; and by the indefatigable exertions of officers and men, the operation was effected over difficult ground without accident, though full of incidents of a most engrossing character, making that night's work memorable in the history of the siege."

During the night of the 10th September, the arming of No. 2 Battery was completed by the arrival of the 18-pounders from Brind's Battery, and No. 3 Battery, for six 18-pounders, under command of Major Scott, was also finished within 180 yards of the Water Bastion. The audacity with which this work was completed under a hot musketry fire, was an earnest of what was to follow. No. 4 Battery, under Major Tombs, consisting of ten heavy mortars, was completed at the same time in the Khoodsee Bagh. The only steps taken by the enemy to break the ring of iron encircling their boasted defences, were to construct an advanced trench parallel to these batteries, and about 350 yards from them, from which they maintained a heavy musketry fusillade throughout the rest of the siege, and to bring into the open in the Taleewarra suburb some field-guns which caused considerable annoyance to Nos. 1 and 2 Batteries by their enfilading fire. Before the guns of No. 2 Battery opened fire, a sortie was made from the Cashmere Gate, which was repulsed with loss, and a constant fire was kept up from the trenches in front. A portion of the first Punjaub Rifles, under Lieutenant Nicholson, brother of the General, was, from the 8th to the 14th, engaged in protecting the battery, being posted behind a low wall in advance, with a reserve of the same corps together with some European infantry at Ludlow Castle, and the other batteries were also guarded by strong parties of infantry.

All being in readiness, the batteries of the left attack opened fire on the 11th, the signal being a salvo from the nine 24-pounders with which Roberts was stationed. The Engineer officer, already quoted, says that this " salvo showed by the way it brought down the wall in huge fragments what effect it might be expected to produce after a few hours. The Cashmere Bastion attempted to reply, but was quickly silenced, and both portions of No. 2 went to work in fine style, knocking the bastion and adjacent curtains to pieces." The fire was kept up with great spirit during the day, and, in the evening, Roberts had a narrow escape of being killed. He and the other officers of the battery, Major Campbell and Captain (now General Sir) Edwin Johnson, were lying under the parapet, reading a newspaper, when a discharge of grape-shot whizzed over the parapet, and a piece struck Major Campbell, who was lying outside, in the thigh, inflicting so severe a wound that he was compelled to surrender the command of the battery to Captain Johnson, Assistant Adjutant-General of Artillery, who, like Roberts, had obtained permission from General Wilson to assist in working the guns of this battery.

No. 3 Battery did not open fire till the 12th, when fifty guns and mortars were engaged pouring a continuous fire of shot and shell on the defences of the rebels, who must have had it brought home to them that the hour of retribution was about to strike. From 10 A.M. on the 11th till the morning of the 14th, when the signal for assault was made, there was no cessation of the fiery hail, which the enemy bore with that resignation to the decrees of fate instilled into the hearts of the followers of the Prophet as an axiom of their religion, and though unable to work a gun from any of the three Bastions so fiercely assailed—the Moree, Cashmere, and Water Bastions— the rebel gunners stood by their field-pieces in the open, which partially enfiladed the British batteries, and showed that the lessons our officers had taught them at Maharajpore, Sobraon, and Goojerat had been turned to account. Not only from these light pieces, but from a gun whose fire was brought to bear from a hole in the curtain wall, from rockets directed from a Martello tower, and a heavy fusillade from their advanced trench and from the city walls, the enemy made a vigorous resistance, and sought to delay the impending hour of doom.

The force of Foot Artillerymen even without relief, being insufficient to man the guns, nearly all the officers and men of the Horse Artillery were sent into the batteries and worked in them until the morning of the assault, when they rejoined their troops. In addition to these, the Carabineers and 9th Lancers furnished a quota of volunteers, " whose intelligence and goodwill rendered their services most valuable." Several infantry officers, who had volunteered their services, had been under instruction for some days before the breaching batteries opened, and were afterwards most usefully employed in the latter. The men of the two field batteries of the force were not taken for the siege guns, as one battery furnished the three divisions of guns for the pickets, and the other was in reserve in camp.

During the bombardment Lieutenant Roberts had another narrow escape. He had charge of the right guns, and on opening the embrasure to fire, while laying one of them, a round shot took off the arm of the gunner who was "serving" the vent and knocked him over, but he escaped without serious injury.

General Wilson now thought the time had come to storm the city, and, during the night of the 13th of September, some Engineer officers stole down and examined the two breaches near the Cashmere and Water Bastions, Lieutenants Medley and Lang the former, and Lieutenants Greathed and Home the latter. Both breaches were reported practicable, and orders were issued that night for the assault to take place at daybreak on the following morning. Four columns of assault were formed; the first, under Brigadier-General Nicholson, to storm the breach near the Cashmere Bastion, and escalade the face of that Bastion; the second, under Brigadier Jones, to storm the breach in the Water Bastion; the third, under Colonel Campbell, to assault by the Cashmere Gate after it had been blown open; and the fourth, under Major (now General Sir Charles) Reid, to attack the Kissengunj suburb and enter by the Lahore Gate. There was also a reserve column under Brigadier Longfield. Lieutenant Roberts now rejoined the staff of General Wilson, as the services of all the officers attached to the Commander-in-Chief would be in requisition during the critical operations connected with the assault.

At 4 A.M., on the 14th of September, the different columns fell in and were marched to their respective places, the heads of Nos. 1, 2, and 3 columns being kept concealed until the moment for the actual assault should arrive. The signal was to be the advance of 200 men of the 60th Rifles, under Lieutenant-Colonel Jones, as skirmishers to the front to cover the heads of the columns. It is not our province to describe the thrilling details of the assault of the breaches at the Cashmere and Water Bastions; the explosion of the Cashmere Gate by the band of heroes, Lieutenants Home and Salkeld, and Serjeants Carmichael, Burgess, and Smith; and the death of the ever to be lamented Nicholson, when, having carried all before him at the point of the bayonet, he proceeded, with the eagerness characteristic of his heroic nature, to clear the ramparts between the Moree Bastion and Lahore Gate, and fell while animating his troops to increased exertions.*

---

* Roberts says it was impossible for any troops in the world—and none finer could be found than the well-seasoned soldiers of the Delhi Field Force—to have carried the Lahore Gate, the narrow streets and passages leading to which were commanded by loopholes and housetops from which a hot fire rained down on the heads of every man who showed himself. In that terrible ordeal Nicholson called on his men for further efforts, and seven officers stepped to the front to show the way. All were shot down save his aide-de-camp, Lieutenant Kennett Dixon, of the Bengal Cavalry. "I shall not forget you, Dixon, should we survive," said the hero, whose majestic form was soon laid low by a bullet. The writer has a special satisfaction in recording this incident of a young officer—his relative—who was killed a few months later heading a charge of the Mooltanee Horse.

The Storm of Delhi.

The storm of Delhi is an oft-told tale, though it is one that reflects undying lustre on the arms of our country.

The only failure throughout the operations of this eventful day was that of the fourth column under Major Reid, which, advancing from the Subzee Mundee suburb towards Kissengunj, in company with the Cashmere Contingent, was compelled to fall back with heavy loss, among the severely wounded being the gallant commandant.

The Cavalry, 600 sabres, under Brigadier Hope Grant, with a troop and a half of Horse Artillery, under Major Tombs, co-operated during the assault by checking any attempt of the enemy to attack the storming columns in flank by a sortie from the Lahore Gate.

The actual loss, among combatants, during the bombardment between the 11th and 14th, was 327 officers and men, including Captain Fagan of the Artillery, as fine a soldier as any in the camp, and during the assault (exclusive of the casualties sustained by the Cashmere Contingent), no less than 66 officers and 1,104 men were killed and wounded, being nearly one-third of the force engaged. The Bengal Fusiliers, of which 250 went into action, lost nine officers, including Major Jacob commanding; and other regiments suffered in proportion. Of seventeen Engineer officers on duty at the assault, ten were placed *hors de combat*, including the three officers, Lieutenants Medley, Greathed, and Maunsell, leading Nos. 1, 2, and 3 columns, and Lieutenants Tandy and Salkeld of the storming party, the former of whom was killed, and the latter died of his wounds.* Lieutenant Roberts had his horse shot during the day. He was going round the position with Captains Norman and Johnson, and came under a heavy fire from a party of the enemy. At the time the horse was killed he had dismounted and was leading the animal.

During the 15th several mortars were got into position to shell the town and palace, a battery was opened from the College Gardens of the Palace, and a breach was made also from the College in the magazine defences. Meanwhile the

---

* During the siege the 60th Rifles lost in killed and wounded 389 men out of 640; the Sirmoor Battalion, 319 out of 540; and the Corps of Guides, 303 out of 550.

enemy kept up a cannonade on our portion of the city from the fortified post known as Selimgurh, and from the magazine a constant musketry fire was maintained on the College compound. At dawn on the 16th, the magazine was successfully stormed by H.M's. 61st Regiment, and Kissengunj was evacuated by the enemy, who left five heavy guns, of which possession was taken by a party sent forward from Hindoo Rao. "We were now, for the first time," says Norman, "enabled to see the immense strength of the insurgents' position here and in Taleewarra, and which they had spared no labour to improve."

Gradually pushing on, but making all secure in his rear before taking another step, General Wilson, on the 17th and 18th, brought his right and left positions at the Cabul Gate and magazine into direct communication by a line of posts; the Bank, Major Abbott's house and the dwelling of Khan Mahomed were also taken, so that his posts were now close to the Palace and Chandnee Chouk. "These advances," says the Engineer officer already quoted, "were not made without opposition both from field artillery and musketry, but, being conducted with great judgment, our loss was trifling." All the mortars, including those captured in the magazine, now played constantly upon the palace and the quarters of the town occupied by the enemy, who, seeing that all further resistance was hopeless, made their escape by the gates at the opposite end of the city. On the evening of the 19th, the Berm Bastion was surprised and captured by a party from the Cabul Gate, and, early next morning, the Lahore Gate and Garstin Bastion were likewise taken and held. By the 20th* the King's palace and Selimgurh, the old Mogul fortress on the opposite side of the town to the Lahore Gate, were captured, and, on the morning of the 21st, a royal salute announced that Delhi had changed masters, and the headquarters of General Wilson were established in the Dewan Khas, or Great Hall of Audience, of the palace.

An extraordinary circumstance is narrated by Sir Hope

---

* The total loss of the Delhi Field Force, from the 30th of May to the 20th of September, was 46 officers and 946 men killed; 140 officers, and 2,655 men wounded; and 30 missing.

Grant in his journal, showing in a striking manner the fatalistic sentiments inspiring the breast of the Mussulman.

As the British troops advanced to seize the King's palace, two sentries were observed pacing their beat, armed and accoutred according to regulation. They took no heed of the advancing enemy, and were bayoneted at their posts. Such indifference in the presence of imminent death is foreign to the Western nature, which yet can boast a superior presence of mind, if not courage. But the doomed sentry acted on the philosophic sentiment of Cæsar, who is made to say by our great dramatist:—

> "It seems to me most strange that men should fear,
> Seeing that death, a necessary end,
> Will come, when it will come."

Meanwhile, Lieutenant Hodson, whose services throughout the siege were of so important a character that it is scarcely an exaggeration to say that no officer of the investing army conduced more to the success of the siege, marching quite round the city, seized a large camp outside the Delhi Gate, hastily evacuated by the rebels, and soon his cavalry had secured the Jumma Musjid, in the heart of the city, where they were speedily supported by the infantry and guns advancing from the opposite direction. Following up his success, the King of Delhi, the miserable descendant of the Grand Mogul, was captured a few miles from the city, on the 21st of September, by Lieutenant Hodson, who, on the following day, marched with a handful of his gallant irregular horsemen, and completed the good work he had accomplished throughout the siege by the seizure of two of the King's sons and a grandson, all deeply implicated in the atrocities committed in the massacres of the preceding May.

Into the vexed question of the shooting of these princes by Lieutenant Hodson we will not enter here further than to remark that—after a careful perusal of Hodson's own account of the affair, of the Memoir of that gallant officer by his brother, of the description of the scene by his subaltern, Lieutenant MacDowell, the only other European eye-witness, who afterwards died the soldier's death, after carefully weighing the considerations that guided Hodson (a man of nerve and not given to panic) in the commission of the act, of the necessity of which he must have been the best judge —we cannot but acquit this gallant soldier of needless bloodshedding. His career at Delhi,[*] achieved as the most brilliant of free lances, was so remarkable that envy was aroused in breasts where it might least have been expected, and, sad to say, this discreditable feeling was not exorcised even by his death, some months later, in the service of his country, when, surely, any blots in his career—if any there were, and Lord Napier of Magdala denied their existence—might have been buried with him in his grave at Lucknow. This estimate of the character of the late Major Hodson is in agreement with that formed by such distinguished soldiers as Sir Donald Stewart, Sir Frederick Roberts, Sir James Brind, Sir James Hills, and many others of his comrades at Delhi.

During the operations between the 14th and 21st of September, Lieutenant Roberts was employed in reconnoitring the streets and defences of Delhi before they successively became the objects of attack, and the valuable service he was thus enabled to render may be gathered from one circumstance. From the information he obtained General Wilson was enabled to take the Berm Bastion in reverse, and also the enemy's position in the Chandnee Chouk, in the heart of the city, without the loss of a man!

A distinguished officer of the Delhi force writes at our request some reminiscences of Roberts at this time. Major Brind says:—"My first acquaintance with Sir Frederick Roberts as a professional associate was in the Peshawur valley. He was at the time aide-de-camp to his father, the late General Sir Abraham Roberts, G.C.B., with whom I had a pleasant acquaintance at Cawnpore in 1833. On my return to Peshawur from active service, the General, then commanding the division, sent his son one or two marches to meet me, and I have a vivid recollection of the interest he took in the splendid battery I had brought safe through a most difficult

---

[*] Mr. Greathed says of him in one of his Delhi letters:—"Hodson keeps an Argus-eye on the rear and left flank, and is always ready for an adventurous ride. He has a rare gift of brains as well as of pluck."

country to the point of our meeting. In those days the roads and ghâts leading to Peshawur offered in many places formidable difficulties to the safe passage of artillery, and it was, therefore, particularly gratifying to receive the General's approval. We were together at Peshawur for a year and a-half, during which time I was in chief command of the artillery force at all our field days there. On these occasions young Roberts acted as my orderly officer most satisfactorily, being then conspicuous as ever after for energy and ready appreciation of field operations.

"We next met in the Delhi Field Force—I in command of the Foot Artillery, and he as Deputy-Assistant Quartermaster-General to the artillery of the force, so we only accidentally came across one another, but it was patent to the Delhi Field Force that this zealous, clever officer never missed an opportunity of serving the cause we were engaged in, and of laying in a stock of practical knowledge that proved so valuable to him in after life. The time at last arrived (and not a day too soon, for the loyalty of the Punjaub was at its last breath, and on it, so far as we all could judge, depended the safety of India) when the actual siege of Delhi became obligatory. Nicholson's success at Nujjuffgur cleared the road for the safe arrival of the siege train, which Major Gaitskill, of the Artillery, had been directed to bring down from Ferozepore, under charge of that indefatigable Officiating Commissary of Ordnance, Captain Gray. It was safely parked in our camp, and made ready for distribution along the line of attack, as the breaching batteries were reported by the chief engineer ready to receive their ordnance and detachments. The Foot Artillery was so weak in officers and men through the casualties of three months' service that the batteries had to be further strengthened by large drafts from the Horse Artillery and European Cavalry, and volunteers from among the commissioned ranks were called for, and in like manner distributed and instructed by battery commanders. The artillery officers on the staff, including Lieutenant Roberts, had also to take their share of battery work. From the 14th of September, he reverted to the Quartermaster-General's department and we had another seven days' and nights' continuous work in clearing the city of the enemy. As my duty required I had to visit batteries—light and heavy—engaged in these operations, during which I found him actively employed."

Long before the close of the siege of Delhi, Lieutenant Roberts had established a reputation in the camp as one of the most promising officers of the Indian Army. Both Generals Chamberlain and Wilson, on whose staff he had acted throughout the siege, except during the bombardment between the 11th and 14th of September, rated his capacity very high, and the latter, in his recommendation to Government, described him as "an active and gallant officer." General Nicholson also had so high an opinion of his capabilities that when, taking time by the forelock, that brilliant officer had demanded of General Wilson (and been accorded) the command of the column that was to pursue the enemy on the fall of Delhi, he selected Lieutenant Roberts to accompany him. Major Campbell and Captain Johnson, under whose immediate command he served during the three days' bombardment, when his battery at Ludlow Castle had the chief work breaching the curtain between the Cashmere and Water Bastions, reported in the highest possible terms of the zeal, intelligence and skill displayed by Lieutenant Roberts.

We boast of the qualities of the Anglo-Saxon race, and when we regard the circumstances under which Delhi was captured there is good cause for self-glorification. Here was a vast city, with defences recently placed in efficient order according to modern military requirements by our own Engineer officers, containing a magazine with a practically inexhaustible supply of ordnance and ammunition, garrisoned by a disciplined force of the three arms, trained and disciplined by our own officers, flushed with success, and outnumbering as three to one the besiegers, who, owing to their paucity, could only beleaguer one-third of the city, while with the remaining two-thirds and the river-face, over which was a bridge of boats under their control, they maintained free communication with the surrounding country, whence supplies and reinforcements were derived to any extent required. It will not be denied, even by our Continental detractors, that no nation but the British would have gravely set about the task of capturing such a city with a single weak division! When the French undertook to subjugate the Arab tribes on the Tunis frontier, they dispatched 30,000 men, though, with a similar European force, scattered throughout the whole Peninsula, we broke the neck of the rebellion in '57, for Delhi was captured by the Indian Army before a soldier arrived from England. What the British soldier did a quarter of a century ago he will do again to-morrow, provided he is intelligently led.* Taken all in all, then, the siege of Delhi is unsurpassed in the annals of war, and bearing in mind that its capture was the turning-point in the suppression of the Mutiny, each one who took part in it may repeat, with just pride, the words of the Latin poet, *Quorum pars magna fui.*

---

* The Egyptian campaign has proved that this anticipation, which recent events in South Africa had, in the opinion of many, tended to disprove, was not hazarded by the writer without warrant.

CHAPTER III.

Lieutenant Roberts takes the Field with Colonel Greathed's Movable Column—The Action at Bolundshur—Narrow Escape of Lieutenant Roberts—The Capture of Allyghur—Roberts is engaged in the Pursuit with the 9th Lancers—The Surprise at Agra of the 10th of October—Roberts's share in the Severe Fighting and Pursuit—The March to Mynpoorie—Skirmish and Pursuit of the Rebels to the Ganges—Arrival at Cawnpore.

No sooner had General Archdale Wilson's gallant army fairly achieved the complete reconquest of Delhi, than a column was formed to clear the Doab of the enemy, and endeavour to open communication with General Havelock at Cawnpore. Lieutenant-Colonel E. H. Greathed, of the 8th (the King's) Regiment, was nominated to the command, and Lieutenant Roberts, who had been serving throughout the siege as Officiating Deputy Quartermaster-General of Artillery, was appointed to the charge of the Quartermaster-General's Department, Lieutenant Norman being placed at the head of the Adjutant-General's Office of the Movable Column.*

The immediate object of the march of Colonel Greathed's column, after clearing the Doab, was to march direct on Cawnpore, as the relief of the Lucknow garrison pressed urgently.

---

* The strength of the column, according to Lieutenant Norman, was as follows:—

1st European troop, 1st Brigade Horse Artillery, four 6-pounder guns, one 12-pounder howitzer; 2nd European troop, 3rd Brigade Horse Artillery, four 6-pounder guns, one 12-pounder howitzer; 3rd Company 1st European Battalion Artillery and No. 17 Horse Field Battery, four 9-pounder guns, two 24-pounder howitzers. Attached to the Artillery, two $5\frac{1}{2}$-inch mortars. Effective rank and file in round numbers—

Detachment of the Corps of Sappers and Miners, detachment of Punjaub Sappers and Miners	200
H.M.'s 9th Lancers	300
Detachment 1st Punjaub Cavalry, 2nd do., and 6th do.	320
Detachment Hodson's Irregular Horse	180
Head-quarters H.M.'s 8th and 75th Regiments	450
2nd Punjaub Infantry, 4th do. (Rifles)	1,200

There was no thought then of going to Agra, the town and cantonments of which were in the possession of the enemy, the European non-combatants and refugees from the surrounding district being crowded into the fort, an old Mogul structure of immense size, now held by the 3rd Bengal Europeans and the late Captain D'Oyley's battery of artillery, both in a numerically weak state.

The Movable Column having a strength of 930 Europeans and 1860 Natives, marched from its encampment outside of the Ajmere Gate on the morning of the 24th of September, and, crossing the Jumna by the bridge of boats, made a march of thirteen miles to Ghazee-ood-deen-nuggur, the point at which the road from Delhi to Meerut branches off the Grand Trunk Road. Lieutenant Roberts's labours as the officer in charge of the Quartermaster-General's Department of an army marching in, practically, an enemy's country, had now begun, but he achieved a marked success in his first venture in a field with which his name during the succeeding twenty years has been so closely identified. His duties required him to proceed in advance of the column to mark out each encampment, to procure information of the enemy's movements, and act on the brigadier's staff during the military operations.

The column halted on the 25th, as the baggage animals were out of condition, owing to the long halt in the unfavourable climate of Delhi, and advantage was taken of the delay to search the baggage of the camp followers for plunder taken at Delhi in order to relieve the cattle. The halt was also utilised to institute an examination of the neighbouring villages, where many rebels were apprehended and executed.

On the 26th, the column marched eleven and a half miles, to Dadra, the people of which were reported by Mr. Clifford, the civil officer accompanying the force, as having plundered the neighbouring village of Secundrabad. Colonel Greathed had surrounded Dadra at daylight by a squadron of the 1st Punjaub Cavalry, under Lieutenant (now General) Watson, and, on the arrival of the main body, the place was destroyed. On the following day the force marched to Secundrabad, ten miles distant. The place had been gutted by the "Goojurs," from Dadra; but the inhabitants, reassured by the presence of the

British, returned during the day in great numbers to the village. The march was continued on the 28th, by the cross road, to the civil station of Bolundshur, seven and a half miles, with the object of attacking the fort of Malagurh, fifteen miles from that place, the residence of the Mussulman Nawaub Wallydad Khan, who had afforded active assistance to the rebels. On nearing Bolundshur, Lieutenant Roberts received information that pointed to a determined opposition on the part of the insurgent force, including regular troops and guns. Major Ouvry, of the 9th Lancers, commanding the cavalry, accompanied by Lieutenants Norman and Roberts, proceeded in advance of the main column, and about a mile from the city encountered the rebel picket of horse, which fell back. On continuing the advance it became evident that a battery had been constructed across the road, not many hundred yards in advance of the point at which our cavalry had arrived; bodies of insurgent cavalry were likewise seen on each flank, but the ground immediately near the battery being covered with trees, compound walls, and the ruined residences of the English civil officers, it was not practicable to ascertain the force of rebel infantry.

The advance party of cavalry was speedily reinforced, and joined by two guns of Captain Remmington's Battery of Horse Artillery, which were brought into action to open on the breastwork in their front, behind which men were constantly passing. But the enemy were too quick, and before our guns could open, commenced a fire of round shot, to which Captain Remmington at once replied. Soon after the remaining guns of his battery arrived, and came into action about a hundred yards to the right of the road. Captain Bourchier's Battery also came up, and, under the direction of Lieutenant Roberts, who had reconnoitred the ground, took ground more to the right, thus bringing its fire to bear on the enemy's flank. The detachments of H.M.'s 8th and 75th Regiments, and 250 of the 2nd Punjaub Infantry, some 700 bayonets, were pushed forward through the gardens and houses of the civil station, and Captain Bourchier's Battery moved on at the same time, supported by a squadron of the 9th Lancers and a squadron 5th Punjaub Cavalry, while Lieutenant Hugh Gough, with his squadron of Hodson's Horse moved on the right of the infantry, and kept in check a considerable body of Sowars. Lieutenant Roberts accompanied Captain Bourchier's Battery, which, coming into action in an advanced position, fired salvoes of grape at the breastworks, and the infantry moving forward, the rebels abandoned their position and fled, leaving a 9-pounder gun behind their breastwork, which was in a good position across the junction of two roads, with trenches for infantry on either flank.* Captain Bourchier says, "By the cross fire which was kept up upon the enemy's battery, their fire was subdued; an advance was then ordered. A few salvoes of grape cleared the front, and the Commanding officer being anxious that the position should be secured, ordered an immediate advance of Artillery. Lieutenant Roberts, of the Artillery, who seemed ubiquitous, brought the order at a gallop. The guns charged and took the battery, the enemy scampering before us as we came up to it. Lieutenant Roberts was first at the guns. A second burst, after clearing our front with grape, brought us to the goal: the enemy flying before us like sheep."

The Cavalry did special good service, and the gallant conduct of the 9th Lancers under Major Ouvry and Captain Drysdale, in clearing the streets of Bolundshur, was worthy that distinguished regiment, which had three officers severely wounded. Lieutenants Probyn, 2nd Punjaub Cavalry, Younghusband, 5th Punjaub Cavalry, and Watson, 1st Punjaub Cavalry, three as gallant and dashing leaders of irregular horse as any army ever boasted, did equally good service in encountering superior bodies of the enemy, who displayed much determination, and made an attempt on the baggage, which was repulsed by the reserve. The British loss in the action was six officers and forty-one men killed and wounded, while that of the rebels, whose force included the 12th Native Infantry and 14th Irregular Cavalry, was not less than 300.

Lieutenant Roberts accompanied the 9th Lancers, which distinguished regiment served under his orders with such credit during the recent Afghan War, and shared the dangers of its brilliant charge in the crowded street, nearly ending his career there and then. While passing under a gateway, in

---

* See Lieutenant Norman's Abstract of Proceedings of Colonel Greathed's Movable Column.

company with Captain Sarel, 9th Lancers, and Lieutenant Anson, A.D.C., their horses got jammed up with hackeries and non-combatants seeking to escape, and a Sepoy took a deliberate aim at Roberts from a window within a few feet, and fired. Providentially his horse, a valuable Wuzeeree charger he had bought from General Nicholson, reared and received the bullet in his head, while his master escaped unhurt.

Lieutenant Roberts received the special thanks of Colonel Greathed, of Major Ouvry, commanding the cavalry, who wrote of " the most valuable information and assistance" he afforded him, and of Captain Bourchier, with whose battery the Deputy-Assistant Quartermaster-General, assuming his double character of a gunner, advanced. That officer reported of his conduct to Major Turner, commanding the artillery of the column, in the following terms : " I should be doing an injustice were I not to bring to notice the assistance I obtained from Lieutenant Roberts of the Artillery, who showed me my ground, and in rapid advance down the road first arrived at the gun we captured."

The enemy being dispersed about 1 P.M., the action having lasted three hours, the baggage was brought up, and camp pitched a mile beyond the town. During the evening information was received that the rebels had evacuated the fort of Malagurh, which was occupied by Lieutenant Baker with a detachment of Hodson's Horse, and, on the following morning, Colonel Greathed, with the Engineers and staff, including Lieutenant Roberts, visited the place. It was a fortunate circumstance that the rebel Nawaub had evacuated the fort, as there were no heavy guns with the column, and only two small mortars for shelling, while the place was of great strength, being surrounded with a deep ditch over twenty-five feet broad. Each face was about 200 yards in length, with a bastion at each angle and in the middle, the mud rampart had a strong parapet all round, and was about ten feet thick at the top, and there were three gateways, one within the other, with narrow approaches.

Some guns and much ammunition were found within the fort, as well as an immense quantity of plundered property. Colonel Greathed halted while the place was being destroyed by

Action at Allyghur.

the Engineers, during which Lieutenant Home, of Cashmere Gate renown, was accidentally killed by a premature explosion, to the great regret of the force. During the halt, carriage was sent for to Meerut for the removal of the sick and wounded, and much good was wrought by the presence of the troops in restoring confidence among the peaceable inhabitants of the district, and of Bolundshur, which was found nearly deserted on their arrival.

The fort of Malagurh being sufficiently destroyed, and a detachment of troops having arrived from Meerut to protect the town of Bolundshur, the Movable Column marched thence on the 3rd of October, to Koorjah, a distance of twelve miles, and, on the following day, to Somna, thirteen and a half miles. Here intelligence was received that the insurgent Mohammedans who, under Mungal and Mytaub Singh, had in the preceding month murdered or expelled the civil authorities, were prepared to oppose the British advance at Allyghur, and, further, that the Rohilcund mutineers had reached Hattrass from Muttra, and by some accounts were going to join the Mohammedan insurgents at Allyghur.

Colonel Greathed accordingly started on the 5th for Allyghur, a distance of fourteen miles, to reconnoitre and learn the road by which the enemy's position could be turned. On approaching the town, the rebels opened fire upon the reconnoitring party with some guns, and it was found that both roads leading to the city from the direction of Bolundshur were in their occupation. Roberts halted with the small detachment of cavalry forming the advanced guard; but was compelled to fall back a little to more advantageous ground, on which a number of the enemy came forward, but gave the cavalry no opportunity of charging. Two guns, under Captain Blunt, now came up and joined the cavalry on the right, and, opening fire at short range, speedily silenced and captured the rebel guns, killing the four men who were working them. The remaining guns of Captain Blunt's battery, moving down the left road, silenced and captured a gun placed at a breastwork newly constructed across the road, but the rebels had disappeared amid the gardens and houses in the suburbs. On the arrival of the infantry a general advance was ordered.

Lieutenants Probyn and Hugh Gough, with their two squadrons, swept round to the right of the city, keeping well away from the walls. Major Ouvry, accompanied by Lieutenant Roberts, with the head-quarters of the cavalry and Bourchier's guns, made a similar detour to the left, passing through the deserted compounds and gardens of the cantonments, and eventually pursued down the Cawnpore road. Major Turner, with three guns, a detail of cavalry, H.M.'s 75th, and the 4th Punjaub Rifles, followed close round the walls to the right, while Colonel Greathed with the rest of the force remained in reserve.

The cavalry on both flanks pursued with vigour for some miles, cutting up the enemy, and Major Turner, pushing round, broke open the city gates and made his way in various directions into the town, taking two guns in position, and destroying a magazine in one of the houses. Moving on thus, he eventually reached the Sasnee Gate, and was there joined by Lieutenant Gough's squadron, which had been quite round the city on the other side. Within the town were to be found only Bunniahs and shopkeepers of all kinds, who testified the most lively joy at the return of the British, and it was very evident that their condition under the rule of the insurgents had not been a prosperous one. Major Ouvry's column, with which was our hero, had a chase after "Pandy" of about 3 miles, and in the high crops with which the country was covered, some hundreds of Goojurs armed with swords and hatchets, were put up like game in an English cover, and 200 bit the dust. Major Turner's column, and the cavalry under Major Ouvry, now moved to the encamping-ground and joined Colonel Greathed, who sent the 2nd Regiment of Punjaub Infantry and a squadron of cavalry to search the town, and bring away any guns and arms that might be found.

A detachment 2nd Punjaub Infantry, with two European officers, was left at Allyghur, and on the 6th the column marched a distance of fourteen miles, to Akbarabad, where dwelt Mungul and Mytaub Sing, twin brothers, Rajpoot chiefs, who had made themselves conspicuous in the insurrection. The cavalry surprised the place, and both the chiefs, with about 100 armed insurgents, were killed. Three small guns were found loaded and in position at the residence of the chiefs, besides property and ammunition of various kinds. The house was blown up and the village destroyed.

The column was halted on the 7th, and, on the following day, marched seven miles across country to Byjygurh, where says Norman, "for the first time we found an apparently thriving town uninjured by the troubles which have desolated everything along and near to the Trunk road." In the course of the day Colonel Greathed received reports (afterwards ascertained to be unfounded) that the detachment left at Allyghur was likely to be attacked, and that night sent off a small reinforcement. He also received urgent calls from Agra, with an intimation that the mutineers from Dholepore were coming to attack that place. Accordingly at midnight on the 8th, seven squadrons of cavalry and the Horse Artillery, with whom Roberts proceeded, marched to Saidabad, and eventually to Kundowlee, a distance of thirty-six miles, and were preparing to proceed to Agra, when intelligence was received that it was not necessary. In this march they passed Hattrass, which had a few days previously been plundered by a large force of 7,000 men, armed with eighteen guns, and several thousand armed "budmashes," passing from Muttra to Oude, under Bukht Khan, the Bareilly Artillery Subadar.

The remainder of the Movable Column came up early in the following morning, and, at sunrise on the 10th October, the whole marched together into Agra, across the bridge of boats and under the fort, the inhabitants of which turned out to see the welcome spectacle. Lieutenant Roberts proceeded in advance of the column to mark out the camping-ground, and was met by the intelligence that the enemy had disappeared. He accordingly made preparations for the camping of the column. So secure from attack did the authorities at Agra consider themselves that Colonel Cotton, the Brigadier commanding the garrison, desired that the camp should be pitched near the church, on a space that would not have held half the force, and would have necessitated dispersion amongst compounds; but after some discussion, and in compliance with Colonel Greathed's wishes, Roberts marked out the camp on the Native Infantry Parade-ground. As the sequel proved, had the column been thus divided, with houses and compounds in front, it must have sustained on that day very severe loss, and perhaps even annihilation, while it certainly could not have attained the success which was achieved.

That the action that ensued was in the nature of a surprise is certainly chiefly attributable to the defective intelligence of the authorities at Agra, and little blame can attach to Colonel Greathed, though it was sought in some quarters to fix it on him, and Brigadier Hope Grant, who was sent to relieve him, says, "Proper precautions had not apparently been taken by our force when it marched in by at once posting pickets and sending out cavalry patrols to examine the country in the vicinity of the camp. The consequence was that before the camp was pitched the enemy opened fire with their guns from three different directions." Mr. (now Sir) William Muir, Secretary to Government, North-West Provinces, writing to Grant from Agra, on the day of the action, imputes no blame to Greathed. He says:—"The enemy came on our camp with artillery on three sides. Greathed's force had hardly got the camp into order. The surprise, however, was only momentary, and the sound and smoke of the artillery discharges show that we have followed them up three or four miles. It was a most complete surprise in one sense to us, but a greater one to them. They could have had no idea that we had so large a force. It entirely justifies the urgent messages we have been sending for Greathed, but his fellows must have been wretchedly tired. They had marched some forty-two miles within thirty or forty hours."

All arms were speedily engaged, some of the troops turning out in their shirt sleeves, but there was no disorder, for the old Delhi campaigners had perfect confidence in their leaders and themselves. While the guns opened fire with vigour and effect, the Punjaub Cavalry, on the right, charged and beat back the enemy, and the 9th Lancers, on the left, met in full career and repulsed a daring charge of the rebel troopers of the 1st Light Cavalry and Irregular Horse. Lieutenant Roberts, having completed his duties, was breakfasting in the fort when he heard of the unexpected inroad of the rebels. Riding quickly to the scene of conflict he found the pickets driven in and Lieutenant Hugh Gough engaged with the enemy, who

The Action at Agra.

were in the camp, in the midst of which hand-to-hand combats were going on. Drawing his sword, Roberts made his way through the combatants to the side of his commander.

During the *mêlée*, a squadron of the Lancers made a brilliant charge on a large body of Sowars on the flank of Blunt's guns, in which Captain French was killed, and Lieutenant Jones received twenty-two wounds, but survived to wear the Victoria Cross. The Punjaub Cavalry, under Lieutenants Watson, Probyn, and Younghusband, equally distinguished themselves by capturing three guns, and the rout of the enemy was soon complete, and he was in full retreat, pursued by all arms, Lieutenant Roberts being with the foremost party of cavalry. On one or two occasions the rebels attempted to make a stand at villages on the Gwalior road, but the British fire was too much for them, and the infantry coming up, their guns were captured. At a point five miles from cantonments the rebel camp was taken, and from thence to the Kalee Nuddee (black stream) the pursuit was one of cavalry and Horse Artillery. Gun after gun was taken, and strings of hackeries captured, fugitive Sepoys being cut down at every yard. On reaching the Kalee Nuddee, which was nearly unfordable, the 1st Light Cavalry, drawn up on the opposite side, made a show of forming a rear-guard, but Captain Remmington's guns speedily coming up, drove them off.

Twelve guns, being all the rebels had brought over, were captured, and between 500 and 600 men were killed, and had the crops not been so high, forming such admirable cover, their losses would have been far heavier. "There never was," says Norman, "a more complete rout, and probably never a hotter pursuit." After securing the guns, and bringing off or destroying the standing camp, the troops returned to the cantonment about seven o'clock, having performed the almost unparalleled achievement of fighting an action and marching sixty-six miles in forty hours, nine miles of which the cavalry did at a trot through high crops or over ploughed fields. Roberts says that he saw a Sikh infantry soldier drinking water in the Kalee Nuddee who had marched fifty miles, and after pursuing to this stream marched back to camp! The British loss was small, consisting of twelve killed and fifty-four wounded, and the result achieved was considerable, a great effect having been produced among the insurgent forces, which consisted of between 6,000 and 8,000 men, including the mutineers from Mhow, part of those from Neemuch, and parties from Delhi, Indore, and Gwalior.

Though the attack was in the nature of a surprise, it was one for both parties, for the rebels had no intelligence of the near approach of Greathed's column, and fancied they were dealing with the Agra garrison, and hence they took the offensive, displaying a dash quite foreign to their method of attack. The disaffected in the city were said to have been engaged to destroy the bridge of boats, but this was frustrated by the rapid advance of the British, and it is probable that their intention to attack such a strong and well-garrisoned fort as Agra was due to the expected co-operation of the Gwalior Contingent, with their siege-train, and four batteries of artillery. But as Norman remarks :—" The most astonishing part of the whole affair was the utter want of information, or rather the incorrect information, of the Agra Government. Within half an hour of fire being opened, the very best authority (as it was supposed) had declared the mutineers to be beyond the Kalee river, and yet, at that very time, they must have been within a mile or so of camp. In fact they crossed the river with guns, ammunition, waggons, &c.—and as the water was by no means shallow and the banks steep, this must have been a work of time—pitched a camp within five miles of the fort, and close to a village, and advanced to the attack past many villages without one word of correct information reaching the Agra authorities, who, indeed, that very morning received intelligence directly opposed to the truth."

Lieutenant Roberts had no small share in the honours of this hard-fought and most laborious day, and had the gratification of seeing his name mentioned in despatches by Colonel Greathed, Colonel Cotton, and Mr. C. B. Thornhill, the Secretary to Government, North-West Provinces.

Colonel Greathed was very anxious to open communication with General Havelock's force, and a detachment, with two guns, having been sent to relieve the party left at Allyghur, the column crossed the river on the 14th of October, and marched on the following day to Mynpoorie, which they reached on the 19th, the last march being twenty-four miles. On the previous day Brigadier Hope Grant arrived from Delhi and took command of the Movable Column, and from this time till the close of his service during the Mutiny, Lieutenant Roberts served on the staff of that distinguished General, who was singularly fortunate in his staff, which included such officers as Wolseley, Roberts, Biddulph, Wilmot, and the late Augustus Anson.

The column made a rapid march of twenty-four miles to Mynpoorie, where resistance was expected, but the Rajah and his followers fled, and some guns and a gun-foundry fell into the hands of the British, also two and a half lacs of rupees, saved by the Rao, his brother, who met the column on the line of march. Brigadier Grant halted on the 20th, and the fort having been destroyed, marched on the following day to Bewer, which, on their approach, was abandoned by a rebel force detached from Futtehgurh by the Nawaub. At Bewer, the junction of the four roads leading to Cawnpore, Meerut, Futtehgurh, and Agra, Brigadier Grant received a letter from Sir James Outram, written in the Greek character, requesting him to push on to Lucknow to his aid with all speed, as they were running short of provisions. He determined, accordingly, not to delay by leaving the road to attack Futtehgurh, and on the 22nd made a forced march of twenty-eight miles to Goorsaigunge, and on the following day pushed on to Meerun-kee-Serai. While Lieutenant Roberts, with his guard, was reconnoitring close to the town, situated on the banks of a stream, he was fired upon by a battery on the opposite side, supported by about 500 infantry, engaged in getting the guns across. General Grant sent to his assistance a squadron of Lancers, two of Punjaub Cavalry, and two guns. Our artillery, getting into action, soon silenced them, and they fled, leaving their guns, which were captured, while the cavalry, fording the river, pursued them for several miles, cutting up a considerable number. Lieutenant Probyn, with the squadron of 2nd Punjaub Cavalry, continued the pursuit as far as the Ganges, into which the remnant of the fugitives were driven. The guns were brought into camp—one 24-pounder howitzer, one 9-pounder, and two brass native guns, 3-pounders, besides ammunition-waggons and two store-carts. During the pursuit Roberts displayed his accustomed ardour, and crossed swords with a rebel sowar, who cut his horse across the flank.

On the 24th of October a forced march of twenty-two miles was made to Poora, and two ordinary marches, on the 25th and 26th, took the column into Cawnpore, where it was directed by Brigadier Wilson, of H.M.'s 64th Regiment, commanding at the station, to halt until orders for an advance on Lucknow were received from Sir Colin Campbell, the newly-arrived Commander-in-Chief.

As the column, barely numbering 3,000 men, marched into Cawnpore, it was surrounded by large bodies of the enemy—the Gwalior Contingent, a highly-disciplined force of 5,000 men, with batteries and a siege-train, in all amounting to thirty-six guns, being encamped on the banks of the Jumna, a few miles distant, and a force under the Nawaub of Futtehgurh of about the same strength, with artillery, in the rear, and other bodies of rebels between the Ganges and Lucknow. But the mutinous Sepoys displayed an unaccountable lack of enterprise, and feared to attack, though burning to destroy the troops destined to save the women and children at Lucknow from the fate that had befallen their unfortunate compatriots at Cawnpore—that name of horror, the sound of which even now, to those who were in India in the Mutiny year,

> "Shall blow the horrid deed in every eye
> That tears shall drown the wind."

Nothing more painful ever met the eye of Roberts and the officers and men of Grant's column, than the scene presented by this once handsome station, now gutted and burnt, with scarce a house standing, but only blackened walls and evidences of slaughter on every hand. There was the house where was enacted the last scene in the unhappy tragedy, with its blood-stained walls and heart-rending inscriptions, telling of the wounds the writers had received, the deaths of those dear to them, and breathing agonizing appeals to Heaven for mercy, and to man for the succour that never came. There was the hospital, which formed the centre of the position on the open plain, defended for twenty-two days by Sir Hugh Wheeler against the artillery and overwhelming forces of the enemy, and, lying about, scraps of letters, children's shoes, ladies' bits of ribbon, and other piteous memorials of the ill-fated occupants; and there was the terrible well, with its contents scarcely covered by a thin layer of earth. Once beautiful women and innocent children lay there in a festering mass, and the echoes of their voices, though stilled in death, called in trumpet-tones to the shuddering visitors who crowded round these sad memorials, to avenge the deed than which the history of all time can show nothing so black or treacherous.

The officers and men of the Delhi Field Force had seen much of bloodshed and the horrors of war during the past few months, but nothing to approach this scene at Cawnpore. As they turned away horror-stricken from the fatal well, there was no need for incentives to steel their hearts against wreaking a full measure of revenge, such as were called to her aid by Lady Macbeth before perpetrating the murder of Duncan.

> "Fill me, from the crown to the toe, top full
> Of direst cruelty. Make thick my blood.
> Stop up the access and passage to remorse,
> That no compunctious visitings of nature
> Shake my fell purpose, nor keep a pace between
> The effect and it."

CHAPTER IV.

Departure of Lieutenant Roberts from Cawnpore with Brigadier Hope Grant's Column for the Relief of Lucknow—Narrow Escape of Roberts from Capture by the Rebels at Buntheera—March upon Lucknow—Roberts as Quartermaster-General of Sir Hope Grant's Division—He leads the Army from the Alumbagh—Is sent by Sir Colin Campbell on a Special Mission to Alumbagh—Is associated with Captain Garnet Wolseley in the Capture of the 32nd Mess-house—The return March to Cawnpore—The Battle of Cawnpore on the 6th of December—The Affair at Serai Ghât.

At Cawnpore Brigadier Grant received an accession of strength, including 350 men of the 93rd Sutherland Highlanders, under Colonel the Honourable Adrian Hope (who fell at Rooyiah, in Oude), which brought up the strength of the column to 3,460 men and twenty guns. With this force he and his officers felt they could accomplish anything, and all were inspired with feelings of self-gratulation when the order came for them to commence their march for the relief of Lucknow. The column crossed the Ganges by the bridge of boats on the 30th October, and pushed on to Bunnee, where the bridge was found to be destroyed, but the river was forded without difficulty. The Brigadier now received an order from Sir Colin Campbell, who arrived at Cawnpore from Calcutta on the 3rd November, directing him to halt until he joined him.

As the ground was unfavourable for camping, he determined to advance a few miles, and, on the morning of 3rd November, sent Lieutenants Roberts and Mayne, of the Quartermaster-General's Department, to select a proper site. In executing this duty Lieutenant Roberts had a narrow escape from capture by the rebels at a village called Buntheera, which we will give in his own words to us:—"I was sent by Sir Hope Grant to select ground for a new camp. We had reconnoitred the country a few hours previously, and finding no enemy, Lieutenant Mayne, Deputy-Assistant Quartermaster-General, like myself, went with a few Sowars on ahead. We arrived on the ground and sent back word to the camp colourmen to come on. While we were waiting and talking to what appeared pilgrims, we were shot at, and on looking round saw a considerable number of the enemy between us and our force. They had been concealed in the village, so we afterwards heard. We put spurs to our horses, but had a narrow escape; my horse, while crossing a ravine, was slightly wounded and fell, and in doing so my sword fell from my hand and cut my left thumb badly."

Had he fallen into the hands of the rebels, a cruel death would have been his fate, for

> "Match'd with them
> The rudest brute that roams Siberia's wild
> Has feelings pure and polish'd as a gem—
> The bear is civilized, the wolf is mild."

The Brigadier sent a portion of his force with guns to drive away the enemy, and they were easily turned out of the village of Buntheera, and retreated in the direction of Lucknow.

The column now occupied the village of Nawabgunj, in the middle of a large plain, where the camp was pitched and a convoy, with suitable escort, was sent to the Alumbagh. Between the 5th and 10th November, when Sir Colin Campbell reached Nawabgunj, and assumed the command-in-chief of all the troops destined for the relief of Lucknow, considerable reinforcements arrived, and the troops available for the advance numbered 6,000 men, with eleven heavy guns, two 18-pounders, eighteen field-pieces, and several mortars.

On the morning of the 12th November, Sir Colin commenced operations by marching to the Alumbagh, a large walled enclosure, about five miles due south of the Residency, the garrison of which consisted of 900 men, forming a portion of the force left by Sir James Outram and General Havelock in their advance to the first relief of the Residency on the 25th of September.

Lieutenant Roberts was with the advance guard, which was attacked by a body of 2,000 rebels, with two guns, but the latter were taken by Lieutenant H. Gough, of Hodson's Horse, in a brilliant charge, and the enemy dispersed. The Alumbagh position having been cleared of the enemy, the garrison was changed, Her Majesty's 75th Regiment, numbering only 300 war-worn soldiers who had served through the siege of Delhi, being placed in garrison there. Depositing his heavy baggage and supplies in the Alumbagh enclosure, and sending back his cattle and wheeled transport to Cawnpore, Sir Colin made his arrangements for marching with the remainder of his force, 4,800 men, without encumbrances, which he proposed to leave in the park of Dilkoosha.*

On the 13th, the advance on Lucknow commenced in earnest, and Lieutenant Roberts, as the head of the Quartermaster-General's Department of the division commanded by Brigadier-General† Grant, reconnoitred the road, and had the honour of leading the army in the advance from the Alumbagh to Dilkoosha, which initiated the operations resulting in the relief of the beleaguered garrison and women and children. As the advance column approached the Dilkoosha park, the leading troops were met by a heavy musketry fire. Reinforcements were pushed on, under the command of Colonel Hamilton, 78th Highlanders, the troops engaged consisting of 2 batteries of Artillery and 3 regiments of Infantry. After a running fight of two hours, the enemy were driven down the hill to the Martiniere, across the garden and park of that college, and far beyond the canal which, running nearly east and west, falls into the Goomtee at a point to the north of the Martiniere. The Dilkoosha and Martiniere were both seized by Brigadier Hope's brigade occupying the gardens and enclosures of the latter, abutting on the canal, Brigadier D. Russell's brigade being on the left, in front of Dilkoosha, and Brigadier Little, with the Cavalry and Bourchier's Battery, occupying the plain in front of the Martiniere.

The enemy however, did not acquiesce in their defeat, but attacked the position with spirit, though without success. Our troops drove them off and advanced across the canal, and, during the fighting, two officers were killed, Captain Wheatley, of the Carabineers, and Lieutenant Mayne, Royal Horse Artiltery, Lieutenant Roberts' companion in the affair at Buntheera.

---

* Dilkoosha signifies "Heart's Delight."

† Hope Grant had been advanced to this rank by Sir Colin Campbell, an old friend with whom he had served in China and on the Sutlej. Sir Colin placed him in command of the whole force, though practically the operations for the relief of Lucknow were conducted by the Commander-in-Chief.

No further advance was made for a few days, but Roberts was selected by the Commander-in-Chief for a duty which showed that he had already made himself a name as an active, capable officer. He writes to us: "The evening previous to the advance from the Martiniere, Sir Colin Campbell sent for me, and said that he had not sufficient reserve ammunition, and that more must be brought from the Alumbagh before morning; he asked me if I could find my way to the Alumbagh in the dark; I replied I thought I could, and was told to go, to take what escort I required and a sufficient number of camels. I took Hugh Gough's and Younghusband's squadrons of Native Cavalry. We had great difficulty in avoiding the enemy's pickets, but we performed the duty during the night, and returned to the Martiniere shortly before daybreak. Sir Colin expressed himself greatly pleased; I had just time for a hasty breakfast when I was ordered to lead the column towards the Secunderbagh."

Storing his heavy baggage and supplies for fourteen days in the Alumbagh, Sir Colin Campbell rested his army, and the advance on the Secunderbagh took place on the morning of the 16th of November, the rear guard, under Colonel Ewart, 93rd Highlanders, having closed up with the column only on the preceding day. Leaving in garrison at Dilkoosha, H.M.'s 8th Regiment, like the 75th one of the Delhi battalions, and therefore entitled to a well-earned repose, early on the 16th Sir Colin advanced direct on Secunderbagh, Lieutenant Roberts leading the column to what proved one of the hardest contested fights of the war.

The Secunderbagh is described by the Commander-in-Chief as a high walled enclosure of strong masonry, 120 yards square, and carefully loopholed all round. It was held in great strength by the enemy, and opposite to it, at a distance of a hundred yards, was a village also loopholed and filled with men. On the head of the column advancing up the lane to the left of the Secunderbagh, fire was opened on them. The infantry of the advance guard was quickly thrown into skirmishing order, to line a bank to the right, and Captain Blunt's[*]

---

[*] Now Major-General C. H. Blunt, C.B.

troop of Bengal Horse Artillery, passing at a gallop through a cross-fire from the village and Secunderbagh, opened fire within musketry range in a most daring manner. As soon as they could be pushed up a steep bank, two 18-pounder guns, under Captain Travers, were also brought to bear on the building. While this was being effected, says the Commander-in-Chief, the leading brigade of infantry, under Brigadier the Hon. Adrian Hope, coming rapidly into action, caused the loopholed village to be abandoned, the whole fire being then directed on the Secunderbagh. After a time a large body of the enemy, who were holding ground to the left of the advance, were driven in, when the 93rd Highlanders pursued their advantage and seized the barracks, and immediately converted them into a military post. While this was going on, the two 18-pounders had been battering the Secunderbagh, which was stormed in the most brilliant manner by the 93rd Highlanders and 4th Punjabees. "There never was a bolder feat of arms," wrote the Commander-in-Chief, who had stormed the breach of San Sebastian, and stood on the ridge at Barrosa; and thus the crime of Cawnpore was avenged at Secunderbagh, within the small area of which over 2,000* dead bodies were counted by the burying parties.

The next point attacked was the Shah Nujeef, a domed mosque, with a garden enclosed within a loopholed wall. The place was first cannonaded for three hours by the heavy guns of Captain Peel's Naval Brigade, an action almost unexampled in war, and then stormed by the 93rd Highlanders, led by Brigadier Hope, supported by a battalion of detachments under Major Barnston, of the 90th Regiment, who received a wound which ultimately proved fatal. This brought the operations of the 16th of November to a close.

On the following morning took place the storm of the 32nd Mess-house, formerly known as the Khoorsheyd Munzil (Happy Palace), a building of considerable size, defended by a ditch twelve feet broad and scarped with masonry, and a strong mud-wall loopholed for musketry. The task of leading the stormers

---

* So says Sir Colin Campbell in his despatch. Bourchier places the number at about 3,000, and Lord Wolseley, who was with the burying party, informed us that the exact number was, by a singular coincidence, 1,857.

was entrusted to Captain Wolseley,* of the 90th Regiment, by Sir Colin Campbell, who mentions that officer's name first in his despatch briefly recording the events of the day. With Captain Wolseley was associated a picket of the 53rd Regiment, under Captain Hopkins, and he was supported by the battalion of detachments formerly commanded by Major Barnston, and now by Captain F. C. Guise,† both of the 90th Regiment.

The difficulty of writing history correctly even when the actors are alive, has received an exemplification in the published accounts of the storm of the Mess-house, one of the most gallant feats of arms performed during the war. The writer, in the first edition of his "Memoir of Lord Wolseley," (published in 1874,) gave an account of this affair derived from the gallant leader of the storming party, who received his instructions from Sir Colin Campbell in person, and it was extracted by Colonel Malleson in his "History of the Mutiny." But in the third and concluding volume of his work, the historian, in correction of this account, inserted an Appendix, in which Captain Hopkins is credited with the honour of having led the storming party across the drawbridge into the Mess-house, and Wolseley is only mentioned as "attacking the houses on the right of the building." Since this was published the writer has been assured by the late Mr. Kavanagh, V.C., who guided Wolseley's party, that his account is absolutely correct, and that Wolseley, and not Hopkins, was the leader of the party that first crossed the drawbridge into the Mess-house. Colonel Malleson, in the Appendix referred to (see pages 505-506, Vol. III.), further states that Captain Hopkins received a flag from Lieutenant Roberts, and himself hoisted it, and on its being shot down, replaced it on the summit of the Mess-house; but the following is Sir Frederick Roberts' account, in a letter to us, of his share of the business :—" I took the flag of the 2nd Punjaub Infantry, by Sir Colin Campbell's orders, and placed it on the Mess-house to show Outram and Havelock where we were. The enemy knocked the flagstaff down three times, breaking the

---

* Now General Lord Wolseley, G.C.B.
† Now Major-General Guise, C.B., V.C.

pole once. The staff is, I believe, still in the possession of the 2nd Punjaub Infantry."

The Motee Mahal was gained the same day by Captain Wolseley's exertions, and a communication opened that evening with the Residency. Lieutenant Roberts accompanied his Chief at the meeting between the three Generals—Sir Colin Campbell, Sir James Outram, and General Havelock—a memorable scene that has been depicted with graphic force by Barker in his famous painting.

Roberts took up his quarters with Brigadier General Grant in the Shah Nujeef, where the occasional welcome of a round shot through the building warned them that their work was not yet ended. The withdrawal of the immense train of non-combatants and sick and wounded and stores, was confided to Sir James Outram, who performed the task with the success that might have been anticipated from his antecedents.

At his own suggestion, Outram remained in command of some 4,000 men and thirty-five pieces of ordnance at the position of Alumbagh, while, on the 27th, the remainder of the army, under Sir Colin Campbell and Brigadier-General Hope Grant, who had continued, throughout the operations connected with the Relief, in immediate command of the division, retraced their steps towards Cawnpore, with the object of sending the Lucknow women and children on to Allahabad and Calcutta. But an unexpected event had occurred at Cawnpore, and in place of a little rest after the weary months of watching passed in the Residency, the sorely tried ladies and children again heard the familiar boom of cannon and rattle of musketry, and found themselves in a beleaguered camp, the garrison of which had no easy task in defeating and dispersing their aggressors.

When Sir Colin Campbell quitted Cawnpore, he left Major-General Windham ("Redan Windham" as he was called) in command of the camp, with strict orders to remain on the defensive. General Windham had at first only 500 Europeans under his orders, but received constant small accessions of strength, until his force numbered between 2,000 and 3,000 men. Hearing of the advance of the Gwalior mutineers from Calpee, notwithstanding the stringent orders of the Commander-in-Chief to stand on the defensive, he resolved to strike a blow. On the 26th of November, he moved out eight miles along the canal in a due westerly direction, and meeting the advance guard of the enemy, consisting of 3,000 men, at a place called Bhowsee, on the Pando Nuddee, he attacked and routed them, capturing three guns. On his return Windham encamped in a position with brushwood on one side and the city in his rear, and the enemy, making a detour in the night, appeared close on his left flank in the morning of the 27th of November. Meanwhile Windham, leaving his camp standing, had advanced in another direction, and found himself suddenly attacked from an unexpected quarter, and was compelled to retreat to his intrenchments, leaving in the possession of the enemy his standing camp with all its contents. That night the rebel force, consisting of the Gwalior Contingent and Koer Singh's men, was joined by the Nana Sahib, and, advancing upon Cawnpore, which fell into their hands, invested the intrenchments, their left resting on the Ganges, and their right on the city at the point where it touches the canal. Doubtless the treacherous and sanguinary monster leading the mutineers promised himself a second "Cawnpore," and the vigour with which the attack was pushed on the morning of the 28th of November, augured well for his hopes, and showed that the rebels had a leader of some ability in the person of Tantia Topee, who now appeared on the scene.

Advancing at dawn with their overwhelming artillery, which had been trained by the late Sir Vincent Eyre, the Gwalior Contingent, Horse, Foot, and Artillery, forming the most highly disciplined native troops in India, reinforced by other levies, making up a formidable army of 25,000 men, with 42 guns, captured the Assembly Rooms, with all its vast collection of private and public stores and ammunition, and, possessing themselves of the Grand Trunk Road, moved down to attack the intrenchments. During the fighting that ensued, the 64th, numbering only 300 bayonets, one of Havelock's regiments in Persia and in his advance up country, made a gallant charge and spiked three guns, but not being supported, were driven back with heavy loss, including Brigadier Wilson and several officers killed. At this time of doubt and disaster, Sir Colin

Campbell arrived on the scene with Hope Grant's weak division, and speedily the aspect of affairs was changed.

The Commander-in-Chief, having made his dispositions for leaving Sir James Outram at Alumbagh, set out on his return march to Cawnpore with the non-combatants and wounded from Lucknow, about 2,000 souls, escorted by the remainder of his troops, some 3,000 men, including the garrison of the Residency. On the morning of the 27th, Sir Colin encamped at Bunnee, about thirty miles distant from Cawnpore, and, about noon of the following day, received a missive from General Windham, headed "most urgent," reporting his critical position in terms that, for a moment, almost unnerved the veteran of a hundred fights. A writer in *Blackwood's Magazine* for October, 1858, gives a graphic account of the position of affairs as the column pressed on to the bridge of boats over the Ganges:—"The impatience and anxitey of all became extreme. Louder and louder grew the roar, faster and faster became the march, long and weary was the way, tired and footsore grew the infantry, death fell on the exhausted wounded with terrible rapidity, the travel-worn bearers could hardly stagger along under their loads, the sick men groaned and died; but still on, on, on, was the cry."

After progressing in the usual order for a short time, the tension became too great for Sir Colin. Leaving the infantry to march on with the convoy, he pressed forward with the cavalry and horse artillery. On reaching Mungulwar, about five miles on the Lucknow side of the Ganges, he halted his troops, directed the artillery to fire salvoes to announce the approach of assistance, and galloped forward with his staff, in mingled hope and fear regarding the condition in which he might find the bridge of boats. As he approached the river, a glance dissipated every doubt on this head. Through the glimmering light, for evening had set in, the bridge was seen to be intact. Flames rising in every direction, mingling with the light of the setting sun, showed that the enemy must have taken the city and a large part of the cantonments, that the tents intended for the ladies and children and the sick and wounded from Lucknow, and the stores of clothing for the defenders of the Residency, must have been destroyed; whilst the artillery fire occasionally directed at the bridge, and the fusillade near the river-bank, proved that a sharp crisis was impending. In a word, to use the language of an officer on Sir Colin's staff, "the veil which had so long shrouded us from Windham was rent asunder, and the disaster stood before us in all its calamity."

Lieutenant Roberts was ordered to communicate with General Windham, and ascertain the state of affairs. Riding at top speed he was the first to cross the bridge of boats leading to the entrenchment, now so hardly beset by an enemy flushed with unaccustomed victory, and communicating with Windham, returned to the Commander-in-Chief and placed him in possession of the situation. Pushing on, Sir Colin crossed the stream, and the language the veteran employed towards Windham on learning the loss of all the stores he had accumulated with such labour, was, to use a mild term, unparliamentary.*

On the 28th the enemy began to bombard the intrenchment, but their opportunity was lost; for, during the 29th, the British troops began to cross the Ganges, and the old chief set to work in his trenchant style to repair the disaster brought about by rashness. By the following evening the whole of his division was on the Cawnpore side of the Ganges, the British resting on the river, and the front and left covering the Grand Trunk Road, which, passing through Cawnpore, unites Delhi, Allahabad, and Calcutta. By the 3rd December, the convoy, "which," says Sir Colin, "had given me so much anxiety, including the families and half the wounded, was finally despatched on its way," and, on the evening of the 5th, every arrangement had been made for a general attack on the enemy the next morning. The city of Cawnpore lay in front of the British camp, the larger portion of the town being on the northern side of the canal running east and west towards the Ganges, and the smaller portion lying on its southern bank. At this time the enemy were on the north side of the canal, which divided them from the British, who occupied also an advanced post, the General

---

* General Windham was superseded by Brigadier Inglis, the commander of the Lucknow garrison, and General Dupuis, R.A., commanding the artillery, was sent to Dum Dum.

Gunj, an old bazaar, of considerable extent, held by Brigadier Greathed.

On the 6th December, the morning of the attack, the British force did not exceed 7,000 or 8,000 men, and that of the enemy amounted to 25,000, with thirty-six guns. The Gwalior Contingent had come westward from Calpee, on the Jumna, a distance of fifty-one miles by the road which, joining that from Delhi, enters the city of Cawnpore on the north; and the Nana Sahib's people had come southward from Bithoor down the Ganges. The rebel camp was about two miles from Cawnpore on the Calpee Road.

There was some desultory fighting on the 5th, in which Lieutenant Roberts took part on Sir Hope Grant's staff; but at 9 A.M. on the following morning, Sunday, 6th December, Sir Colin had his force, with thirty-five guns, ready disposed for action, and commenced operations for the dispersal of the enemy by a heavy bombardment from the works near the Ganges to the east of Cawnpore, with the object of inducing the rebels to believe that the attack was to be made in that quarter. Brigadier Greathed's three regiments were reinforced by the 64th, and he was directed to occupy the General Gunj, the bazaar on the canal, opposite the enemy's centre, where he had been posted for some days. The rest of the British force, consisting of an artillery brigade, including Captain Peel's heavy guns, a cavalry brigade, under Sir Hope Grant, and three weak infantry brigades under the Hon. A. Hope, Walpole, and Inglis of Lucknow, were drawn up in contiguous columns, and effectually masked from the observation of the enemy.

Soon after eleven all was ready. The infantry then deployed in parallel lines fronting the canal. Hope was in advance in one line, Inglis in rear with the second. General Grant was sent with the cavalry and horse artillery to cross the canal by the bridge a mile and a half to the westward, and to threaten the enemy's rear. Immediately to the left of Brigadier Greathed was another bridge across the canal, which was crossed by Walpole, who drove the enemy from some brick-kilns. The Sikhs and the men of the 53rd did the same on the left, and then the whole line advanced, with Peel's heavy guns. Sir Colin Campbell wrote; " On this occasion there was the sight

The Pursuit after the Battle.

beheld of 24-pounder guns advancing with the first line of skirmishers."

The troops were soon over the canal, and the enemy were driven back at all points. His camp two miles in rear, and covering his line of retreat, was reached and taken at one o'clock in the afternoon, and his rout was complete. For fourteen miles along the Calpee road the enemy was hotly pursued with cavalry and artillery, and Sir Colin Campbell expressed his belief that not one gun or ammunition waggon which had been on the right of the enemy's position, escaped.

Lieutenant Roberts rode by the side of his chief in this chase and capture. Captain Bourchier commanding No. 17 Battery, which first took up the pursuit, says:—"Gun after gun is spiked, cartloads of ammunition lay strewed along the road; Pandies are bolting in all directions. For two miles without a check the pursuit was carried on by the battery alone, accompanied by Sir Hope Grant and his staff. Four times in that distance did we come into action, to clear our front and flanks, until General Grant, thinking wisely we were too far from our supports, determined to wait until the cavalry arrived. A halt was called; not until it was required, for the horses, though in the condition of racers, had felt the pace. A small cloud coming nearer and nearer is seen on the left. The head of the cavalry column debouches from a grove. The order for a further pursuit is given. The cavalry spread like lightning over the plain in skirmishing order, and Sir Colin takes the lead. The pursuit is continued to the fourteenth milestone, assuming all the character of a fox-hunt."

Meantime, as the Commander-in-Chief passed the enemy's camp, he ordered General Mansfield, his Chief of the Staff, to secure it, and take the position of the Subadar's Tank, which stood in rear of the rebel left. Owing to a defect in Mansfield's arrangements, the enemy escaped with their guns down the Bithoor Road. The rebel centre, however, finding themselves taken in rear and their camp captured, abandoned the town by the same road, and so ended the battle of Cawnpore.

Sir Colin Campbell selected General Hope Grant to deal the final blow by dispersing the enemy concentrated at Bithoor, the seat of the Nana Sahib, and capturing his guns. The complete manner in which the task was executed justified the choice, and Lieutenant Roberts, who participated in the succeeding operations received his meed of praise from his immediate Chief.

Giving his wearied men one day's rest, soon after noon of the 8th December, General Grant marched from Cawnpore with a compact force of 2,800 men, consisting of Brigadier Hon. Adrian Hope's Infantry Brigade—the 42nd and 93rd Highlanders, and 4th Punjaubees—and 520 sabres, with eleven guns.

Lieutenant Roberts, who accompanied the column as head of the Quartermaster-General's Department, had a difficult task in obtaining information from the natives passed on the road, as to whether the rebels in the retreat had conveyed the guns to Bithoor, or were about to cross into Oude by the ferry, called Serai Ghat, twenty-five miles up the river. At length he learned from one man that six guns, including a 24-pounder, which had been captured but was subsequently lost, had been conveyed by the latter route. Sir Hope Grant resolved to march thither, and the same night, leaving his baggage under a guard, started by a cross country road for Sheorajpore, three miles from Serai Ghat. Soon after marching a rebel sowar was captured, from whom information was obtained that the guns, which formed the chief object of the expedition, were still on the banks of the river. The General and his staff, with a small Sikh escort, pushed on and soon saw the enemy, on which he sent back orders for the remainder of his cavalry and the artillery to come up immediately, and the infantry to follow. On the arrival of the cavalry and guns, the General pushed on over very difficult and swampy ground, in which the 24-pounder that had been lost on the 6th, was discovered embedded up to the axle.

The men worked with a will, and soon the leading guns of Captain Middleton's battery, under Lieutenant Warren, reached sounder ground and opened fire, advancing to within 500 yards of the rebels clustered on the river's bank. Presently the remainder of the battery and Captain Remmington's troop of horse artillery arrived, and came into action at a range of 200 yards. The enemy, consisting of a confused mass of guns, bullocks, baggage, and men, soon gave way, and fled along the marshy banks of the river, where they were pursued and cut up by the Irregular Cavalry.

In this well arranged affair, fifteen guns, belonging to the Gwalior Contingent, were captured. Sir Colin Campbell, writing to congratulate Sir Hope Grant on the following day, said : " It is impossible to over-estimate the advantage to our interests, military and political, which will result from the taking of the only guns remaining with the Gwalior Contingent. All the discontented chiefs with their rabble of villains, will lose hope and heart at once on learning the result of your pursuit and attack of the body of men protecting the guns that had been left to them, with the loss of the latter. All this is matter for real rejoicing, and will cause great satisfaction in Calcutta."

In his report Brigadier-General Grant specially referred to the services rendered by Lieutenant Roberts, and the Commander-in-Chief endorsed his acknowledgments in a letter to Lord Canning, the Governor-General.

CHAPTER V.

Roberts gains the V.C. at Khodagunj—Occupation of Futtehgurh on the 2nd of January, 1858—A Day's Pig-sticking—The Army crosses into Oude—Arduous Nature of Roberts's Duties on the Staff—Storm of Meeangunj—Roberts's Humanity—The Siege of Lucknow—Operations Trans-Goomtee—The Action of Koorsie—Roberts is invalided and returns to England.

FROM Serai Ghat the column marched on the 11th to Bithoor, the residence of the infamous Nana Sahib, which was completely destroyed, the temple and palace being blown up, and the contents burnt—and thus Bithoor, with its terrible memories, became a thing of the past. Sir Hope Grant marched on the 24th December for Mynpoorie, halting for Christmas-day at Chahbepore, where he was joined by the Commander-in-Chief with the main force from Cawnpore. Pursuing their course on the following day to Poonwah, they arrived on the 30th at Goorshaigunj.

Learning that the rebels had partially broken down the suspension bridge over the Kala Nuddee, Sir Colin Campbell, on the first day of the new year, detached a force, with engineers, to repair it, and the work was so rapidly executed that, by the following morning, the bridge was pronounced practicable. The Commander-in-Chief went down to examine the position, and was received by a heavy fire of musketry and field-pieces from the enemy, who, coming up in great force from Futtehgurh during the night, had taken up a position in the village near the head of the bridge. Sending for the brigades under Hope Grant and Greathed from Goorshaigunj, some four miles distant, the Commander-in-Chief directed Brigadier Hope to cross the river and hold the enemy in check.

On the arrival of the main force, the village of Khodagunj was stormed by General Grant, who was accompanied by Lieutenant Roberts. The cavalry, in *échelon* of squadrons, first charged the enemy as they emerged from the village, and then followed in hot pursuit, sabring the flying foe at every stride. The scene enacted at the battle of Agra was repeated, and the rebels, fleeing in panic, did not even halt on reaching Futtehgurh, but fled into Bundelcund, leaving eight guns and much stores in the hands of the victors. Says the writer in *Blackwood* already quoted:—" Then despair seized upon the rebel mass; breaking their ranks, throwing aside their arms, they fled in wild confusion; but the horsemen were upon them and amongst them, and the slaughter was terrible; for several miles they rode along spearing and cutting down at every step; and the progress of their swift advance might be marked by the smoke of exploded tumbrils curling up amidst the dark green trees."

In the pursuit a very gallant young officer of Irregular Cavalry, Lieutenant Younghusband, met his death, and the subject of this Memoir performed an act of personal gallantry which secured him the Victoria Cross, that most coveted of all military distinctions.

While following up the retreating enemy with the ardour of a fox-hunter across country, Lieutenant Roberts saw two Sepoys making off with a standard. Putting spurs to his horse he overtook them just as they were about to enter the village, and made for them sword in hand. They immediately turned at bay and presented their muskets at him. It was a critical moment, as one of them pulled the trigger, but a merciful Providence had preserved the young officer to render priceless services to his country, and add a glorious page to her history. The cap snapped almost in Roberts's face, and, the next moment, he laid the Sepoy carrying the standard dead at his feet by a tremendous cut across the head, and seized the trophy as it fell from his lifeless grasp. Meantime the companion of the standard-bearer made off into the village. But this was not the only exploit performed by Lieutenant Roberts on this 2nd of January.

Following up the rebels, he came up with a group, consisting of a Sikh Sowar and a rebel Sepoy standing at bay with musket and bayonet. The cavalryman with his sword felt himself no match for the foot-soldier armed with what Napier calls " the queen of weapons;" but Roberts, on arriving on the scene, did not wait to count the odds, if they were against him, but rode straight at the Sepoy, and with one stroke of his sword slashed him across the face, killing him on the spot.

For these two acts of personal prowess Brigadier-General Grant recommended him for the decoration of the Victoria Cross, which was conferred on the following 14th of September, by a General Order of the Commander-in-Chief, issued at Allahabad.

On the rebels being completely dispersed, the cavalry returned to camp after a hard day's work, and, on the following morning, a march of twelve miles brought the army to Futtehgurh, which was found deserted by the mutineers, as well as a strong fort on the banks of the Ganges, in the midst of the town which it commanded. The town of Furruckabad, three miles distant, also surrendered without firing a shot; and the Nawab, Azim Khan, who had committed frightful atrocities on the occasion of the massacre of Europeans at Futtehgurh, was hanged, and his body left on the gallows as a warning to the townspeople.

The day after his arrival at Futtehgurh, the Commander-in-Chief was joined by Walpole's and Seaton's brigades, escorting an immense convoy, when the force placed at his disposal numbered over 10,000 men. The task set before Sir Colin Campbell in undertaking the operations terminating with his arrival at Futtehgurh, had been accomplished; the Doab had been cleared of the enemy, communications with the Northwest Provinces had been reopened, and to complete the pacification of the country, there remained the formidable task of the reconquest of Rohilcund and Oude, into which the rebels had been driven as birds into a net by the fowler. The Commander-in-Chief, therefore, made preparations for the final capture of Lucknow, which had become a vast stronghold, requiring a large army and a siege-train for its reduction.

Sir Colin Campbell, with his staff, escorted by some cavalry and horse artillery, broke up his camp on the 1st of February, and, making double marches, reached Cawnpore in three days. General Grant followed on the same day with the remainder of the force, when the column retraced its steps towards the Kala

Nuddee, passing over the ground which was strewed with the unburied corpses and skeletons of the rebels killed a month before.

On the 3rd of February, when a halt was made near Kunoge, Sir Hope Grant, who was a keen *shekari* and fearless rider, indulged in a day's "pig-sticking" to the gratification of his staff, among whom were horsemen not inferior to himself. The sport afforded a pleasant relaxation from the tedious marches and more exciting operations of war, and was improvised on an extensive scale. On arrival at the ground, on a tongue of land between the Kala Nuddee and the Ganges, thirty-five elephants, marshalled in line, moved through the high grass, the pig-stickers armed with lances riding in front. The sport was indifferent, but there was excellent opportunity for the reckless riding over ground invisible a yard in front, which characterises this species of Indian hunting.

General Grant made the following entry in his journal of an incident of the day's sport:—"We singled out a young boar, and I was on the point of spearing him, when Augustus Anson, my aide-de-camp, and Roberts, Deputy Assistant Quartermaster-General, full of ardour, dashed up at a gallop, as if they were riding for their lives, and simultaneously cannoned against both flanks of my horse, fairly lifting him off his legs and shutting me up completely. However, strange to say, the horse did not roll over. After all, the young gentlemen did not spear the pig; he was run into by some dogs which held him fast, as he was not full grown, until we came up and despatched him. We afterwards put up a large fox, which gave us a fine chevy. Three greyhounds followed him up splendidly for about a mile and a half, until one of them caught him by the brush and rolled him over, but could not hold him. Reynard then doubled and escaped."

After this interlude in the more serious game of war, the march was resumed and the column proceeded to Surajpore. On arriving here General Grant received a message from the Commander-in-Chief, requesting him to join him at Cawnpore. Accompanied by his staff, he started after breakfast and rode into the station, when he received instructions from Sir Colin Campbell to assume temporary command of the whole army between Cawnpore and Bunnee during his absence at Allahabad, where he was about to proceed to confer with the Governor-General, who had taken up his headquarters at this city, so as to be in communication with the army during the approaching operations in Oude.

On Sunday, the 7th of February, Grant's division arrived at Cawnpore, and, on the following day, the General crossed the Ganges and took up his command at Oonao, where the army was gathering for the capture of Lucknow.

It was no light task transporting the vast train of ammunition, artillery, and stores, with the camp followers and *impedimenta* considered necessary for an Indian Army until the gallant subject of this Memoir demonstrated by his advance on Cabul after Cavagnari's murder, and on his more renowned but less arduous march on Candahar, that Oriental warfare can be undertaken under conditions more nearly approximating to those enforced in the armies of the West, and with increased efficiency and a due regard to the health of British troops, even though there is some sacrifice of the comforts of life in a cantonment. Lieutenant Roberts's duties at this time were of a very arduous character, superintending the passage of troops and stores across the bridge of boats, and marking out the camps of the respective brigades on the vast level plain at Oonao, where a halt was made pending the arrival of the Commander-in-Chief.

An officer who was present with Grant's force, gives the following description of the extent of this encampment:—
" The encampment around Oonao was a very large one, as the immense parks of artillery and ordnance stores had been massed here, and the enormous quantity of ground covered by the army and its belongings is incredible, and would not be believed out of India. A division of the army, and that not a very large one, moved from one side to the other of Oonao, a distance of two miles, and it took eight hours from the time the advanced guard left the old ground till the rear guard arrived at the new encampment; true they were escorting a large part of the siege train, and, besides the guns and mortars, they had carts upon carts of ammunition, each drawn by five bullocks, which again required carts upon carts more, also drawn by five bullocks each, to carry food and fodder for these numberless bullocks.

The Naval Brigade, for instance, which had only sixteen guns—but they are monsters—and ten rocket tubes, had no less than 800 bullocks attached to the guns and their belongings. Besides bullocks there are elephants, camels, horses, ponies, goats, fowls, geese, &c., and camp followers innumerable. Every officer has from four to twelve servants, and the men also have several attached to each company, for a private in India cannot draw his own water, nor cook his own victuals, nor could he, till lately, clean his own boots, nor shave his own chin, but shoe-cleaners and barbers were attached to each regiment. There is a bazaar also which follows every corps, and which is under the control of the commanding officer. It supplies all the things which are required by soldiers on a campaign, such as soap, tobacco, &c., also gram* for horses." Bad as this state of affairs was in 1857, it was far worse in the days before the time of Sir Charles Napier, whose soldierly instincts induced him to cut down the establishments which encumbered the march of an Indian Army.

While at Oonao, General Grant undertook a *dour* (or flying expedition) to clear the country north of the Cawnpore and Lucknow road of insurgents, especially at a stronghold called Futtehpore Churassie, twenty miles distant, on the banks of the Ganges, where the Nana was supposed to be. The column, consisting of some 3,000 men,† quitted camp on the 15th of February, and, marching over a difficult country, intersected by nullahs, arrived at Futtehpore. Roberts reconnoitred the fort, which was found to be deserted, but the cavalry succeeded in cutting up some fleeing rebels, from whom two guns were captured. After destroying the town and blowing up the fort, as well as another stronghold six miles distant, the column marched to Bunghurmow, the inhabitants of which sent a deputation expressing their loyalty and promising to furnish supplies. The General spared the place, but a portion of the 53rd Regiment were guilty of looting, which he punished by

---

* A species of vetch.
† The 34th, 38th, and 53rd Regiments; two squadrons of the 7th Hussars, two squadrons of the 9th Lancers; Anderson's and Turner's troops of Horse Artillery, an 18-pounder, and an 8-inch howitzer, and a company of Sappers.

summarily flogging a dozen of them who were caught *flagrante delicto*.

On Sunday, the 21st, the column arrived at Sultangunj, and, two days later, were before Meeangunj, which 2,000 rebel infantry, besides some cavalry, had made preparations to defend. The town, of rectangular shape, was surrounded with a high loop-holed brick wall, with circular bastions at the angles and along the sides; the gates also were fortified with ditch and palisade. The General, with Roberts and the other members of his staff, rode forward to reconnoitre. A suitable spot for breaching having been selected, an 18-pounder and 8-inch howitzer were dragged forward by elephants to effect a breach, while Captain Turner's troop of horse artillery took up a position to sweep the walls, and the cavalry were sent round to intercept the fugitives, the infantry being kept in the rear ready to storm. After about two hours' firing a practicable breach was reported, and the 53rd were ordered to advance, and marched cheerily to the assault, thinking little of what the poet calls

"That awful pause, dividing life from death."

Some sharp fighting took place, but the rebels were beaten at every point, and, as they issued from the gates on the other side of the town, were pursued by the cavalry, who cut them down relentlessly. The slaughter at Meeangunj was great, for no quarter was expected or given, and every man found with arms in his hands or seeking to escape was shot or sabred. Corpses strewed the plain and streets of the town, which was burning in different parts. Captain (now Admiral) Oliver Jones, of the Royal Navy, a gallant officer, who was present with the force as a volunteer, speaking of the distressing scenes he witnessed, describes one in which the subject of this memoir figures in a manner most creditable to his humanity: "Roberts, the Assistant Quartermaster-General, was giving directions about burning a part of the town, when an old, infirm man, who was sitting at the door of a house, entreated him to spare it, saying, ' that yesterday morning he was the happy father of five sons, three of them lie there, pointing to three corpses, where the other two are, God only knows; that he was old, and a cripple, and that if his house was burned he would have nothing left but to lie down and die.' Roberts, who is as good as he is brave, gave directions for sparing the old man's house, and I hope that the two missing sons have escaped, and have returned to comfort his few remaining days."*

As the author of "Don Juan" cynically observes:

> "However habit sears
> Men's hearts against whole millions, when their trade
> Is butchery, sometimes a single sorrow
> Will touch even heroes."

Captain Jones, in another part of his interesting journal, which was published on the conclusion of the war just as he penned it on the spot, writes of Roberts in terms which those who have served with or under him on active service can vouch are not exaggerated: "He is one of those rare men who, to uncommon daring and bravery in the field, and unflinching hardworking discharge of duty in the camp, adds the charm of cheering and unaffected kindness and hospitality in the tent, and his acquaintance and friendship are high prizes to those who obtain them."

After a day's rest the column resumed its march, and, on the 1st March, reached Buntheera, where Sir Colin Campbell had arrived shortly before from Allahabad. On the arrival three days later of Brigadier-General Franks, who, in thirteen days, had marched from the other side of Oude, a distance of 130 miles, and beaten the enemy in four general actions, the force placed at the disposal of the Commander-in-Chief consisted of 20,000 men,† the greater portion Europeans, with 180 pieces of ordnance, forming the finest army assembled under any British General in India. General Hope Grant was placed in command of the cavalry division, and, accompanied by Roberts, proceeded with the Commander-in-Chief, on the 2nd March, when he moved from Buntheera to put into execution his plan of campaign.

Sir Colin took with him the second division of infantry,

---

* "Recollections of a Winter Campaign in India in 1857-58," by Captain Oliver J. Jones, R.N.

† This was exclusive of the Nepaul troops under Jung Bahadur, which brought up the number to 40,000.

under Sir Edward Lugard, the head-quarters of the artillery division, under Sir Archdale Wilson (of Delhi), and three troops of horse artillery, two 24-pounders and two 8-inch howitzers of the Naval brigade, under Captain Peel, R.N., and the head-quarters of the cavalry division, with Little's Brigade. Passing the fort of Jellalabad, the force, after a skirmish, seized and occupied the Dilkoosha palace and the Mohamed Bagh, where batteries were erected to keep down the fire of the enemy's guns along the canal. Lieutenant Roberts accompanied his Chief, who was engaged in placing the outposts entrusted to his care by the Commander-in-Chief, who placed great reliance on General Grant's well-known ability in effecting this duty, one of the most important in the conduct of the operations of war. Both Sir Frederick Roberts and Lord Wolseley, who served at different periods on Sir Hope Grant's staff, have expressed to the writer how much they owe to their late chief in the matter of outpost duty, and both these distinguished Generals put in practice, the one in Ashantee and Egypt and the other in Afghanistan, the lessons learnt in the school of war under this careful cavalry officer. While engaged in placing the guns, the Generals and their staffs were exposed to a biting fire, and Brigadier Little was severely wounded.

The canal referred to runs into the Goomtee, and formed the outer line of defence on the southern and eastern sides, the bridges over it having been broken down, and an earthen rampart, with bastions mounted with guns, having been constructed on the inner face.

Lucknow was defended by a second line of works, starting from the Goomtee in front of the Motee Mahal palace, and covering the 32nd Mess-House, the building called the Imambara, and the street known as Huzrutgunj. The third or inner line of defence was in front of the great palace and enclosure called the Kaiser Bagh, which, as well as the buildings of the outer line, had been greatly strengthened and mounted with guns by the rebels during the period the city had been in their undisputed possession, while the houses in the streets leading to them had been loopholed. In short, preparations had been made for a desperate defence, to overcome which the British commander had to undertake siege operations, the conduct of

The Siege of Lucknow.

which was placed in the hands of Brigadier Robert Napier, of the Bengal Engineers, better known to fame as Lord Napier of Magdala.

The Commander-in-Chief, seeing that the rebel leaders had neglected defending the Goomtee—probably anticipating that the advance would be made either by the route adopted by Havelock in September, 1857 (by the Charbagh bridge and through the centre of the city), or by the Secunder Bagh and Shah Nujeef, the road by which he himself advanced in the following November—decided to send a division across the river to operate from that side, so that he might take all the fortified works in reverse. The command of this force was entrusted to Sir James Outram—it could not have been placed in better hands—and Sir Hope Grant, who accompanied him as second in command, was directed to superintend the passage of the river by two pontoon bridges which the engineers threw across with great celerity. The Commander-in-Chief was very anxious to secure the uncontested passage of the Goomtee, as the operation, always a dangerous one over a broad and swift stream unless executed before the enemy has intimation of what was intended, might have caused heavy loss. It was to have been carried out on the night of the 5th March, but some delay occurred in bringing the troops and guns over the sedgy, heavy ground at Bibiapore, on the banks of the river. Sir Hope Grant and his staff, on all preparations being completed, rested on the ground smoking philosophically, and the Commander-in-Chief, on coming up, was very irate that the passage of the troops was not in progress, as he apprehended opposition.

But the enemy, though close at hand and mustering in overwhelming force (some place the number in Lucknow at 50,000, or even 100,000), knew not what was in progress, or lacked initiative and enterprise, as they did all through the Mutiny.

> "Hark! through the silence of the cold dull night,
> The hum of armies gathering rank on rank!
> Lo! dusky masses steal in dubious sight
> Along the leaguer'd wall and bristling bank
> Of the arm'd river, while, with straggling light,
> The stars peep through the vapours dim and dark,
> Which curl in curious wreaths."

The troops forming Sir James Outram's division arrived after midnight, and, by daybreak of the 6th March, had crossed the Goomtee with all their guns and stores, an operation reflecting great credit on all concerned in carrying it into effect, including Lieutenant Roberts, on whom the brunt of the duty fell.

Advancing towards Lucknow a cavalry skirmish took place, in which Major Percy Smith, of the Bays, was killed, and the division encamped that evening within four miles of the city. On the following day, as Sir Hope Grant, accompanied by his staff, rode down the Fyzabad road to reconnoitre, the enemy opened fire with artillery, whereupon he brought up some cavalry and guns. Under orders from the Commander-in-Chief, Outram remained in his camp till the 9th, when he attacked the enemy's works in two divisions, that on the right being under the command of Sir Hope Grant, and the left under his personal direction.

The action was commenced by a fire from two heavy batteries, mounting twelve guns, constructed by the British during the previous night, within 600 yards of the rebel works on the old race-course; and Sir Hope, advancing his infantry, under Walpole, on the right, took the enemy's position in reverse, but found that the guns had been removed. Outram, with the left column, crossed the Kokrail stream, captured the Chukur Kotee (Yellow House), the key of the position, as it enfiladed the enemy's works on the right bank of the Goomtee, and pressing forward, driving the enemy before him, occupied the left bank as far as the Badshah Bagh, and effected a junction with Sir Hope Grant. The buildings and works on the banks of the river were now occupied, and, under cover of a heavy musketry fire, two batteries were erected to enfilade the works in rear of the Martiniere and keep down the rebel fire. Profiting by this success, the Commander-in-Chief captured the Martiniere without resistance, and the whole line of works up to Banks's house, which was captured on the following day.

On the 10th Sir James Outram was engaged strengthening his position, his batteries keeping up a fire on the Kaiser Bagh and other works, and Sir Hope Grant sent out strong parties of cavalry to prevent supplies being brought into the town, and some smart skirmishing took place. During the night Outram erected fresh batteries, which played on the Kaiser Bagh and enfiladed the enemy's works, and, on the following morning, he advanced and captured the works covering the iron bridge, leading to the Residency, and the stone bridge, leading to the Muchee Bhawun, as well as a camp between these two points, during which Lieutenant Moorsom, his Deputy-Assistant-Quartermaster-General, a very accomplished officer, was killed. Outram was now occupied erecting fresh batteries of heavy guns and mortars to play on the Kaiser Bagh, which was, in a measure, the enemy's citadel.

Meanwhile, on the other bank, the buildings forming the second line of defence fell to the brilliant valour of the troops under the personal direction of the Commander-in-Chief. The Secunder Bagh and Shah Nujeef, which had been so severely contested in the memorable Relief of the previous November, were captured without opposition, and, by nightfall on the 11th, the series of palaces and enclosures known as the Begum Kotee, were stormed by the 93rd Highlanders and 4th Punjaub Rifles with their wonted dash, though the brilliancy of the achievement was dimmed by the loss of that gallant and most admirable soldier, Hodson, whom the Commander-in-Chief, who attended his funeral, described as surpassed by no officer of his army.

On the 14th the Imambara, having been breached, was stormed by detachments of the 10th Foot and Ferozepore Regiment of Sikhs, who, following up the fleeing rebels, entered the Teera Kotee and Mess-house, and soon the Motee Mahal and other palaces, and the Kaiser Bagh itself, were won, when the demon of plunder seized the troops, and an indescribable scene of rapine ensued. The 14th was the decisive day in the operations resulting in the capture of Lucknow. The slaughter had been terrible, and as when, "on the gentle Severn's sedgy bank," Mortimer engaged Glendower, so now, when Christian and Pandy met in desperate conflict, the Goomtee

> "Ran fearfully among the trembling reeds,
> And hid his crisp head in the hollow bank,
> Blood-stain'd."

Unhappily, owing to over-caution on the part of the Commander-in-Chief, the success was not so complete as it might have been, as when Outram applied for leave to advance across the iron bridge and intercept the retreat of the enemy, he was directed only to do so if it could be done "without the loss of a single man." The proverbial difficulty of making omelets without breaking eggs prevented the gallant "Bayard of India" from carrying out an advance which would have made the operations of the day complete.

On the 15th Sir Hope Grant proceeded, under orders from Sir Colin Campbell, to Seetapore, with 1,100 sabres and twelve horse artillery guns, to pursue the enemy in that direction, and Brigadier Campbell was directed to move in co-operation from Alumbagh along the Sandila road, but the movement left open the Fyzabad road, by which the enemy in large numbers effected their escape, thus requiring the subsequent protracted operations in Oude which resulted in considerable loss, due more to disease and heat apoplexy than the sword. Sir Hope was recalled after making one march, and, on the 19th, co-operated from the left bank with Outram (who had crossed the river with Douglas's brigade and captured the Residency and other buildings) in the attack on the Moosa Bagh; the rebels, who held the stronghold in great force, abandoned it, and, owing to the unfortunate inaction of Brigadier Campbell, whose splendid force of cavalry was suffered to remain idle, effected their escape unmolested.

Lucknow was now once more in possession of the British, and, on the 22nd of March, Sir Hope Grant was directed to proceed to Koorsie, twenty-five miles distant, on the Fyzabad road, where a strong force of the enemy had taken post. At midnight he marched with a brigade of the three arms, and, on coming up with the enemy, attacked them with spirit; in this affair Captain (now General Sir) Samuel Browne, commanding two squadrons of Punjaub Cavalry, and Captain Cosserat, commanding a detachment of Watson's Horse, displayed conspicuous gallantry, the latter officer being killed. The column now returned to Lucknow, in command of which Sir Hope Grant was placed with a fine division.

The action at Koorsie was the last at which Lieutenant Roberts was present during the Mutiny, in the three principal episodes of which, the Siege of Delhi, and the Relief and Siege of Lucknow, he had taken so distinguished a part. His health had long been indifferent, but his brave heart and high sense of duty kept him up while there was the incentive to exertion derived from an urgent demand for his services. Now that the neck of the revolt was broken, his health completely gave way, and he was ordered to proceed to England on medical certificate. He, accordingly, gave over charge of the Quartermaster-General's Department to Captain Garnet Wolseley, of the 90th Regiment, and thus for a second time—the former occasion being at the capture of the Mess-house in November, 1857—these two officers were associated together, whose names within the past few years have been much in the mouths of their countrymen as the two Generals (excluding Lords Napier and Strathnairn, by reason of their age), on whom this country chiefly relies as the future leaders of her armies, should any emergency arise.

Lieutenant Roberts proceeded to Calcutta, and, on the 3rd of May, embarked in a Peninsular and Oriental steamer, in company with several wounded and sick officers. On his arrival at Alexandria he took the Austrian Lloyd's steamer to Trieste, and thence journeyed through Switzerland to England. It was more than six years since he quitted his native land, and Wordsworth's lines on landing in England well expressed his feelings, as they have those of many a returning wanderer from home :—

> "The cock that crows, the smoke that curls, that sound
> Of bells,—those boys who in yon meadow ground
> In white-sleeved shirts are playing,—and the roar
> Of the waves, breaking on the chalky shore,—
> All, all are English."

The past twelve months had been, indeed, eventful in the life of our hero. The "battles and sieges" in which he had participated, and the "hairbreadth escapes" he had experienced during that period, were sufficient to render any career extraordinary, and he emerged from the campaign a veteran in war though still young in years. But what were the rewards he received at the hands of a grateful country for his meritorious services? He had entered the war as a subaltern, and a subaltern he remained at the end, without promotion or brevet, according to the inexorable "rules of the service," until in due course he should obtain his captaincy. In common with every private soldier he was awarded the medal with three clasps, and he had earned that decoration, "for valour," which, though only of bronze, is of priceless value in the estimation of every one privileged to wear Her Majesty's uniform. But beyond repeated thanks from every General Officer under whom he had served, as also from the Commander-in-Chief and the Governor-General in Council, he had received nothing save what his humbler comrades in the ranks had shared. As Byron writes of a battle field and its rewards :—

> "Here the still varying pangs, which multiply
> Until their very number makes men hard
> By the infinities of agony,
> Which meet the gaze, whate'er it may regard—
> The groan, the roll in dust, the all white eye
> Turned back within its socket—these reward
> Your rank and file by thousands, while the rest
> May win, perhaps, a riband at the breast!"

CHAPTER VI.

Lieutenant Roberts returns to India—Is employed in Charge of the Viceroy's Camp—Lord Clyde's Letter to Lord Canning recommending Roberts—Promotion to a Brevet-Majority—On Tour with Sir Hugh Rose—Is ordered on Special Service to Umbeyla—Critical State of Affairs on the North-West Frontier in 1863—The Action of Laloo—The Capture of Umbeyla—The Burning of Mulkah—Major Roberts Compiles a Route Book for the Bengal Presidency—Returns to England on Sick Leave—On his return to India proceeds to Abyssinia with the Expedition under Sir Robert Napier—Major Roberts's Services in Abyssinia.

LIEUTENANT ROBERTS remained only twelve months in England, and, on the 17th of May, 1859, shortly before his return to India, married Miss Nora Henrietta Bews, daughter of Captain Bews, of the 73rd Regiment, afterwards Paymaster-General of Constabulary. The issue of this marriage was six children, of whom three survive—a son, Frederick Hugh Sherston, born 8th July, 1872, and two daughters.

In June, 1859, Lieutenant Roberts quitted England for India, travelling overland, and, on reporting himself, was attached to Army Head-Quarters for the purpose of taking charge of the Camp of the Viceroy, Earl Canning, during the customary tour in the approaching cold weather. Hitherto he had only held an acting appointment in the Quartermaster-General's Department, but, immediately after the capture of Lucknow, Lord Clyde, in recognition of his meritorious services and his marked aptitude for the duties of this important branch of the staff, placed him on the permanent establishment, to which he had been gazetted on the 15th April, 1858. The Quartermaster-General was Colonel (now General Sir) Arthur Becher, who was head of the Department at the Siege of Delhi, where he was seriously wounded, and now welcomed his old associate in that arduous struggle, during which he had formed a high opinion of Roberts's capacity and aptitude for organization.

The terms under which Lieutenant Roberts was recommended by the Commander-in-Chief to the charge of the Viceroy's Camp were of a nature that were specially complimentary to him. Writing privately to the Viceroy from Simla on the 29th August, 1859, Lord Clyde said: "With respect to Major Garden, whom your Lordship proposed to be the Quartermaster-General with your Camp, should you particularly wish for that officer, of course he is at your service, but Colonel Becher, the head of the Department, has observed that as Major Garden is the next senior officer to himself in the office, it will be more convenient for the Service, if equally agreeable to your Lordship, that Lieutenant Roberts should attend your camp. Believe me, &c., CLYDE." "P.S.—Lieutenant Roberts is a particularly gentlemanlike, intelligent and agreeable young officer."

And so, doubtless, Lord Canning found the young artillery officer, while the mode in which he discharged the arduous duties of his post was such as to elicit the commendation of his lordship, and the surprise even of those accustomed to the efficiency of the Quartermaster-General's Department in India. We have been assured by one qualified to know, that the arrangements for the camp were simply perfect, and only those can appreciate the labour, who are conversant with the details of a Viceregal progress in India, with its large body of troops, the thousands of camp followers and servants, the daily march, and the durbars, with the elaborate etiquette and attendant formalities as regards the reception and precedence of the princes and nobles, with whom such ceremonies assume an importance inexplicable to any European mind save, perhaps, that of the chamberlain of a third-rate German court.

The Viceroy's first tour was of a very extended character, embracing a visit to Cawnpore, Lucknow, Futtehghur, Agra, Meerut, Roorkee, Delhi, Umballa, Lahore, Jullundur, Umritsur, Peshawur, Sealkote, and Cashmere. The tour of 1860-61 was to Jubbulpore, and thence through the Central Provinces. On the 12th November, 1860, Lieutenant Roberts was gazetted to his regimental captaincy, and thus having attained qualifying rank, on the following day he was promoted to a brevet-majority for his services during the Mutiny, so that he was addressed

The Umbeyla Campaign.

for only one day as a captain. In the winter of 1861-62, and again in the following winter, Major Roberts accompanied the Commander-in-Chief, Sir Hugh Rose, in his several tours through the Derajât and Central India, and the gallant soldier, whose march from Bombay to Gwalior, in 1858, forms one of the most striking episodes of the quelling of the great Sepoy revolt, formed, like his predecessor and all who were thrown into official contact with the hero of the second Afghan War, a high opinion of his military capacity.

From the close of the Mutiny to 1863 not a shot was fired in India, but, in the latter part of that year, the Indian Government were involved in what is known as the Umbeyla Campaign. The column destined to subdue the tribes in that remote corner of the British Empire, was commanded by Sir Neville Chamberlain, but the campaign was more protracted than was anticipated, and the gallant mountaineers offered so desperate a resistance to the passage of our troops, and our losses were so severe, that large reinforcements were ordered to the front, and at one time the Viceregal Government and Sir Hugh Rose himself were anxious lest the movement should spread, involving a costly and extended struggle with the fierce and fanatical tribes in that portion of the North-West frontier.

In November of this year Major Roberts received orders from the Commander-in-Chief to proceed, in conjunction with Colonel (now General Sir) John Adye, of the Royal Artillery, to the British camp at Umbeyla on special duty, to represent Army Head-Quarters, and make himself generally useful to the officer in command. Before Roberts's arrival at the British camp some desperate fighting took place in the dark glens and steep mountain sides of the Umbeyla defile, the nine miles of which it took the British troops some two months to force, and none of those engaged are likely to forget the hand-to-hand combats at the "Crag" and "Eagle's Nest" pickets. Before the close of that brief campaign some 25,000 troops were in motion north of the Jhelum, and our loss was 19 officers and 238 men killed, and 47 officers and 672 men wounded. In the action of 20th November Sir Neville Chamberlain, who had displayed his wonted impetuous valour, received, with his usual fortune, a severe wound, the eighth in the service of his country. Colonel Hope, his second in command, was also dangerously wounded.

At the time Major Roberts arrived at the British camp the position of affairs was indeed critical, and Major James, C.B., an officer of great ability and experience, who had just arrived from England, and assumed political charge of the expedition, reported to Government : " The excitement was spreading far and wide. The Momunds on the Peshawur border were beginning to make hostile demonstrations at Shubkudder, for the first time since their signal defeat near the same place, in 1852, by the late Lord Clyde. Rumours were also reaching me from Kohat of expected raids by the Wuzeerees and Othman-Khail. Emissaries from Cabul and Jellalabad were with the Akhoond, who had been also further reinforced by Ghuzzun Khan, the Chief of Dher, and 6,000 men. On December the 5th the Momunds made a raid into our territories at Shubkudder, in repelling which Lieutenant Bishop was killed."

So threatening had the aspect of affairs become that the Lieutenant-Governor of the Punjaub telegraphed to Sir Neville Chamberlain and Major James, authorizing the retirement of the troops. Though suffering greatly from his wound, the gallant Chamberlain, supported by the opinion of his political coadjutor, declined to retire, rightly judging that the effect on our prestige would be disastrous ; and Sir Hugh Rose, (Lord Elgin, the Governor-General, being then in a dying state),* strenuously opposed so pusillanimous a course, but was overruled by a majority of the Council, and, on the 25th November, orders for withdrawal, involving a humiliating confession of defeat, were actually issued, when Sir William Denison, Governor of Madras, who arrived from that Presidency to assume temporary charge of the government, induced the Council to reconsider their decision, and, on the arrival of General Garvock† with a brigade, raising the force to 9,000 men, operations were resumed and crowned with complete success.

Once more Roberts found himself on that North-West frontier in which he had gained his earliest military experiences, and where and in the countries beyond he was to earn for

---

* Lord Elgin expired on the 20th of November.
† The late General Sir John Garvock, K.C.B.

himself undying fame as one of England's most daring and successful Generals. Speaking to us of the North-West frontier, he enlarged on the advantages it affords to the Indian Service as the great training school of our officers. It is the only department in which young officers have a chance of earning distinction, as they are there placed in positions of responsibility at an early age, and the manner in which they acquit themselves of this responsibility is the measure of their capacity. Nearly all our best officers have been reared on the North-West frontier, from Sir Henry Lawrence and Major Broadfoot to the Lumsdens, Coke, Watson, Probyn, Sam Browne, Daly, Hodson, the Battyes, Brownlow, Keyes, Abbott, and Cavagnari.

At daylight of the 15th December, General Garvock, leaving 3,000 men to guard his camp, marched out with the remainder, divided into two brigades, under Lieutenant-Colonel Wilde, C.B.,* of the Guides, and Colonel W. M. Turner, C.B., of the 97th Regiment. Major Roberts accompanied the General, and witnessed the succeeding operations, which had for their object the capture of Laloo, two miles beyond the Crag picket, and of Umbeyla, at the Chumla valley end of the pass. On arriving before Umbeyla it was found that the enemy, with standards flying, had taken up a position in great force on the conical peak of one of the spurs running up from the Chumla valley, dominating the whole ridge and the village nestling at its feet. On the arrival of the troops Colonel Wilde's Brigade was told off to make the direct assault on the peak, the natural strength of which was greatly increased by breastworks all the way up the mountain; the second brigade being detailed to turn the right of the position and storm the village of Laloo.

All being ready, at the signal, the British troops, with their Sikh, Pathan, and Goorkha comrades, raised a cheer, and rapidly crossing the intervening open ground, commenced to scale the steep ascent with admirable *élan*, the 101st Regiment, gallantly led by Colonel Salusbury, being conspicuous in the advance. The determination to win evinced by these veteran soldiers struck terror into the hearts of the mountaineers, who sought to stop their assailants by a rapid musketry fire and

---

* The late General Sir Alfred Wilde, K.C.B., Member of the Council of India.

hurling rocks on their heads; but all was in vain, and the breastworks were carried in succession at the point of the bayonet, the almost inaccessible peak itself being soon crowned by the victorious soldiers of the Queen. In the meantime Colonel Turner was equally successful, and the village of Laloo fell into the hands of the 7th Fusiliers and the native corps of his brigade, and the hillmen were driven down the steep glens and through the pine woods clothing the Chumla valley. Not anticipating such vigorous action, a large force of the enemy had attacked the camp from the Umbeyla Pass, but were repulsed.

Following up his success, early on the following morning Colonel Wilde, accompanied by Major Roberts, who, throughout the operations, proceeded sometimes with one brigade, sometimes with the other, wherever the work promised to be the hottest, marched down the hills on Umbeyla with the brigade of Infantry, and 400 sabres, commanded by Colonel Probyn, who, anticipating a fight in the valley, had brought up his regiment from Eusofzye, and afforded the mountaineers the unwonted spectacle of troopers leading their horses down a breakneck declivity, and then, on gaining the valley below, mounting them in readiness for action. The enemy were drawn up in front of Umbeyla, but with one brigade in front, and Colonel Turner's brigade, which had made a *detour* by Laloo, on their flank, they fell back under cover of the broken ground. Later in the day, as Colonel Turner, with his Sikh regiments in line, and a wing of the 7th Fusiliers in support, was advancing from Umbeyla towards the hills which divide the Chumla and Bonair valleys, several hundred Ghazees, or fanatic swordsmen, who had been concealed at the base of the ridge, made a furious attack on the British line, but were exterminated almost to a man. From the slopes and crests above many thousands of the hillmen witnessed this scene, which was the last military incident of this brief campaign, and, as they dispersed under the shell fire from the guns of Captain Griffin's battery, stationed in the valley beneath, they tacitly owned that they were no match for such soldiers. That the fighting during these two days had been severe was attested by the British loss, which was 172 killed and wounded.

End of the Umbeyla Campaign.

The alliance of the chiefs against us was now broken up, the Bajourees returned to their fastnesses, the Akhoond of Swat, that fanatical semi-ecclesiastical semi-military enemy to our rule, seeing that the game was up, returned with his followers to his valley, and the chiefs of Bonair, relieved from their allies, agreed to terms. Nothing now remained but to destroy the town of Mulkah, the *teterrima causa belli*, the nest whence these birds of prey issued, some twenty-five miles distant. This place became the seat of the Wahabee fanatics who, driven from Sitana in 1858, by a British force commanded by Sir Sydney Cotton, had returned thither four years later, and established themselves at Mulkah, on the north side of the Mahabun mountain, that vast natural stronghold, extending about thirty miles from east to west, whose rugged and steep ridges rise to an altitude of 8,000 feet.

Instead of despatching a brigade to destroy Mulkah, General Garvock, anxious to terminate the war, resolved on the somewhat hazardous step of sending to this cradle of treachery and fanaticism some British officers, with an escort, to witness its destruction, which was to be effected by the Bonair chiefs. Major Roberts, Colonel Adye, Captain Jenkins, commanding the Guides, and some other officers accompanied Colonel Reynell Taylor, the Commisioner of Peshawur, to Mulkah, which was found to be a large village, standing on a northern slope of the Mahabun, with numerous workshops and a powder factory.* The place was burnt on the 22nd December, in presence of the British officers and of the natives, who collected near the spot, and, with feelings of bitter resentment, watched the destruction of their homes. On the return of the British officers, the force broke up its encampment, and marched to the plain of Eusofzye within our borders, on the Christmas-day of 1863. For his services Major Roberts was mentioned in despatches by General Garvock, who expressed to him and Colonel Adye, his "best thanks for their aid on many occasions."

Major Roberts returned to his duties in the Quartermaster-General's Department, and, during the following year, was employed in compiling a new Route-book for the Bengal Presi-

---

* See Colonel Adye's "Sitana."

dency. This work was published in January, 1865, when the author received the thanks of the Governor-General in Council, and of the Commander-in-Chief.* In the words of Colonel Norman, the Military Secretary to the Government of India, when conveying the thanks of the Viceroy, Major Roberts displayed " care and ability " in the compilation of this useful work, and the service is rendered the more meritorious from the circumstance that it was written at a time when he was suffering from liver complaint, which necessitated a return to England in the month succeeding the publication of the book.

Major Roberts sailed by the Cape route in Messrs. Green's ship, the " Renown," and, in March of the following year (1866), returned overland. On his reporting himself he was posted to the charge of the Quartermaster-General's Department in the Allahabad Division, where he served under Generals Troup and Beatson, until October, 1867, when he was ordered to proceed once more on active service.

Our Government having resolved to chastise Theodore, "Negoos," or Emperor, of Abyssinia, for imprisoning several British subjects, including Consul Cameron and Mr. Rassam, Assistant Political Resident at Aden, who had been dispatched in July, 1864, with a letter from the Queen to Theodore, it was not until the 13th of August, 1867, that Lord Derby's Cabinet, yielding at length to the persistent representations of Brigadier-General William Merewether, at that time the able Political Resident at Aden, finally resolved on a military expedition to

---

* From Colonel Paton, Quartermaster-General, to the Secretary to the Government of India. Fort William, 31st of January, 1865.

"I am instructed in forwarding for submission to Government a copy of the new edition of ' Routes in the Bengal Presidency,' to state that His Excellency the Commander-in-Chief desires most fully to acknowledge the exertions and services of Major Roberts, V.C., Assistant Quartermaster-General, attached to this office, by whom the work has been entirely compiled and carried through the press."

From Colonel H. W. Norman, C.B., Secretary to the Government of India, Military Department, to the Quartermaster-General. Fort William, 18th of February, 1865.

"In reply to yours, dated 31st ult., I am directed to acquaint you, for the information of the Commander-in-Chief, that the Right Honourable the Governor-General in Council very cordially concurs in His Excellency's acknowledgments of the care and ability displayed by Major Roberts, V.C. Assistant-Quartermaster-General, in the compilation of the New Route Book for this Presidency, a copy of which accompanied your letter."

compel Theodore to release his prisoners. This remarkable man was favourably inclined to the British, and his two chief officers, killed in his service, were Englishmen; but his pride was deeply hurt by no answer being sent for some years to a letter he addressed to Her Majesty, and he gave rein to his savage nature, which had been soured by recent defeat—an unwonted experience to one who was above all things a gallant soldier, and was of the opinion of Hector that—

> "The field of combat is the sphere for men;
> Where heroes war the foremost place I claim,
> The first in danger as the first in fame."

The command of the army was entrusted to Sir Robert Napier, the Commander-in-Chief at Bombay, from which Presidency the expeditionary force was drawn, with the addition of a Bengal brigade, to the command of which Brigadier-General Donald M. Stewart* was appointed, with Major Roberts as head of his Quartermaster-General's Department. In nominating him, the Commander-in-Chief, Sir William Mansfield, under date 30th September, 1867, addressed the Government of India in the following terms:— "Sir William Mansfield would recommend Major F. S. Roberts, V.C., now Assistant-Quartermaster-General, Allahabad Division, for the post. This officer is eminently qualified for the appointment by his activity and well known military qualities, as well as by his experience in the Quartermaster-General's Department in peace and war for nearly ten years."

The following were the troops drawn from the Bengal Presidency to take part in the Abyssinian Campaign, and placed under the command of Brigadier-General Stewart. No. 5 Battery 25th Brigade, Royal Artillery, and Mountain Battery with mortars attached, Major A. H. Bogle, R.A.; 10th Bengal Cavalry (Lancers), Major C. H. Palliser; 12th Bengal Cavalry, Major H. H. Gough, V.C.; 21st Punjaub N.I., Major J. B. Thelwall; and 23rd Punjaub N.I. (Pioneers), Major C. F. Chamberlain. The Bengal troops† took mule transport with

---

* Now General Sir Donald Stewart, Bart., G.C.B., Commander-in-Chief in India.

† The total strength of the Bengal Brigade was 38 officers, 77 warrant officers, and 2,436 non-commissioned officers and men, besides camp followers.

them, so that they were in a condition to move forward almost immediately after landing at Zoolla; and, in addition to complete transport for the corps proceeding from Calcutta, the Punjaub Government collected a large number of mules and ponies, which embarked at Kurrachee for the seat of war. For the conveyance of the Bengal contingent of troops and stores, forty-three* transports (twenty-four sailing vessels and nineteen steamers) were taken up by the Marine Department at Calcutta, and on Major Roberts devolved the superintendence of the arrangements for embarkation, which were concluded without a hitch.

On the 16th of September a reconnoitring party, under command of Brigadier-General Merewether, C.B.,† left Bombay for Massowah to select a landing-place for the force, and fixed on Zoolla, the ancient Adulis, in Annesley Bay; and, on the 7th of October, an advance brigade, under Colonel Field, 10th Bombay N.I., sailed from Bombay. Sir Robert Napier landed at Zoolla on the 2nd of January, 1868, and took over the command from Sir Charles Staveley, commanding one of the two divisions.

At this time the greater portion of the expeditionary force had arrived, including a detachment of the 23rd Punjaub Pioneers from Calcutta, which was attached to the brigade, stationed at Zoolla, under Brigadier-General Schneider. On the 25th of January, 1868, Sir Robert Napier proceeded to the front, and Sir Charles Staveley remained temporarily in command at Zoolla. On the 27th of January the 21st Punjaubees arrived at Zoolla, and, on the following day, the remainder of the Pioneers, who marched up to the Senafe Pass to join their comrades.

On the 9th of February, Major Roberts arrived in the "Golconda," on board which was the 5th Battery 25th Brigade, R.A., with a strength of eight officers, and 139 non-commissioned officers and men, and though the greater portion marched no

---

* The total number of transports employed in this expedition was 205 sailing vessels, and 75 steamers, besides native craft and lighters and barges, and the total number of seamen and others employed on board vessels in the transport service was 14,255.

† The late Sir William Merewether, K.C.S.I., C.B., Member of the Council of India.

farther than Senafe, a detachment, with two eight-inch mortars, under Major Roberts's Addiscombe friend, Major James Hills, performed excellent service at the capture of Magdala. On the same day the first detachment of the 12th Bengal Cavalry arrived, and proceeded to the front, and the remainder were landed between the 18th and 28th of February, and a detachment of 100 men, under Major Gough, shared in the attack on Magdala. The 10th Bengal Cavalry, with a strength of 460 officers and men, and 463 horses, landed on the 6th of March, and, with the 12th, was employed in keeping open the communications between the Antalo and the Takazze river.

Major Roberts was placed in charge of the Quartermaster-General's Department at Zoolla, and, as the pressure of work gradually increased, it was found that his services were too urgently required at Zoolla to permit of his going inland.* On the 23rd of February Sir Charles Staveley left the port of disembarkation for the front, and Brigadier-General Donald Stewart temporarily assumed command at Zoolla, until the arrival of Major-General Russell, Political Agent and Com-

---

* Captain H. M. Hozier writes in his "British Expedition to Abyssinia":—"At Zoolla beat the heart from which the life-stream flowed that must pulsate through the long artery of the line of communications, and carry food to the farthest outposts. . . . . . The army throughout the campaign depended almost entirely for everything, except meat and firewood, on the ships and on the Senafe depôt stored from the harbour. Never were operations carried on in a country so unfavourable for war; the very base of operations, where at the end of January there was a population of about 12,000 men and animals, had to be supplied with water from the condensers and from the shipping. An accident to a delicate piece of machinery, or the breaking of the valve of a pump, caused the stock of the precious fluid to run short, and inflicted a great inconvenience on the camp, where the water had to be doled out in daily portions of limited quantity, and a reduction of the ration told heavily on man and beast. A storm of sufficient severity to drive the condensing ships away from their anchorage would have caused a terrible calamity. To provide against such an accident, every effort was made to provide a reserve of water in a great reservoir, which was formed partly of ships' tanks and partly of a tank sent in pieces from England put together on the spot. There was no timber in the country, there was no stone near the sea coast, every block of coral and every beam of wood for the construction of piers or storehouses had to be imported; every inch of rope had to be brought from the ships; every yard of road had to be made to allow the convoys to pass; every boat had to be brought to the coast for the disembarkation of troops and stores, for none were found there, though a liberal supply was expected by some who should have been better informants. The boats that there were could not at first approach the beach, as the water shoaled slowly and the beach was very flat."

mandant at Aden. At Zoolla, under these officers, Major Roberts laboured till the end of the campaign with an indefatigability beyond praise. We have been assured by an officer well qualified to form an opinion, from having served at Zoolla throughout the Abyssinian campaign, that nothing could exceed the zeal and success with which the subject of this Memoir performed the very arduous duties committed to his charge. As an ardent soldier, confident in his ability to be of service at the front, he longed to be with the advance, and when the news of the capture of Magdala and death of Theodore, on the 13th of April, arrived in the camp, Roberts must have experienced a natural disappointment that he was toiling in the less glorious, though equally essential, duties of his department; but he had learned the secret of success in his profession, as in every other, to do with all his heart and ability the work allotted to him, and with patience to wait for the time when such good honest service will bring its reward—the opportunity for displaying in a more prominent capacity the military aptitude he felt within him, and of which those who had watched his career recognized that he was possessed.

By the 1st of April there was landed in Abyssinia 10,800 fighting men, and 14,500 camp followers, and the total number of persons re-embarked at Zoolla for Suez and India on the conclusion of the campaign, was 42,699, of whom 4,868 were embarked before the 18th of April, the date on which the news of the fall of Magdala was received at Zoolla, and 37,831 were embarked after that date. The total number of animals landed at Zoolla was 36,094,* of which 14,842 were re-embarked, the remainder being either disposed of at Massowah by Mr. Munzinger, the British Consul, or having died during the campaign. Colonel Phayre, head of the Quartermaster-General's Department, proceeded to the front, leaving Major Roberts as senior officer at Zoolla, so that the chief portion of the work of disembarkation of this vast mass of men and animals devolved on Roberts, who, on the 21st of March, had received instructions, through Major-General Russell, to make the necessary arrangements for their despatch. This he com-

---

* Of this total there were 2,538 horses, 44 elephants, 17,943 mules and ponies, 5,735 camels, 8,075 bullocks, and 1,759 donkeys.

pleted without hitch or miscarriage, though suffering almost continuously from ill-health, caused by over-work and the tropical heat of the burning plain on which Zoolla is situated, aggravated by a limited supply of water, and "perpetual clouds of dust lodging in every pore."

On the 13th of April the gloomy tyrant of Abyssinia saw the power he had built up at the cost of hecatombs of his countrymen, slain in battle or murdered in captivity, passing away from him as the soldiers of the 33rd Regiment and Engineers stormed his mountain fastness. Theodore had truly waded through seas of slaughter to the throne, and of him may be used the words Byron applied to another warrior :—

> "The greatest chief
> That ever peopled hell with heroes slain,
> Or plunged a province or a realm in grief."

True to his nature, his last act on the previous night was to order hundreds of his enemies, captives in Magdala, to be hurled headlong from the summit of the cliff at the back of that fortress, which fulfilled the purposes of the Tarpeian rock at Rome, and having thus satisfied his lust for blood, he awaited the morrow with unabated resolution. When the gateway of his stronghold was forced and British soldiers poured in upon him, the tyrant resolved not to outlive his disgrace, but putting a pistol into his mouth, blew out his brains. Like the Homeric hero who falls beneath the spear of "the godlike Thrasimed":—

> "He sinks, with endless darkness cover'd o'er,
> And vents his soul, effused with gushing gore."

On the 22nd of May, while on the march down from Magdala, Sir Robert Napier, through his Assistant-Quartermaster-General, wrote to General Russell in the following terms of Major Roberts's services :—"I have the honour, by desire of the Commander-in-Chief, to request that you will be so good as to convey to Major Roberts, V.C., Assistant-Quartermaster-General at Zoolla, the thanks of His Excellency for the efficient manner in which he has performed his duties since the date of his arrival at Zoolla. His Excellency has received with pleasure most favourable reports regarding the able and energetic manner in which Major Roberts has carried on the duties of this department at Zoolla, and it has been a source of regret to the Commander-in-Chief that he has been unable to avail himself of Major Roberts's services in the front. His Excellency however considers that work performed by those at Zoolla has been as valuable to the interests of the expedition as any duty they might have been called upon to perform with the advanced portion of the army."

Two days later General Russell received a telegram directing Roberts to proceed to Bombay to arrange for the return of the troops, which was, however, countermanded, as Roberts had rendered himself indispensable, and was a *persona grata* with the naval and transport authorities, who fully appreciated his geniality, resource, and powers of organization, which were the wonder of every person with whom he was thrown in contact. General Russell wrote an urgent letter requesting that he might be allowed to remain at Zoolla, which was granted. No one knew so well the value of these services as General Russell, who, from being on the spot, had the best opportunities of judging of the capacity of the officer in charge of his Quartermaster-General's Department. The following was the letter he addressed to Colonel Phayre on this occasion :—" Major Roberts has for some months conducted the duties of the department at Zoolla ; during the time I have held command he has done so most entirely to my satisfaction. He has lately had very arduous duties in surveying and allotting vessels and arranging embarkations, and has, in his communications with the Naval and Transport authorities, carried on the duties to the satisfaction of all. Major Roberts has taken such interest in the embarkation, and has been so energetic, I had hoped he might have remained to see the whole embarkation carried out, but as his services are required elsewhere, I think it just to represent to His Excellency the Commander-in-Chief the good services he has performed."

In sending Major Roberts a copy of the above letter, General Russell wrote :—" You will see how I appreciate your energy ; I have to thank you for your valuable assistance to me."

On the 2nd of June Sir Robert Napier arrived at Zoolla,

and, on the 10th, accompanied by Major Roberts and other officers, embarked in H.M.S. " Feroze " for Suez, whence he proceeded to England to receive the honours that were so justly his due, and the Abyssinian Expedition came to an end. The 25th Bombay N.I., remained as a guard for the stores, and, on the embarkation, on the 17th of June, of the last of these and the followers, the headquarters of the regiment quitted Zoolla. On the following day, the rear-guard, being two companies of the 25th Regiment, embarked, and Annesley Bay returned to its normal condition of solitude, save for the presence of a guard of Egyptian troops to look after the railway* and sundry sheds and trucks left behind.

During the campaign now brought to a conclusion, while other officers of the Quartermaster-General's Department were enjoying the excitement of active service and the invigorating breezes of the Abyssinian highlands, it was Major Roberts's fortune to work on the burning plain of Zoolla, but his heroic struggles against the disabilities of a constitution always weakly, and now borne down by lassitude and fever, were appreciated and recorded by those who had witnessed his self-sacrificing efforts, or had the discernment to contrast to his advantage these qualities with the self-assertion of others more highly placed.

Sir Robert Napier paid Roberts the high compliment of selecting him to carry his final despatches to H.R.H. the Duke of Cambridge, and his letter to the Military Secretary at the Horse Guards, written at Zoolla on the 5th of June, though very flattering to Major Roberts, was only his due. He said, " I have the honour to acquaint you for the information of His Royal Highness the Field Marshal Commanding-in-Chief, that I have selected Major Roberts, V.C., Royal Artillery, to convey, for submission to His Royal Highness, the continuation of my despatch of the 12th May, reporting the concluding operations and re-embarkation of the troops which composed the Abyssinian

---

* From returns by the Quartermaster-General's Department it appears that the railway from Zoolla to Koomayli, twelve miles in length, conveyed in three months 9,000 tons of commissariat stores, 2,400 tons of *matériel*, 10,000 troops and 14,500 followers, with 2,000 tons of baggage, the whole without accident or delay.

Expeditionary Force. I would beg of you to be so good as to bring Major Roberts to the favourable notice of His Royal Highness. He performed the duties of Assistant-Quartermaster-General at Zoolla throughout the campaign. It was not possible to spare this officer from his important office at our base with the duties of which he was thoroughly acquainted. It will be, I am sure, satisfactory to His Royal Highness to learn that, although the orders for the re-embarkation of the force were issued near Magdala, and the greatest portion of the troops had to traverse several hundred miles to reach their ships, the embarkation took place nearly on the dates fixed. The regiments generally embarked within forty-eight hours after their departure from Senafe, marching fifty-five miles through the passes to Koomailee, whence they were conveyed by rail to the pier at Zoolla, and immediately sent to sea. By this they were spared any unnecessary exposure in the extreme heat of Zoolla. I beg to forward for submission to His Royal Highness a copy of a demi-official letter* from Major-General Russell, commanding at Zoolla, relative to the manner in which the embarkation was carried out, and also an extract from a report from that officer on the highly valuable assistance afforded him by Major Roberts at all times, and more especially in the re-embarkations referred to in General Russell's letter."

Roberts left Sir Robert Napier at Suez, and, proceeding from Alexandria *viâ* Brindisi, with the despatches with which he was entrusted, hurried across the continent, and landed in England after an absence of ten years. His feelings on treading again

---

* From Major-General Russell, commanding at Zoolla, to the Military Secretary to the Commander-in-Chief Abyssinia Expeditionary Force, dated Zoolla, 3rd of June, 1868.

"From Major Roberts, V.C., the Assistant-Quartermaster-General, I have received most valuable assistance, and he has conducted the duties of the department at Zoolla most entirely to my satisfaction. He has lately had very arduous duties in surveying and allotting vessels and arranging the re-embarkation of the troops, and has in his communications with the Naval and Transport authorities carried on the duties to the satisfaction of all. He has taken such interest in the re-embarkation and has been so energetic and efficient that I submitted a request for him to be permitted to remain at Zoolla and complete the re-embarkation, which request has been granted. I am specially indebted to him for his very valuable assistance."

Roberts Compiles the Transport Regulations.

the soil of his native country were, doubtless, not inaptly expressed by the lines of Coleridge :—

> "If aught on earth demands an unmixed feeling,
> 'Tis surely this—after long years of exile,
> To step forth on firm land, and gazing round us,
> To hail at once our country and our birth-place."

On the arrival of Sir Robert Napier in England, he participated in the banquets and fêtes that were given to the successful General.

For his services during the campaign, Roberts received the brevet rank of lieutenant-colonel, and, while in England, was offered by Sir William Mansfield, the Commander-in-Chief in India, the post of First Assistant-Quartermaster-General at Army headquarters, and, in February, 1869, sailed for India and took up the appointment in the following month. At this time Colonel P. S. Lumsden was Quartermaster-General, but during the two succeeding winters, in the absence of his chief, Colonel Roberts was in charge of the department, and, with his usual energy, employed such leisure as he could command in compiling Parts I. and II. of the Transport Regulations, "By Sea," and "By Rail." He writes to us, "I felt there was a great want for transport regulations, and I compiled Parts I. and II. which form the basis of the present regulations as used in India."

Colonel Roberts added to the Mutiny medal, with three clasps, and the India medal for the Umbeyla campaign, the medal for Abyssinia.

Alone among our wars this campaign is remarkable for having been brought to a conclusion, not absolutely without spilling a drop of blood—for seventeen officers and men were wounded at the action of Arogie, and fifteen at the capture of Magdala—but without the loss of a single life in action on the British side. Lord Napier merited all the honours and encomiums he received for his conduct of the operations in what has well been called an "Engineers' War," though it was scarcely less a Quartermaster-General's War, for the difficulties of transporting supplies along the 400 miles intervening between Zoolla and Magdala, were of a nature that may be said, without exaggeration, to be almost unparalleled. To Colonel

Roberts the experience he had gained in this campaign was priceless, and no long time elapsed before he was in a position to put in practice the lessons he had learned under a master in the art of mountain warfare. To a man who (to paraphrase a famous saying) "was an excellent official if you will, but a soldier above all," the *kudos* he gained as being "indispensable" at Zoolla, must have been dashed by the thought that he was not present at the capture of the stronghold of the Abyssinian Emperor. To a soldier combining the impetuous valour that gained him the V.C., with the strategic skill of which he has given such striking examples in Afghanistan, the perils of the assault were the most congenial experiences of military life, and he would agree with the fiery Hotspur :—

> "Send danger from the East unto the West,
> So honour cross it from the North to the South."

CHAPTER VII.

The Looshai Campaign—Description of the Country and Cause of the War —Colonel Roberts fits out the two Columns of the Expeditionary Force—He joins General Bourchier at Cachar—March of the Cachar Column—Arrival at Tipai Mookh—Attack on the Kholel Villages led by Colonel Roberts—Further Operations against the Looshais—Action of the 25th of January, 1872—Colonel Roberts Commands at the Capture of Taikoom—Arrival at Chumfai—Conclusion of Peace and Return of the Column to India—Roberts is appointed Quartermaster-General at Army Head-quarters—His Services in that Capacity—Lord Lytton and General Roberts—Roberts is nominated Commandant of the Punjaub Irregular Force and Special Commissioner on the Scinde-Punjaub Frontier.

IN 1871 the Indian Government was involved in hostilities with the wild tribes on the south-east frontier of Bengal, known by the common name of Looshai, and Colonel Roberts's services were again brought into requisition. Their country, almost a *terra incognita,* is situated between the southern extremity of the Cachar district and the northern boundary of the Chittagong Hill Tracts, and consists of a belt of land about 100 miles in length, traversed by high ranges of mountains running nearly due north and south. On the Chittagong side of the Looshai portion of the country, these mountains are more or less inhabited, but towards the Cachar frontier the broad and swampy valleys are almost entirely devoid of population, a result due not so much to their unhealthiness as to the raids of more powerful neighbours.

The Looshais, says Colonel Roberts,* are a family of the great Kokie tribe, who may be found in Independent, or Hill, Tipperah, which bounds the Looshai country on the west. The Looshais first raided on British territory in 1850, and, in January of the following year, Colonel Lyster, political agent

---

* See " Narrative of the Cachar Column, Looshai Expeditionary Force," published in vol. ii. of the "Journal of the United Service Institution of India," in which the author minutely describes the organization of the Expedition.

in the Cossyah and Jynteah Hills, and Commandant of the Sylhet Light Infantry, marched from Cachar with a small force, and penetrated their country a distance of 100 miles, inflicting severe punishment and releasing 400 captives, but he expressed his "confirmed impression that this robber tribe will not cease to infest the frontier until they shall have been most severely dealt with." Matters remained tolerably quiet until 1862, when aggressions occurred in Sylhet, culminating in 1868-69 in a series of outrages on the tea-gardens of Cachar, when the Government despatched two columns, under Brigadier-General Nuthall and Major Stephenson, 7th Native Infantry, with twenty days' provisions. But the expedition started too late in the season, and was ill-organized, and returned without meeting with opposition or effecting any of the objects sought to be attained.

The Supreme Government now tried the policy of conciliation, and, on the 20th December, 1869, Mr. Edgar, Deputy Commissioner of the district, accompanied by Major Macdonald of the Survey Department, and a small escort of police, left Cachar and visited Soonai and Beparee Bazaar, the centre of the territory of Sookpilal, the most powerful of the chiefs raiding on British territory, who paid him a visit on the 23rd March, and discussed the question of the boundary between the Looshai and British States. In the following December, Majors Macdonald and Graham, the Civil Officer, were deputed to proceed with a small police escort on a friendly mission to the country of the Sylhoos, situated to the south of Sookpilal's territory, and Mr. Edgar penetrated to Dullesur, where he had an interview with Sookpilal, who, on the part of the western chiefs, agreed to the boundary clearly defined in a "sunnud," or written engagement, but declared that he could not negotiate on behalf of the tribes to the east of the Soonai river. But the old chief was acting with duplicity, and at this time the Sylhoos and Howlongs, tribes to the north and north-east of the Chittagong Hill Tracts, and the north-eastern Looshais, under Lalboorah, entered Sylhet and Cachar, destroying villages and property, killing the coolies and Mr. Winchester, a tea-grower, whose daughter, six years of age, was carried off. To recover this second little Helen of Troy, "the direful spring

Origin of the Looshai Expedition.

of woes unnumbered," a considerable force was assembled, and the Indian Government found itself involved in hostilities.

At this time Lord Napier of Magdala, the Commander-in-Chief, accompanied by Brigadier-General George Bourchier, C.B., commanding the eastern frontier, whose name has appeared before in these pages, happened to be on a tour of inspection through the district, and, under his lordship's instructions, the Brigadier-General proceeded to Shillong to take steps for the protection of that frontier, and despatched a small force up the Soonai river, which succeeded in ensuring the safety of Mr. Edgar, then returning from his mission to Sookpilal. On the 24th February the Commander-in-Chief, having inspected Dibrooghur and the other stations on the Brahmapootra, reached Cachar, and, as the season was too far advanced for active operations, in conjunction with the General commanding the district, he made arrangements for defending the frontier, forts and stockades being established at suitable points, with roads communicating between them.

Acting on the recommendation of Lord Napier, the Supreme Government, on the 30th June, 1871, directed the Military Department to organize an expedition in the Looshai country, to consist of two columns, starting from Cachar and Chittagong, with the forces of the Rajahs of Munnepore and Tipperah acting in co-operation, while the services of Sookpilal were to be brought in requisition on the north, and of Rutton Pooea, a powerful chief, on the south, from which side the Chittagong column would attack. Lord Napier, in the previous March, had impressed on the Government that all the details connected with the organization and equipment of the force and supply of carriage, should be carefully considered beforehand, so that there might be no chance of failure, such as had lately overtaken some mountain expeditions.

On the 13th July his lordship was definitely called upon to submit his proposals for giving effect to the measures decided upon against the Looshais, and, four days later, the Commander-in-Chief submitted his scheme, the main features of which were that each column was to consist of 1,500 picked men from the Regular Native Infantry, half a Peshawur Mountain battery, with two steel guns, and two $5\frac{1}{2}$-inch mortars carried on elephants, and one company of Sappers and Miners. No tents were to be carried, each fighting man being supplied with a waterproof sheet, and baggage and camp followers were to be reduced to a minimum, every one being rationed by the Commissariat. These recommendations were adopted, as well as others suggesting that the co-operation of the Munnepore and Tipperah Rajahs should be limited to the protection of their own frontiers, the opening out of roads, and maintaining communications through their own territories. The Commander-in-Chief also strongly insisted on the Political Officers with the columns acting in subordination to the Generals, and Colonel Roberts writes :—" This move was attended with the happiest results ; indeed, it is not too much to say that to it, as much as to the efficiency of the troops, the ultimate success of the expedition was due."

The suggestions of the Commander-in-Chief having received the approval of Government, orders were at once issued to the several departments concerned, and, by the beginning of September, the fitting out of the two columns had been fairly commenced.

The experience Colonel Roberts had acquired during fifteen years' service in the Quartermaster-General's Department, and more recently in the Abyssinian campaign, was now to be put to the test, and the completeness with which he fitted out this small expedition was an earnest of what he could do on a larger scale and in a more important crisis, and evidenced that he possessed the qualities for a successful chief of which the " sage Polydamas " declared that Hector, with all his valour, was deficient.

> " To few, and wondrous few, has Jove assign'd
> A wise, extensive, all-considering mind."

Lord Napier, who had formed, from personal observation in Abyssinia, a high estimate of the energy and professional capacity of Colonel Roberts, placed the entire preparation of the columns in his hands, and the result was that nothing could be more complete and efficient than the organization and equipment of the expedition. For this service he received from the Commander-in-Chief, through his immediate chief,

Colonel R. S. Lumsden, "the expression of his Excellency's approbation of the highly satisfactory manner in which the duties entrusted to you for the preparation of the Looshai expedition and its despatch from Calcutta, have been carried out."

Colonel Roberts was appointed Senior Staff Officer of the Force, and, having despatched the stores and equipment of the columns by the 3rd November, joined Brigadier-General Bourchier, commanding the Cachar column* (his old comrade at Delhi), at Silchar, the Sudder, or principal station of the district. The Chittagong column was commanded by Brigadier-General Charles Brownlow, C.B., but with its operations we are not concerned.

On arriving at Silchar, Colonel Roberts, accompanied by Colonel Nuthall, of the 44th Native Infantry, went out to explore the route over the Burban range, but the difficulties appeared so great that it was decided that the advance should be made by the alternative route, round by Luckipore and the banks of the Barak. On the 21st November, a wing of the 44th Native Infantry marched to Luckipore, and, on the 23rd, General Bourchier and his staff followed with one wing of the 44th and the Sappers, when road-making towards Tipai Mookh commenced, a labour which never ceased until the end of January, by which time 110 miles had been completed. This last-named place had been fixed upon as the base of operations for the left column, after a lengthy discussion, as it was believed that from there the tribes of the chiefs about to be

---

* The Cachar, or left, Column consisted of :—" Half Peshawur Mountain Battery, Captain Blackwood, R.A.; one company Sappers and Miners, Lieutenant Harvey, R.E.; 500 men of the 22nd Punjaub Native Infantry, Colonel Stafford; 500 of the 42nd Assam Light Infantry, Colonel Rattray, C.B.; 500 44th Assam Light Infantry, Colonel Hicks: and 100 police, under Mr. Daly. There were 1,400 coolies, under Lieutenant-Colonel Davidson of the Commissariat; also a Coolie Corps of 800 men for the carriage of the Sepoys' baggage, under Major Moore. In addition 600 Coolies joined during the campaign to replace casualties. There were 121 elephants, and 32 others arrived later ; of which 20 died in the campaign. The Staff Officers, besides Colonel Roberts, were Captain Thompson, Brigade-Major, and Captain Butter, Aide-de-Camp. Dr. Buckle, Inspector-General of Hospitals, was in medical charge, and Mr. Edgar was Political Officer of the Column, acting in subordination to the General. The Topographical survey was under Captain Badgley, and the telegraph under Mr. Pitman.

coerced—Vonpilal, Poiboy, and Vonolel—could be most easily reached. Had the meeting of the two columns been the primary object of the expedition, a more westerly course, either by the valley of the Soonai or the Dullesur, would have been adopted, but it was hoped that, by whichever route the columns advanced, they would be able to effect a junction after the Looshais had been sufficiently punished.

For the greater part of this way there was not even the vestige of a path, and many a long and weary reconnoissance was made by Colonel Roberts before the best line for the advance could be selected. The troops, however, worked with a will, and the Sappers, under Lieutenant Harvey, traced out the road, which was widened to a suitable extent by the leading wing of the 44th Regiment, the other corps following in succession by wings, each doing their share. Colonel Roberts writes of the work done under somewhat adverse circumstances:—" Notwithstanding the extreme heat of the climate, and the difficult nature of the country, which was one succession of rolling hills covered with dense jungle and huge creepers, and intersected by numerous rivers and watercourses, a good road from six to eight feet wide was constructed, with a gradient easy enough for laden elephants to travel over."

This sort of campaigning is not exhilarating, and is more trying for regular troops than the excitement of battle, when discipline and superior arms inspire confidence. Byron justly speaks of

"The nightly muster and the silent march
In the chill dark, when courage doth not glow
So much as under a triumphal arch."

On the 29th November, General Bourchier arrived at Mynadhur, on the farther side of the Burban range, where commissariat stores for three months had been collected, and ordnance and other stores were rapidly arriving. Here, also, a telegraph had been carried, and a daily post established, so that by the first week in December, headquarters were in postal and telegraphic communication with Calcutta. Between Mynadhur and Tipai Mookh, four camps close to the Barak bank, were established, each consisting of comfortable huts made by the troops and coolies, the framework consisting of bamboo leaves, and grass, fastened together with strips of bark, and the interior furnished with a low raised bamboo floor for sleeping purposes. As opposition was expected, General Bourchier, accompanied by Colonel Roberts, reconnoitred the place, which was found to be deserted, when it was occupied and made the base of operations. Tipai Mookh (the junction between the Tipai and Barak) is eighty-four miles from Cachar, but in this short distance the river Barak had to be crossed four times.

By the 4th December preparations for an advance were completed, and headquarters marched two days later; but the difficulties as to roads and water on the route were so considerable that the Toweeboom river, distant twenty miles from Tipai Mookh, was only reached on the 22nd of the month. Crossing the river, the column encamped a little above its junction with the Tipai. During the advance, small bodies of Looshais were encountered, but they retired on the approach of the reconnoitring parties. General Bourchier determined at once to attack the Kholel villages before the people had time to strengthen them, and, early on the morning of the 23rd, leaving a guard in camp, marched with the remainder of the troops up the hill. Colonel Roberts, with fifty men of the 22nd Punjaub Native Infantry, under Major Stafford, led the advance up the ascent, which was very steep, and through thick jungles. On arriving at a clearing in the forest, where was a stockade, Colonel Roberts collected the troops, who, owing to the narrowness of the path, straggled up, and could not keep any proper order, and advanced towards the work in which the enemy had taken up a position. As the detachment emerged into the open, the Looshais fired two volleys, which wounded two men, but before the Punjaubees could reach them with the bayonet, they had evacuated the place and disappeared into the jungle. The work, which was full of rice, was destroyed, and the column continued its toilsome chase after the enemy, who were driven from stockade to stockade.

The tactics adopted by the enemy were to post themselves at the top of each ascent, fire a volley, and retreat; but, nevertheless, the British troops were able to inflict some loss upon them, as was evident by the traces of blood that marked their line of flight; though they took care to remove their slain, as, according to a superstition prevalent among them, the man who loses his head in battle becomes the slave of the victor in the next world.

Storehouses full of grain were found in each stockade, and were destroyed, together with the contents. Advancing in this way for several hours, through thick jungle, with an occasional hamlet, the column came upon a large village, which the General determined to occupy, as there was a good stream of water close at hand. He accordingly sent back to Tipai for the baggage. Meantime, accompanied by Roberts and his staff, he took a detachment of the 44th higher up the hill, to look for the Chief Kalhi's principal village, which had been seen from the camp on the Senbong range. The ascent was very steep, the village being situated at an elevation of 3,300 feet above the point left in the morning. The Looshais made an attempt to defend the village, but the 44th drove them out, and the place was burnt, when the detachment retraced its steps to the village fixed upon for occupation. During the day the losses had been only two men killed and four severely wounded.

The troops were so exhausted by their exertions that it was with great difficulty the pickets could be prevailed upon to construct breastworks, though materials in abundance were at hand. Throughout the night the Looshais kept up a harassing fire under cover of the forest which surrounded the village, and as soon as morning dawned, a party moved out to clear the ground near the pickets. Later in the day the General proceeded, with Colonel Roberts and sixty-two men of all ranks, being all that were available for the duty, to attack another village a short distance to the south, which was carried with a rush, the enemy evacuating the place after firing a volley.

Christmas day was spent burning the stockades and granaries in the neighbourhood, and, at night, the officers celebrated the day in the fashion usual among Englishmen in all parts of the world, and under the most depressing circumstances. All the officers assembled at the headquarters mess, and dined at a table "raised in a conspicuous position, with candles burning before them and Looshais firing from the jungle close by."*

---

* "The Looshai Expedition," by Lieutenant R. G. Woodthorpe, R.E.

Though some of the sentries were wounded, none of the officers, though presenting such excellent marks, were hit, and that "music hath charms the savage breast to quell," was proved by a singular circumstance. When, after dinner, the officers in turn favoured the company with a song, the auditory included the fierce children of the forest, who stopped firing when each song commenced, and resumed it on its conclusion.

When starting from Tipai, on the 23rd, it was understood that the route to Lalboorah's village lay by the Voombong mountain and the new Kholel villages, but from a closer inspection of the country it became evident that they had taken the wrong road, and that it would be necessary to retrace their steps to the Toweeboom, and take a fresh departure thence for old Kholel, a collection of deserted villages near Pachowee, visible at some distance on the opposite bank of the Tipai. As there were only 250 fighting men available, and the nature of the country necessitated proceeding in single file, it was difficult to guard the long line of sick, wounded, and coolies; but the retirement was planned by Colonel Roberts, and executed with skill and success, and reflected great credit on all concerned. By 10 o'clock on the 26th the preparations were complete, and the column marched, Colonel Stafford's detachment of the 22nd Punjaubees leading, a detachment of the 44th, under Captain Lightfoot, guarding the coolies and non-combatants, and Colonel Nuthall and Captain Robertson bringing up the rear with the remainder of the 44th. As the rearguard, accompanied by General Bourchier and Colonel Roberts, quitted the village, after setting it on fire, the Looshais entered at the other end, yelling and screaming like fiends, but were kept off by the steady fire of the skirmishers of the 44th. All the way down the hill, a distance of five miles, to the river, the savages endeavoured to get past the rearguard to attack the coolies with the baggage, but, says Roberts, "they were invariably baffled by the little Goorkhas, who, extending rapidly where the ground allowed, retired through their supports in admirable order, and gave the enemy no chance of passing.

On the 27th and 28th December, Colonel Roberts was employed reconnoitring the route, and, on the following day, the General, accompanied by his staff and Mr. Edgar, and taking with him a wing of the 22nd Punjaubees, under Colonel Rattray, which had joined the camp, returned to the Kholel villages that had been burnt to show the natives that it was not fear that had caused the retirement. Here an envoy was received from the Chief named Poiboy, soliciting peace, and a cessation of hostilities was arranged. Meanwhile the Sappers and Goorkhas commenced road-making, and, on the arrival of a sufficiency of supplies for a further advance, the General, with Colonel Roberts and his staff, left the camp on the 6th January, 1872, and halting at the Sapper camp for the night, arrived at the river Tuitu on the following morning.

On the 8th, headquarters, with the Sappers, marched to a deserted village on the Kholel range, called Daidoo, where a wet night was passed, there being no shelter, or bamboos to construct huts, and the rain coming down in torrents. On the following day camp was formed at Pachowee, officially known as No. 9, where an agent arrived from Sookpilal with a message from that Chief and Khalkom that they would soon come in to make their submission. The General sent him back with an intimation that he would not delay his march, and a road was at once commenced to Lalboora, through Poiboy's country. Three miles from No. 9 post were the deserted villages of old Kholel, where is the tomb of Vonpilal, the once powerful Looshai chief, who ruled over Daidoo, Poiboy and Kholel. On the 13th, the 22nd Regiment arrived, and, three days after, the two steel guns (the mortars were never brought to the front), and also Major Moore, bringing the Goorkha coolies, of whom nearly 300 had died of cholera since leaving Calcutta. All the troops of the Cachar column, with the exception of a guard at Mynadhur, were now distributed at the posts between Tipai Mookh and No. 9.

On the 17th, the General and staff, including Colonel Roberts and Mr. Edgar, leaving behind a guard of fifty men, marched from Pachui, with a wing of the 44th, and, crossing the Tuivai, and passing a stockade where 200 men armed with muskets were collected, ascended to Chepui, a height of 2,200 feet above the river's bed, where the column passed the night in some unfinished houses. Here the troops remained till the 22nd, Colonel Roberts employing the interval in reconnoitring.

A Smart Skirmish.

The villagers sought to mislead him by pointing out a roundabout route, but, says Lieutenant Woodthorpe, "Colonel Roberts, feeling convinced that there must be a more direct road, was untiring in his endeavours to discover it, and at last success rewarded his efforts." As the time did not admit of constructing roads, General Bourchier determined to use the country paths, taking on only the artillery elephants, the supplies being brought on from Chepui by coolies.

On the 22nd January the advance was continued along a rocky path to Station No. 11, whence Colonel Roberts, taking a guide with him, reconnoitred the roads which diverged shortly after reaching the camp. He resolved to adopt the road across the Tuila and over a spur of the Surklang, but Poiboy, expecting the invaders would use the route by Gnaupa, had fortified several strong points, and determined to make a stand. On arriving at the next camp the General and Colonel Roberts went on ahead to reconnoitre, and, on the 25th, the force came into collision with the enemy.

The advance, consisting of fifty men of the 44th, accompanied by the General and his staff, had advanced about half a mile from camp, and were climbing over a steep, rocky part of the path, when suddenly a heavy fire was opened upon them, the General's orderly being killed, and the General himself receiving wounds in the left arm and hand. There was a sharp struggle on the bank of the purling, swiftly-flowing brook, whose waters ran stained with blood, while the fierce yell of the Looshai mountaineer was answered by the wild cry of the little Goorkha, who was not less at home on the rocky hill-side, which reminded him of his sequestered valleys in distant Nepaul. Thirteen Looshais fell almost in one spot in the stream, victims to the terrible "kookrie," or knife, which these hardy mountaineers wield with such dexterity. One young Looshai, panic-struck at the fate which had befallen so many of his countrymen, was seen, in trying to make his escape up the slippery rock, to lose his footing, and before he could recover himself was cut down at one blow by a Goorkha. As when Sarpedon fell beneath Patroclus' "never-erring dart"

> "The Fates suppress'd his labouring breath,
> And his eyes darken'd with the shades of death."

On General Bourchier being disabled, Colonel Roberts temporarily assumed the command, and the troops dashing into the stream, drove the enemy up the hill and through the jungle. After having his wounds bound up, General Bourchier followed the column, which had pushed on rapidly for the village by a path running along the face of a precipice. At this point a stockade had been constructed, but the enemy were so panic-striken that they abandoned it and fled wildly towards another large stockade, which they prepared to defend ; the position was, however, turned by a party of the 44th, and the Looshais, finding themselves taken in flank, abandoned the stockade and the village of Kungnung, 200 yards beyond, and disappeared into the forest and down the hill-side. In this spirited affair the British loss was only two killed and five wounded, and that of the Looshais over sixty. Speaking of Colonel Roberts's services the General reported :— " At the outset I was wounded by two slugs in the left arm and hand, and although not disabled for the rest of the subsequent advance, I was so at one time, and have to thank Colonel Roberts and my staff for carrying out the details which ended so successfully."

As the attack thus successfully repelled had been made by Poiboy's men, the General determined to burn the village of Taikoom, and, at noon on the following day, despatched Colonel Roberts in command of a small column, consisting of 100 men from the 22nd and 44th regiments, and the two mountain 7-pounder guns, which had only arrived that morning in camp. During the course of the reconnoissance made two days before, it was apparent that, owing to the nature of the country, these guns, if conveyed by elephants, could not be conveyed to Taikoom in one day, so it was decided that they should be carried by coolies. Accordingly, six men were told off to each gun, which weighed only 150lbs. apiece, six to each carriage, two for each wheel, and four for the ammunition boxes, each containing nine rounds. By noon the small column, under the command of Colonel Roberts, was on the march towards Taikoom, which lay due east. The path descended for about a mile and a half till it reached the bend of the stream just below the saddle connecting Muthilen, a great hill rising to an altitude of 6,000 feet, with the Soorklang, a wild mass of peaks, whence, ascending again, it joined the path reconnoitred by Roberts on the 24th.

Passing a stockade containing granaries, Colonel Roberts continued his march between two spurs of the neighbouring hills, about a mile beyond which, on the farther side of a valley, was a strong stockade, built across a road which it quite commanded, and having on its right flank a steep rocky ravine, in which a large party of the enemy were collected. As the nature of the ground did not permit of a direct attack with the limited force of infantry under his command, Colonel Roberts resolved on making a flank movement, a feature of military tactics with which these unsophisticated hillmen were unacquainted. This entailed a fatiguing march over steep spurs, at one time attaining a height of 6,000 feet, but, at length, the party came out on the road, about a mile beyond the stockade. The Looshais, on finding their position turned, retired to Taikoom, upon which Colonel Roberts continued his march with all expedition, but it was five o'clock before he came in sight of it.

The village, which contained about 200 houses, surrounded by a strong palisade, is situated on the top of a small hill, and was found to be full of men, who were collected in a large open space at the upper end. The position Colonel Roberts took up completely commanded the village, from which it was some 1,200 yards distant, and the guns were brought into action on a level space on the right of the road. Captain Blackwood, who was in command, opened fire, and his practice was so good, the second shell bursting amid a group of men, that, after a few rounds, Colonel Roberts led the infantry in person, and entered the village at one end as the enemy evacuated it at the other. Taikoom was set on fire, and as it was past six o'clock, the troops, having secured some live stock, which were slaughtered by the Goorkhas, commenced the return march, guided by the light of the moon. Camp was reached in safety at 11 P.M., every officer and man being thoroughly fatigued. Thus successfully terminated Colonel Roberts's first independent command, which was an earnest of what he was capable of doing.

General Bourchier, in forwarding to Lord Napier of Magdala, a copy of Colonel Roberts's despatch, observes:—" I need scarcely add one word to what he has described therein, except acknowledging in the warmest terms the services on this and every occasion of this distinguished officer; the distance he had to travel was more than anticipated, and he did not return to camp until half-past ten at night. This was the first occasion on which the guns had been taken into action, and while I was perfectly confident in the officer to whom I had entrusted this expedition, I felt somewhat anxious, being unable to witness their first effect upon the enemy."

The Quartermaster-General at army headquarters, in forwarding enclosures from General Bourchier, referring to Colonel Roberts's services, to the Military Department of the Government of India, says, Lord Napier desires " to draw the attention of Government to the skilfully and judiciously planned, and ably and boldly executed operations therein set forth, and to the praiseworthy services of Lieutenant-Colonel Roberts, V.C., and the other officers brought to notice by the Brigadier-General."

On the 29th January, 1872, a telegram was received at Kungnung, announcing that Sookpilal had delivered up the child, Mary Winchester, to General Brownlow, commanding the right, or Chittagong, column, and, during the following two days, the Looshais arrived in camp, bringing in the indemnity in kind, demanded from Poiboy for his share in the attack of the 25th.

On the 1st February, General Bourchier, accompanied by his staff, including Colonel Roberts and Mr. Edgar, marched with a detachment of the 22nd and 44th regiments for Chelam, Poiboy's chief village, taking the road along the steep slope of the western face of Muthilen. On the following day the column arrived at Chelam, which was perched on the side of a hill at an elevation of 5,800 feet, and consisted of about 200 houses enclosed in a strong stockade, with two other smaller villages, also stockaded, on other peaks. Chelam, which had just been vacated by its inhabitants, was occupied by the troops, who made themselves comfortable in the houses in which the fires were still smouldering, and there being a plentiful supply of pigs, the hill coolies killed as many as were required, and Europeans and natives alike revelled in a plethora of pork, for which viand the Goorkha has a great predilection. During the night a fire occurred, which consumed twenty-five houses and some of the public buildings, but it was extinguished by the exertions of the soldiers and camp followers.

In order to obviate the danger to life and property from a recurrence of these fires, Colonel Roberts was sent, early on the following morning, to search for a suitable camping ground, and one having been selected, the troops moved thither, and huts were quickly constructed, the cold—for the thermometer marked one degree above freezing-point at night—rendering a bivouac out of the question. As one of the chief objects of the expedition was to effect the reduction of the village of Chumfai, 110 miles distant from Tipai Mookh, belonging to the powerful chief, Lalbourah, General Bourchier commenced collecting twelve days' supplies for his force, and telegraphed his intention to General Brownlow, viâ Calcutta, so that if possible the two columns might effect a junction at that spot. A wing of the 42nd arrived at Chelam on the 11th January, and the General, making up his flying column to 400 men, drawn from the 22nd and 44th regiments and artillery, with the two guns, on the following day marched from Chelam, leaving Colonel Rattray to occupy the camp. Baggage had been reduced to the utmost extent, the officers taking with them only two blankets, one change of clothes, and a few cooking utensils.

The route, as before, was along the sides of mountains and across ravines and valleys, but everywhere the fortified villages were deserted, and the stockades unoccupied. One of these, at Tulcheng, was of considerable strength, and displayed great ingenuity, as there were flanking defences. On the 16th February the column entered Lalbourah's valley of Chumfai, having an elevation of nearly 5,000 feet, and, on the following day, took possession of Lungvel, the deserted village of Vonolel, in which was that chief's tomb, a curious structure, decked with horns and human heads, according to Looshai custom. At this spot the British flag was hoisted amid hearty cheers, and General Bourchier, addressing the troops, said that they had reached the limit of their march into the enemy's country.

The village, which consisted of 1,000 houses, was fired, and the troops retired to pitch their camp in the valley below, where, on the following day, the General received a deputation of headmen from Chonchim, who came to make their submission. The British terms were, the surrender of Lalbourah, or of three headmen in his place, the admission of Government agents to their villages if required, the surrender of captured firearms, and the payment of a fine in kind. After the meeting General Bourchier took with him 150 men and ascended the hill to Chonchim, which was strongly stockaded and filled with armed Looshais, and for a time it seemed as if a resort would have to be made to hostile measures, but after a parley the General and his staff with twenty men were admitted into the enclosure. Thus the submission of the tribe was complete, and could not be explained away by the sophistries barbarous chiefs employ in such cases to explain their humiliation.

In the evening the troops returned to Chumfai, and parties were sent out on the following day, to make a cursory examination of the country. The British terms were all complied with, three muntris, or chiefs, being chosen as hostages, and then, as agreed on by telegraph with General Brownlow, on the night of the 20th February, rockets were sent up to advise him of their position, but were not visible owing to the height of the intervening mountain ranges, the distance between the two columns being some fifty miles as the crow flies. It was a subject for regret that the meeting of the columns, which was one of the original intentions sought to be attained in framing the plan of campaign, was not effected; but for this the Cachar force was in no way to blame, as it attained the objective point of its march. According to Captain East, the accomplished Chief Staff Officer of the Chittagong column, the results to be attained by a junction of the two columns did not warrant a march over more than eighty miles of unknown and mountainous country, inhabited by independent tribes.*

---

* The following, to borrow General Brownlow's own language, were the results of his four months' campaign:—"The complete subjection of two powerful tribes, inhabiting upwards of sixty villages, of which twenty that resisted were attacked and destroyed; the personal submission of fifteen chiefs, and their solemn engagement on behalf of themselves and tributaries for future good behaviour; the recovery of Mary Winchester, and the

End of the Campaign.

On the evening of the 21st, further signals, blue lights and rockets, were sent up from the Murklang hill, which received no response, and, on the morning of the 22nd February, the homeward march was commenced, to the satisfaction alike of the European officers and Sepoys.

The withdrawal from the Looshai country was conducted without any *contretemps*, a result due to the admirable arrangements of Colonel Roberts, who also earned the thanks of the officers of the column for the regularity with which throughout the expedition, the *dawk*, or post, was despatched, " not a day having passed," says an officer of the force, " without despatching the dawk, and scarcely a day without receiving the letters and papers."

Tipai Mookh was reached on the 7th March, and as the heat was great and cholera prevailed, the column proceeded thence by boat, but the dreaded pestilence pursued the troops after their arrival at Cachar, and even up country to the hill-station of Shillong. There was much sickness also, due to the privations endured by the force, which had campaigned without tents, and two officers, Captain Harrison, 42nd Native Infantry, and Captain Cookesley, Royal Artillery, belonging to the half-battery, who was the photographer of the column, died from the effects of climate. The former officer was quite unfit to proceed on active service, and was on his way to Calcutta to return to England, but when his regiment was ordered to the front, got his leave cancelled in the hope of gaining some glory in a campaign which could not afford much scope for military distinction. But as Byron says:

> "Oh, glorious laurel! since for one sole leaf
> Of thine imaginary deathless tree,
> Of blood and tears must flow the unebbing sea."

---

liberation of upwards of 150 British subjects, who had from time to time been made captives. In addition the operations of the column, which, by frequent departures from the main line of advance, covered a large area, enabled the officers of the Survey to triangulate 3,000 square miles of country, more than half of which was surveyed in detail, and also to complete the connection between the Cachar and Chittagong districts." To effect this success, the casualties of Brownlow's column were trifling, and consisted of seven killed and thirteen wounded; from sickness, there were thirty deaths amongst the fighting men, and amongst the coolies and followers, 118.

A large number of officers suffered from ill-health, including General Bourchier* and Colonel Roberts, who writes to us that "the privations were great, and the climate of Looshai most trying." To the invaluable services of his Chief Staff officer the General did no more than justice when he recorded them in the following terms in his final despatch to the Quartermaster-General at Army headquarters:—"Lieutenant-Colonel Roberts's untiring energy and sagacity are beyond all praise; working without guides, even without map and geography, thwarted by the Looshais, whose game was to delay our progress, he seemed never at a loss; but not only in his own department was it that he exerted himself. Whether piloting the advance guard through the trackless forest, or solving a commissariat or transport difficulty, his powerful aid was willingly given."

Colonel Roberts received the thanks of the Governor-General in Council, was awarded the Companionship of the Bath,† and added a clasp, inscribed Looshai, to the Indian medal gained at Umbeyla, making the fourth decoration he had won

---

* General Bourchier issued a valedictory order to the column on its arrival at Cachar, dated 19th March, in which he expressed his thanks to the officers and men, and added:—"The Brigadier-General has unfeigned pleasure in according his belief that its discipline, energy, and devotion to the Service could not have been surpassed. From the beginning of November, when the troops were first put in motion, to the present time, every man has been employed in hard work, cheerfully performed, often under the most trying circumstances of heat and frost, always bivouacking on the mountain side, in rude huts of grass or leaves, officers and men sharing in the same accommodation, marching day by day over precipitous mountains, rising at one time to 6,000 feet, and having made a road fit for elephants from Luckipur to Chipowee, a distance of 103 miles. The spirits of the troops never flagged, and when they met the enemy, they drove them from their stockades and strongholds until they were glad to sue for mercy. The history of the Expedition from first to last has been sheer hard work. Each regiment has shared in actual fighting, the 44th more than either of the other corps (22nd and 42nd Native infantry); but to the officers in the rear most important duties were assigned in protecting a line of communications extending over 110 miles from Tipai Mookh to Vonolel's stronghold of Chumfai, and watching through spies the attitude of the inhabitants of the neighbouring villages, conveying provisions and the post, and keeping the road constantly patrolled. The Frontier Police did equally good service with the troops in this way. Each field-officer in the rear had assigned to him a certain number of posts for which he was responsible, and to their vigilance may be attributed the fact that our communications have not for a day been interrupted."

† Both Brigadier-Generals Bourchier and Brownlow received the K.C.B. for their services in Looshai.

in the service of his country. So remarkable had been these services that we find his name mentioned twenty-three times in despatches up to the close of the Looshai campaign; but when he again took the field it was as a writer of despatches, describing military achievements of so exceptionally brilliant a character that they will be for ever inscribed in the page of history.

Colonel Roberts rejoined Army headquarters as Deputy Quartermaster-General, to which promotion he had been gazetted in the previous January while campaigning; and, in the following winter, 1872-73, accompanied the Commander-in-Chief, Lord Napier of Magdala, on his tour through the Punjaub and to the camp of exercise held at Hussan Abdul.

In the ensuing February, on the departure for England of Major-General P. S. Lumsden, C.S.I.,* Colonel Roberts was appointed to officiate as Quartermaster-General, and he performed the duties for a period of five months to the satisfaction of the Commander-in-Chief and of the Viceroy, Lord Northbrook, who, on receiving a copy of a circular memorandum on "Intelligence and Topography," drawn up by Colonel Roberts for the information of the officers of his department, wrote to him, on the 19th July, through his military secretary, in the following terms:—"His Excellency desires me to thank you for it, and to take the occasion of your handing over charge of the Quartermaster-General's Department to Major-General E. B. Johnson, to express to you the sense he entertains of the ability and thoroughness which mark several important papers which you have recently prepared, and which have been brought under his notice."

On the 17th March, 1874, on Major-General E. B. Johnson's† transfer to the post of Adjutant-General in India, Lieutenant-Colonel Roberts again "officiated" as Quartermaster-General, as by the rules of the Service he was ineligible for holding the substantive appointment until he became a full Colonel, and the office carried with it the local rank of Major-General. It was recognized that Roberts, from his services

---

* Now Sir Peter S. Lumsden, K.C.B., C.S.I., A.D.C.
† Now General Sir Edwin Johnson, K.C.B.

and abilities, was the only possible head of the department in which he had graduated for seventeen years, and so the appointment was kept open until the 31st January, 1875, when, on obtaining the qualifying rank of Colonel, he was confirmed in the office by Lord Napier of Magdala, in a letter to the Secretary to the Government of India, in which his lordship wrote:—
"The duties of the Quartermaster-General in India require attainments of a character which can only be possessed by officers of long Indian experience, and His Excellency considers himself fortunate at the present time in being able to nominate an officer of such ability and varied experience in the field and quarters as Colonel Frederick Roberts, C.B., V.C.*

In laying down the chief command of Her Majesty's forces in India, on the 10th April, 1875, Lord Napier of Magdala, referring to General Roberts's services, expressed himself in Army Orders as follows:—"I cannot sufficiently express my obligations to the Adjutant-General, Major-General Lumsden, the Quartermaster-General, Major-General Roberts, and their departments, and to my Military Secretary, Colonel Dillon. It would be impossible to enumerate the many occasions on which I have been indebted to them for their opinions or suggestions for the benefit of the Army." And his lordship's successor, Sir Frederick Haines, found the Quartermaster-General of the Army equally valuable as an adviser of varied experience and great sagacity.

In the cold season of 1876-77, General Roberts accompanied the new Commander-in-Chief on a tour of inspection of the Punjaub and Scinde frontiers, and thence proceeded with him to Bombay before returning to Army headquarters.

In 1873-74 broke out one of those terrible famines which periodically desolate the fairest provinces of our Indian Empire, and the mitigation of which—for prevention is impossible until we can regulate the rainfall, or cover the country with a network of railways and canals, and, moreover, induce the people to use the latter—forms one of the great tests of successful Indian administration. In February, 1874, on the outbreak of

---

* By Governor-General's Order, dated the 26th April, 1875, Colonel Roberts was confirmed as Quartermaster-General, and received the local rank of Major-General whilst holding the appointment.

the Tirhoot famine, General Roberts was sent by Lord Northbrook to Patna, to assist the Commissioner with his advice. After giving his opinions on the measures to be adopted, he left one of his assistants, Colonel Macgregor,* to carry his proposals into practice.

How changed are the sentiments with which Government officials now administer India, from those in the times when the agents of the East India Company turned to their advantage seasons of scarcity to secure a monopoly in the trade in cereals,† and when the author of the "Pleasures of Hope" could write :—

> "Rich in the gems of India's gaudy zone,
> And plunder piled from kingdoms not their own,
> Degenerate trade! thy minions could despise
> The heart-born anguish of a thousand cries;
> And lock, with impious hands, their teeming store,
> While famished nations died along the shore."

General Roberts had hitherto mostly exhibited his aptitude for the post of Quartermaster-General in the tented field, or in the routine duties of the onerous office, during which his energetic nature found scope in the compilation of transport regulations, route-books, or other military topographical works, which are so essential for the modern requirements of war. But he was to exhibit his singular capacity for organisation in another field, and one of a nature that, in any country but India, would be confided to the civil department. We have seen how admirably he conducted the duties of executive officer of Lord Canning's camp when that Viceroy undertook his tour through Central India and the Punjaub, soon after the conclusion of the Mutiny. The experience he then gained in the ceremonial duties attendant upon the reception by Her Majesty's

---

* Now Major-General Sir C. M. Macgregor, K.C.B., C.S.I., C.I.E, Quartermaster-General at Army Headquarters in India.

† The author of a "Short History of the English Transactions in the East Indies" says:—"Some of the agents saw themselves well situated for collecting the rice into stores. They did so. They knew the Gentoos would rather die than violate the principles of their religion by eating flesh. The alternative would, therefore, be between giving what they had or dying. The inhabitants sunk;—they that had cultivated the land and saved the harvest at the disposal of others, planted in doubt—scarcity ensued. Then the monopoly was easier managed—sickness ensued. In some districts the languid living left the bodies of their numerous dead unburied."

representative of the great feudatory Indian princes, was to be exercised on a still larger and more important scale in the preparation of the camps and management of the durbars held at Delhi on the occasion of the memorable visit to India, in 1875-76, of His Royal Highness the Prince of Wales, and the Imperial assemblage on the 1st of January, 1877, when the Viceroy, Lord Lytton, with more than Eastern pomp and circumstance, declared to the assembled princes and potentates the assumption by Her Majesty of the title of Kaiser-i-Hind, or Empress of India.

To a practical soldier like Roberts, the continuous durbars, with their elaborate etiquette, must have been most wearisome, and doubtless the endless succession of scenes of Oriental pomp, which amused and elicited the wonder of the groundlings, palled on one who found a more congenial sphere for his talents on the arid sands of Zoolla, or the lonely valleys and difficult passes of the Looshai country. General Roberts superintended the preparation and arrangements of the Royal and Vice-regal camps to the entire satisfaction of the Prince of Wales, whom he first met at Calcutta, and of the Viceroy. In connection with the Imperial assemblage he was also specially appointed by Lord Lytton a member of the general committee for devising and carrying into effect the requisite measures in pursuance of the Government policy.

The energy and powers of organisation displayed by General Roberts attracted the notice of Lord Lytton, who was led to form a very high opinion of his capacity, and from that time an intimacy sprang up between these two remarkable men, which ripened into a warm personal friendship; and when the post of Commandant of the Irregular Force stationed on the Punjaub Frontier (which is under the direct control of the Viceroy, and not of the Commander-in-Chief), became vacant by the retirement of Brigadier-General (now Sir) Charles Keyes, Lord Lytton offered him the appointment, with the additional duties of Special Commissioner in the Scinde-Punjaub frontier. Thus, in accepting the double post, Roberts found himself once more connected with the force, in a mountain battery of which he commenced his military career. The offer of the appointment was due to the circumstance that Lord

Lytton, while in England, had seen a report of General Roberts on Afghanistan, which displayed great familiarity with the military aspect of the Afghan question, then forcing itself prominently into public notice.

The appointment of General Roberts was hailed with approval by all India, as it was generally acknowledged that than Roberts there was no fitter man in the army for the post of Warden of the Marches, the occupant of which should be a soldier combining with military experience a certain measure of the sagacity of the statesman.

Whatever may be said against the Indian career of Lord Lytton, and the success or failure of his policy, it should be noted in his favour that he correctly gauged the military talents of General Roberts, and when the time came for assigning the chief commands in one of the most important wars undertaken during the present reign, he nominated him to one of the three columns about to take the field for the invasion of Afghanistan, and, moreover, in spite of the grumblings of an influential minority at so young a general being placed in command, took care that his requirements to place his small force in a state of efficiency were attended to. Lord Lytton's discrimination in appointing General Roberts was generally acknowledged, even before the massacre of the Cavagnari mission demanded the despatch of an army of retribution; and the victorious advance from the Shutargardan Pass to Cabul, one of the most remarkable achievements of our arms since Waterloo, showed that a great soldier had arisen in the military firmament, which the renowned march from Cabul to Candahar, crowned with the rapidly delivered battle under the walls of that city, made manifest to the whole world, even the phlegmatic German temperament being roused into approval.

CHAPTER VIII.

The Afghan War—General Roberts is Appointed to the Command of the Kurram Field Force—Constitution of the Field Force—Brief Description of the Kurram Valley and its Inhabitants—The Advance from Thull into Afghan Territory—The Occupation of the Kurram Fort—The Operations of the 28th November—Reconnoissances and Preparations for the Attack on the Peiwar Kotul.

It is foreign to our purpose to enter into a disquisition on the political events which led to the war with Afghanistan. These events are viewed by Englishmen of Conservative or Liberal bias, in such opposite lights, and have afforded so measureless a field for envenomed discussion on the platform and in the press, that we, in our anxiety to avoid such combustible materials, will confine ourselves to the military events so far as they affect the hero of this memoir.

General Roberts, at the time of the outbreak of hostilities with the Ameer Shere Ali Khan, had made for himself such a name in his profession that it was generally allowed in Anglo-Indian society, as well as by the best and most active section of the officers of the Indian Army, that, in the event of war, his name would be found among those submitted by the military authorities to the Viceroy for a high command. In a remarkable degree he commanded the confidence of the Indian public and Army, but though his merits were not equally appreciated at Army Headquarters, where they should have most commanded recognition, in the Viceroy Roberts had a friend more powerful than the Commander-in-Chief, and one who correctly gauged the capacity of the young General.

In September, 1878, when the Afghan Commandant at the Fort of Ali Musjid, in the Khyber Pass, refused to admit the passage ("forcibly repulsed," as Lord Lytton declared in his summary of events) of the Mission under Sir Neville Chamberlain, of the advent and importance of which he had been duly notified by a letter from the Viceroy, his lordship, after proffering to the Ameer Shere Ali Khan, "a last opportunity of escaping the punishment merited by his acts," issued a formal Declaration of War against the ruler of Afghanistan, while absolving the sirdars and people of that country "from all responsibility for the recent acts of the Ameer," and expressing the determination "to respect their independence, and not willingly to injure or interfere with them."

Early in October a column for field service in the Kurram Valley was formed at Kohat, where General Roberts, who then held the command of the Punjaub Frontier Force, arrived on the 9th of that month, and assumed command. On the issue of the Declaration of War, an amended Government General Order, dated 9th November, was issued, constituting a column*

---

* General Roberts's staff consisted of Major W. Galbraith, 85th Regiment, Assistant-Adjutant-General ; Major H. Collett, Bengal Staff Corps, Assistant-Quartermaster-General (whose assistants were Captain R. G. Kennedy, Bengal Staff Corps, and Captain F. S. Carr, 5th Punjaub Cavalry); and Captain G. T. Pretyman, R.A., and Lieutenant Neville Chamberlain, Central India Horse, aides-de-camp. The Commanding Engineer was Lieutenant Colonel Æneas Perkins, R.E. ; Lieutenant-Colonel A. H. Lindsay commanded the Artillery ; the Principal Medical Officer was Deputy-Surgeon-General F. F. Allen, C.B. (succeeded at a later period by Deputy-Surgeon-General Townsend) ; the Commissariat Department was under Captain A. R. Badcock ; and the Superintendent of the Transport Department was Major D. Moriarty, Bengal Staff Corps, and from the 18th December, Major A. P. Palmer, 9th Bengal Cavalry. Captain A. S. Wynne was Superintendent of Field Telegraphs, but was subsequently succeeded by Captain E. Straton, 22nd Regiment. Colonel G. Waterfield was Chief Political Officer to the column, but he and his successors, Colonel J. Gordon, C.S.I., and Captain R. H. F. Rennick, were invalided, when Captain A. Conolly, Bengal Staff Corps—a name having an intimate but melancholy significance in our relations with Afghanistan—became head of the department. The Survey was under Captain R. G. Woodthorpe, R.E., who had campaigned with Roberts in Looshai, and the Chaplain's Department consisted of the Rev. J. Jolly, 72nd Highlanders, and the Rev. J. W. Adams, who was attached to the General's personal staff throughout the entire operations of the war, and rendered excellent service on many critical occasions.

The following were the troops forming the Kurrum Field Force:—Engineers—7th Company Bengal Sappers and Miners ; 23rd Bengal Native Infantry (Pioneers), Colonel Currie ; Engineer Field Park. Artillery—F Battery, A Brigade, Royal Horse Artillery, Lieutenant-Colonel Stirling ; G Battery, 3rd Brigade, Royal Artillery, Major Sidney Parry; No. 1 Mountain Battery, Captain Kelso, and No. 2 Mountain Battery, Captain G. Swinley. Ordnance Field Park, Captain Colquhoun, R.A. Cavalry—10th Hussars, 1 squadron, Captain Berkeley ; 12th Bengal Cavalry, Colonel Hugh Gough, C.B., V.C. First Infantry Brigade, Brigadier-General A. H. Cobbe.—2nd Battalion, 8th Regiment, Colonel Barry Drew ;

to be assembled in the Kurram Valley, under the command of Major-General Roberts, which was to act in combination with, though independently of, two other columns, intended for the invasion of Afghanistan by the Khyber and Bolan Passes, which were placed under the command respectively of Lieutenant-General Sir Samuel Browne, K.C.S.I., C.B., V.C., who had served with Roberts in Sir Hope Grant's Division during the Mutiny, and Lieutenant-General Donald Stewart, C.B., a comrade of his on the Staff at the siege of Delhi, and the commander of the Bengal Brigade in the Abyssinian campaign. Until General Stewart assumed command of the Candahar *corps d'armée*, Major-General A. S. Biddulph, R.A., held command of a smaller column called the "Quetta Field Force."

The Kurram Valley, on the borders of Afghanistan, had been visited by Sir Neville Chamberlain in 1856, when he marched a force to punish the people who had raided within our territories, and again, in the following year, Colonel (now General Sir) H. B. Lumsden travelled by this route when he proceeded on his mission to the Ameer Dost Mahomed Khan, just before the Mutiny. The scanty information gained by these officers was compiled into a Manual for the use of the force by Major Collett, of the 23rd Pioneers, General Roberts's Assistant-Quartermaster-General. The valley receives its name from the Kurram river, which at Thull has a bed about 500 yards broad, and at the Kurram fort only half that breadth, but in the winter months the river itself shrinks to very narrow proportions, being only about forty feet wide, with a depth of three feet. The entire valley to the north is dominated by the Sufeid Koh range of mountains, having an average altitude of 14,000 feet, from which spurs run out enclosing narrow valleys of great beauty, but affording in their sterility a scanty subsistence to their hardy inhabitants, who only cultivate the land along the banks of the river or its feeders. The average width of the Kurram valley, at its broadest part, is about twelve

---

29th Bengal N.I., Lieutenant-Colonel J. H. Gordon ; 5th Punjaub N.I., Major McQueen. Second Infantry Brigade, Brigadier-General J. B. Thelwall, C.B.—72nd Highlanders (now known as the 1st Seaforth Highlanders), Lieutenant-Colonel F. Brownlow ; wing 21st N.I., Major Collis ; 2nd Punjaub Infantry, Lieutenant-Colonel Tyndall ; and 5th Goorkha Regiment, Major FitzHugh.

Description of the Kurram Valley. 135

miles, and towards Keraiah it narrows to about two miles on either side the river, the intervening distance between it and the Sufeid Koh range being filled up with an upland valley called the Hurriab, which descends gradually from the Peiwar Kotul towards the west, a distance of twelve miles, to Ali Kheyl, near the Kurram river, and is bounded on the south by a high range of mountains, which occupies the space between the Hurriab and Kurram valleys, both of which were carefully surveyed by British officers during the occupation.*

The Turis, who were the original possessors of the Kurram valley, were much oppressed by their Afghan rulers, and hailed General Roberts as a deliverer, and at no time during the occupation of the Kurram valley did they give any trouble. The few villages at the head of the valley are inhabited by a people called Chumkunnies, and beyond the border are the lands of the Mangals, further on again along the river banks being the Ahmed Kheyl and Hassan Kheyl section of Jajis, whose territory extends close to Ali Kheyl, at the west end of the Hurriab valley. The mountainous district to the south of this valley belongs to the Mangals, whence they harry the villages on either side.

There are several passes from the Hurriab to the lower valley of the Kurram, which were explored, including the Sappri defile, from Ali Kheyl to Keraiah, a very difficult pass, in which a rear-guard of our troops guarding a convoy experienced some loss. The village of Ali Kheyl, in the Hurriab valley†, which has an elevation of 6,800 feet, consists of about fifty houses, inhabited by Jajis, and is surrounded with cultivation and fruit trees. About a mile from the village is a level "merg," or plateau, divided into three parts by ravines about two miles long and 400 yards wide, and between it and the village a spur from the mountain Matungi, which, as well as the nearest portion of the plateau, General Roberts caused to

---

* See Major Colquhoun's work, "With the Kurram Field Force," to which, and to Sir Frederick Roberts's despatches, of which copies were supplied to us by the General, we are indebted in the compilation of the following pages.

† The Afghans did not attempt to hold the Valley of Hurriab, which was inhabited by Jajis who are Soonies like themselves, the Turis being of the Sheeah sect of Mahommedans, between whom, all over the East, the feeling is as bitter as between Protestants and Roman Catholics.

be fortified with redoubts and intrenchments to protect the camps which were placed on the plateau. From the southern face of the Sika Ram, of which the Peiwar Kotul forms a spur, descends a watercourse, known as the Spingawi, or the White Track, which, joining another watercourse, runs to the south into the Kurram river, passing the village of Peiwar on the right hand, and leaving the deserted Afghan cantonment of Habib Killa on the left, as it debouches into the plain. This watercourse was the road used by General Roberts on the night of the 2nd December, in his attack on the Peiwar Kotul, which has an elevation of 8,500 feet above sea level.

No description could do justice to the wild and difficult nature of the country about the Peiwar Kotul, with its tremendous mountain defiles and narrow plateaus, only reached by a track winding through a pine forest, and amazement at General Roberts's success is not confined to those who formed a portion of the force with which he effected his brilliant capture of the Peiwar Kotul on the 2nd December, but is shared by all military critics. A very competent one, General C. L. Showers, who afterwards went over the ground with the victor as his guide, assured us that the Afghan position was apparently impregnable, and an attack on disciplined troops, such as those of the Ameer stationed in the Pass, with the limited means at Roberts's disposal, appeared an act of rashness which only success could justify.

The mass of mountains to the left of the Kurram river culminates in a peak called Saratiga, whose spurs and branches, says Major Colquhoun, fill up the whole of the ground between the road from Ali Kheyl to Cabul by the Pass of the Shutargardan ("Camel's Neck") and the road to Ghuznee. The great Ghilzai tribe—who are just now paramount in Afghanistan, having defeated their ancient rivals, the Dooranees, whose cause is identified with Ayoob Khan—have fixed their boundary at a place known as Karatiga ("Black Rock") on the southern side of the Shutargardan, and have spread over the crest of the pass unopposed by their weak neighbours, the Jajis. Other formidable passes in the vicinity are the Hazardarakht ("1,000 trees"), and Surkhai Kotul. At the foot of the Shutargardan runs the Logar river, with the usual belt of vegetation marking its course, and on the further side of the river lie the Pughman mountains, the southern continuation of the mighty Hindoo Koosh. At the foot of the hills on the Afghan side the road goes over an open plain, and crossing a low spur known as the Shinkai Kotul, then turns westward to Kooshi, a large village where General Roberts was joined by Yakoob Khan in his memorable dash on Cabul, after the massacre of the Cavagnari Mission. The city of Cabul, which is only thirty-seven miles distant from Shutargardan, as also the course of the Logar, which flows into the Cabul river below the capital, is shut out from view by a spur that closes the valley of the "Camel's Neck."

Starting from Kurram Fort, and proceeding along the bed of the river past the Chumkunnies and the Suffee Mangals, the Ahmed Kheyl district is reached, in which lies the Ghuznee, or Surki river, with a Kotul, or saddle, over which is the road to Ghuznee. Another track turns off from this road and leads to Cabul. The road down the valley from Ali Kheyl joins the first of these roads at the Ghuznee river, which is the road taken by those great conquerors, Genghiz Khan and Timour the Tartar, when invading India.

"The physical difficulties of the road between the Peiwar Kotul and Kooshi," says General Roberts, "are certainly far greater than any which present themselves in the Khyber route. Doubtless in time they could be materially lessened, and at no very considerable outlay; but the construction of a really good cart road between the points indicated would be a matter of great difficulty and vast expense. In the event of our re-occupying the Kurram valley, and a line of railway being constructed to the foot of the Peiwar Kotul, there would only remain a distance of ninety miles between it and Cabul, though the difficulties of this short space are almost insurmountable at certain seasons of the year save to an enterprising commander." To such an one, General Roberts is of opinion, even during the months from the middle of December to the end of March, the Shutargardan would not be impassable, so that he adds "practically troops quartered in the upper portion of the Kurram valley are capable of being pushed on to Cabul all the year round."

But though the Peiwar Kotul, Ali Kheyl and the tableland of the Hurriab are admirably suited for the location of troops, General Roberts deprecated the continued occupation of Kurram valley as it "proved very unhealthy to native troops, throughout the valley pneumonia and fever being very prevalent." On the other hand, the military advantages of the Kurram valley route to Cabul are, in General Roberts's opinion, great and manifest. From Rawul Pindee to Kohat and Thull the country, though sparsely inhabited, is under British jurisdiction, and from Thull to Peiwar Kotul the territory belongs to the friendly Turis, now declared independent of the Ameer. The Shutargardan passed and Kooshi reached, "the force enters the rich and fertile valley by the Logar, where supplies are procurable," and from thence "Cabul is approached by the least defensive and least difficult line, a defile within five miles of Cabul being the only point at which an effective stand could be made, and this could be turned by the Indki route."

Of the races of the Kurram valley, the Bungash occupy the lower portion as well as the fertile plains of the Miranzai valley, within the British border between Thull and Kohat, and muster 15,000 fighting men. The powerful Afreedee tribes inhabiting the mountainous district between the Miranzai and Kurram valleys, are the Orakzais, who are subdivided into Alizais and Alisharzais, and the Zymookhts, about 5,000 men. The Turis of the Kurram valley, divided into five clans or sections, and the Jajis, chiefly inhabiting the Hurriab, each muster an equal number of fighting men, and many of the latter opposed Roberts's advance at the Peiwar Kotul. The Mangals, a powerful tribe, inhabit the country to the south of the Kurram river, and might number 20,000 fighting men; and the territory to the south of the Khost valley is the *habitat* of a section of the Waziris, one of the most powerful and the bravest of the tribes on our north-west frontier, who extend from this point to Thull and thence eastward towards Bunnoo, and south as far as the Gomul Pass, their main road into India. Finally there only remains to mention the Jadrans, a cognate tribe to the Mangals, inhabiting the western hills of the Khost valley.

Kohat, where General Roberts joined the Kurram Field

Force placed under his orders, is a cantonment lying to the south of Peshawur, from which it is separated by a range of mountains. On assuming command of the force on the 9th October, General Roberts set to work with characteristic energy, organizing it for the advance, and, this completed, on the 18th November reached Thull, sixty-three miles distant, whither he had already despatched the greater portion of the force.

Between the 9th October, the date of his arrival at Kohat, and the 18th November, when he reached Thull, General Roberts's labours had been great, and he had infused into his force some of his own energy and a sense of perfect confidence in their leader. The orders he issued during his stay at Kohat, while engaged organizing the small division which proved such an efficient weapon in his hands, are multifarious, and embrace every provision for the efficiency and comfort of his men, no detail being considered too trivial or unimportant. His European troops were the 2nd Battalion 8th Regiment, and a wing of the 72nd Highlanders. The former corps had arrived from Rawul Pindee, and, owing to sickness, chiefly fever, was scarcely in a fit state to take the field; the battalion had been only a short time in India, and was composed of young and unacclimatized soldiers.

General Roberts, like Sir George Pollock, a brother officer of the Bengal Artillery and former commander of an army invading Afghanistan, almost daily visited the hospitals and personally inquired into each case. The effect was remarkable on both doctors and patients. The former looked forward to the visits, and the men began at once to improve. General Roberts's speciality always has been organization, and now everything was prepared, even to the postal arrangements, which were as perfect as in Looshai, before a move in advance was made. During the day he would work for many hours without cessation in organization and correspondence, and during the morning and evening he was ubiquitous, inquiring into everything, and permitting no minutiæ of detail to escape his notice.

At Thull, two months' supplies of provisions were collected, and preparations made for the advance across the frontier, on receipt of the reply to the ultimatum addressed by Lord Lytton to the Ameer Shere Ali; and, on the 20th November the

General issued orders for an advance into Afghan territory on the following morning. This was effected by the 29th Punjaub N.I. crossing the river by a trestle-bridge, with the 10th Hussars and 12th Bengal Cavalry acting as flanking parties; and thus "the Rubicon was passed," and the invasion of Afghanistan commenced.

The Afghan fort of Kapiyang was found deserted by Colonel Gordon, who commanded the advance, which was accompanied by the General. The cavalry followed in pursuit, but without overtaking the enemy, and the Infantry, with No. 1 Mountain Battery, followed, and encamped that night at Ahmed-i-Shama, eight miles distant. On the two following days a further portion of the troops, under the command of Colonel Stirling, R.H.A., and Brigadier-General Cobbe, joined the advance, and the General moved from Kapiyang, with headquarters, on the 23rd, to Hazir Pir, a distance of fifteen miles, where the troops in advance were now encamped, the fort in the rear being occupied by Brigadier-General Thelwall, who moved up from Thull. The difficulties of the first portion of the road between Ahmed-i-Shama and Hazir Pir were very great. There was no road for the wheeled guns of the battery of Horse Artillery, and the advance, under Colonel Gordon, consisting of the 23rd Pioneers, wing of 5th Punjaub Infantry, and the company of Sappers, had to make a passage for the guns under the General's personal directions. The troops, therefore, got no further than the village of Esoar, four miles from Hazir Pir, to which place General Roberts proceeded with headquarters.

As he passed along the road, the headmen of the villages paid their respects, and, on approaching Hazir Pir, he found a repast in the native style, prepared for him, spread out *sub tegmine fagi*. The villagers also turned out with milk, eggs, and dried fruit, which they offered to the troops for sale, and supplies of grass and fuel were also brought in abundance. General Roberts held a durbar of the leading men in the lower Kurram valley, and assured them of the friendly feelings entertained towards them by the British Government, and promised his protection so long as they committed no act of hostility.

On the following day, Sunday, the 24th November, the General marched to an encamping ground about a mile distant

Arrival at the Kurram Fort.

from the southern end of the Durwazi (Gate) Pass, with Headquarters and the following troops:—Squadron 10th Hussars, 12th Bengal Cavalry, No. 1 Mountain Battery, 29th Punjaub N.I., and Wing 5th Punjaub N.I. The march presented no difficulties, and the country was uninhabited, though streams of water, stocked with fish, were crossed. During the day intelligence was received of the evacuation of the Kurram Fort by the Ameer's troops, who were retreating by the Peiwar Kotul, and, on the following morning, the General moved across the Durwazi Pass—which leads over the chain of mountains which bounds the Kurram valley on the south, and has an ascent of about five miles, and a descent of three miles—and occupied the Kurram Fort, which was found in good condition, save for the roofing which the Turis had carried off as soon as the place had been evacuated by Shere Ali's troops. On the same day Brigadier-General Cobbe marched from Hazir Pir to the camp at the Durwazi Pass, and Brigadier-General Thelwall took his place from Ahmed-i-Shama.

Camp was pitched on an open plain between two nullahs, about half a mile to the west of the Kurram fort, a mud work about 120 yards square, with round bastions at the corners, a keep in the centre, about fifty square yards, and only one gateway protected by an outwork. The thickness of the outer wall was about 6 feet, height 20 feet, that of the keep being 10 feet higher; outside the wall was a broad *fausse braye*,* about 12 yards wide, to the edge of the ditch, on the west and south sides of which were parapet walls. The Governor's quarters were in one of the bastions, which was raised into a three-storied house, but, like the rest of the fort, with the exception of a small mosque, it had been wrecked by the Turis; both these buildings were used as hospitals as soon as the necessary alterations and repairs had been effected. About a quarter of a mile distant from the Kurram fort, was a walled barrack enclosure, about 100 square yards in extent, having stables for horses as well as huts for the troops, which was known as the Upper Fort. These military works were found useful for storing the Commissariat, Engineer, and Ordnance park stores,

---

* A *fausse braye* is a kind of counter-guard, or low rampart, for the protection of the lower part of the main escarp in the rear.

as well as for a hospital. In the vicinity was a large fruit garden, amply stocked, and a two-roomed edifice, surrounded with a verandah, which was transferred to the political officers for use as a Court-house.

General Roberts was received, on approaching the fort, by Mahomed Noor, one of the leading men of the valley, who came to pay his respects, escorted by a following of mounted men and footmen. Having completed the inspection of the fort, the General, accompanied by two squadrons of the 12th Bengal Cavalry, proceeded to reconnoitre in the direction of the Peiwar Kotul, twelve miles distant. On approaching the village of Peiwar, two other villages were seen to be in flames, and a report was brought that the Ameer's troops, consisting of three regiments of infantry, with twelve guns, had evacuated the cantonment of Habib Killa, about a mile to the east of Peiwar, through which they were passing. General Roberts was able, by the aid of glasses, to see the enemy retiring towards the valley leading to the foot of the Peiwar Pass, but his means did not permit of an attack, and he retired to the camp at Kurram.

On the following day, the 26th November, the General issued orders for the advance, which was to be made "as light as possible," officers' baggage being limited to half a mule load, and two officers occupying one tent of 80 lbs. The soldiers were to have one tent of two palls (having a superficial area of 512 square feet and a height of 8 feet) between 40 Europeans, 50 Sepoys, and 60 camp followers; and a bell tent between 25 British soldiers or 20 natives. The troops selected for the advance were put in orders on the 26th, on which day Brigadier-Generals Cobbe and Thelwall crossed the river and came into the Kurram Camp, so that the whole Division was now massed ready for the advance. A small garrison was detailed to hold the fort, and the remainder of the force, which General Roberts held in readiness to accompany him in the first critical operation of the war, numbered 83 officers and 969 effective European soldiers of all ranks, and 2,854 effective Native troops, with nine 9-pounders, and four 7-pounders.

We have seen how the French required 50,000 men to subdue the Arabs of the small territory of Tunis, each of the operating columns exceeding the strength of General Roberts's entire force, and in contrast we find a British General, with the utmost confidence, advancing against one of the strongest positions in the world with less than 4,000 men, of whom only one quarter were Europeans. That a favourable result accrued was due mainly to the genius of the commander, who possessed the true admixture of caution and dash, and whose dispositions were admirably framed for the operation in hand. But none the less was it a desperate undertaking, for we remember a distinguished member of the Indian Council informing us during the brief interval that elapsed between Roberts's departure from his camp and the report of his victory, that he and his colleagues were " very anxious " for the safety of the force.

At 5 A.M. on the 28th November, the morning being very dark and the cold severe, the troops formed up in two parallel columns,* and before six the start was made, General Roberts marching at the head of the left column, which arrived about ten, near Habib Killa, having made a fatiguing march of fourteen miles. On his arrival the General received intelligence, which afterwards proved to be false, that the Afghans had abandoned their guns at the foot of the Peiwar Kotul, and were retreating in disorder, and he determined, without loss of time, to make the march of seven miles and take possession of the guns. General Roberts sent Brigadier-General Cobbe to the left with his brigade, with instructions to turn a ridge forming the southern boundary of the valley, through which was the road from the village of Peiwar to the Kotul, and to seize the Mangal village of Turrai ; and Brigadier-General Thelwall was ordered to move in support of the left column by proceeding past the village of Habib Killa up the regular road to the Pass.

---

* Left column.—One squadron 12th Bengal Cavalry ; two guns No. 1 Mountain Battery ; four companies 5th Punjaub N.I. ; remainder of the 1st, or Brigadier General Cobbe's, Brigade, consisting of 5th Punjaubees ; 23rd Pioneers ; 29th Punjaub N.I. ; 8th Regiment ; and two guns, F Battery, A Brigade, Royal Horse Artillery, on elephants.
Right Column.—One squadron 12th Bengal Cavalry ; two guns No. 1 Mountain Battery ; four companies N.I. ; remainder of 2nd, or Brigadier-General Thelwall's, Brigade, consisting of 5th Goorkhas ; wing 72nd Highlanders ; 2nd Punjaub N.I., and two guns F Battery, A Brigade, Royal Horse Artillery, on elephants.

General Cobbe carried out his orders with the 5th and 29th Punjaubees and two mountain guns, and, as the enemy were seen on the side of the spur, he moved down towards the village of Turrai, but the remainder of the brigade, disposed in support, did not round the southern side of the spur, but keeping to the north, eventually met the right brigade as they moved up the road. General Cobbe, in descending the mountain path towards Turrai, finding the passage into a valley, called "the Punch-Bowl," barred by precipices, had to make a retrograde movement, which always excites the warlike ardour of Pathan mountaineers, who are in their element in harassing warfare, but rarely make a direct attack on regular troops unless in overwhelming force. A party of them now moved down from a spur and commenced an attack, as the 29th N.I., with a wing of the 5th Punjaubees in support, moved towards the village.

It was 2 P.M. when General Roberts arrived at Turrai, and at the same time the right brigade came in. Observing that an engagement was in progress between our men and the Afghans, which formed no part of his programme, the General proceeded with the 5th Goorkhas to the assistance of General Cobbe, and the force was withdrawn by alternate regiments. The loss in this affair was slight, and included Lieutenant A. Reed, of the 29th N.I., severely wounded. At 3 P.M., during General Roberts's absence, the camp was marked out by Brigadier-General Thelwall, in some terraced fields below the village, and the troops were waiting the arrival of the baggage, when the Afghans, having sent to the main ridge in the rear for a gun, opened fire with shell at a range of 1,700 yards, which was replied to by the guns of F Battery, A Brigade, Horse Artillery, which also fired on some riflemen who were annoying a picket of the 5th Punjaubees. It accordingly became necessary to move back the camp, and a spot was selected $1\frac{1}{4}$ miles in the rear, but it was not until a late hour that the different corps could find their baggage and take rest, after a very fatiguing day and a march of more than twenty miles over difficult ground.

That General Roberts should pitch his camp under fire of the enemy's guns was a proceeding so completely at variance with the military antecedents of so experienced a soldier, and the war correspondent of one of the London daily papers having, in conversation with us, animadverted upon the General's strategy in this respect, we asked General Roberts for the true story, and he, with that soldierly frankness which is so distinguishing a feature of his character, far from taking offence at the outspoken question and the opinions that had given rise to it, described, in the following words, the circumstances under which his camp became exposed to the enemy's fire, necessitating a retrograde movement:—"Having received information that the enemy were in a hollow and could not get their guns away—which proved incorrect, as at this time the Afghan army was securely entrenched on top of the Peiwar Kotul—I sent Brigadier-General Cobbe's Brigade round the enemy's right to prevent their getting on the crest of the Peiwar Kotul, while Brigadier-General Thelwall's Brigade was directed to attack in front, so as to get the enemy between two fires. Soon the advance regiment of Cobbe's Brigade got under fire from the enemy's flanking positions near the Peiwar Kotul, when I went on to see what was happening in the front, leaving orders for the main column to be halted and pitch tents at a point about two miles from the foot of the ascent to the Kotul. This order was not carried out, and during my absence in front with the leading regiments of Cobbe's Brigade, some of the baggage animals were allowed to come too far in advance, and the camp was marked out on a spur which proved to be within the range of the enemy's guns on the Kotul. On seeing this, I ordered the baggage animals to be taken to the rear, and camp to be pitched on the spur I had first selected. This movement gave rise in the minds of those ignorant of the facts, to the opinion that there had been a retirement, which was due to a misconception on the part of the Brigadier-General who had been ordered to pitch the camp in a safe position."

On the following morning a portion of the camp was moved to a more suitable spot, and the troops were given a day's rest in order that the supplies might be moved up and the necessary reconnoissances made. Colonel Æneas Perkins, Commanding Royal Engineers, Roberts's friend at Addiscombe, for whose services he had specially applied, escorted by two companies of the 23rd Pioneers, proceeded up the valley beyond the north picket, with the object of ascertaining whether the ridge was connected with the Peiwar Kotul. Colonel Perkins reported that a deep valley lay between the picket ridge and the Kotul itself, and that it was impossible to direct an attack from this side.

A second reconnoissance, conducted by Major Collett, Assistant-Quartermaster-General, accompanied by his assistant, Captain Carr, and Captain Woodthorpe, R.E., escorted by two companies of the Pioneers, proceeded to ascertain the practicability of the route by the Spingawi ravine. Marching by a road unsuited for wheeled guns, they reached the summit of a ridge about five miles distant from the British camp, overlooking the Spingawi nullah. It was ascertained that "the road up the Kotul itself appeared to be on the same ridge as the Peiwar Kotul, and that a force working from the former towards the latter would pass over a series of dominating positions." Major Collett was of opinion that the enemy did not occupy the Spingawi Pass in force, though there was a picket and a gun on a commanning knoll to the south of the Pass, and one apparently on the Kotul itself. Colonel Gordon, with a company of his regiment, the 29th N.I., reconnoitred the south ridge of the valley, and ascertained that it was continuous with the main ridge, and that an attack could be conducted along it.

During the day the troops were engaged making roads in the camp, which was wretchedly situated, being surrounded by a thick oak jungle, but no better site could be found without moving back three or four miles towards the village of Peiwar, and the camp itself was protected from attack by strong pickets on the hill sides. That the enemy were mustering in considerable strength to meet the apprehended attack on the Peiwar Kotul appeared certain, from the circumstance that their position had been considerably extended on both flanks, but little information could be procured.

At dawn on the following morning, the 30th November,—as Montague says:—

"So soon as the all-cheering sun
Should in the further East begin to draw
The shady curtains from Aurora's bed,"—

General Roberts was astir, and proceeded to reconnoitre in the direction Colonel Perkins had taken, being accompanied by Colonel Currie, 23rd Pioneers, and Captain Richard Kennedy,* Deputy-Assistant-Quartermaster-General, an officer of singular promise, in whom his commander recognized a soldier, who, had he lived, must have attained great distinction in his country's service. Colonel Gordon again reconnoitred the hills on the enemy's right, and Major Collett and Captain Carr made a secret reconnoissance,† unaccompanied by troops, from the village of Peiwar up the regular road to the Spingawi, and succeeded in reaching a point about $1\frac{1}{2}$ miles distant from the Kotul, and getting a fairly good view of the approaches thereto. General Roberts carefully considered the reports of these officers, and, on the evening of the 30th, decided to abandon any attempt at attacking the Peiwar Kotul in front, which would certainly entail great loss. He would however make a feint in front on the Peiwar Kotul, to be developed into an attack at the proper moment, while the real attack would be a flanking movement to the right rear round by the village of Peiwar, and thence by the Spingawi ravine to the plateau of hills on the right of the Peiwar Kotul. This, which was to be the main attack, he resolved to conduct in person, but he kept his councils to himself, the only officer whom he brought into his confidence being Major Collett, who, from his reconnoissances, was conversant with the road as far as the Spingawi plateau.

Having formed his plans, including the portioning off of the regiments, without reference to any one, at 4 P.M. on Sunday, the 1st December, General Roberts convened a meeting in his tent of the brigadiers, officers commanding regiments and batteries, and chief staff officers, and laid before them in detail his plans. In his address to the assembled officers, General Roberts enjoined on them the strictest secrecy, as were his intentions to get wind, the consequences would be fatal to success. He requested them not to speak of them to any one, and not even to look in the direction of what he

---

* The late Colonel Kennedy, who met with a premature death by drowning soon after his return to Ireland from service in Afghanistan.
† See Sir F. Roberts's despatch of the 5th of December, 1878.

intended should be the main attack. He pointed out the difficulties of a long night march, where so much depended on discipline and endurance, and enjoined upon his hearers the absolute necessity for silence in the ranks, and, above all, that the regiments should keep touch of each other in the darkness, as otherwise they might lose their way, and cause a miscarriage of the enterprise. The entire force at his disposal to capture a strong position defended by a superior force of regular troops with artillery, was 3,314 men, of whom only 899 were Europeans.

The night march by the Spingawi Pass, he proposed to undertake himself with Brigadier-General Thelwall's Brigade, the direct attack on the Peiwar Kotul to be made by Brigadier-General Cobbe. In order to encourage the belief among the enemy that the attack was to be a front one on the Peiwar Pass, General Roberts sent ostentatious reconnoitring parties to both flanks of the Peiwar Kotul, and directed a party of pioneers, under an engineer officer, and a covering party of the 8th Regiment, to construct a battery near the village of Turrai, in advance of the camp. The enemy fired shells at this detachment from the Kotul battery, but without doing much damage. General Roberts discovered that the Afghan strength was concentrated on the centre and right, while their left, which was to be the objective point of the turning movement, was comparatively weak. So well was the secret kept that not only the Afghans expected a front attack on the Kotul, but every man in camp anticipated that the morrow would see them engaged in storming by a direct movement the formidable Pass, behind which lay the enemy in unknown strength. In order to strengthen this impression, the half battery of G battery, 3rd Brigade, Royal Artillery, and the squadron of the 12th Bengal Cavalry, which had been brought from the Kurram Fort on the previous day, were paraded in full view of the enemy.

CHAPTER IX.

The Midnight March up the Spingawi Ravine—Treachery in the Ranks—The Capture of the Spingawi Pass—Advance along the Ridge and Severe Fighting—General Roberts is Wounded—The Night Bivouac in the Mountains—Occupation of the Peiwar Kotal—Account of the Operations by an Officer of the Staff—General Roberts Reconnoitres the Shutargardan Pass.

THE operation in which General Roberts was about to embark was one calculated to daunt all but the very brave. Behind the wall of rock that barred his advance lay an enemy of whose numbers and composition he could gain no information. The regular army of the Ameer Shere Ali numbered "at least 50,000 men, with over 300 guns and ammunition in abundance,"* and in a country where every adult male bears arms, the nucleus afforded by the garrisons of the posts stationed in the Kurram could be strengthened at short notice by large numbers of tribesmen, who would flock with religious ardour to war against the infidel invader. The Afghan force of regulars that had retired before the British Army, was known to consist of 1,800 men, with 11 guns, and, by the end of November, reinforcements of infantry and a battery of artillery had arrived, while they had the advantage of superior artillery, and an almost impregnable position, besides the aid of the warlike mountaineers and tribesmen.

Not until after "tattoo" were the troops of the turning force, drawn from Brigadier-General Thelwall's brigade, warned to be ready to march. At 10 P.M., the column, under the immediate command of General Roberts, numbering 43 officers and 2,220 men, with the hospital dhoolies and ammunition mules in rear of each regiment, marched off in silence, without sound of drum or bugle, and, passing from the light of the camp fires, which were kept brightly burning, disappeared into

---

* See General Roberts's Memorandum, dated "Cabul, 29th May, 1880."

the darkness, and commenced the march for the Spingawi nullah by the circuitous route of the village of Peiwar in the rear.

The 29th Punjaubees, 5th Goorkhas, and Mountain Battery, under Colonel J. Gordon, 29th P.N.I., led the column, followed by the wing of the 72nd Highlanders, 2nd Punjaub Infantry, 23rd Pioneers, and four guns of the F-A Horse Artillery, on elephants, escorted by two companies of the Pioneers, under General Thelwall. The first part of the march to Peiwar was about three and a half miles, over broken ground, the tracks, for there was no road, passing through oak jungle, and crossing many ravines and stony watercourses, before the cultivated ground surrounding the village was reached, when the road ran along a terrace on the cultivated slope to the edge of the Spingawi nullah. A watercourse flowed swiftly along the bed of the nullah, the banks of which and the boulders on the slope were thickly covered with ice, rendering the descent tedious and difficult for man and beast. It was fortunate that General Roberts started as early as 10 P.M., which was done with the intention of giving the troops time to rest on the road, as it was correctly surmised that, owing to the slow rate of progression, the Spingawi Pass, involving a further march of at least six miles from the village of Peiwar, would be reached none too soon to allow of a surprise at early dawn.

There was a cutting wind blowing, the elevation at starting being 7,000 feet, while the ascent was continuous to the top of the Pass, which had an elevation of 9,400 feet. The labour of keeping one's feet or holding up the horses was excessive, owing to the broken nature of the road, and the boulders with which it was covered, while the difficulties of the march were much increased by the extreme darkness of the night. But the men kept on bravely, and there was no murmuring, all looking forward with eagerness to the hour of conflict, and placing implicit confidence in the skill of their leader. Owing to the darkness and the difficulties of the road, which had only before been traversed by Major Collett, the 2nd Punjaubees lost touch of the 72nd Highlanders, and, instead of turning up the nullah, crossed it, thinking the turning point was further on. The 23rd Pioneers and the Horse Artillery followed in their track, and it was not for some time that Brigadier-General Thelwall, riding at the head of this portion of the column, became aware of the absence of half his force. On discovering this fact he sent his orderly officer, Lieutenant Turner, of the 8th Regiment, to bring them back, which that officer did after a ride of two miles; owing to this mishap the Brigadier-General, and the 2nd and 23rd Regiments and four guns with him, were practically "out of the hunt." The further the column marched, the worse appeared the road, if the bed of the nullah could be dignified by the term, as it was, says General Roberts, "nothing but a mass of stones, heaped into ridges and furrowed into deep hollows by the action of the water."

After General Roberts had advanced with the troops still accompanying him for a mile and a half up the nullah, an incident occurred, which showed the risky nature of the operation in which the column was engaged, and nearly caused the miscarriage of the surprise which the General had prepared with such care. From the ranks of the 29th Punjaub N.I., marching at the head of the column, suddenly a shot was fired, quickly followed by a second. What could this mean but treachery? General Roberts found himself confronted with a danger on which he had not counted. With everything against him in conducting a critical operation, save his skill and the valour of his troops, it was a terrible revelation thus flashed on him from the rifles of his own men, but the trial found him equal to the occasion. Colonel Gordon, commanding the 29th, halted his regiment, and the General, who was riding close behind the advance party, immediately ordered the 5th Goorkhas and two companies of the 72nd Highlanders to pass them and head the column. But it was feared that the mischief had been done, and the alarm had been given to the Afghans, though this was not so, owing to the accidental circumstance of the direction of the wind and the conformation of the hills at this spot preventing the sound travelling towards the enemy's position.* But this Roberts knew not at the time, and his anxiety at the success of his plans was greatly in-

---

* Major Colquhoun says, that it was afterwards ascertained that "an Afghan sentry heard the shots, and woke up the commander of the post who took no action in the matter, hearing no further cause for alarm."

creased, though he had no hesitation or thought of changing them. Like Hotspur,

> "He walk'd o'er perils as on an edge,
> More likely to fall in than to get o'er."

But such dangers acted as a spur to his ardent nature, and he took the course great spirits adopt in crises when lesser men fail—he "plucked the flower, safety, out of the nettle, danger."

Colonel Gordon endeavoured to discover the men who had fired their rifles, but none of their comrades could or would identify them. One of the native officers of the regiment examined the rifles of several men, and found out some which had recently been discharged, but being a co-religionist he sought to screen the delinquents, and affected not to have discovered them.

During the Umbeyla Campaign, the Punjaub regiments engaged at the Mahabun, were mostly recruited from Pathans, and proved faithful to their salt under the most trying circumstances, as they have on numberless occasions in our border wars, and no doubt was now entertained of their fidelity; but this deed of treachery revealed a new source of dread, and, but for a fortunate circumstance, the well-laid plans of the British General might have been baulked, and a sanguinary struggle, if not a repulse, might have changed the fortunes of the campaign. But General Roberts had embarked his fortunes and the lives of the handful of troops with him, in the perilous task of snatching a victory by a surprise, and he resolved to prosecute the attempt to the end at whatever hazard. As Cassius said before Philippi:—

> "Why now, blow wind, swell billow, and swim bark!
> The storm is up, and all is in the hazard."

The advance was now resumed, the 5th Goorkhas and two companies of the 72nd Highlanders leading, and about four in the morning the main bed of the watercourse was quitted, and the march was continued along the ravine to the left, at the top of which, distant three miles, was the Spingawi Kotul. The General had intended to halt the column for an hour or two in order to rest the men, but owing to the distance that yet remained to be traversed being greater than was anticipated, he had to abandon the intention.

Plodding doggedly along, the troops made their way up the ravine, the obscurity of which was scarcely relieved by the light of the stars, and, at length, shortly before six in the morning, the head of the column reached the foot of the pass, where the track left the ravine and turned up the spur. The guides, who had led the troops up to this point, were dismissed at their own request, and the men moved on expecting momentarily to fall in with the enemy. Presently, just as day was breaking, the challenge of a double sentry was heard, and two shots, fired in rapid succession, warned every one that the struggle had begun. The order, "Front form companies," rang out on the morning air, and an advance party of the 5th Goorkhas, gallantly led by Major FitzHugh and Captain Cook, made a rush for the first stockade, fifty yards up the hill, while the remainder of the regiment extended and swarmed round the flanks of the obstacle.

Sir Frederick Roberts has given us the following account of the advance up the Spingawi ravine, and the act of treachery by the 29th Punjaub Native Infantry, which nearly proved fatal to the success of his operations:—"I was going along just in rear of the advance, and began to be aware that gradually the pace was becoming slower and slower, with great straggling among the men of the 29th Regiment, and as I had given special orders that the regiments were to keep touch, I halted the column to find out if the remainder of the troops were with me. On the return of the staff officer, whom I had sent back for this purpose, I found that the 5th Goorkhas, the four companies of the 72nd Highlanders, and the mountain battery were following the 29th, but the remainder of the column had lost touch; the 23rd Pioneers I did not see again till 11 A.M. on the following day, and Brigadier-General Thelwall till 1 P.M.

"While the column was halting, I heard two shots fired in the ranks of the 29th, and immediately gave orders to Colonel Gordon to find which men of his regiment had been guilty of the act. He reported that he could not identify them. I then said that the 29th could no longer lead the advance because of the slow pace at which they marched, and ordered the Goorkhas and Highlanders to head the column. This caused some delay, and I became anxious, as it was necessary we should reach the Spingawi Pass before daylight, which broke about six o'clock. I asked Colonel Villiers the time. Taking out his watch he said, 'Three o'clock.' This reassured me, as it would give time to reach the enemy's position before daylight; but soon after he came to me and said he had made a mistake, that it was four o'clock. This renewed my anxiety, as we were travelling over ground unfamiliar to us. The Goorkhas were now leading, and soon a further delay occurred owing to the regiment taking a wrong road, which at this point bifurcated. I halted the column and sent an officer to find them, and they soon returned, but this caused a further delay of half an hour.

"The ground now began to ascend rapidly, and I knew from this that we must be nearing the final slope. I now told Major FitzHugh, commanding the 5th Goorkhas, that I should give him no further orders, but that he was to move on rapidly, and on reaching the foot of the Afghan position he was to give the order, 'Front form companies,' and go at the enemy as hard as he could, and I promised to support him with the 72nd Highlanders and other regiments as fast as I could bring them into action. At the first streak of dawn I heard the order, 'Front form companies,' and a few seconds after the enemy began firing."

The firing became general on both sides, and the dense pine woods were illuminated by the discharges of the rifles, for daylight was only just beginning to break. The Afghan fire is described to us by one who was present, as a perfect rain of bullets, but it was almost ineffective, as, owing to the steepness of the hill, the bullets passed over the men's heads. With admirable dash the Goorkhas stormed the stockade after a brief hand-to-hand struggle. The Afghans fell back on a second stockade, eighty yards in the rear, but the spur here being a little wider, the flanks of the stockade were turned, and the agile little Goorkhas, assisted by the Highlanders, under Colonel Brownlow, were in the midst of the stalwart Afghans, who speedily gave way.

Meantime General Roberts directed Captain Kelso to take his mountain battery to the front, which that officer did with great gallantry, and himself advanced up the hill with the remaining companies of the wing of the Highlanders, who, forcing their way through the timber that grew on the precipitous sides of the spur, came up on the right flank of the advance, and pushing on in support of the latter, followed the fleeing Afghans up the hills to their last defences near the crest. From the second stockade to the crest of the hill the ground was open, "the track ascending in short zigzags," while the crest itself was covered by the enemy, who kept up a heavy musketry fire on the troops, and also maintained an ineffective shell fire. The obstacles of the attack were increased by the felled timber lying across the slope of the hill, and by a knoll on the flank protected by shelter-trenches, which it was necessary to take as it occupied a commanding position.

The Goorkhas and Highlanders pressed up the hill, and soon captured the third stockade, the Afghans suffering heavily, though they succeeded in removing the gun which commanded the line of advance. The 29th Punjaubees were in support, and, later, repelled an attack on the right flank, while General Roberts, on foot, accompanied the 72nd Highlanders on the right, and seized the knoll which commanded the ground above the third stockade. At this time the force suffered a loss in the death of Captain Kelso. This officer, following the Goorkhas and Highlanders, had brought two of his guns into action in the battery vacated by the Afghans, and not being aware, owing to the dim light, that the enemy had temporarily returned to the first stockade, after the advance had pushed up the hill, was proceeding through the work with his chief native officer to find a position for one gun on the knoll, when too late he discovered his mistake, and as he turned round was shot through the back of the head and fell dead on his face. Immediately afterwards the 29th Regiment advanced, and a second time turned the enemy out of the stockade.

Meantime, the Highlanders, led by Colonel Brownlow, and accompanied by General Roberts, pushed up the ascent, the enemy falling back till they were driven among the pine woods which clothed the spur. The Goorkhas also carried on a front attack up the hill above the last stockade, when a party of Afghans charged down, but were met by the gallant Captain

Cook, who rescued Major Galbraith, the Assistant-Adjutant-General from death at the hands of a powerful Pathan.* The fighting was severe throughout, and within the first, or great, stockade, seventy-eight dead bodies of Afghans were found, proving that they had defended the position with resolution.

The troops were now formed up on the edge of the "merg," or small grass plain, beyond the last stockade. By 6.30 the whole of the Spingawi stockades had changed hands, and the line of the enemy's defence was completely turned, while he withdrew towards the Peiwar Kotul, and along the edge of the woods to the north. General Roberts heliographed the news of his success to Brigadier-General Cobbe, and instructed him to co-operate vigorously from below in attacking the Kotul. Having re-formed the troops on the crest of the hill, he sent for the supports, which were still some way in the rear, under the command of Brigadier-General Thelwall.

After giving the men a rest, at 9.30 General Roberts, feeling the importance of pressing the enemy while they were dispirited, determined to push on without waiting for the supports. Sending word to General Thelwall to come to his assistance, he marched with the troops then with him—the 72nd, Goorkhas, and 29th—to dislodge the enemy from the dense woods surrounding the plateau in the direction of the Peiwar Kotul, in which they had sought shelter.

The 29th now led the way, followed by the Goorkhas, the 72nd, and the mountain battery, under Lieutenant Jervis. The column crossed the plateau unopposed, and then plunged into the pine wood on the rocky hill-side in skirmishing order, a species of fighting which tries the discipline and courage of troops, who are less under the leadership of their officers. The men skirmished through the forest and over rocks and bushes in a way that spoke well for their training, driving the enemy before them, and reached the crest of the hill, a very steep acclivity, with slopes towards the Peiwar, which afterwards received the name of Picnic Hill, as the troops later in the day dined here out of the contents of their haversacks,—and were

---

* For this act of gallantry Captain Cook received the V.C., but did not long survive to enjoy the distinction and a brevet majority he had well earned, as he fell at Cabul, in December of the following year.

soon met by a hot fire from the Afghans assembled in great strength on an equally steep hill on the opposite side of the narrow valley, only fifty yards in breadth at this point.

General Roberts took up a position, amid a heavy fire, on the left of the line in rear of the 29th, opposite the neck which communicated with the hill on which the Afghans were crowded in great strength, but from which they would have to be driven if the Peiwar Kotul was to be stormed. The enemy exhibited great hardihood, and relying on their numbers, which enabled them to extend along the crest of the hill, a mile to the left and half a mile to the right of the neck, and also on the strength of their position, poured in a hot fire, and even charged down the hill towards the British troops, but each time were driven back. Though the time for the advance had not yet arrived, as the attack in front, by Brigadier-General Cobbe, was not developed, it was foreign to General Roberts's nature to act only on the defensive, and he directed the 29th to proceed down the hill and, covered by the fire of the mountain guns, attack the enemy on the opposite slope, and sent word to the Goorkhas and Highlanders to act in support.

The Punjaubees succeeded in reaching the top of the opposite hill, but unfortunately the Goorkhas and Highlanders lost their way in the dense forest, and there being no support, the 29th were driven back. General Roberts accompanied the last company of the regiment, and was about halfway up the opposite hill, believing the Goorkhas and Highlanders were close behind, when he met the 29th rushing back, having been driven down by the Afghans, who were in overwhelming force. The General had sent one after the other all the members of his Staff, including even the chaplain, Rev. J. Adams, to find out where Brigadier-General Thelwall was with the supports, and where the Highlanders and Goorkhas had strayed to, but neither his officers returned with news, nor did the wished for troops make an appearance.

The position now became very critical. In vain the General sought by voice and example to rally the panic-stricken Punjaubees. With his wonted valour, freely exposing his person, he was now the centre of a storm of bullets, and that he escaped death was a marvel, though a contusion in the hand from a spent bullet bore evidence to the personal danger to which he was exposed.

At this time General Roberts's attention was attracted by an act of devotion towards himself, which should find a place in this personal record. When returning up Picnic Hill from the Afghan position, after vainly endeavouring to rally the discomfited Punjaubees, on turning round to look back, he beheld his Sikh orderly, Dhyan Singh by name, of the 5th Punjaub Infantry, walking close behind him with his arms stretched out to cover the body of his master, exposed to the Afghan fire across the narrow valley, which, as before said, was only fifty yards in width. Officers who have served on the North-West frontier can recall many instances of a like devotion on the part of those serving under them, whether Sikhs or Pathans, and it is a disgraceful calumny to say that the virtue of gratitude is unknown to the inhabitants of the Indian Peninsula.

At this anxious moment, when all seemed lost, as neither General Thelwall, with the supports, nor the Highlanders and Goorkhas, had made an appearance, a party of the 23rd Pioneers appeared, coming down the hill, under Colonel Currie, who informed General Roberts that Major Anderson, of his regiment, was close by with more of his men. The Pioneers were soon under fire, and a few minutes afterwards, Major Anderson was killed, a little to the left; but his death was avenged by Colonel Currie, who drove back the enemy. This timely assistance saved a further retirement, and soon afterwards the Goorkhas and Highlanders, finding the right direction by the sound of the heavy firing, returned to the hill, having lost their way in the dense wood.* Even now the 2nd Punjaub N.I., and the four Horse Artillery guns, forming, with the Pioneers, General Thelwall's brigade, had not arrived.

The action had proceeded for two hours all along the front, with great expenditure of ammunition, but with small loss, owing to the cover, when a portion of General Cobbe's troops came on the scene, and their presence prevented the necessity

---

* General Roberts said he afterwards tried to find out whither the Highlanders had wandered, but no one could explain, though the denseness of the forest and the want of guides was perhaps a sufficient excuse.

A Further Flank Movement.

of driving the enemy from their strong position by a front attack. The 5th Punjaub N.I. and 2nd Battalion 8th Regiment had been detailed for the front attack on the Peiwar Kotul, and the former, in order to co-operate with the flank attack, began ascending one of the principal spurs that run down from the range between the Peiwar and Spingawi Passes. Leaving camp before dawn, the Punjaubees were six hours reaching the summit, when, guided by the sound of the firing, Major Macqueen, the commanding officer, accompanied by Colonel Perkins, commanding Royal Engineers, who gave most valuable information regarding the enemy's position on the Peiwar Kotul, led his men up to the rear of the hill where the duel was progressing between the British and Afghan main forces.

General Roberts, acting on the information brought by Colonel Perkins, sent two mountain-guns to shell the Afghan camp, which was exposed to view by an opening in the woods, the range being about 1,000 yards across the face of the precipitous Peiwar range. The shells set fire to the tents and caused a panic among the men and animals, which was increased when, about noon, the elephants arrived with the four Horse Artillery guns, under Colonel Stirling, which were brought into action on the left of the hill that the Afghans had lately held so tenaciously. On the arrival of the 2nd Punjaub N.I., which had been absent, with the remainder of the supports, from the fighting line, General Roberts ordered them to hold the crest of the hill, while the troops, who had been marching and fighting continuously for more than fourteen hours, rested and refreshed themselves with the cooked provisions they had brought in their haversacks, and hence the hill, that had witnessed such hot work, received the name of Picnic Hill.

General Roberts says:—" I walked across to the hill lately held by the enemy for the purpose of reconnoitring, the horses of the mounted officers having been left at the foot of the ascent; but it was impossible to pursue the Afghans in this direction through the thick forest and undergrowth, and as guides could not be had, and as there were only two or three hours more daylight, I decided to make a further flank movement with the object of getting still further round the enemy's rear, and to make an attack on the following morning. Leaving the 2nd Punjaubees on Picnic Hill, on the north of the Kotul, and the 29th to hold the hill overlooking the Spingawi and protect the field hospital which had been established there, I took the remainder of the troops I had brought with me from camp, including 5th Punjaub Infantry, and proceeded on the endeavour to get round the enemy's rear." Just before dark he reached a hill having an elevation of nearly 10,000 feet, where he bivouacked, amidst intense cold, the thermometer marking 25 degs. of frost.

Though the troops, the 5th Goorkhas leading, commenced the march from Picnic Hill at 2 P.M., it was four before the head of the column emerged from the forest on to the open slopes above the highest cultivation in the Hurriab Valley. No enemy was in sight, and as the short December day was already closing in, and the troops were quite worn out with their exertions, the General gave the order to bivouac, and soon huge fires were lit, and afforded the troops the only means of keeping out the piercing cold of this elevated spot. General Roberts shared the discomfort of his men and shivered in his greatcoat; but he had the added trouble caused by anxiety as to the absence of news from Brigadier-General Cobbe, of whom he had not heard since Colonel Perkins left him in the morning, as owing to the intervening hills, he had been unable to communicate by heliograph with the camp after the first signal in the morning reporting the capture of the Spingawi Pass.

About eight o'clock in the evening, however, the General's anxiety was relieved by a hastily scribbled note from Colonel Waterfield, Political Officer with the Force, announcing that six companies of the 2nd Battalion 8th Regiment, under Colonel Barry Drew, were in possession of the Peiwar Kotul. The column for the front attack,* numbering 30 officers and 838

---

* The column consisted of the 8th Regiment; 5th Punjaub Infantry; 12th Bengal Cavalry; 2 guns F—A, R.H.A.; 3 guns G—3, R.A.; and the Turi and other levies. General Cobbe received general instructions to open fire on the enemy about 6 A.M.; to get his troops into position in front of the Peiwar Kotul by 8.30, and to storm the place when the flank attack had become sufficiently developed to shake the enemy's defence.

The Front Attack.

men, under command of Brigadier-General Cobbe, had moved from camp at 5.30 A.M., and about seven o'clock, having reached the last spur (separated from the Peiwar Kotul by a glen), became engaged with the enemy, whose artillery also opened fire on our guns, which returned the compliment with vigour. The duel went on till about ten o'clock, when the enemy, trying to outflank the skirmishing line of the 2nd Battalion 8th Regiment, a squadron of the 12th Bengal Cavalry charged across the line of fire and forced them to retire. An hour later General Cobbe was wounded in the leg, when the command devolved on Colonel Drew. The Afghans held their ground in the Kotul, until, panic-stricken at the success of the further flank movement made by General Roberts, and fearful of having their line of retreat cut off, they evacuated the Kotul, which was occupied at 2.30 P.M.

So hastily had the enemy abandoned their position that they left their tents standing, and dinners ready cooked, and the road towards Ali Kheyl was strewed for some distance with guns, limber boxes, and other *matériel*. The camp was plundered by the Turis, who had been directed to move in co-operation on the enemy's right, but kept out of harm's way until the camp was in the occupation of the British. Colonel Hugh Gough, commanding the cavalry, proceeded in pursuit of the enemy, but they had had too long a start, no signs of them were visible, and the cavalry returned to the camp at the foot of the hill, whence tents and rations were sent for the men of the 8th Regiment, who passed the night on the Kotul.

The loss in the action, which was chiefly confined to the column under General Roberts's immediate command, was twenty-one killed, including two officers—Major Anderson, 23rd Pioneers, and Captain Kelso, R.A.—and seventy-two wounded, including two officers—Brigadier-General Cobbe and Lieutenant Monro, 72nd Highlanders. The enemy, though occupying a defensive position, suffered far more heavily, and the wounded, who were removed, crowded the villages in the Hurriab Valley, while six field-pieces and twelve mountain-guns were captured.

The victory achieved was in every way a remarkable one. The Afghans had everything in their favour—an almost impregnable position, perfect knowledge of the ground, superior numbers, and a stronger force of artillery, with an ample supply of provisions and ammunition; but all were neutralised by the genius of the British General and the valour of his troops.

An officer of the Staff who was by General Roberts's side throughout the operations that resulted in the capture of the Peiwar Kotul has given us the following interesting account of the proceedings:—

"On the 28th of November we reached the foot of Peiwar Kotul about three in the afternoon. The General had information to the effect that the enemy were entrenched at the entrance of the Pass, and had six guns. The whole force at the General's disposal marched from Kurram at 5 A.M., reached the ground opposite the Afghan cantonment of Habibkila about 10 A.M., when dispositions were made for attacking what was supposed to be the enemy's position. Colonel T. Gordon, commanding the 29th P.N.I., was ordered to proceed to the left, and turn their right flank, and he was given his own regiment, the 5th P.I., under Major McQueen, and two mountain guns. Brigadier-General Cobbe, with the 28th Foot and four mountain guns, was ordered to advance on the enemy's centre; and the General, with Thelwall's brigade, moved against the enemy's left.

"The ground was covered with a kind of dwarf ilex, which grew like a thick shrub rather than a tree, and which was well calculated to conceal even a large body of men. It was also intersected by several deep ravines. Along this ground, then, Thelwall's brigade advanced, and we were on the tiptoe of expectation, believing that the enemy were close in front, and that at any moment we might see the leading men of our skirmishers open fire. But on we went, and still there was no sign of the enemy. Then the ground was reached where they were said to be entrenched, but still no sign of either enemy or entrenchment, and the idea that the Afghans had fled began to gain ground amongst those of us who were new to Asiatic methods of warfare. At last a bit of open ground was reached, where there were signs of the enemy's last encampment, and a halt was made.

The Staff Officer's Account.

"We had seen Colonel Gordon, with part of his force, cross a hill on our left and dip down into a valley behind a spur just in front of us, and we could see Colonel McQueen, with part of his regiment, holding a commanding position on this spur. Glasses were directed towards the top of the Kotul, but nothing could be discerned at first, and the idea that the enemy had fled, or had moved back to some stronger position, began to gain ground. Meanwhile, the General had directed a search to be made for water, and the open bit of ground to be examined with a view to encamping on it for the night.

"About this time officers with good glasses detected men moving about on the top of the Kotul, and the dress of these men was so like that of our 29th P.N.I. that many declared them to be our men, who had worked round through the valley behind the spur on the end of which was Major McQueen. All doubt, however, as to whether they were friends or foes was soon dissipated as the sounds of very heavy firing reached us from the gorge or narrow valley along which Colonel Gordon had advanced.

"The General immediately sent Captain Kennedy, A.Q.M.G., back to stop the baggage, and to choose a place for a camp a little further down the pass, and giving directions as to what was to be done on the spot where he then was, he sent an officer to McQueen to hold his position till Colonel Gordon and the force with him had retired, for the General had determined not to attack the enemy's position that day, it being far too strong to attempt to take at that late hour in the afternoon, with troops who had been marching from before daylight. One great point effected by Colonel Gordon's move, and by the advance of the whole force to the foot of the Pass, was that the whole of the enemy's position in our front was unmasked. The General himself, and some of his Staff, went up the valley by which Colonel Gordon had advanced, and when he saw the strength of the enemy's position he ordered the 5th Punjaub Infantry to advance and cover the retirement of Colonel Gordon's force. This was most satisfactorily accomplished, the whole of the casualties amounting, I think, to only eleven. The artillery and rifle fire was exceedingly heavy for a considerable time, and the small number of casualties on our side is another instance of how ineffectual a heavy fire often is from a very elevated position.

"The troops were all got back comfortably into camp, and we were all thoroughly satisfied at having found the enemy at last, though his position was much stronger than we should have supposed. The General seemed satisfied that he had now got them within striking distance, and next morning he prepared for a thorough reconnoissance of the different spurs which led from the Peiwar Kotul into the plain below. Those on the right and left of our camp were carefully examined, and towards evening the impression gained ground that the General would probably order the attack along the spur on our left, the highest point of which was held by a picket of McQueen's regiment. Our camp was almost under the spur on our right, where we had a very strong picket also of 23rd Pioneers. These pickets were inspected continually, as well as those in front and rear of our camp, by Lieutenant-Colonel the Hon. G. Villiers,* whom the General had appointed Superintendent of Outposts. Next day reconnoitring still went on, and the General himself went up to the picket of the 23rd Pioneers, and from that commanding position was able to get a very good view both of the enemy's position and of the spur on our left, along which it was thought he would probably deliver his attack on Monday, the 2nd December, as the General said he would rest quietly until that day in order to give the troops, who had had some very harassing marches, time to recover from the effects before tasking their energies with the attack of so strong a position as that chosen by the enemy. But he had not as yet said how, or at what hour on Monday he would attack.

"On Sunday morning there was divine service in the open air just a little out of range of the enemy's artillery. The General and all his Staff attended, and there was a very large number of communicants. Towards the middle of the day an attempt was made to throw up an earthwork in front of our position, which had the desired effect of leading the enemy to suppose that the principal attack would be made on their centre and along the high road that led to the top of the Kotul. This

---

* Colonel Villiers was Military Secretary of the Viceroy, and subsequently did good service in Zululand, under Sir Garnet Wolseley.

attempt was, I believe, ordered to be carried on until it drew the enemy's fire, when the working party was to retire. About four in the afternoon the General summoned all officers commanding brigades, regiments, and batteries to a council in his own camp, and he then explained to them that he had had the road leading to the Spin Gawai Kotul carefully reconnoitred by Major Collett, Assistant Quartermaster-General to the Division, and Captain Carr, Deputy-Assistant Quartermaster-General of Cavalry, and that the report was so favourable he had determined upon making his chief attack on that point. He then explained how this was to be done, and all the details of the movement had been so carefully worked out by Major Collett that no little point was forgotten.

"The General's plan, briefly, was this:—Not to warn the troops till 1 P.M., when the regiments appointed for the attack were all to turn out without any noise or speaking, and without sound of drum, bugle, or trumpet. The fires in the camp were to be kept alight, and all the tents were to be kept standing. The men were each to carry one day's cooked rations, and the march was to continue all night till about 4 A.M., when it was calculated we should be tolerably close to the Spin Gawai Kotul. It was then intended to halt until a little before dawn, when it was proposed to time the movement so that the attack should be actually delivered at dawn.

"Brigadier-General Cobbe was left in command of the camp with the 2nd battalion 8th Foot, four guns G battery 3rd brigade Royal Artillery, and two guns F battery A brigade Royal Horse Artillery, and one squadron of cavalry. With this force he had orders to attack the enemy's centre as soon as he found the enemy's left had been turned at Spin Gawai.

"A few minutes after ten General Roberts, with the remainder of his force, marched off in silence. There was a little moonlight for the first hour, but that help to marching soon vanished, and the troops marched on as best they could in the darkness, in the teeth of a cutting wind. The road lay up the bed of the Spin Gawai Nullah, which was covered by huge boulders, over which the men had to pick their way as best they could.

"The march proceeded without incident till about 2 A.M.,

when two shots were fired by men of the 29th P.N.I., apparently with the intention of giving warning to the enemy of our approach. Their object, however, was frustrated by two causes. First, the wind blowing strongly down the Nullah prevented the sound from travelling upwards, and secondly, the conformation of the hills at that particular spot was unfavourable to sound travelling in the direction of the enemy. This conduct of the two men of the 29th P.N.I. necessitated a change in the order of the march. The 5th Goorkhas and a company of the 72nd Highlanders, under Colonel Brownlow, took the place in front that had hitherto been held by the 29th.

"As soon as this arrangement was made the line marched on again in the darkness, and without incident or mishap, until the foot of Spin Gawai Kotul was reached. So little did the enemy suspect our approach that our leading men had actually come within a few hundred yards of their advanced double sentry before they were aware of our presence. Two shots fired by the double sentry gave the alarm, and then rang out the orders on our side for the attack. It was still quite dark, and under the pine trees, through which our men advanced, the flashes of our rifles and those of the enemy from the big stockade on the top of the Pass lit up fitfully the whole scene. This stockade was gallantly taken by the 5th Goorkhas and the company of 72nd Highlanders, and two other stockades on the left of the enemy's position were also attacked and taken. The two guns of No. 1 Mountain Battery, under Major Kelso, who had taken up a position, by the General's direction, on a knoll that commanded the stockade, contributed greatly to the rapid success of the movement. The firing having ceased, and it being still almost dark, Major Kelso advanced with one gun through the stockade, hoping to get a shot at the retreating enemy, but the force which held the stockade, finding that they were unpursued in the darkness, and that the line of attack had followed the direction of the two stockades on their left, returned again to their first position in the big stockade. These men were dressed so much like our 29th P.N.I. that Major Kelso, seeing them in the stockade in the dim light of the early dawn, supposed they were men of that regiment, and did not discover his mistake till he was close upon them, when they fired and shot him through the head. A similar mistake was also made by Captain Woodthorpe, R.E., at whom they also fired, but he escaped almost by a miracle, the hilt of his revolver and part of his coat being shot away, and for some months afterwards he bore on his skin the mark or burn which the graze of the bullet left upon it.

"The enemy's return necessitated the taking of the stockade a second time, which was done by the 29th P.N.I., and the whole position, held so strongly by a very large body of the enemy, was in our hands a little before 7 A.M. As an instance of the difficulty of shooting down hill, I may mention that very few of our men were hit during the advance up the hill. The enemy's fire was very heavy and well sustained, but was just too high to be destructive to our people. They themselves, though occupying what appeared to be a secure position inside the big stockade, suffered heavily, and seventy-eight dead bodies were counted next day lying in and around the stockade.

"As soon as the Spin Gawai Kotul was in our hands the troops were formed up, and an advance made across the open ground in the direction of Peiwar Kotul. The 29th P.N.I. led the advance, and every effort was made to press on the retreating enemy as fast as possible. Leaving the 'merg,' the line of advance lay along thickly-wooded spurs, covered with a great deal of undergrowth. After some distance had been traversed our advanced skirmishers suddenly drew the fire of the enemy, who, having retreated from Spin Gawai, had joined their comrades at Peiwar, and now took up a strong position on the route we were following to Peiwar Kotul. General Roberts never hesitated, but he sent back at once for the 5th Goorkhas and 72nd Highlanders, and with a view to encouraging the men of the 29th P.N.I., went down the hill with them, and up the opposite side under a very heavy fire. With this small force he actually reached the top of the hill occupied by the enemy; but there was delay in getting up the 72nd and the 5th Goorkhas, caused by the thick undergrowth and the nature of the ground, which both prevented the regiments seeing what point to make for, and the officers of the General's staff sent in quest of them, from finding them easily. In consequence of this short delay the men of the 29th P.N.I. were forced to retire to the opposite hill, which we then held with the Goorkhas, 72nd, 23rd Pioneers, and 2nd P.I., all of whom had now come up. Holding this position, General Roberts then tried to open communication with General Cobbe's force, which it was understood was at this time attacking the enemy in front. But the nature of the ground prevented the signallers from opening communication.

"Shortly afterwards, Colonel Perkins, R.E., and Major McQueen, 5th P.I., who were in the front attack, contrived to ascend the spur to the right of their line of attack, and to join General Roberts, thereby giving him full information of what had taken place in front up to the time when they left. After consulting with them and the commanding officers of the force he had with him, the General resolved to get round in the rear of the enemy, and to leave a regiment, the 2nd P.I., to hold the position he then occupied. Before making this move two mountain guns were brought into action at a spot pointed out by Colonel Perkins, who, on his road up, had observed that the enemy's camp at the Peiwar Kotul would be exposed to artillery fire at that point.

"The General, about one o'clock, commenced his march to the flank and rear of the enemy, and this movement, being observed by them, caused at once their retreat on all sides within our view; but their position was so extended that we could not tell how far the retreat was general, nor whether it included the force opposed to Cobbe's brigade. It was impossible with our tired troops, who had been marching all night and fighting all day, to follow up an enemy who took no *one* line of retreat, but fled in many directions. The General, therefore, having completed the flank movement, and got in rear of the enemy's position, bivouacked for the night on a hill above the village of Gandigan.

"At this time we did not know how completely the flank movement had routed the enemy, but we afterwards learned that the enemy, seeing it, and fearing it would cut off their retreat, had all of them fled precipitately. Meanwhile, the front attack, finding that the enemy's fire had altogether ceased, began to advance in the direction of the road leading up to the Kotul, their attack hitherto having followed the line of a spur on the proper left of that road. Colonel Waterfield and Colonel Hugh Gough were, I believe, the first to reach the top of the Kotul, which they found utterly deserted. This was about 3 P.M. Immediately afterwards the troops followed, under the command of Colonel Drew, 2nd battalion 8th Foot, and occupied the ground lately held by the Afghans on the top of the Kotul. About 8 P.M. a messenger from Colonel Waterfield (or Colonel Gough, I forget which) reached us, with a letter which informed the General that the enemy had fled, and that what remained of their camp was in the possession of Cobbe's brigade."

General Roberts had a cheerless bivouac on the night of the 2nd of December, and, on the following morning, he moved his force, comprising four guns, Royal Horse Artillery, and two mountain guns, wing 72nd Highlanders, 5th Goorkhas, and 23rd Pioneers, to the open ground about half a mile from Zabberdasht Killa,* where the camp was pitched on the arrival of the tents from the camp at the foot of the Peiwar Kotul. During the afternoon the 2nd Punjaub N.I. joined him from Picnic Hill, and the 29th N.I. were sent back to the standing camp on the other side of the Kotul. General Roberts was of opinion that it would be useless to attempt the pursuit of the enemy over a hilly and, in parts, thickly-wooded country, as they had not retreated in a compact body, but, like the Israelites of old, fled " every man to his city, and every man to his own country." During the forenoon he rode, with his Staff, to the Peiwar Kotul, and carefully examined the position, of which his admirably designed and executed strategy had dispossessed the enemy. Along the whole line of the narrow pass, extending from Zabberdasht Killa to the Kotul, appeared the usual indications of a precipitate flight. He describes it as " a place of enormous natural strength, and the enemy's dispositions for repelling any attack on it from the front were very complete and judicious. It is also evident, from the enormous stores of ammunition and supplies which have been captured, that it was the intention of the Afghan Government that their troops should remain here for the winter, and that they fully expected to be able to maintain their position against the British

---

* Zabberdasht means "high-handed," and Killa is a fort.

forces." The strength of the enemy on the 2nd December was ascertained to be 3,500 regular infantry with 18 guns, and a large number of tribesmen. After an interview with Colonel Drew he rode down the hill to the camp, and directed that the hospital, which was under the protection of the 29th Regiment, should be moved back to the Kurrum Fort, where he had established the base hospital.

On arriving at headquarters General Roberts sat down at a little camp-table, in the open air, to write the despatch announcing his splendid achievement, and his Aides-de-Camp and the officers of his Staff wrote as best they could at the same table, sending news of their safety to anxious relatives and friends. They were not long thus occupied when an orderly came to announce that the trench was ready for the reception of those who had fallen on the previous day, upon which the General immediately left his writing, and, accompanied by the officers of his Staff, followed the bodies to the grave, where they were interred with as much ceremony as the circumstances permitted. Towards evening he returned to his camp near Zabberdasht Killa, and, writes the officer of his Staff, already quoted, "while riding back it was a matter of general comment how admirably the enemy had chosen their position at Peiwar, and also a matter of congratulation that so difficult a task had been performed with the loss of so few officers and men." On the following day, the 4th December, the bodies of the two officers killed, Major Anderson and Captain Kelso, were committed to the grave, on a little hill between Zabberdasht Killa and Gandigan, in the presence of the General and other officers.

During the day General Roberts issued a congratulatory order* to his gallant troops, and, on the 7th, he had the grati-

---

* The following is General Roberts's order to his troops :—"Major-General Roberts congratulates the Kurrum Field Force on the successful result of the operations of the 2nd December against the Peiwar Kotul, a position of extraordinary strength, and held by an enemy resolute and well armed. Not only had the enemy the advantage of ground, but also of numbers, as they were largely reinforced from Cabul the evening previous to the attack. A position apparently impregnable has been gained, a considerable portion of the Afghan army has been completely routed, and seventeen guns, with large stores of ammunition and supplies, have been captured. The result is most honourable, and could only have been attained by troops in a high state of discipline, capable of enduring hardships, and able to fight as soldiers of the British Army have always fought. Major-

fication of announcing to them the following telegram from her Majesty the Queen, forwarded through the Viceroy, who added his " warm congratulations on the success achieved :"—" I have received the news of the decisive victory of General Roberts and the splendid behaviour of my brave soldiers with pride and satisfaction, though I must ever deplore the unavoidable loss of life. Pray inquire after the wounded in my name. May we continue to receive good news."

The troops halted in their positions on the 3rd December, when the 5th Punjaub N.I., under Major MacQueen, proceeded to bring in a large quantity of provisions left by the Afghans in the neighbouring villages, and the 2nd Battalion 8th Regiment furnished working parties to assist in taking the captured guns back to the camp for transmission to the Kurram Fort, a work of no small difficulty, owing to the steepness of the hill, but which was facilitated by using the long drag-ropes employed by the Afghans in bringing the ordnance up the ascent.

Preparations were now commenced for halting the troops that were to remain at the Kotul, the company of Sappers and Miners being ordered up from Kurram to assist in this and road-making, and three guns of G Battery, 3rd Brigade R.A., were ordered for the defence of the position. Brigadier-General Thelwall was placed in command of the troops* remaining for the winter at and near the Peiwar Kotul, and at ten o'clock on the morning of the 6th December, General Roberts marched from the camp at Zabberdasht Killa to Ali Kheyl, with the remainder of the troops,† the column being temporarily under the command of Colonel Barry Drew until Brigadier-General

---

General Roberts deeply regrets the brave men who have fallen in the gallant discharge of their duty, and feels for the sufferings of the wounded. In Major Anderson, 23rd Pioneers, and Captain Kelso, Royal Artillery, the Major-General has lost two personal friends, and the Government two valuable officers." The Commander-in-Chief, Sir Frederick Haines, also telegraphed his congratulations to General Roberts.

* At the Peiwar village, 12th Bengal Cavalry; at the Camp, near the village of Turrai, 29th Punjaub N.I.; at the Kotul, the 8th Regiment, three guns G Battery 3rd brigade Royal Artillery, and a company of Sappers.

† Advance-guard — detachment, 12th Bengal Cavalry; wing, 23rd Pioneers, No. 1 Mountain Battery. Main body—72nd Highlanders, 2nd Punjaub N.I., 5th Punjaub N.I., and 5th Goorkhas. Rear-guard—Four guns F Battery A Brigade Royal Horse Artillery, on elephants; wing, 23rd Pioneers.

Cobbe returned to duty. The march to Ali Kheyl, a distance of twelve miles, was made without much difficulty, the road being in the river-bed or along the bank, and camp was pitched on the plateau beyond the village.

On arriving at Ali Kheyl, General Roberts, at 1 P.M., proceeded to examine the road in the direction of the Shutargardan Pass, taking with him as escort 250 men of the 72nd Highlanders, 250 of the 5th Goorkhas, and two guns of the Mountain Battery, the whole under the command of the late Lieutenant-Colonel Brownlow, who fell at Candahar, on the 1st September, 1880, in the last action of the war. The first march was made to Rokian, a distance of three and a half miles, and, on the following day, the General marched to Jaji Thanna, a force in support, consisting of the 2nd and 5th Punjaub N.I., under the command of Lieutenant-Colonel Tyndall, of the former regiment, with the two remaining guns of the Mountain Battery, taking the place of the escort at Rokian. The cold was intense, the thermometer marking 5° Fahr. at 7 P.M., but the weather was clear, and there was no snow. On the 9th, General Roberts and Staff, escorted by fifty men of the Highlanders, and an equal number of the Goorkhas, leaving his camp standing, pushed on to the crest of the Shutargardan, a distance of about ten miles, and eagerly scanned the Logar Valley and the road that led to Cabul, some fifty miles distant.

Between the Peiwar Kotul and Dreikula, a point eight miles beyond Ali Kheyl, the route lay through the country of the Jajis, who had fought against the British in the action of the 2nd December, but who were so completely at the mercy of the invaders that they were glad to make terms with Colonel Waterford, the Political Officer, who proceeded to Ali Kheyl, and promised them good treatment if they assisted the transport of the force, which they continued to do for some months without giving cause for complaint. Beyond Dreikula to the Shutargardan, says General Roberts, " the country was absolutely uninhabited, though Jajis, Mangals, and Ghilzais can collect there in considerable numbers to oppose the advance of a force, both in the Hazardarakt defile and on the slopes of the Shutargardan."

The Government had decided that the Shutargardan was to be the limit of the advance into Afghan territory at the present season of the year, and so General Roberts, after wistfully regarding the land of promise from the summit of the Afghan Pisgah, returned to Ali Kheyl, leaving on the further slope of the Shutargardan a battery of brass guns, which the Afghan reinforcements, under Wali Mahomed Khan, had abandoned when, climbing the ascent, they met the flood of their retreating countrymen, and swelled its volume instead of stemming the tide.

General Roberts returned, on the 10th December, to Ali Kheyl, where a company of the 29th Punjaubees was permanently quartered, and the 2nd and 5th Punjaub N.I., and the four guns of the Horse Artillery, marched for Kurram, to which the General decided to return by the northern route, over a range of hills occupied by the hostile Mangals, with the object of exploring the country between the Hurriab and Kurram valleys, and of acquiring a knowledge of an important route by which the Peiwar Kotul could be turned.

CHAPTER X.

General Roberts returns to Kurram by the Sappri Defile—Attack by the Mangals on the Baggage Escort—Preparations for the Occupation of the Kurram Valley during the Winter—The Court-Martial on the Treacherous Soldiers of the 29th Punjaub N.I., and Roberts's General Order to the Force—Disposal of the Troops into Winter Quarters—Expedition into the Khost Valley—The March from Kurram to Hazir Pir, and thence into the Khost Valley—Occupation of the Fort of Matun—Action of the 7th January and Defeat of the Mangals—Reconnoissance by General Roberts of the Khost Valley.

GENERAL ROBERTS marched from Ali Kheyl by the Sappri, or Manjiar defile at 9 A.M. on the 12th December, with a force consisting of the 5th Goorkhas, wing 72nd Highlanders, the 23rd Pioneers, and the Mountain Battery. The operation of marching a considerable force, with its long baggage train, through a defile held by a hostile tribe of mountaineers is one of the most difficult in war, and it was not effected on the present occasion without some loss, which included two excellent officers.

The village of Sappri, distance seven miles from Ali Kheyl, was reached about mid-day. The road was difficult and wild, and led along the Hurriab river till the Kurram was reached, on the right bank of which it continued, until, after passing the two villages of Kermana, it again recrossed the bed of the Kurram, and lay up a narrow glen, a part of the route being through a pine forest.* General Roberts had received information that the Mangals intended defending a defile and pass about two miles beyond the larger village of Kermana, and, at four in the afternoon, pushed on the 23rd Pioneers to occupy the Kotul and bivouac near the village. An hour after midnight the tents were struck, and at 3 A.M., the night being bitterly cold and dark, the General resumed his march with the

---

* See Major Colquhoun's "With the Kurram Field Force."

troops in the following order :—Advance Guard : two companies of the 23rd Pioneers. Escort for the baggage, four companies. Baggage. Mountain Battery. Wing, 72nd Highlanders. Rear-guard : 5th Goorkhas.

The track of the Kotul was steep and difficult for the camels, owing to the frozen water rendering the footing very slippery, and it was not until past 8 A.M. that the rear-guard began the descent from the top of the Kotul. No enemy was in sight, and it was hoped that the early hour of the march had defeated any intentions they may have entertained to attack the baggage ; but this anticipation was not verified by the result. The descent of the pass was even more difficult for the camels than the ascent, and the road was about as suitable a one for a surprise as could be conceived. " The gorge at the foot of the hill, " says the military historian already quoted, " extended for five miles, the track for the first part ran through a deep ravine with perpendicular walls, which narrowed in places to but a few yards, over-hanging the path till they seemed to meet, and made a gateway or tunnel through which the road passed.

The ordinary precautions in forcing a pass, of crowning the hills on either side, could scarcely be put in practice, as these in their turn were commanded by other ridges running parallel to the ravine, while there were ample facilities for a lurking ambush in the side ravines which broke into the road, if that could be called so which was a rough and stony watercourse. But this part of the road was passed in safety, and as the more open part was reached, some of the Mangals were seen perched high up on the sides of the mountains, looking at the line of march defiling below.

On reaching the valley, the troops, with the exception of the Goorkhas, were allowed to push on ahead of the baggage, and make their way to the camp which was to be pitched at the village of Keraiah. But all danger was not yet at an end, and the mountaineers, seemingly regretting that such a chance of looting should escape them, began collecting in small detached parties, which gradually closed in on the rear of the column. No duty in war is more difficult or hazardous than escorting a convoy through a long pass in the occupation of a predatory tribe. Byron graphically describes such a scene :—

> "The rest in length'ning line the while
> Wind slowly through the long defile;
> Above, the mountain rears a peak,
> Where vultures whet the thirsty beak,
> And theirs may be a feast to-night,
> Shall tempt them down ere morrow's light."

Captain F. Goad, Transport Officer, was in charge of the baggage, and was walking close to a small party of the guard, consisting of a sergeant and three men of the 72nd Highlanders, when some of these Mangals approached salaaming and making signs. The sergeant in charge, named Green, apprehending treachery, asked leave to fire, but Captain Goad, under the impression that the hillmen were inspired by amicable intentions, refused permission. Immediately afterwards the Mangals fired a volley, and Captain Goad fell wounded with a bullet through both legs. Sergeant Green picked him up, and, having placed him under cover of a rock, prepared with his three men to defend the unfortunate officer against the enemy pressing on them now from all sides; and so close and accurate was the fire of these brave men that they succeeded in killing several, and driving off the remainder of their assailants.[*]

The firing now became general, as the Mangals, seeing their anticipated prey escaping from their clutches, attacked the rear-guard, which was hotly engaged under the command of Major Fitz Hugh, of the 5th Goorkhas. Captain Powell, of the same regiment, received two wounds, which subsequently proved fatal. The scene at this time, as the escort, dismounting, sought to keep the enemy at bay, and the latter, sheltering behind every rock and inequality of ground, maintained a hot return fire upon the British troops, may be well described in that passage in the "Giaour:"—

> "With steel unsheathed, and carbine bent,
> Some o'er their courser's harness leant,
> Half shelter'd by the steed;
> Some fly behind the nearest rock,
> And there await the coming shock,
> Nor tamely stand to bleed
> Beneath the shafts of foes unseen
> Who dare not quit their craggy screen."

On General Roberts hearing of the attack on his rear-guard

---

[*] For his gallantry Sergeant Green received a commission in his regiment.

he despatched the main body of the Goorkhas back to assist in driving off the enemy, but this had already been done before their arrival, and Major Fitz Hugh had the satisfaction of bringing his convoy in safety into camp without the loss of a single camel.

On the following day, the 14th December, General Roberts, leaving his troops in camp at Keraiah, proceeded, accompanied by his staff, to Kurram, a distance of twenty-one miles. The road, which lay along the bank of the Kurram river, was covered with boulders, and was altogether too rough for guns or wheeled transport. The General determined, if possible, to punish the marauders who attacked his baggage in the Sappri defile, and sent Mr. A. Christie, of the Civil Service, Assistant-Commissioner, to Keraiah, to enquire if an attack on their villages was possible, and also despatched Captain Kennedy, Deputy-Assistant-Quartermaster-General, to reconnoitre up the river with the same object; but the result of these enquiries proved that there were no villages sufficiently large to be worth the trouble of destroying, and, furthermore, it was ascertained that the attacking party was not wholly composed of Mangals, but was recruited from the Jajis and Chumkunnies, and that some of the Ameer's soldiers, defeated on the 2nd December, took part in the attempt on the baggage.

General Roberts issued a complimentary order, thanking the 5th Goorkhas for their "great gallantry and steadiness" in the affair of the 13th, "when passing through the most difficult defile the Major-General had ever seen." On this day Captain Goad died of the wounds received in the Sappri Pass, and, on the 16th, was buried at Kurram, whither his body was brought from Keraiah, with military honours, in the presence of the General and his staff. On the same day the troops stationed at Keraiah, under the command of Colonel Drew, left for the Kurram fort, where they arrived in two marches.

General Roberts arranged for the protection of the wire between his head-quarters and Thull, which had been frequently cut of late, detachments of troops being posted at Suddar and Ahmed-i-Shama, and agreements were made with the head men of the villages, who were to supply armed men for the purpose of patrolling the intermediate sections of the line, an arrangement which worked well. Meanwhile the process of hutting the 2nd Battalion 8th Regiment at the Peiwar Kotul proceeded apace, and three redoubts and block-houses were commenced on commanding positions, while the hill-sides were cleared of trees where necessary, and the Sappers and Miners were engaged in making a practicable road to the Kotul for laden animals. In order to provide against the contingency of a sudden attack from the direction of the Hurriab, detachments from the 12th Bengal Cavalry and 2nd Punjaub Infantry were stationed at Zubberdasht Killa, and, in his orders and arrangements generally, General Roberts took all the precautions for the safety and comfort of his soldiers and camp-followers, the care of his camels and other transport animals, and the security of the Kurram valley, that military skill and experience could suggest.

The troops throughout the valley had to be on the alert, and on the night of the 16th December, the cavalry post at Ibrahimzai, three and a half miles from Suddar, was fired into by some men of the Orakzai tribe, who were reported to be assembling in the adjacent hills. The General immediately strongly reinforced the post, which he placed under the command of Lieutenant-Colonel Cochrane, of the 8th Regiment, and, on the 18th, he rode thither accompanied by his staff, and, having enquired into the affair, proceeded to Suddar, where he caused the destruction of the house of a Moollah who had incited the people against the British rule, the owner taking care to be *non est inventus*.

As soon as he had a little breathing time, General Roberts convened a general court-martial to bring to justice the soldiers of the 29th Punjaub N.I., who had been guilty of treachery during the eventful night of the 2nd December, while making the flank march on the Peiwar Kotul. The Court-martial assembled on the 20th December, at the Kurram fort, for the trial of Sepoy Hazrat Shah, "for having unlawfully loaded and discharged his rifle with intent to communicate intelligence to the enemy." The prisoner was found guilty of the charge, and was condemned to death by hanging. Another Sepoy, Mira Baz, of the same corps, was tried for a similar offence, but was acquitted, though he was brought in guilty on the second count, which charged him with firing his rifle, "thereby causing risk of disclosing to the enemy the position of the column, and producing alarm and confusion in the same;" and was sentenced to be imprisoned with hard labour for two years. Before the same Court-martial, on the following day, Jemadar* Razan Shah, of the 29th Punjaub N.I., was charged with having, on the same occasion, "after becoming aware that Hazrat Shah, of his company, had unlawfully fired his rifle, with intent to communicate intelligence to the enemy, omitted to disclose the same to his commanding or other superior officer, and not having reported any of the circumstances of the case until the 5th December following." The Jemadar was found guilty, and sentenced to be transported for seven years. Before the same Court-martial, on the same day, seventeen other soldiers of the 29th Punjaubees, were arraigned for "having, in time of war, on the 2nd December, whilst the regiment was engaged with the enemy near the Spingawi Kotul, quitted their regiment without leave and returned to camp, and having thus remained in camp without authority until the return of the regiment on the following day." The whole of the prisoners were found guilty of the charge, and were sentenced, five of them to transportation for 14 years, eight for 10 years, two for 7 years, one to be imprisoned with hard labour for 2 years, and one for 365 days.

General Roberts confirmed all these sentences, and issued a general order, dated the 23rd December, which he directed to be read at the head of each Native Regiment under his command, in Urdu and Pushtu, in which, while expressing his sorrow "for the stain reflected on a gallant and distinguished Regiment, by the misconduct of some of its members," he described the act of the Sepoy under sentence of death as one "of gross treachery, and which, had it succeeded, would, in all probability, have involved, not only his own Regiment, but the rest of the force associated with it, in one common disaster." The sentences passed on the deserters, the General declared, "were not more than the crime deserved; indeed, the Court-martial would have been justified in sentencing one and all of

---

* Jemadar is a native officer of the rank of Lieutenant.

the prisoners to death." Finally, he expressed his trust that the sentences "will serve as a warning, and that all native soldiers who enlist in the service of Her Majesty the Queen of England and Empress of India will clearly understand, that while in that service, they must loyally and faithfully carry out all and every duty they may be called upon to perform."

On the following day, at 11 A.M., the sentence of death was carried out on Hazrat Shah, in presence of the troops of the Kurram Field Force, who were formed up in a hollow square, and the prisoner met his fate with the stoicism of his race. There can be no doubt that the execution proved a salutary lesson to the native soldiers, who were incited by the Moollahs, and the proclamations of the Ameer, preaching a "Jehad," or holy war, to place the requirements of their religion before the duties they owed to the State whose salt they had eaten.

After the execution, the 5th Punjaub N.I. marched for Thull and Kohat, with the convoy of sick and wounded, the ordnance captured on the Peiwar Kotul packed on elephants, and the prisoners sentenced to transportation and imprisonment. On their departure the troops prepared to move into winter quarters, as it was evident from information received that no attack would be made from Cabul on the British positions in the Kurram valley, while the inhabitants of this valley were satisfied to exchange the mild *régime* of the conqueror for that of their Afghan oppressor. The 5th Goorkhas and one company of the 72nd Highlanders, under Major Fitz Hugh, were detailed to occupy the Kurram Fort, where the supplies and ammunition were stored, the remaining three companies of the Highlanders being quartered at the Afghan cantonment near Peiwar, called Habib Killa, after the nearest village (but afterwards re-christened Peiwar), while they were enabled to give a support, if required, to the garrison of the Peiwar Kotul, which consisted of three guns G Battery, 3rd Brigade, R.A., four companies of the 8th Regiment, and the 2nd Punjaubees.

General Roberts had determined to proceed on an expedition into the Khost valley, with the object of "investigating its resources in men and supplies, and to ascertain to what extent the combination of the inhabitants of the country against us could affect our line of communications." There were subsidiary considerations that influenced the General—who had no intention of annexing the Khost valley, though subsequently it was formally surrendered to him by the Afghan Governor—in undertaking this expedition; among which were the exploration of the road from the west end of the valley to Ghuznee, and to discover the practicability of despatching a force for the punishment of the Wuzeerees, who had been giving some trouble on our frontier, and whose chief town, Kanigoram, was not far distant. The Khost country was marked on the map as a blank, and the streams that run into the Kurram valley at Hazir Pir were only defined at their embouchure. Captain Carr, Deputy-Assistant Quartermaster-General, had reconnoitred to a little distance beyond the first march into the valley, and reported the country open and accessible for cavalry, but beyond this it was a perfect *terra incognita*.

On the 27th December, General Roberts struck his camp near the Kurram fort, and marched with a squadron of the 10th Hussars, F Battery, A Brigade, R.H.A., the 29th Punjaub N.I., and No. 1. Mountain Battery, to Ibrahimzai, a distance of 15 miles, on the way threading the Darwaza Pass, in which a few camp followers were killed by a body of 60 or 80 marauders, who, however, were driven off by a working party of the 23rd Pioneers, and three of their number captured. The road lay for the first part along the banks of the Kurram, and then crossed the Kermanah River. About six miles from Kurram was a large fort and a walled village, like others in this country, where preparation for defence is the only protection against oppression. As General Roberts passed this and the other fortified villages on the road, the walls were lined with women and children, while the men collected on the bank below and respectfully saluted the lord of the invincible legions.

At two o'clock, camp was pitched near the village of Ibrahimzai, and, on the following morning, the 28th December, General Roberts marched with headquarters and wing of the 12th Bengal Cavalry to Hazir Pir, a distance of about sixteen miles, the road being through or along cultivation the whole way, except when crossing some ravines. On the way Suddar was passed, where a company of the 21st Punjaub N.I. was employed making a road to Hazir Pir, a mile above which the column crossed the Kurram River at a ford. At Hazir Pir was already encamped a force under the command of Colonel Cochrane, of the 8th Regiment, consisting of No. 2 Mountain Battery, 5th Punjaub Cavalry, and the 21st Punjaub N.I., who were located on a site sheltered from the north wind by a low range of hills, at the angle formed by the confluence of a stream which drained the valley leading to Khost.

On the 2nd January, 1879, at nine in the morning, General Roberts commenced his march for Khost, with the following troops, which were drawn chiefly from that portion of the Kurram Field Force that had not yet been engaged, and had been concentrated at Hazir Pir:—Squadron 10th Hussars, three troops 5th Punjaub Cavalry, Nos. 1 and 2 Mountain Batteries, 21st and 28th regiments of Punjaub N.I., and wing of the 72nd Highlanders, 200 men, who had marched up from Kohat. The Infantry was in command of Colonel Barry Drew, the Cavalry, of Colonel Hugh Gough, C.B., V.C., ; and the Artillery, of Lieutenant-Colonel A. Lindsay, R.A. Nearly 900 camels accompanied the column for the carriage of supplies, as the productions of the country were as unknown as its topography. In the camp at Hazir Pir were left three guns, F Battery, A Brigade, R.H.A., one company 8th Regiment, wing 12th Bengal Cavalry, and wing 29th Punjaub N.I.* The 23rd Pioneers, who were engaged road-making in the Darwaza Pass, were under orders to proceed, on its completion, to the camp at Hazir Pir.

The first day's march of the Khost column was ten miles to Jaji Maidan, a cluster of about ten villages, situated in a basin formed by low hills, forming the head of the valley leading to Khost. This valley or basin, which has a breadth varying from three to five miles, though fertile, is quite uncultivated, owing to the insecurity of life and property, for between the

---

* The remainder of the Kurram Field Force was disposed as follows for the winter:—At Thull, 3 guns F Battery, A Brigade, Royal Horse Artillery, one troop 5th Punjaub Cavalry, one company 8th Regiment, and wing 29th Punjaub N.I.; at Kurram Fort, one company, 72nd Highlanders, half troop 12th Bengal Cavalry, and 5th Goorkhas. At the Peiwar Kotul and vicinity, three companies 72nd Highlanders; wing, 8th Regiment, three guns G Battery, 3rd Brigade, Royal Artillery, one squadron 12th Bengal Cavalry, 2nd Punjaub N.I., and company of Sappers and Miners.

Entry into the Khost Valley.

Afghan rulers and the freebooters inhabiting the mountains that dominate the valley, the industrious husbandman (if the term can be applied to the inhabitants of any part of Afghanistan and its appanages) had little chance of reaping the fruits of his toil. Camp was pitched near the chief village in the rice fields, which are dry and suitable at this season. The people were very civil, and the camp was abundantly supplied with provisions.

On the following morning the march was resumed, for five miles over open country, when it became rough and steep, the hills closing in on the road on either side. So slow was the rate of progression, the cavalry having to go in single file, that it was nearly noon before the rearguard marched out of camp, the Jaji villagers watching with interest the progress of the never-ending column. The scene from the Kotul was extensive and not wanting in beauty. At the end of the descent lay the plain of the Khost country, with a distant blue line of mountains blocking the horizon to the south, and smaller ranges in front. General Roberts reached the summit of the Pass about noon, but as, owing to the nature of the road, the camels of the Commissariat convoy, carrying fifteen days' provisions for the column, could not arrive till dark, he gave instructions that they should be halted at the village of Dhani, about one mile on the Jaji Maidan side of the Kotul, and, in order to guard against an attack of Mangals, a squadron of the 5th Punjaub Cavalry, No. 1 Mountain Battery, and the 21st Punjaub N.I., were halted as an escort.

The remainder of the force pitched camp at Nar, one of the Bakh group of villages at the northern end of the Khost district, the total distance traversed from the Jaji villages being eleven miles, four miles of which, from the Kotul to a nullah, were very difficult. The headmen of the village showed a want of friendliness in not presenting themselves before the General, who thereupon sent for them, and warned them to be careful against displaying hostility towards the British, and promised them good treatment if they behaved well; at the same time the prices to be paid for stores were settled with them.

During the 4th of January a halt was made at Nar, to which the Commissariat camels and escort marched on the following morning without molestation, and advantage was taken of the rest by that indefatigable and excellent surveyor, Captain Woodthorpe, R.E., who commenced the survey of the country, which, beginning at the highest hill of the range, was prosecuted during the stay of the column in Khost, until the whole of the country was mapped out. Hence, although owing to political considerations, which demanded its ultimate abandonment, the result of the invasion of this hitherto unknown valley was *nil*, at least geographical science benefited largely, and what was a blank on our map is now accurately delineated.

General Roberts's attention was again drawn to the careless way in which the camels were loaded, and he issued a stringent order on this vital question of transport, directing regimental officers to see personally to proper loading, the neglect of which, apart from humanitarian considerations, not only causes the deaths of these valuable animals, and consequent loss to the Exchequer and crippling of the mobility of a force, but in traversing passes, or marching in single-file, necessitates the halt of the entire column while one load is being re-adjusted.

On the 5th January, at the usual hour for marching, 9 A.M., the force proceeded, and as the country was open, the baggage marched in two broad columns, under a guard, the mules on one side and the camels on the other, so that the march of seven miles was concluded by 1 P.M. The road lay across a plain, past a fortified serai and village, and across the Kam Khost, or little Khost River, to the village of Khubi, containing about 1,000 souls, near to which the camp was pitched. General Roberts, accompanied by his Staff, proceeded to reconnoitre the road over the pass in the range, which would form the morrow's march, but observing a party of horsemen, whom he concluded were the Governor of the Khost district—with whom he had been in correspondence for some weeks—and escort, coming to pay his respects to him, he rode back to camp, as a meeting in the road might have borne the appearance of his advancing to meet the Sirdar halfway.[*]

---

[*] The particulars of the marches and events in this expedition to the Khost country are derived from Major Colquhoun's work, "With the Kurram Field Force," and from General Roberts's despatches, of which he kindly sent copies of this and his other campaigns in Afghanistan from Calcutta to the author.

His conjecture was correct, and, at 3 P.M., the Acting-Governor, Akram Khan by name, came with a large number of attendants and principal maliks, or headmen, and was received by the General in the Durbar tent. The Sirdar was about forty-five or fifty years of age, and the expression of his face was not of a character to inspire confidence. He had not been long in Khost, having previously served for seven years in the Kurram valley as Deputy-Governor under Sirdar Wali Mahomed, whose deputy he was now at Khost. During the interview, which was brief, Akram Khan promised, on the arrival of General Roberts at Matun, to make over to him the fort and all the records of the Khost country.

On Monday, the 6th January, the column marched with the baggage animals and camp followers, under an escort, in the centre, the force being divided into two equal portions in front and rear. The road, after passing for three miles across an open plain, led over a kotul, and then for about two miles through some low hills, till the plain was reached, in which are situated Matun and numerous other villages. As the baggage column defiled through the Pass, flanking parties crowned the heights on either side. On reaching the brow of the slope overlooking the Matun valley, the squadron 10th Hussars, which formed the advance-guard, halted, when the Governor and his escort rode up, and was soon joined by General Roberts, who, escorted by the Hussars, proceeded in company with Akram Khan towards Matun, about three miles distant. On arriving within half a mile of the fort, the General halted the Hussars on the open ground where the camp was subsequently pitched, and, accompanied by his staff and only a few files of the 10th, rode into the fort up to the door of the keep, where the Governor had his private quarters.

The fort of Matun, which is about eight miles distant from Khubi, is described as a square walled enclosure, with circular corner bastions, the length of the side being about one hundred yards. The interior was occupied by huts along the outer walls, which were used as barracks and stables. Over the gateway leading into the fort, which was reached by a road crossing the exterior ditch, was a suite of rooms, which was occupied by the Governor's brother. In the centre of the fort was the keep, a smaller square enclosure, with round towers at two of the angles.

As General Roberts neared the fort, the garrison, consisting of 200 juzailchees, or matchlock-men, were drawn up at the entrance, in two lines, "with red silk triangular banners at the end of the lines." The British General was greeted by the beating of tomtoms, and, as he rode through the gateway, each man saluted by raising his hand to his forehead. General Roberts dismounted at the entrance to the keep, and, accompanied by his staff, was conducted to a room on the ground floor, having access to the garden, which occupied the centre of the enclosure, above the level of which it was raised some three feet. The floor was covered with a coarse felt cloth, with strips of a superior quality arranged around three sides for visitors to sit or recline, but the General preferred to remain standing. Tea, without milk, according to the Afghan manner, was handed round during the interview, which lasted about half an hour, at the conclusion of which General Roberts and his staff remounted their horses and returned to the escort. The great defect of the fort as a military position was the absence of water, which appeared to be derived from the surface irrigation canal passing close by it; but as this could be easily diverted from the point of its leaving the Matun river, an attempt had been made to find water inside the fort, and a well had been dug to a depth of about sixty feet, but without result.

The whole of the force having arrived, the camp was pitched, facing outwards, the headquarters tent being in the centre, thus obviating the necessity of rear-guards. General Roberts, forewarned by Akram Khan, who stated that he had received information of large numbers of Mangals assembling, and that they were being joined by some of the inhabitants of the Khost valley, with the object of attacking the British camp, took every precaution against a surprise.

The attitude of the people was unfriendly, and the Maliks, even when summoned to attend General Roberts, appeared uneasy, and asked permission to return before they accompanied him to the camp. The General had hoped that, as had happened with the Turis and Jajis of the Kurram valley, the people would soon become reassured, and accept the presence of the British troops as inevitable, but Akram Khan undeceived him, and stated that the moollahs, of which the district possessed a large number, famous for their fanaticism, had been engaged in fanning the religious prejudices of the people, who were summoned to attack the camp and expel the invaders.

Before night closed in, the Mangals commenced to assemble in the neighbouring villages in the valley, upon which the General instructed Colonel Waterfield, the political officer with the column, to send "purwanas," or written notices, to the Maliks, warning them that if the camp was attacked, summary and severe retribution would be exacted on the villages which had harboured the Mangals or other persons having hostile intentions towards the British. This at first had the desired effect, for before midnight nearly all the Maliks from Matun, as the cluster of walled villages is called, came into camp and informed the General that the Mangals had departed for their homes, and they offered to remain in camp as hostages for the good behaviour of the villagers.

The night passed quietly, but, on the following morning, some Maliks whom General Roberts had sent to ascertain if the Mangals had really dispersed to their homes, returned with the information that the men were on their way when they were met by large numbers of their tribesmen proceeding to Matun, and that the whole had returned. They also announced that other hillmen were assembled in the valley, and that the camp would certainly be attacked that night by many thousands of men. On receipt of this intelligence the General sent out a troop of the 5th Punjaub Cavalry, under Major J. C. Stewart, accompanied by Captain Carr, Deputy-Assistant-Quartermaster-General, to endeavour to ascertain the real state of affairs. The troop had not ridden two miles when it was fired upon, and soon it became clear that the enemy had collected round three sides of the camp. "It was evident to me," says the General in his despatch, "that the time had arrived when prompt and vigorous action was required to ensure our safety. The strength of the column, which amounted to about 2,000 men, all told, was insignificant in comparison with the number we might find arrayed against us. We were separated by many miles of difficult country from our nearest support, and I judged it to be a matter of urgent necessity that the tribes who had dared to organise an attack on our camp should receive speedy and severe punishment." It became apparent that a hot day's work was in store for the British force, as these fierce hillmen, whose country had never yet suffered the humiliation of a hostile visit from the conquerors of India, were anxious to measure themselves against the invaders of their valley. On his part, General Roberts completed his arrangements with deliberation, and the troops, which had been directed to fall in about 9.30 A.M., to repel an attack from the north-west, were dismissed, as it became apparent that the enemy's plan of action embraced a simultaneous onslaught from all sides. At about noon a stampede of grasscutters and camelmen from the north-east direction, where no enemy had been observed, showed that the Mangals had completed their movement of surrounding the British camp.

In the first instance General Roberts reinforced Major Stewart's troops with all his disposable Cavalry, under Colonel Gough, retaining only 25 sabres, and sent in support six companies of the 28th Punjaubees, under Colonel Hudson, and No. 2 Mountain Battery, under Captain Swinley. These troops operated to the north-west of the camp, where the enemy appeared in greatest strength. The villages in the plain were found to have been evacuated by the enemy, who occupied in great force the low hills at the foot of the mountains. The 10th Hussars, 70 sabres, under Major Bulkeley, dismounting, took up a position on the crest of some low mounds, and opened fire on the enemy, as did the 5th Punjaub Cavalry, 130 men, from the foot of some detached hills on the right. The Afghans retired, on which the cavalry took up an advanced position, and a troop of the 5th Punjaubees, under Major Williams, made a brilliant charge up another hill, in the centre of the enemy's position, and, rapidly dismounting, commenced to harass them in their retreat. The cavalry kept up so close and effective a fire that the enemy gave way at all points and fled up the rocks, and nothing remained for the 28th Punjaubees to do on their arrival, though the Mountain Battery made excellent practice, and completed their dispersion. A prominent object in the sky line was a Malik, who fearlessly displayed a banner as a rallying point to his followers, until a well-directed shell utterly destroyed him, and in Homeric phraseology,

" Everlasting slumber closed his eyes."

While these troops operated to the north-west of the camp, where the enemy appeared to be in greatest strength, the right, or eastern, flank was protected by a wing of the 21st Punjaub N.I., under Major Collis, and two guns of No. 1 Mountain Battery; the other wing of the 21st Punjaubees, under Captain Carruthers, and the remaining two guns of No. 1 Mountain Battery, covered the rear of the camp, and the front and left flank were defended by the wing of the 72nd Highlanders, under Lieutenant-Colonel Clarke. The whole of the troops in and around the camp were placed under the command of Colonel Drew, who was directed to hold his own until Colonel Gough had disposed of the enemy in his front, which he did in the manner to be expected of an officer of his military talent and experience.

General Roberts having made his arrangements for the defence of the camp, started off to watch the progress of the attack on the heights, under Colonel Gough. He was only accompanied by his staff, as by some mistake the twenty-five men of the 5th Punjaub Cavalry, who should have remained in camp under Colonel Drew's orders, had marched with their regiment; and he left with that officer his personal escort of eight Sowars. Immediately after he quitted the camp, says an officer who was present, the enemy, who occupied the villages towards the north-east, began to show themselves, on which Captain Morgan's two guns were brought into action, and threw shells amidst the masses with such excellent effect, that they retreated towards the villages in their rear, and to the south. This they were enabled to do without hindrance, as the few Sowars sent out against them were brought up by a water-course, impassable in this direction. The enemy opened a heavy fusilade in the rear to the south, from some old Afghan cavalry lines and a walled village, and the fire was returned by the left wing of the 21st Punjaubees, and two guns of No. 1 Mountain Battery, supported by Captain Spens's detachment of

Highlanders. The shell fire quickly dislodged the tribesmen, who retreated beyond the range of the guns, while the discharges of musketry became brisk and roused the echoes on the hillside in that lonely valley. Byron describes a similar scene :—

> "And pealing wide or ringing near
> It echoes on the throbbing ear,
> The death shot hissing from afar;
> The shock, the shouts, the groan of war,
> Reverberate along that vale,
> More suited to the shepherd's tale."

Meanwhile, Colonel Gough's attack on the enemy in the north-west having succeeded in driving them to the mountain top, he retired the force under his command slowly and steadily, and so cowed were the enemy that they made no attempt to harass him. Before this, General Roberts, who had witnessed the fighting, ordered a troop of the 5th Punjaub Cavalry, under Major Stewart, to follow him, and returned to camp about 2.30, when he directed the wing of the 21st Punjaub N.I., with the detachment 72nd on their flank, and the mountain guns, to follow up the enemy retreating to the east and south-east, and to burn the villages which had harboured them during the night. Colonel Drew proceeded with the main body for about three miles and burnt five villages, which were found to be deserted, and Captain Carruthers, with the left wing of the 21st, occupied and burnt a village in the south-east direction, and also a second village, which was first shelled, as the enemy appeared inclined to make a stand. Crossing the Matun river a third village was fired, the guns meantime shelling a crowd of the enemy, who streamed across the plain to the spurs of the range which closed the valley to the south. The troop of the 5th Punjaub Cavalry, under Major Stewart, which had followed General Roberts to camp, made a very effective charge on a large body of the enemy, who were escaping from the rear of a village in which Captain Carruthers' wing of the 21st was advancing. Major Stewart rode them down, killing over 20 of their number, and many more would have fallen beneath the "tulwars" of the Punjaubee horsemen but that they got away to the stony bed of a broad nullah, commanded by a high bank, lined with matchlock-men whose fire compelled Major Stewart to withdraw his men. Soon the 21st came up, and the advance was continued against a village beyond the bank, into which the enemy had retired. On seeing themselves again threatened, the tribesmen evacuated the village, but a party of about 80 of them, finding their retreat cut off, ran back, and, after some parley, surrendered. On examining them, Colonel Waterfield, the political officer, discovered that they did not belong to the Khost country, but were Waziris. Accordingly, they were taken to the camp, and General Roberts directed that they should be placed under charge of the 21st Punjaub N.I., as it was his intention to demand a ransom of fifty-eight rupees per man from the Garbaz section of the tribe to which they belonged.

In the evening, General Roberts sent for the headmen of Matun, and told them that they had brought this punishment on themselves, that it had been his earnest desire to have avoided all bloodshed, and that they must now see the futility of attempting to withstand disciplined troops, though greatly inferior in numbers. During the next few days the headmen of the Khost district came into camp, and the General impressed on them the views he had enunciated to the Matun maliks, and assured them they had nothing to fear so long as they abstained from hostile acts, the sole object he had in view in entering their country being to oust the government of the Ameer of Cabul. "There is evidence," wrote General Roberts to the Viceroy, "that the combination against us was widespread, and that if a severe example had not been made of those who fought against us on the 7th inst., the ill-feeling would have extended. It might, under the circumstances, have become impossible to leave any portion of my small column here. The aspect of affairs is now changed; the headmen of nearly all the neighbouring villages have come in, and the remainder are reported to be anxious to submit." But the change was more apparent than real, and the opinion, in which Colonel Waterfield concurred, that "an adequate force could now be left here with safety, provided that the troops in the Kurram valley are maintained in sufficient strength to keep open our long line of communications," was soon proved to be fallacious. The sturdy tribesmen were irreconcilable in their enmity, which perhaps was not surprising, as the punishment they had received was undoubtedly severe, though similar to what it has always been the custom to mete out to refractory hillmen in our dealings on the north-west frontier. Burning the habitations of the Khostwallies in the depth of winter appears a harsh measure to our English views, but it was no more than the people merited, and such as they anticipated, for the troops found them all deserted; but the nearest villages to the west were left uninjured, as the inhabitants had acted up to their engagements, and warned the camp followers not to proceed beyond their protection, while those further off in this direction, which had afforded shelter to the enemy, were spared, as it was considered that sufficient punishment had been inflicted.

It was estimated that the combined tribes taking part in this attack, numbered 6,000 men, of whom 2,000, chiefly Mangals, attacked the camp from the north-west. The Jadrans and Waziris, with the Khost people in league with them, were engaged on the south and east sides. The defeat of the combined tribes had been complete, and the effect of it was apparent during the remainder of the stay of the British troops in the Khost country; while it had been achieved with the nominal loss of only two killed and six wounded.

It would appear that this attack was part of a combination against the infidel invaders, by the Mangals and Jajis, as, at the same time, taking advantage of the absence of the column in Khost, these tribes organized an onslaught on the Peiwar Kotul. 4,000 of them, assisted by 2,000 of the Hasan Kheyl section of the Jajis, advanced against the British blockhouses on the crest of the Pass. But Brigadier-General Thelwall—warned of their approach by the gallant and able Captain Rennick, of the 29th N.I., political officer at Ali Kheyl, who kept at his post with only twenty men—ordered up reinforcements from Kurram and Habib Killa, and though, on the 6th January, a body of 1,500 of the enemy approached close to the British position, they feared to make the attack, and retired on finding all preparations complete for their reception.*

---

* General Roberts had received a report from General Thelwall of this intended attack on the 6th of January, and sent 200 Goorkhas to his assistance, but he telegraphed to Government that as everything had been placed in a state of defence at Peiwar Kotul, he saw no necessity for calling on Kurram Fort for assistance.

An Attempted Rescue.

During the evening of the 8th January the Waziri prisoners made a desperate attempt to escape, which was frustrated, though not without some loss of life. About 7 P.M., it being dark, the moon not having risen, one of them managed to escape from the guard, a strong party of the 21st Punjaub N.I., under a Subadar, but was shot dead by the picket near which he passed. Instantly a shot was fired from the bank of a watercourse, showing that the attempt was part of an organized effort to effect a rescue, upon which the whole of the eighty-six prisoners, "who were secured by their hands being tied to ropes which were picketed down to tent poles, rose as one man, and began to try to free themselves, crying out, 'Now is the time to run.'" Subahdar Makkan Singh, in command of the guard, called out to the prisoners in Pushtoo to sit down or they would be fired upon, but without avail, and those of the prisoners who succeeded in freeing themselves rushed at the sentries and tried to deprive them of their arms. The native officer gave the order to fire, and on receiving a volley, which told with fatal effect on the struggling mass, they threw themselves flat down, and quiet was immediately restored. On separating the dead and wounded from the untouched it was found that nine had been killed, including three who had managed to clear themselves of their bonds, one had escaped, and fourteen were wounded, five mortally, and one severely, leaving sixty-three uninjured. The wounded were carefully attended to, and the remainder of the survivors, by General Roberts's directions, divided into three parties under separate guards. The firing created an alarm in the camp, but perfect order prevailed; the troops fell in and took their appointed stations in case of a night attack, "and in less than five minutes from the first alarm, every one was at his post."

During this affair a party of horsemen, under a friendly Malik, who were passing along the south-west flank of the camp, failed to return the challenge of the sentry, who fired at them, when the chief was wounded in the shoulder. The night's proceedings were concluded by the cavalry being sent to scour the neighbourhood of the camp, and as they returned with the report that no enemy was in sight, the troops were dismissed and quiet reigned once more around.

During the 9th detachments were sent out to bring in the grain from the deserted and partially burnt villages, and a considerable body of men were observed on the low ranges of hills to the north, who had come from Yakubi to loot the camp, as they had been informed that the Mangals had gained a glorious victory in the fighting of the 7th, and they naturally desired to share in the plunder; but on arriving at the end of the pass overlooking the plain, they found to their amazement the tents standing and all secure in the British camp. So confident had they been of the truth of the intelligence brought to them that, headed by their Maliks, they treacherously seized and ill-treated a small party of eight Sowars left under their protection to guard the mail to Hazir Pir. On learning the true state of affairs the Maliks restored to the troopers their horses, arms, and clothes, of which they had robbed them, though this did not satisfy the Sowars, who loading their carbines, forced the two Maliks who had ill-treated them to accompany them to the camp. There an investigation was made into the circumstances of the case, and the Maliks were tried by a General Court-martial presided over by Colonel Gough (the offence being against the Military law), and were sentenced to seven years' transportation.

General Roberts, having resolved to make a reconnoissance in force towards the west end of the valley, occupied the fort of Matun, some rooms in which were utilised as a hospital, tents being pitched within the area for the remainder of the sick. Colonel Collis was placed in command of the fort with his regiment, the 21st Punjaub N.I., and a troop of the 5th Punjaub Cavalry, under Captain Vousden; and Mr. A. Christie, Bengal Civil Service, remained with him, as Political Officer.

CHAPTER XI.

General Roberts makes a Tour of the Valley—Army Signalling in Khost—Durbar of the Headmen of the Khostiwals and Mangals—Evacuation of Matun and Return March to Hazir Pir—Preparations for the Advance on Cabul—Reconnoissance by General Roberts—Conclusion of the Treaty of Gundamuck—Arrival at Ali Kheyl of the Cavagnari Mission—General Roberts Returns to Simla.

On the morning of the 13th January General Roberts, accompanied by Akram Khan, marched with the following troops:—Squadron 10th Hussars, three troops 5th Punjaub Cavalry, Nos. 1 and 2 Mountain Batteries, left wing 72nd Highlanders, and 28th Punjaub N.I. The first day's march was to Dehgan, a village six miles distant from the camp, the route being across the river Matun and over a deep watercourse and a nullah, on the opposite bank of which the people assembled in great numbers as though to oppose the crossing, but, on inquiry, it was found that their object was the peaceful one of selling supplies to the strangers, whose custom of paying for all they required, when they could take what they wanted, was one that baffled their philosophy. The prices asked were four annas (sixpence) for a fowl, and four or five shillings for a sheep.

The column halted at Dehgan for a day, and General Roberts, escorted by a troop of the 10th Hussars, and one of the 5th Punjaub Cavalry, rode across the plain on which the camp was pitched, to the village of Durgai, at the southern end of the valley, occupied by the Thunnies. The General was respectfully received by the villagers, and, assembling the head men in an open spot in the centre, he addressed them in English, his words being translated, sentence by sentence, by Mahomed Hyat Khan, Assistant Political Officer, warning them against any act of hostility, and holding them responsible for keeping him advised of any projected raids by their brethren in the hills. The headmen presented the General with a sheep as a peace-offering, after receiving which he rode through the village with his staff and a small party, and, passing round it, rejoined his escort.

Thence General Roberts rode to another village in the west end of the valley, about four miles from Dehgan, where he again assembled and addressed the headmen, and then proceeded to a third village, where he repeated his warning, and rested his horses for an hour. Camp was reached about 4.30, when he was greeted with intelligence of an apprehended attack by the Mangals that night. But though 2,000 of them had, it was reported, sworn on the Koran to attack the camp, the night passed without any alarm, though shelter-trenches were thrown up, and other arrangements made to receive them. On the following day the column returned to Matun.

As there was little forage for the camels, 400 of them, whose loads had been consumed, were sent back to Hazir Pir, under escort of a body of Turis of the Kurram valley, and, on the 18th, a convoy, with fifteen days' supplies, for which the General had sent, arrived from Hazir Pir, escorted by the 23rd Pioneers and a detachment of the 5th Goorkhas, under Captain Cook, which latter returned on the following morning escorting the remainder of the camels whose loads had been consumed.

On the 19th January, the survey party, under Captain Woodthorpe, escorted by a detachment of the 28th Punjaub N.I., proceeded to survey the southern range which lay in Waziri territory, their safety being guaranteed by the chief of the Atakheyl section of the Waziris, Keeput by name, who arrived in camp with some followers, and, after paying his respects to the General, accompanied the surveyors. Captain Wynne, Superintendent of Army Signalling, who accompanied the survey party, on reaching the highest peak of the range, named Lazam, heliographed to the camp, twenty miles distant, and also to Bunnoo, on the British side of the frontier, a distance of thirty miles from the peak, where the message was read by Colonel Noel Money, commanding the 3rd Sikh Regiment, who fortunately had been instructed in the code, and Colonel Godby, commanding the Punjaub Frontier Force, who happened to be

A Threatened Attack.

at Bunnoo at the time, flashed back to General Roberts, through Captain Wynne, the intelligence that the Mahsood Waziris had raided and burnt Tank. Taking advantage of this means of communication, General Roberts heliographed to Lord Lytton, then at Calcutta, and the messages from the distant Khost valley, over vast ranges of mountains, reached the Viceroy within two hours, truly one of the most astonishing instances of army signalling on record.

General Roberts had determined to raise local levies, chiefly from among the friendly Turis, to hold the valley on the departure of the British troops, and on the arrival of Captain Arthur Conolly, of the Meywar Bheel Corps (a name that has an honoured, though painful, memory in our relations with Afghanistan), who had great experience in converting the wild tribes of the Indian peninsula into disciplined soldiers, directed him to embody and command 200 horse and 200 foot, in which he succeeded, though the subsequent abandonment of the valley involved their disbandment.

During the 20th January, General Roberts inspected the cavalry under Colonel Gough, and directed that a royal salute should be fired in honour of the surrender of Candahar, and the day concluded with races and athletic sports for the men. On the following day, the 23rd Pioneers marched on their return to Hazir Pir, by the eastern road, which they were directed to improve, as the General intended to return to Kurram by it. On the 22nd January, General Roberts, accompanied by his staff, and escorted by a troop of the 10th Hussars, rode towards the east end of Khost, and examined the villages, the largest in the valley, assembling and addressing the headmen as to their duties and responsibilities towards the dominant power, and returned in the afternoon after a ride of over twenty miles. Information was received on the 23rd that an attack on the camp was meditated by the Mangals, who had collected in great force about twelve miles distant; and to be prepared against a night attack, General Roberts ordered the exposed sides of the camp to be defended by an entrenchment thrown up 100 yards from the tents, and so admirably did the different regiments and batteries work, under the direction of Captain Colquhoun, R.A. (in the absence of Colonel Perkins,

R.E.), that before dark the camp was reported secure, an earthen bank, 3½ feet high, and the same width, having been thrown up in exposed parts, which, with the saddles of 1,200 camels, formed a breastwork that would defy a rush of Mangals on any part of the camp. The cavalry were sent out to reconnoitre, but returned without finding any large body of the enemy, though the villagers at the north end of the valley were defiant, and the enemy were doubtless concealed in the houses; during the day the survey party came back, having completed the examination of the Khost ranges, and connected their work with the triangulation of the Trigonometrical Survey of India.

General Roberts received in the afternoon a deputation from a party of Mangals who had settled in the Keraiah end of the Kurram valley, asking for a share in the distribution of money and turbans to those who had behaved well to British rule, and were dismissed fairly satisfied at the extent to which this request had been complied with. During the night of the 23rd, some star shells were fired to show the Mangals and other would-be enemies that the British were ready for them; the effect was excellent, the light from the shells illuminating a space, 800 yards by 400, for a distance varying from 400 to 600 yards. During the two succeeding days the defence of the camp was completed, under Lieutenant Spratt, R.E., by an earthen rampart being thrown up in place of the camel saddles, the construction of a new bastion, with abattis, at the southeast angle, filling the ditches with water, and other works. In the afternoon of the 25th January, General Roberts held in the Durbar tent an assembly of the headmen of the Khost valley, with those of the Mangals and Jadrans who cared to attend. The General, in a speech translated by Mahomed Hyat Khan, first addressed the Khost chiefs, to whom he described the arrangements that would be made on the evacuation by his troops of the valley, which would be placed temporarily under the administration of Shahzada Sultan Jan, who had been employed at Kohat in the Punjaub commission, and who would be supported, if necessary, by the British troops at Hazir Pir. General Roberts also took advantage of the opportunity to enlarge on the faithlessness of Russia towards the Ameer

Durbar of Hill Chiefs.

Shere Ali, whose troops, defeated in every encounter, had received aid neither in men nor money from that Power. Leaving Colonel Waterfield, the Political Agent, to confer with the headmen individually, and bestow rewards on those who had rendered services, the General addressed the chiefs of the hillmen, wild, fierce-looking fellows, with unkempt hair and dirty garments, but armed to the teeth, and told them in a good-humoured way that if they wanted more fighting he and his men were ready for them, but that he advised them to keep quiet. The durbars were concluded by a dinner to the headmen, for which twenty sheep were slaughtered, and the distribution of a few rupees to each man to pay his expenses.

On the 26th, General Roberts received a letter from Sirdar Wali Mahomed, son of the late Ameer Dost Mahomed by a Turi woman, and half-brother of Ameer Shere Ali, reporting his escape from Cabul, and arrival by the Shutargardan Pass at Rokian, six miles from Ali Kheyl. The General immediately sent instructions to Captain Rennick, Political Officer at Ali Kheyl, to treat the Sirdar with consideration, and escort him to Hazir Pir, where he would meet him. All the arrangements for the evacuation of the Khost valley being complete, and the Shahzada Sultan Jan having been installed as temporary Governor, on the 27th January, the thermometer marking eight degrees of frost, the return march was begun, the first stage being to the village of Sabbri, twelve miles distant.

The road from Matun lay past three detached hills, near the village of Madhi Kheyl, on the crest of the centre one of which was a field-work, said to have been made by Timour in one of his invasions of India, and, skirting the range and crossing several ravines and watercourses, the road led through a pass, about seven miles from the camp, to the banks of the Kam Khost river, across the river, and over another gorge leading into the Sabbri valley. A halt was made here on the 28th, while General Roberts reconnoitred in the direction of Thull, and the survey party took observations from the hill, about four miles to the north-east of the camp. At 10 that night the General received an express from the Governor left at Matun, reporting that the Mangals were gathering to attack the fort, with the intention of killing him and the garrison. The General quickly formed his plans, which were to remove the Khost garrison and leave the distracted valley to the tender mercies of the Mangals, or whoever chose to harry it; and, at daybreak on the 29th January, leaving as many troops as he could spare in camp at Sabbri, under the command of Brigadier-General Drew, he started for Matun with a detachment 72nd Highlanders, the squadron 10th Hussars, 5th Punjaub Cavalry, No. 2 Mountain Battery, and 28th Punjaub N.I.*

Starting at 6.15, the General arrived at the deserted camp at Matun at 9.30, when the Mangals were observed on the skirts of the hill where they had been previously defeated, but expecting an easy prey in the levies, they were evidently disinclined to try conclusions with a powerful enemy. Loading some camels he had brought with him, with grain from the fort, the General sent them in advance, under charge of the Turi levies, and, after the column had breakfasted, commenced to retire, as evacuation having been decided upon, no object would have been gained by attacking the enemy, for they could not be followed up to the hills, as General Roberts's troops had already marched twelve miles, and he was desirous of returning to his camp that day. The Mangals, who were in great force, estimated at quite 6,000, had meanwhile ventured out into the plain, about two miles off, and formed a line a mile in length, and it must have been a source of disappointment to the General, who had already once chastised them severely, that the exigencies of the public service, and the necessity for husbanding the strength of his men, prevented him from attacking them. With the limited force at his disposal it required military capacity in the commander, and steadiness on the part of the troops, to effect a retirement before these savage mountaineers, whose guerilla tactics are conducive to successful attacks on a retreating force.

The Mangals remained drawn up in anticipation of an attack, and General Roberts encouraged the belief by advancing his cavalry, which took up a position about a mile from the enemy, who commenced skirmishing in regular order, under

---

* The troops left in the camp, which was placed in a condition to repel an attack, were 200 men of the Highlanders, No. 1 Mountain Battery, and the 21st Punjaub N.I., being a total of about 1,000 men.

Evacuation of the Khost Fort.

the direction of mounted leaders, one of whom, riding a white horse, was killed by a lucky shot from the Martini-Henry of a trooper of the 10th Hussars, which had been thrown forward, in skirmishing order, about 600 yards in advance of the 5th Punjaub Cavalry. Shortly before noon the General commenced the retirement by moving off the 28th Punjaub N.I. and mountain battery, and when they had increased their distance from the Mangals to about three and a half miles, the cavalry retired, leaving the enemy in doubt as to the object of this movement. They accordingly halted, fearing to be drawn into the open plain, where the British horsemen could ride them down, and only discovered their mistake as the troopers trotted off and rejoined their comrades. Then the Mangals swarmed into the deserted entrenchment and fort, while the column, making its way unopposed, reached the camp at Sabbri about five in the afternoon, after a most fatiguing day. Precautions were taken to guard against a night attack, but none was attempted.

The march was resumed on the following day, the 30th January, and General Roberts, escorted by a troop of the 5th Punjaub Cavalry, pushed on to Hazir Pir, about twenty-four miles distant from Sabbri. The troops, under Brigadier-General Drew, made a long march of nearly twenty miles, passing through a defile in the hills intervening between the Khost and Kurram valleys, and encamped at Baghzai on the following day, making the short march of four and a half miles to Hazir Pir.

On the 1st February Sirdar Wali Mahomed, accompanied by some Maliks from the Logar valley, and escorted by Captain Rennick, from Ali Kheyl, arrived at Hazir Pir. General Roberts and Captain Conolly, now Acting Political Officer, and the General's aide-de-camp, Lieutenant Neville Chamberlain, a well-known name in Afghan annals, welcomed the Sirdar, and at noon, on the arrival of the *cortége* at the camp, Roberts, accompanied by his staff, met the Wali Mahomed at the end of the headquarters street of tents, and conducted him to his own tent, where a guard of honour and the band of the 21st Punjaub Native Infantry were drawn up to salute the distinguished guest. The General invited the Wali to dinner, but this, so far as the Sirdar was concerned, was little more than a Barmecide repast, as his Mussulman prejudices prevented him from partaking of anything more than bread and water with unbelievers.

The Indian Government appeared to consider the Wali Mahomed in the British camp as a matter of considerable political importance, which subsequent events hardly justified, as the Wali was a man of no ability, and by his descent from a low-born Turi woman could have but slight pretensions to the Ameership of a people like the Afghans, who think so highly of "blue blood." Under orders from the Viceroy, on the 4th February the Sirdar started for Jellalabad, *viâ* Thull, Kohat, and Peshawur, in order to confer with Major Cavagnari, Chief Political Agent, and with Sir Samuel Browne, commanding the Khyber column.

On the day before the Wali's departure, General Roberts, being desirous of examining the roads, rode to Ahmed-i-Shama, returning by another route through the hills. During the day, also, the 29th Punjaub Native Infantry, which had been encamped at Hazir Pir during the past month, marched for Thull, and the squadron 10th Hussars, greatly to the regret of their comrades in the late campaign, proceeded to join the head-quarters of their regiment with Sir Samuel Browne.

On the 4th February General Roberts broke up his camp at Hazir Pir, and, escorted by No. 2 Mountain Battery and the 28th Punjaub Native Infantry, started for Kurram fort and the Peiwar Kotul, leaving in camp three guns F Battery A Brigade Royal Horse Artillery, left wing 72nd Highlanders, 12th Bengal Cavalry, wing 5th Punjaub Cavalry, and wing 21st Punjaub Native Infantry. General Roberts entered the Kurram river at a ford, where it was 50 yards wide and 3 feet deep, and, visiting the village of Suddar, where the headmen petitioned him to remit the fines imposed for their ill-treatment of the troopers placed under their protection, a request he refused, arrived at Ibrahimzai, where his camp was pitched. On the following day Kurram was reached, and on the 7th, General Roberts, having inspected the upper and lower forts, marched with the same escort for the Peiwar Kotul and Habib Killa; on the same day Brigadier-General Cobbe, who

The Punjaub Chiefs' Contingent.

had sufficiently recovered from the wound received on the 2nd December, left for Thull, and did not return to the command of the 1st Brigade until the 2nd March following. General Roberts, after inspecting the British Camp and positions, proceeded to Thull (at this time garrisoned by the half F Battery A Brigade Royal Horse Artillery, wing 14th Bengal Lancers, and 19th Punjaub Native Infantry), and thence to Kohat, his base of operations.

At this time the Government placed at the General's disposal for keeping up the communications of the Kurram Field Force, a contingent offered by the Punjaub Chiefs, of whose services he was glad to avail himself, as it set free his forces for field operations. The contingent was commanded by Brigadier-General Watson, C.B., V.C., an officer of acknowledged gallantry and ability, who had served at Delhi and Lucknow, and was an old comrade and personal friend of the commander of the Kurram Field Force. Half of the contingent, which arrived at Kohat on the 9th February, was sent to Bunnoo on the 13th, and the remaining half marched for Thull on the following day, and arrived in time to be inspected by General Rooberts on the 19th.*

After the inspection the General left for Kohat†, 63 miles distant, which he reached on the following day. During his rest at Kohat, General Roberts turned his attention to preparing for the much desired forward movement in the spring, and forwarding two months' supplies to Kurram, for which, besides camels and local transports, 2,000 carts, each drawn by 4 bullocks, and carrying 20 maunds, or 16 cwt., were employed, the journey there and back occupying nearly a fortnight. These

---

* While at Thull General Roberts made a new disposition of the Kurram Field Force. The 2nd Brigade was to consist of the troops in advance of Kurram from Habib Killa to Ali Kheyl ; the 1st Brigade, all other troops across the frontier, at Kurram, Hazir Pir, and on the road from Kurram to Thull. The troops in British territory at Thull and Kohat to be under Brigadier-General Watson.

† The following was the Kohat garrison at this time :—Squadron 9th Lancers, half G Battery 3rd Brigade Royal Artillery ; left wing, 2nd Battalion 8th Regiment ; headquarters wing, 14th Bengal Lancers, and 5th Punjaub Infantry. During General Roberts's stay at Kohat the 92nd Gordon Highlanders and 2nd Punjaub Native Infantry joined the Kurram Field Force. The command at Kohat was held by Colonel Osborn Wilkinson, 3rd Bengal Cavalry.

arrangements completed, and having inspected the 92nd Gordon Highlanders—that magnificent Regiment whose name is identified with the most brilliant achievements of British arms in Afghanistan—which joined the Field Force under his command, General Roberts left Kohat, and, on the 4th of March, issued from Headquarters at the Kurram Camp, the orders for the movement of his troops preparatory to their reassembly at Kurram on the 15th of the month.

On 11th March, General Roberts, with his staff, arrived at Shinnak, 26 miles from Thull, where he was met by Brigadier-General Watson, who had been making a flying visit to Kurram Valley and Peiwar Kotul, and they proceeded in company to Thull, to receive the Commander-in-Chief, Sir Frederick Haines, who was expected to make an inspection of the Kurram Field Force. On the arrival of his Excellency with the Headquarter Staff of the Army, General Roberts accompanied him to Kurram, where, on their arrival on the 22nd, they were received by Brigadier-General Drew, and in the afternoon the troops assembled there were inspected, when their smart appearance elicited the encomiums of Sir Frederick Haines, who, on the conclusion of the inspection, called the officers to the front, and complimented General Roberts on the gallantry and good conduct of his men. During his visit the Commander-in-Chief inspected the Fort and Regimental Hospitals, and, accompanied by General Roberts, went to Habib Killa, where he inspected the 72nd Highlanders, No. 2 Mountain Battery, and 2nd Punjaub Infantry, and thence rode to the Peiwar Kotul, where the garrison, consisting of half of the 9th Battery 3rd Brigade, Royal Artillery, and a wing of the 2nd Battalion 8th Regiment, were inspected, and the party made their way through six inches of snow to one of the Block houses in the Pass. On the 26th of March the Commander-in-Chief left Kurram on his return to India, and was accompanied by General Roberts as far as Shinnak, whence he rode back the twenty-six miles to Kurram, in one day, amid pouring rain, which made the road across the cultivated land as heavy as a bog.

During the next few days the 72nd Highlanders and 23rd and 28th Native Regiments marched to Ali Kheyl, in the

Preparations for the Advance.

Hurriab Valley, as it was desirable to occupy that place before the melting of the snow from the Shutargardan Pass permitted its seizure by the enemy, and the 67th Regiment, C. Battery 4th Brigade, Royal Artillery, and Headquarter wing 14th Bengal Lancers, were pushed on into the Kurram Valley, the 5th Goorkhas and 21st Punjaub Native Infantry, which were to form part of the force held in readiness for the apprehended march on Cabul, being moved up. Carriage for supplies and stores was now, as always, the great difficulty, owing to the death of the camels, and the scarcity of suitable mules; but all difficulties were overcome by the energy impressed into the officers of the Transport Department by the example of General Roberts, who appeared to be ubiquitous, personally inquiring into everything, and encouraging every one to increased exertion. There being a paucity of animals for the transport of Ordnance Stores, the General ordered the Artillery horses and mules to be employed, and natives were engaged to carry the ammunition, about 200 tons, over the Peiwar Kotul itself.

On the 1st of April General Roberts established his headquarters at Byan Kheyl, in the Hurriab Valley, on the further side of the Peiwar Kotul, where he went to inspect the roadmaking, and on the 6th, returned to Kurram from visiting Ali Kheyl where, three days later, he was joined by the 92nd Higlanders and half of the 9th Battery 3rd Brigade, Royal Artillery.

On the same day the General, accompanied by Colonels Gough and Lindsay, commanding the Cavalry and Artillery of the Force, rode out to pay a visit to a leading Turi Chief, Noor Mohamed, who lived in a fortified village about six miles from Kurram. The Chief happened to be absent, but the General was received by his representative, who offered for his acceptance a handsome carpet, which, however, he declined. Noor Mohamed returned the visit next day, attended by a following of horse and footmen. General Roberts, desirous of winning the confidence of all classes, paid a visit, two days later, to the camp of a large number of Ghilzyes, returning to the Logar valley with their flocks, who appreciated the honour, and hospitably received the "Lord Sahib."

Throughout his stay in the Kurram and Khost valleys General Roberts adopted what would appear to more timid natures the hazardous course of throwing himself on the good faith of the fierce hillmen. He habitually attended Durbars and Jirgas of chiefs, sometimes numbering 200 or 300 armed men, with an escort of four Goorkhas and two Sikh orderlies of the 5th Punjaub Cavalry, who were kept in the background, and though his life was exposed to the knife or musket of any fanatic desirous of earning immortality by slaying an unbeliever, or of the avenger of blood smarting at the loss of a relative killed in battle, yet he reckoned correctly on the chivalry of his foes, and led what might be called a charmed life when conversing freely with the ferocious sectaries, any one of whom had it in his power to plunge his knife into the heart of the British general who had overthrown his people in battle, and robbed his country of her independence.

An immediate advance on Cabul being expected, the General, after an interview with the commanding officers of the regiments and batteries of his force, published a divisional order regulating the scale of carriage for all ranks. The Kurram Field Force was strengthened by the arrival of half C Battery 4th Brigade, Royal Artillery—bringing with them thirty-seven elephants for carrying the 9-pounder guns over the mountains —and the 67th Regiment, which had been sent from the Madras Presidency. The General went out to meet the new arrivals, and welcome them to the force under his command. Other reinforcements arrived during the next few days, including the 11th Bengal Native Infantry, and the Punjaub chiefs' contingent, consisting of the three arms, numbering nine British officers and 2,560 men, with seven guns, the whole under Brigadier-General Watson; the 2nd Brigade also received a new commander in Brigadier-General Forbes, General Thelwall having returned to India on sick leave. Deputy-Surgeon General Townsend also became Principal Medical officer of the Division, while the signalling department received a new chief in Captain Straton, 22nd Regiment, a gallant officer, who rendered excellent service to General Roberts during the remainder of his campaign in Afghanistan, and fell at Candahar on the 1st September, in the last action of the war.

Preparations for the Advance.

Meanwhile the regiments and batteries were being pushed on over the Peiwar Kotul into the Hurriab valley, and at 5 A.M. on the 20th April, General Roberts, accompanied by Colonel Colley (the late ill-fated General Sir George Colley), private secretary to the Viceroy, who had arrived at Kurram on the previous day, started off to ride to Rokian, in the defile beyond Ali Kheyl, and returned to the Peiwar Kotul, where they passed the night, having covered during the day no less than seventy miles of ground, including the Pass, a feat which speaks highly for the powers of endurance of both these distinguished officers, as the cold was severe and the weather inclement.

On the following day they returned to Kurram by the Spingawi route, the first visit the commander of the Field Force had paid to the scene of his memorable achievement of the 2nd December.

Undeterred by the heavy fall of snow and wretched weather, General Roberts, whose sleepless activity was the wonder of all witnesses, on the succeeding day, accompanied by Brigadier-General Watson, rode to Badesh Kheyl, seventeen miles distant, returning the same day to inspect the camels, 2,700 in number, assembled there, of which only 1,900 were passed as fit for service by a committee presided over by Major Mac Queen, 5th Punjaub Native Infantry. Every point relating to the advance and the efficiency of the force he proposed to take with him was carefully considered; and as the European portion of the Kurram garrison would be small, he took steps to render the forts defensible.

By the 29th April the arrangements for the advance from Ali Kheyl, including the storing of provisions and ammunition, and the ordnance and Engineer parks, were complete, and, on the following day, the General established his headquarters at that place, where the greater portion of the Kurram Field Force was now assembled.* The camps of the 1st and 2nd Brigades,

---

* The following was the constitution of the Kurram Field Force :—Royal Artillery under Colonel G. H. Lindsay. F Battery A Brigade Royal Horse Artillery, G Battery 3rd Brigade Royal Artillery, No. 2 Mountain Battery. Cavalry Brigade, under Colonel H. H. Gough, V.C., C.B., squadron 9th Lancers, 12th Bengal Cavalry. 14th Bengal Cavalry (Lancers). First Brigade Infantry, under Brigadier-General Cobbe, 72nd Highlanders, 5th Goorkhas, 23rd Pioneers, 28th Punjaub Native Infantry, 7th Company Sappers and Miners. Second Brigade, under Brigadier-General H. Forbes,

with the former being the headquarters, and with the latter the Artillery, were pitched on two plateaus and fortified, being surrounded by loose stone walls, with picket towers on commanding sites. The spur jutting out from Matungi, between the two plateaus and the village of Ali Kheyl, had been crowned with a series of works, the highest of which consisted of picket towers protected by ditches and scarps; also a redoubt, with emplacements for guns and parapets for infantry, and other positions on the slope of the hill were also occupied. General Roberts inspected all these works, and, on the 1st of May, accompanied by Brigadier-General Watson, rode up the Hazardarakht defile as far as Dreikulla.

On the 3rd of May a grand parade of all the troops* at Ali Kheyl and Byan Kheyl was held, and was witnessed by a concourse of the native population of the neighbourhood; but the effect of the review was much marred by a heavy thunderstorm, with rain and hail. In the afternoon the General, accompanied by the brigadiers, political officers (Colonel T. Gordon, C.S.I., and Captain Rennick) and Staff, held a durbar, which was largely attended by the headmen of the Hurriab valley. Turbans and dresses of honour as rewards for friendly conduct were distributed, and then the General made a speech, which was translated into Pushtoo by Mahomed Hyat Khan, C.S.I., Assistant-Political Officer, in which he assured his audience of the intention of the British Government to annex the Kurram and Hurriab valleys, a determination which was altered at a later period. He also warned the Jajis to keep on their good behaviour, or he would pay a hostile visit to their most secluded vales.

92nd Highlanders, 5th Punjaub Native Infantry, 21st Punjaub Native Infantry. The Kurram Valley Reserve, under Brigadier-General Watson, V.C., C B., half C Battery A Brigade Royal Artillery, No. 1 Mountain Battery, 5th Punjaub Cavalry. First Infantry Brigade, 2nd Battalion 8th King's Regiment, and 11th Bengal Native Infantry. Second Infantry Brigade, 67th Regiment, and 29th Punjaub Native Infantry.

* The strength of the Kurram Field Force, including the Punjaub chiefs' contingent, was as follows on the 1st of May :—212 British officers and 3,511 European soldiers of all ranks, exclusive of five officers and 95 men sick and wounded; 9,180 native officers, non-commissioned officers, and men effective, and 259 in hospital; grand total, 13,269; 15 9-pounder and 12 mountain guns; 4,673 public, and 2,230 private, camp followers. Of animals for the service of the guns and cavalry there were 2,613 horses, 277 mules, 26 bullocks, and 58 elephants. Also 800 grass cutters' ponies.

Advantage was taken of the halt by the Survey department to examine the Shutargardan, and a party returned by the Thabai pass, which enters the Hazardarakht defile at Jaji Thanna, a route which was pronounced impracticable for camels. Survey parties, under Captains Woodthorpe and Martin, with a strong escort, also explored the neighbouring country, including the range between the Manjiar Pass and the Peiwar Kotul; also the Jahtra Pass, opposite Byan Kheyl, and the ranges overlooking the Ahmed Kheyl villages, by which much valuable information was procured, and a considerable tract of country, with the course of the Hazardarakht, or upper Kurram River, mapped out.

On the 9th May, the General, with his staff, rode to Shaluzan, to select a site out of some that had been examined by Major Collett, the head of the Quartermaster-General's department, and a few days later proceeded to the Kurram valley, returning to Ali Kheyl on the 14th. On the following day he issued a lengthy order detailing the system on which the Transport was to be worked from the 1st June.

But all these preparations appeared as if they were to end in naught, for, on the 13th May, intelligence was received in camp that Yakoob Khan had accepted the terms on which was based the instrument known in history as the treaty of Gundamuck, thus concluding all probability, as it was mistakenly supposed at the time, of a further prosecution of hostilities. On the following day the chiefs of the Ahmed Kheyl section of the Jajis, who had been consistently hostile to the British, came into camp and made their submission, saying that they had been informed that they were freed from allegiance to the Ameer of Cabul.

General Roberts, now that there was slight chance of an advance on Cabul, occupied himself in conducting a series of reconnoissances, by which he personally gained an intimate knowledge of the surrounding mass of mountains, with their peaks and passes, within two days' march of the British camp at Ali Kheyl. Accompanied by his staff he made a reconnoissance in force, on the 22nd May, of a peak on the south-western side of the camp, between the points visited in the reconnoissances of the 10th and 17th of the month. The escort consisted of four companies of the 72nd Highlanders, two companies of the 3rd Goorkhas, with a reserve of two companies of the 92nd Highlanders, two companies of the 21st Punjaub Native Infantry, and two guns of No. 1 Mountain Battery; and some of the lately hostile Ahmed Kheyls accompanied the party, with which also went the survey officers. The peak which General Roberts ascended, had an altitude of 10,300 feet, whence a magnificent view was obtained, and signals were exchanged with the camp and reserves by means of an intermediate party on the further side of the Sappri valley, overlooking Ali Kheyl. So important were the results obtained in these reconnoissances that the General issued a divisional order, in which, after thanking the troops, and the officers for their sketches and reports, he declared that "the results obtained possess a political, in addition to their topographical, value, and the people of this country now understand that the paths over their precipitous mountains can be traversed by British troops as easily as by themselves."

On the Queen's Birthday (24th May) General Roberts held a grand parade of all the troops forming the Kurram Field Force, the regiments and batteries coming up from Peiwar to take part in the display. On the ground, drawn up in three lines, were 5,500 infantry, 1,200 cavalry, with twenty-seven guns and two Gatlings. After the usual three cheers and *feu-de-joie*, the General rode up to the 5th Goorkhas, and decorated Captain Cook with the Victoria Cross for his gallantry on the 2nd December, in saving the life of Major Galbraith, Assistant-Adjutant-General, and conferred on two native officers and seven non-commissioned officers and men of the regiment, the 3rd class Order of Merit, for distinguished gallantry at the Peiwar Kotul. He then addressed Major Fitz Hugh on the pleasure it afforded him to have his distinguished regiment under his command, and eulogized Captain Cook as an officer of established reputation in the Punjaub Frontier Forces before the present campaign. A march past of the division concluded the ceremony, and during the day, the orders for the return of the troops to the Kurram valley were published.

On the following day the division broke up, and on the 26th General Roberts marched with headquarters to Shaluzan, where

Brigadier-General Watson, on behalf of the Punjaub chiefs, gave an open air luncheon to General Roberts and his staff, and about 100 other officers, who were regaled on luxuries such as they had not enjoyed since the commencement of the campaign. When the company had done justice to the delicacies spread before them, General Roberts made a speech, thanking the Punjaub chiefs for the assistance they had afforded the government, to which General Watson returned thanks, and then proposed the health of the gallant commander of the Kurram Field Forces, which was drunk with enthusiasm. During the day a telegram was received, reporting the signature of the treaty of Gundamuck.

General Roberts returned to Kurram and thence to the Peiwar Kotul, inspecting the site of an artillery camp halfway between Shaluzan and the Peiwar (or Habib Killa) cantonment. Having ordered a re-distribution of troops on the return of the Punjaub Chiefs' Contingent* to India on the 31st May, the General returned with headquarters to Ali Kheyl; and, on the 1st June, rode up the Lakkerai Pass, a distance of eighteen miles, with the object of meeting Captain Strahan, R.E., and Major Stewart, Guide Corps, who had been sent from Gundamuck to report on the road; but after waiting some time, he returned to camp, and a telegram was afterwards received, reporting that they had been unable to cross the pass as their baggage animals had been seized by robbers. But Mr. Scott, of the Survey Department of the Khyber column, reached the summit of the Peak of Sikaram, whence he saw the Kurram and Hurriab valleys spread out like a map at his feet, but though a lookout was kept at Ali Kheyl in anticipation of a heliographic signal, he was unable for some reasons to communicate with the signallers below.†

---

* On the 2nd of June General Roberts issued a farewell order, expressing "his high appreciation of the valuable services rendered by Brigadier-General Watson, and the officers, non-commissioned officers, and men, during the three months they had been under his command, when they were employed in escorting convoys and protecting the line of communication." So excellent had been the behaviour of the men, both in camp and on the line of march, that he added, "Their conduct has not been the subject of a single complaint by the inhabitants of the country, and their steadiness and good discipline reflect honour on those chiefs whom they serve."

† Captain Colquhoun's "With the Kurram Force."

On the 2nd June General Roberts, escorted by two companies of the 92nd, four companies of Goorkhas, and two mountain guns, marched on a reconnoissance of the country of the Ahmed Kheyl section of the Jajis, which had not yet been visited, though visible from the ranges to the south of Ali Kheyl. The people did not appear friendly, and the chief failed to put in an appearance to pay his respects, on which the General sent a native assistant political officer to require his presence, when he came into camp, which was pitched for the day at a ridge called Dobozai. Accompanied by his staff, and an armed escort of the villagers, locally called a "badragga," the General ascended a spur running south from Saratiga (white rock), a peak forming the centre of a series of spurs, which spread out like a fan from the neighbourhood of the Shutargardan. The view from this point was of a sea of mountain chains and peaks, the Zermatt valley in Afghanistan being visible, but the General was unable to see Ghuznee, which lay on the further side of a low range of hills which bounded the horizon to the south-west. As soon as the Mangals in the valley below saw the party on the ridge which overlooked their country, they raised the alarm, and began to collect with the object of intercepting their return, on which the General, who besides the "badragga," was accompanied by only a few orderlies, returned to camp, and thence proceeded to Ali Kheyl that night.

In order to complete his knowledge of the network of mountains to the south of the Hurriab valley, General Roberts proceeded, on 6th June, with his staff, and some officers of the survey, escorted by two companies 28th Punjaub Native Infantry, and No. 1 Mountain Battery, and a "badragga" of Jajis, to explore the route by the Ishtiar Pass, which, starting from Byan Kheyl, leads across the range, and emerges in the upper Kurram valley. In order to co-operate against an attack by Mangals, the 12th Bengal Cavalry, and 300 men of the 5th Punjaub Native Infantry had been ordered on the 1st June to march from the camp at Peiwar to Keraiah, in the upper Kurram valley. The destination of the reconnoissance was kept secret, so that no opposition was experienced. The pass was found to be less steep and rugged than the Manjiar defile, and the camp was pitched in a broad open valley, at the west end of the range that slopes down from the Peiwar Kotul. On the following day the march was made to Keraiah, eight miles distant, near the mouth of the Manjiar Pass. The survey officers connected their survey of the Kurram valley with that of Khost, which lay to the south, on the other side of the range of mountains, and several reconnoissances were made in this direction across the Kurram river. On the 15th June the last of these was to be made, enabling the survey officers to map the course of the Kurram river between Keraiah and the country of the Ahmed Kheyls, the chiefs of whom, Zaib and Cassim, the headmen of the Hassan Kheyls, were in camp, and guaranteed the safety of the party with which General Roberts intended to proceed. A part of the road, however, passed through the territory of the Lajji Mangals, who sent into camp ten hostages for their good behaviour.

General Roberts started with the survey officers and an escort, consisting of No. 1 Mountain Battery, a detachment of the 12th Bengal Cavalry, and the 5th Punjaub Native Infantry, and was about entering a difficult gorge by which the Kurram river enters the valley, one mile and a half from camp, when a man of the "badragga," consisting of Chumkunnies, who owned this part of the river bed, observed that the Mangals would make an objection to the advance of the party the General intended to take with him, which consisted of only the survey officers, eight men of the 5th Native Infantry under Major Mac Queen, and four orderlies of his escort. General Roberts sent the Assistant-Political officer, Mahomed Hyat Khan, to ascertain if this was so, and on his reporting the road clear, the party continued their march, and reached the first Mangal village, two miles further on, where the headmen paid their respects to the General.

Pushing on along the hillsides, a body of Mangals were seen about 400 yards distant, who assumed a hostile attitude, on which the General ordered a halt, as the Ahmed Kheyl villages, which were the goal of the expedition, lay three miles higher up, and it would have been unwise, if not impossible, to have pushed on there against opposition, while their return would have been cut off. Accordingly, a halt was called under a plane-tree, at the entrance of a glen leading to the bed of the river, while an attempt was made to bring the Mangals to terms; but they refused to permit the passage of the party. While the General was discussing the matter with the headmen, under the shade of the plane-tree, suddenly a party of Mangals poured in a volley from a peak overlooking the glen. Had it not been for a wall of rock, thirty feet high, which screened most of the party, few would have escaped. Colonel Mark Heathcote and Major Collett, both officers of the Quartermaster-General's Department, had narrow escapes, and one sapper and a nephew of the Hassan Kheyl Chief, were wounded.

The General had already taken the precaution to order the return of the survey party, and had sent word to the supports to be ready to advance, if necessary, and now gave the order to retire, which was done with order and deliberation. Meanwhile the *badragga* had disappeared, and the enemy swarmed down from the peak, and kept up a hot fire on the small escort, which, under the leadership of Major Mac Queen, managed to keep them off until the supports were reached.

On the return of General Roberts to the camp at Keraiah, the Mangal hostages were sent to Kurram for detention till their tribe had paid a fine of 1,000 rupees for breaking their engagements.* The maliks of Keraiah were also sent prisoners to Kurram for failing to warn the General of the treachery of their neighbours.

On the 17th of June the camp at Keraiah was broken up, and General Roberts returned to Shaluzan, whence the head-quarters were moved to the Peiwar Kotul, as being more salubrious. In the second week of July, Brigadier-General Dunham Massy arrived to relieve General Roberts, and take up the command of the advanced brigade of the Kurram Field Force, now reduced by the breaking up of the 2nd Brigade, commanded by Brigadier-General Forbes, Brigadier-General Cobbe, commanding the 1st Brigade, having been appointed to command at Agra. On the 15th July arrived Major Cavagnari,

---

* The Mangals made their submission on the 5th of July, and paid up 500 rupees, expressing their inability to pay the remainder, which was remitted.

C.B., the recently appointed Envoy to the Court of the Ameer Yakoob Khan, and, on the following day, the remaining officers of the Mission, Mr. Jenkins, C.I.E., Secretary, Surgeon-Major Kelly, and Lieutenant Hamilton, V.C., of the Guide Corps, who commanded the escort of fifty men from the infantry, and twenty-five from the cavalry, of his own regiment.

General Roberts and Major Cavagnari proceeded together to Ali Kheyl, the 5th Punjaub Infantry escorting the rest of the Mission, which encamped near Zubberdusht Killa. In order to impress the natives with a proper sense of respect due to Her Majesty's Envoy, and also to give as many officers as circumstances permitted the opportunity of visiting the Shutargardan Pass, General Roberts detailed a strong force, under Brigadier-General Massy, consisting of two companies from each of the three British regiments, a squadron of the 12th Bengal Cavalry, 4* guns No. 2 Mountain Battery, and the 5th Goorkhas, which marched on to Dreikulla, ten miles up the Hazardarakht defile, where they were joined, on the 18th July, by the General and Envoy from Ali Kheyl.

The camp was pitched that afternoon at Saratiga,† and in the evening Major Cavagnari gave a farewell dinner to General Roberts, at which mutual good wishes were exchanged between the host and his guest, which subsequent events too sadly belied. On the following morning, the 19th July, Sirdar Khusdil Khan, formerly Governor of Afghan Turkestan, deputed by Yakoob Khan to welcome the British Envoy, arrived at the camp. He was received by General Roberts and Major Cavagnari, and as soon as all was ready, the cavalcade started on the mission for the Afghan camp at Cassim Kheyl, in the Shutargardan plain, and General Roberts, accompanied by his staff, and all the officers on leave, marched for the Pass, from the summit of which they viewed the Logar valley and the road to Cabul, which all thought with a sigh they were not to traverse.

---

* The two mountain batteries had used only four guns during the campaign, but when the preparations for the advance on Cabul were in progress they were made up to the strength of six guns.
† Saratiga derives its name from a light-coloured cliff near, forming the boundary of the Jaji territory.

On his return, General Roberts visited Khusdil Khan, who received him with ceremony, but created anything but a favourable impression, owing to the sinister expression of his face and want of cordiality. Among the chiefs accompanying the Sirdar was Padshah Khan, chief of the Eastern Ghilzyes, whom the late Ameer Shere Ali had appointed Wuzeer, or Prime Minister, and who had received gifts from the British for his friendliness towards them. After the interview a dinner was served in the Afghan fashion, in large trays raised about six inches off the ground, but the *cuisine* was by no means despicable, and the *menu* was varied, though there was only one spoon on each tray, and no plates or knives and forks, the former being represented by large "chupatties," or flat cakes of flour, and the latter by the fingers of each guest. Only four chairs were provided—for the Sirdar, the General, the Envoy, and his secretary, the remaining officers participating in the banquet having to sit cross-legged on the floor. After the guests had washed their hands in basins passed round by the attendants, tea was served, and then hot milk, sweetened and spiced, completed the entertainment.

On this day General Roberts was gazetted, in London, to a Knight Commandership of the Bath, and never had the honour been more worthily earned, and many officers of the staff and of the force under his orders received decorations and promotion. Major Cavagnari was also made a K.C.S.I.

Sir Frederick Roberts remained for the night at Cassim Kheyl, and, on the following morning, bade farewell to his entertainer, and the ill-fated British Envoy, who, with his officers and escort, was seen no more by his countrymen. As the newly-made Knight of the Star of India watched the last of the gallant array that disappeared from view with Sir Frederick Roberts, it may well be a subject of speculation whether such thoughts presented themselves to his mind as Shakespeare puts into the mouth of Henry IV., who gloomily exclaimed, when insurrection, which he had employed to overthrow the unhappy Richard, raised its head to eject him from the throne,

> "O heaven! that we might read the book of fate,
> And see the revolution of the times."

Though, recognizing the wisdom that hides our fortunes under the pall of futurity, the King adds—

> " If this were seen,
> The happiest youth—viewing his progress through,
> What perils past, what crosses to ensue—
> Would shut the book, and sit him down and die."

Sir Frederick Roberts returned to Ali Kheyl, where he held a farewell durbar of the chiefs of the surrounding tribes and clans, to whom, in the name of the Government, he made presents. Handing over the command of the Kurram Field Force in its diminished strength, to Brigadier-General Massy, he left the scenes of his triumphs and returned to Simla, where he had been summoned as a member of the Army Commission, which Lord Lytton had assembled for the purpose of considering the reorganization of the Indian Army.

CHAPTER XII.

Massacre of the British Mission at Cabul—Receipt of the Intelligence by Sir Frederick Roberts at Simla—He Proceeds to take the Field—Arrival at Ali Kheyl—Preparations for the Advance on Cabul—Sir Frederick Roberts Moves across the Shutargardan Pass—He Experiences a Narrow Escape—Arrival at Kooshi—Interview with Yakoob Khan—Proclamations of Sir Frederick Roberts to the Army and the People of Cabul.

Sir Frederick Roberts was received at Simla with much distinction by the Viceroy, Lord Lytton, who gave a grand banquet in his honour, at which, in the presence of the highest dignitaries of the State, his Lordship designated his guest, "the hero of the Afghan War," a title he had fairly won as the victor of the Peiwar Kotul, by far the most brilliant and prominent achievement of the campaign, which, as regards the Khyber and Bolan columns, was rather barren of military exploits. But hardly had the congratulations of the General's friends and well-wishers ceased to sound in his ears, and scarcely was the ink dry on the proclamation of the Viceroy, announcing the conclusion of the peace of Gundamuck, than that much-vaunted instrument was torn to shreds by an act of more than Oriental treachery, and the pæan of triumph sung by the Viceroy was turned into expressions of horror and lamentation at the fall of his friend, Sir Louis Cavagnari, and the gallant officers and men who composed the mission to Cabul.

Before proceeding with the narrative we will interpolate a brief account of the circumstances attendant on the perpetration of this tragedy, as they bear on the relations that later existed between Yakoob Khan and Sir Frederick Roberts.

On the conclusion of the treaty of Gundamuck the Ameer Yakoob Khan returned to Cabul, accompanied by Habibulla Khan, the Mustaufi, or Finance Minister, Daoud Shah, his

Massacre of the Cavagnari Mission.

Commander-in-Chief, and a native agent in the employ of Sir Louis Cavagnari, named Buktiar Khan, who was entrusted with the duty of preparing for the reception of the British mission. Sir Louis Cavagnari, after bidding farewell to Sir Frederick Roberts, on the 19th of July, proceeded by the Shutargardan pass to Cabul, which he entered on the 24th of July, having been received *en route* with the utmost consideration and ceremony by the Ameer's ministers and troops, and in his reception by Yakoob Khan was treated with every mark of esteem and honour. Unfortunately Buktiar Khan died a few days before the Envoy's arrival at Cabul, and the death of so tried an agent was a great loss to Sir Louis; but beyond some trivial disputes in the Bazaar between the Ameer's troops and the Envoy's escort, all went well, and, says the Viceroy in his letter to the Secretary of State for India, dated September 15th, 1879, detailing the events preceding the massacre, the Envoy's last private letter, dated 30th of August, concluded with the words: "I personally believe that Yakoob Khan will turn out to be a good ally, and that we shall be able to keep him to his engagements." The Ameer spoke with pleasure of his proposed visit to the Viceroy, in which he was to be accompanied by the Envoy, and on the 2nd September, Sir Louis Cavagnari despatched a telegram to Lord Lytton, the last received from him, concluding with the words, "all well."

On the following day the British Residency in the Bala Hissar, or Citadel of Cabul, was attacked by three regiments, called the Ordal Regiments, who had come to the pay office in the Bala Hissar to receive their arrears, and on hearing that they were not to be paid in full, two of the regiments attacked the Residency, and being joined by the mob, succeeded in setting the buildings on fire and destroying its defenders after a desperate resistance.

The news of this extraordinary outrage was conveyed to Ali Kheyl, in the form of a letter addressed by Yakoob Khan to Sir Frederick Roberts. In the first, dated 4 P.M., the 3rd September, the Ameer reports the attack, at 8 A.M., on the Residency by the troops and "people from city and surrounding country," and adds that he had sent without avail his son and Daoud Shah, whom he reported as "dying;" and the second letter, dated 4th September, reported that the attack on the Residency had gone on from " morning till evening," when the building was set on fire, but added, that he had no " certain news " of the fate of the Envoy, and that he himself, "with five attendants, had been besieged." The statements of the messenger who brought these letters, an uncle of Padshah Khan, the great Ghilzye Chief, left no doubt as to the fate of the mission and escort.

In Sir Louis Cavagnari, Sir Frederick Roberts lost a personal friend, of whom Lord Lytton spoke in no exaggerated terms when he said, that " by his life and death he had bequeathed to the Service he adorned a splendid example, and to the Empire for whose interests he lived and died, the grateful guardianship of his honoured memory and spotless name." But he did not die unavenged, for his friend the British General swiftly appeased his manes, as did Achilles those of Patroclus:

"Whole hecatombs of Trojan ghosts shall pay."

Thousands of Afghans bled for the treacherous deed enacted on the 3rd September, and the *fainéant* monarch—who surveyed the scene from his palace windows while he despatched messengers, and ultimately his Commander-in-Chief, Daoud Shah, the only honest man of them all, to check his mutinous soldiery—suffered for his want of good faith by the sacrifice of his throne.

The fate of Lieutenant Hamilton, V.C., who commanded the escort, an officer young in years, but of great distinction and still higher promise, was especially tragic, and had in its circumstances all the elements of the heroic. Standing at bay, sword and revolver in hand, the heart of the young hero quailed not, while he confronted the surging mob thirsting for his blood.

A melancholy interest attaches to some lines, displaying considerable poetic merit, written, shortly before his death, by Lieutenant Hamilton, and sent from Cabul on the 25th of that August, eight days before he was massacred:—

"THE VILLAGE BEHMARU."

(Scene of outbreak of Cabul disaster, 1841. Revisited, August, 1879.)

> "Though all is changed, yet remnants of the past
> Point to the scenes of bloodshed, and, alas !
> Of murder foul ; and ruined houses cast
> Their mournful shadow o'er the graves of grass
> Of England's soldiery, who faced a lot
> That few, thank Heaven ! before or since have shared ; --
> Slain by the hand of treachery, and not
> In open combat, where the foe ne'er dared
> To show themselves. The fatal, honest trust
> Placed in an enemy who loved a lie
> And knew not honour was a trust that cost
> The lives of those that gave it. Yet to die
> Game to the last, as they did, well upheld
> Their English name. E'en now their former foe
> Frankly avers the British arms were quelled
> By numbers only and the cruel snow.
> 'Tis forty years since British soldiers turned
> To look their last on this now peaceful scene,
> Whose lingering gaze spoke volumes as it yearned
> For vengeance due to treachery so mean.
> And vengeance true did Pollock, Sale, and Nott
> Deal with a timely and unerring hand
> As they with victory effaced the blot
> Which first had dimmed the annals of our land.
> And, now, while standing here, where side by side
> Fell many fighting with a fruitless bent,
> Regret were uppermost were't not for pride
> Which gives no place for weaker sentiment.
> And Pride might well be foremost if one thought
> That though fair Fortune smiled not for awhile,
> How England's fame shone brighter as she fought,
> And wrenched lost laurels from their funeral pile,
> And rose at last from out misfortune's tide
> Supreme—for God and right were on her side."

Sir Frederick Roberts was at Simla, engaged on the Army Commission to which he had been appointed before the outbreak of the war, when, at 1 o'clock on the morning of the 5th September, he was suddenly roused from his sleep with a telegram from Captain Arthur Conolly, Political Officer at Ali Kheyl, announcing the astounding news of the murder of the British Envoy at Cabul, with the other members of the Mission, and all save nine men of the escort. Sir Frederick immediately sent the telegram to Lord Lytton, and proceeded in person shortly afterwards to Government House. The Viceroy settled with him the composition of the force that was to be launched against the city of Cabul, and a meeting of the Council was summoned, at which the Commander-in-Chief attended.

General Roberts's achievements in the first phase of the Afghan War pointed him out as the man for the crisis that had arisen, and Lord Lytton, who had hailed him as "the hero of the Afghan War," now that hostilities had so unexpectedly broken out, with a discrimination that does his judgment infinite credit, selected the young General for the Command of the Force that was to vindicate the outraged name of England. It was a high honour, but Roberts's whole career pointed to him as the man pre-eminently fitted to cope with the emergency that had arisen. As Warwick says:

> "There is a history in all men's lives,
> Fixing the nature of the times deceased,
> The which observ'd, a man may prophesy,
> With a near aim, of the main chance of things
> As yet not come to life."

Those who had watched Roberts's career since he made his name at Delhi, recognized in him the man of the hour, and public opinion fully endorsed the Governor-General's action in appointing him to the command of the army of retribution, in spite of the claims of seniority. It was admitted that the campaign in the Kurram Valley had introduced to the world a soldier of uncommon excellence, one combining the caution of Nestor with the fiery valour of Achilles, "*impiger, iracundus, inexorabilis, acer.*"

In the afternoon of the following day, the 6th September, Sir Frederick Roberts started for Ali Kheyl, with orders to advance rapidly on Cabul with a force of about 6,500 men. He travelled post by night and day, taking the rail to Jhelum, and thence proceeding by mail-cart and riding, and arrived at Thull on the 10th September, and at Ali Kheyl on the 12th. Meanwhile Brigadier-General Massy had been instructed by telegraph to occupy the Shutargardan Pass, and General Stewart, who had evacuated Candahar, was directed by the Viceroy to return to the city, whilst Jellalabad was re-occupied, and a reserve of 5,000 men assembled between Rawul Pindee and Peshawur.

By the 11th September, the 5th Goorkhas, 23rd Pioneers,

and No. 2 Mountain Battery, the whole under Colonel Currie, commanding the Pioneers, acting under Sir Frederick Roberts's instructions, were securely entrenched on the crest of the Shutargardan Pass. As it was a matter of the greatest importance that every facility should be afforded for the easy passage of the artillery across the Shutargardan, Sir Frederick Roberts telegraphed orders on the 9th September, directing the 7th Company of Sappers and Miners, then at Shaluzan, to march with all speed towards the Pass. This order was executed promptly, and by the 13th inst. they were at work on the Sirkai Kotul, a steep and awkward ascent about three miles beyond the summit of the Pass.

Sir Frederick Roberts was accompanied, or followed, by the following officers whom he had selected for high command. Brigadier-Generals H. T. Macpherson, C.B., V.C., and T. D. Baker, C.B., to command the two infantry Brigades; Brigadier-General J. Gordon to command the column of 4,000 men holding the country from Shutargardan to Thull; Brigadier-General H. Gough, C.B., V.C., to be Road Commandant. Brigadier-General D. Massy, now commanding at Ali Kheyl, was nominated to command the Cavalry Brigade. He selected as Chief of the Staff, Colonel C. M. Macgregor, C.B., of the Quartermaster-General's Department, an officer, though young in years, of great military experience and considerable talent.

General Baker proceeded, on the 13th September, to take command of the troops at Shutargardan, the position at which was strongly entrenched, and every precaution taken against a surprise. With the energy that distinguished this gallant officer while serving under Sir Garnet Wolseley in Ashantee, he made a reconnoissance on the 16th, as far as Shinkai Kotul, but met with no resistance. Two days before, Nawab Sir Gholam Hussein Khan passed thourgh Shutargardan and proceeded to Ali Kheyl where he joined Sir Frederick Roberts. This distinguished native officer was proceeding from Candahar to Cabul, to assist Sir Louis Cavagnari, but fortunately heard on the road of the massacre of the British Mission.

Sir Frederick Roberts's first consideration was transport for the force of between 6,000 to 7,000 men, whom he was going to take with him to Cabul. With the usual want of forethought at Army Headquarters, where a renewal of hostilities was not anticipated, the animals of the transport department of the Kurram Field Force were suffered to fall below the strength essential to maintain its efficiency. Sir Frederick Roberts writes :—" Transport was the great difficulty which had to be met. Owing to the continuous and hard work to which the animals had been subjected, their numbers had steadily but rapidly diminished until, at the commencement of the month of September, there remained about 1,500 mules, 500 sickly camels, and 800 bullocks, or barely sufficient to enable the Commissariat to feed the force which it was presumed would remain in the Kurram valley for the winter. It is true that a large number of pack bullocks had been despatched for the Commissariat service in the valley, but of these many had been knocked up by the journey from the Punjaub, or were suffering from semi-starvation to such an extent as to be practically useless." As he said to the writer, " On arriving at Ali Kheyl I found that there was only transport for half the force I was to take to Cabul. Little provisions were in store, and there was no communication with the Khyber Column." And yet within about six weeks, his communications would be transferred by the snowing up of the Shutargardan route to that by the Khyber.

In his endeavours to improvise a transport Roberts had the support of the Viceroy, a functionary whose word is law in our despotically-governed dependency. By Lord Lytton's orders, the Peshawur district was swept clean of transport cattle, but still the number was insufficient, owing to the enormous loss among the camels and the improvidence of the Indian authorities, who, not anticipating a renewal of hostilities, had suffered the transport to lapse into its chronic state of unpreparedness. Sir Frederick Roberts, and, before his arrival at Ali Kheyl, the able political officer, Captain Conolly, exerted themselves to procure carriage, and his old allies, the Turis of the Kurram Valley, and the Jajis, brought in all the animals they could spare, with drivers, and Padshah Khan, the Ghilzye Chief, whom Sir Frederick had met in the previous July, gave his aid, so that the commissariat were enabled to collect a considerable amount of supplies at the Shutargardan, "quite sufficient," he says, "to relieve any anxiety as to the immediate want of the troops left there, and to move still larger stores forward for the force advancing upon Cabul."

The position of Yakoob Khan, brought on by his vacillation and timidity, if not treachery, was not an enviable one at this time, between his countrymen who hated him for signing an ignominious treaty and receiving a British Envoy, and the British Government, whom he knew would call him to strict account for suffering the murder of their representative.

In order to conciliate Sir Frederick Roberts, he sent to Ali Kheyl the Mustaufi, Habibullah Khan, and the Wuzeer, Shah Mahomed, with a letter declaring his fidelity to the British alliance, and announcing his intention of seeking the protection of the British Commander; but the real object of the visit of these ministers of the Ameer was, in Sir Frederick's opinion, to use their influence in preventing him from getting supplies, to blind him as to the real state of affairs, and, above all, to seek by every argument in their power to deter him from advancing on Cabul. The Ameer's ministers arrived at Ali Kheyl on the 23rd September, and during their stay, which extended over three days, were treated with becoming consideration and respect. In their conversations with Roberts and his political officers, they pretended that their master desired the assistance and protection of a British force, but at a later period; while at the same time they wrote to Lord Lytton deprecating an immediate advance, and secretly used all their influence to deter the Jajis, Turis, Ghilzyes, and others from furnishing supplies.

In the Commander of the Cabul Field Force these wily Orientals found one versed in the treacherous ways of Easterns, a man whose open, truthful nature did not blind him to the insincerity and downright lying which is unblushingly practised among Asiatics of the governing class from Constantinople to the wall of China. Taking this view of the Afghan character in general, and that of the two emissaries of Yakoob Khan in particular, Sir Frederick Roberts was civil to them, but let them clearly understand that they did not blind him by their protestations and pretences, and that as soon as he had collected sufficient supplies for the advance he would move on Cabul without fail.

It would be almost impossible to exaggerate the difficulties of Sir Frederick Roberts's position at this time. With a force of

6,500 men, and with supplies and transport for only one half that number, he was required to advance upon Cabul before a fall of snow had rendered the Shutargardan impassable, and mete a swift and crushing punishment on that city and the Ameer's Army for their treachery towards a British Ambassador. During the winter, once across the Shutargardan, he would be thrown on the resources of the country and the supplies forwarded by the line of the Kyber Pass, with open enemies to contest his hold of the country, and secret foes in his camp. He could not also blind himself to the difficulties of the march on the capital. The Afghan Army, so carefully raised and disciplined by Shere Ali, had not yet been broken by defeat on their own soil, and the populace were numerous, fanatical, and inured to the use of arms. They had taken up positions selected by themselves of enormous strength, while the Intelligence Department of the British General was defective, and he was embarrassed by the attitude, and, a few days later, by the presence of the Ameer, as whose ostensible ally he was about to restore his authority over his rebellious capital.

Sir Frederick Roberts's orders from the Viceroy requiring him to keep on terms with the Ameer, he wrote to him a conciliatory letter from Ali Kheyl, to which he received a reply, suggestive, in the General's opinion, of a guilty conscience, and in this view he was strengthened by the conduct of Yakoob's envoys, and, at a later date, of the Ameer himself, who, Sir Frederick knew, though he was obliged to treat him as a friend and ally, was seeking from the vantage point of the British Camp to thwart his every move.

In contrasting to us the difficulties and achievements of his world-famed march from Cabul to Candahar, in August, 1880, with the advance on Cabul, in September to October of the previous year, Sir Frederick Roberts expressed his opinion that the latter was incomparably a more arduous and brilliant feat of arms, and this opinion, he added, would be endorsed by every competent military critic; but the world was struck by the boldness and rapidity of the masterly advance through Afghanistan, bringing to mind Napoleon's march into Italy, or across Spain in pursuit of Sir John Moore, while the swift reconnoissance of the 31st August, and battle of the following day, was quite in the "*veni, vidi, vici*" style, so familiar to every schoolboy, and commanded the popular applause, which, indeed, it well merited.

So successful were the arrangements made by Sir Frederick Roberts for collecting supplies, that, before the snow had cut off his communications with Ali Kheyl, three or four months' supplies were collected for his troops and camp followers, and six weeks' forage for his animals. By the 18th September he had firmly established on the summit of the Pass the 72nd Highlanders, 5th Goorkhas, 23rd Pioneers, No. 2 Mountain Battery, and the 7th Company of Sappers and Miners. In addition 200 men of the 5th Punjaubees were posted in the walled serai at Karatiga, $1\frac{1}{2}$ miles from the Sirkai Kotul.

On the 24th September, while at Ali Kheyl, Sir Frederick Roberts issued the following general order to the troops under his command:—

"The Government of India having decided that the Kurram Field Force shall proceed with all possible despatch to Cabul, in response to his Highness the Ameer's appeal for aid, and with the object of avenging the dastardly murder of the British representative and his escort, Sir Frederick Roberts feels sure that the troops under his command will respond to the call with a determination to prove themselves worthy of the sacred duty entrusted to them and of the high reputation they have maintained during the recent campaign.

"The Major-General need address no words of exhortation to soldiers whose courage and fortitude have been so well proved. The Afghan tribes are numerous, but without organization; the regular army is undisciplined, and, whatever may be the disparity in numbers, such foes can never be formidable to British troops. The dictates of humanity require that a distinction should be made between the peaceable inhabitants of Afghanistan and the treacherous murderers for whom a just retribution is in store, and Sir Frederick Roberts desires to impress on all ranks the necessity for treating the inoffensive population with justice, forbearance, and clemency. The future comfort and well-being of the force depend largely on the friendliness of our relations with the districts from which our supplies must be drawn; prompt payment is enjoined for all articles purchased by departments and individuals, and all disputes must be at once referred to a political officer for decision. The Major-General confidently looks forward to the successful accomplishment of the object of the expedition, and the re-establishment of order, and a settled government in Afghanistan."

The first shot fired in the campaign was on the 22nd September, when a combined attack was made by Mangals and Ghilzyes upon a telegraph party whilst on the march between the Sirkai Kotul and Karatiga. Between 200 and 300 of these tribesmen attacked the party, who were escorted by eleven sepoys of the 5th Punjaub Infantry, and killed seven of the latter, one telegraph linesman, twelve muleteers, and five coolies, and captured the eighty-four mules intended to convey the telegraph poles from Karatiga to Shutargardan. They also attacked a party of 50 men of the 72nd Highlanders, stationed in a block-house on the Sirkai Kotul, but were repulsed with loss. A detachment of this regiment from Kazim Kheyl was sent in pursuit of the marauders, but without success.

On the 24th Brigadier-General Baker moved from Shutargardan with a column,* and, passing through Dobandi, which was found to have been deserted by its inhabitants, crossed over the Shinkai Kotul, and reached Kooshi the same evening, thus securing the entrance into the Logar Valley.

Three days later Sir Frederick Roberts moved from Ali Kheyl to the Shutargardan in company with the headquarters of the Cavalry Brigade, one squadron 9th Lancers, 5th Punjaub Cavalry, 28th Punjaub N.I., and a detachment of the 5th Punjaub Infantry. The infantry were directed to bring up the rear, whilst the General, with his staff and the cavalry, pushed forward in order to reach Kazim Kheyl or the Pass before dark. On the road he had a narrow escape, and the event proved that the tribesmen all along the line of route were in a dangerous state of excitement. About 10.30 the General was fortunately joined by twenty-five men of the 92nd Highlanders, whom Colonel Perkins had taken the precaution to send from Karatiga to act as an advance guard, in consequence of a rumoured gathering of Mangals and Ghilzyes in the Hazardarakht defile. At 11 A.M., whilst halting to allow

---

* The following troops accompanied General Baker:—F Battery A Brigade Royal Horse Artillery; 12th Bengal Cavalry; 2 guns No. 2 Mountain Battery; one Company 72nd Highlanders; 7th Company Sappers and Miners; 5th Goorkhas, and 23rd Pioneers.

the luggage to come up, General Roberts received a report that 2,000 Mangals barred his advance, occupying the Pass between Jaji Thanna and Karatiga, and Captain Vousden, 5th Punjaub Cavalry, who was ordered to reconnoitre, reported that the enemy held in force both sides of the ravine half a mile beyond Jaji Thanna. Suddenly a large party of Mangals, who had been lying in ambush, fired a volley at the General and the headquarter staff, and Deputy Surgeon-General Townsend, head of the Medical Department, was severely wounded by a bullet which entered his right cheek. The Highlanders and a troop of dismounted Lancers cleared the northern side of the gorge, but the enemy clung to the precipitous hills on the south, and some time elapsed before they were driven from their position. The 28th Punjaub Native Infantry, on arriving, held a commanding hill until the rearguard had passed.

General Hills, C.B., V.C., Roberts's old Addiscombe friend, who had joined him at Ali Kheyl, having received leave from the Commander-in-Chief to accompany him to Cabul in an unofficial capacity, describes the narrow escape General Roberts had on this occasion:—" We pushed forward towards the pass, when suddenly we were confronted with a party of Afghans, who had taken up a position commanding the road, which lay up the dry bed in the Hazardarakht defile. Waiting till the headquarters came up, the enemy let drive into the 'brown' of them. I was riding alongside Townsend, who received a slug in his cheek, and General Roberts was a little ahead. Roberts dismounted the Lancers, and they, and the company of the 92nd, fortunately sent from Shutargardan, drove them off."

Meanwhile a smart affair had been in progress in the direction of Karatiga, whence had been despatched a small detachment consisting of eighteen men of the 92nd Highlanders and forty-five of the 3rd Sikhs, led by Colour-Sergeant Hector Macdonald and Jemadar Shere Mahomed. This gallant band fought their way up a steep spur commanding the Hazardarakht defile, and drove off the enemy, inflicting severe loss, and thus cleared the way for the General and his staff.

These events showed that caution would be necessary, and Brigadier-General Macpherson, commanding the troops that moved, on the 29th September, from Ali Kheyl to join the General, took precautions to guard the large convoy of 1,500 laden animals he was escorting. A feeble attack was made in the Hazardarakht defile on the rear-guard of the column by a small party of marauders, but they were beaten off by the 67th Regiment.

Pushing on, Sir Frederick Roberts only rested one night at the Shutargardan Pass. A General Officer who accompanied him described to us the rapidity of the movements of his friend, who, in order to economize transport, made the cavalry horses carry rations and arms, while the men walked beside their steeds over the Pass. On the 28th September General Roberts reached Kooshi, where the Ameer Yakoob Khan, accompanied by his eldest son, by Sirdars Yahya Khan, Daoud Shah, the Mustaufi, Wuzeer Gholam Mahomed Khan, and a suite of forty-five persons, with an escort of 200 horsemen, had arrived on the preceding day, and been received by Brigadier-General Baker, commanding the advance. Sir Frederick Roberts paid a formal visit to the Ameer, accompanied by his staff, Brigade Commanders, and by Major-General James Hills. He was received by Daoud Shah, late Commander-in-Chief, and conducted into the presence of the Ameer, where the usual inquiries as to health were made, after which the British General left. During the course of the afternoon the Ameer, accompanied by his son and the nobles of his suite, returned the visit.

Sir Frederick replied to the Ameer's pleading for delay, that not even for one day would he defer his march on Cabul, and the latter returned to his tent, having failed to convince or turn his host, whose suavity of manner was only equalled by his determination, the pressure of the iron hand being apparent beneath the velvet glove. Yakoob's treacherous attitude in the British Camp may be described in the words Cassius used of Antony:

"The posture of your blows are yet unknown,
But for your words, they rob the Hybla bees,
And leave them honeyless."

Roberts firmly declined to delay his advance or listen to the pleadings of Yakoob, to whom his reply was similar to that of Octavius:

"I draw a sword against conspirators;
When think you that the sword goes up again?
Never till Cæsar's three-and-thirty wounds
Be well avenged."

Roberts's Determination of Character.

Yakoob Khan, who now practised deception, had himself learnt by painful experience to value aright the word of an Afghan ruler. Though Shere Ali guaranteed his safe conduct by an oath on the Koran, yet even the father, when he got his son into his power, threw him into a dungeon, where he pined for many years in darkness and solitude.

Transport was the weak point of the situation, and only fourteen days' supplies could be taken, but with such tried Regiments as the 72nd Highlanders and 5th Goorkhas, and magnificent corps like the 92nd Highlanders and 67th Regiment, commanded by Brigadiers like Baker and Macpherson, General Roberts had no fear as to the result of his daring move, while his soldiers on their part reciprocated the feeling of confidence.

On the 29th September the Cavalry Brigade, under General Massy, with two guns of the Horse Artillery, two Companies 72nd Highlanders, and the 5th Punjaub Infantry, moved from Kooshi to Zerghan Shah to collect supplies. The same day the rear-guard, under General Macpherson, marched to the Shutargardan, and next day arrived at Kooshi. On the 1st October the last of the troops intended for the advance on Cabul arrived at Kooshi from Ali Kheyl, when the force* at Sir Frederick Roberts's disposal numbered 192 officers, 2,558 Europeans, and 3,867 natives, with 18 guns.

---

* The following were the troops that accompanied Sir Frederick Roberts to Cabul :—

Divisional and Brigade Staff Officers, 60.

	Officers.	Men.
F Battery, A Brigade, R.H.A.	7	118
G Battery, 3rd Brigade, R.A.	7	137
No. 2 Mountain Battery	3	223
9th Lancers	4	118
5th Bengal Cavalry	7	325
12th Bengal Cavalry	6	328
14th Bengal Cavalry	7	407
67th Regiment	18	686
72nd Highlanders	23	746
92nd Highlanders	17	717
5th Punjaub Infantry	8	610
23rd Pioneers	6	671
28th Punjaub Native Infantry	8	636
5 Goorkhas	7	574
7th Company Sappers and Miners	3	95
Two Gatling Guns	1	34

Also about 6,000 camp followers and 3,500 transport animals.

On the preceding day Sir Frederick went to Zerghan Shah, where he met Wali Mahomed Khan and several other Sirdars, chiefly Barukzyes, from Cabul, all of whom professed great friendship for the Indian Government. The rapidity with which the two Batteries of Horse and Foot Artillery had crossed the Shutargardan Pass, hitherto deemed impracticable for wheeled guns, filled these Sirdars and all Afghans with astonishment.

Sir Frederick returned to Kooshi the same day, and, on the 1st October, issued the following notification to the Troops, impressing upon them the necessity for discipline and self-restraint :—" Sir Frederick Roberts desires general officers, and officers commanding corps, to impress upon all officers under their command the necessity for constant vigilance in preventing irregularities likely to arouse the personal jealousies of the people of Cabul, who are, of all races, most susceptible as regards their women. The deep-seated animosity of the Afghans towards the English has been mainly ascribed to indiscretions committed during the first occupation of Cabul, and the Major-General trusts that the same discipline so long exhibited by the troops under his command will remove the prejudices of past years, and cause the British name to be as highly respected in Afghanistan as it is throughout the civilized world."

The references to the personal jealousies of the people of Cabul, and the "indiscretions committed during the first occupation of Cabul," referred to a delicate subject touched upon by Sir John Kaye in his " History of the first Afghan War," which greatly incensed against their conquerors the Afghan nation, who, like all Mahomedan nations, are sensitive as regards their women.

In his general order, issued at Ali Kheyl on the 24th September, Sir Frederick Roberts, with the humanity for which he was conspicuous, enjoined on his army, "the necessity for treating the inoffensive population with justice, forbearance, and clemency," and, on the 3rd October, he issued a proclamation to the people of Cabul, copies of which were sent in advance of the column, requiring those who had taken no part in the massacre of the Cavagnari Mission, and the well-disposed, and especially the women and children, to arrange for their safety by either coming into his camp or by removing from the city. In conclusion, he gave warning that, after the receipt of this proclamation, "all persons found armed in or about Cabul will be treated as the enemies of the British Government."*

A little before noon on the 2nd October Sir Frederick Roberts, accompanied by the Ameer and his Sirdars, marched with two infantry brigades from Kooshi for Zerghan Shah, where Generals Baker and Massy were posted. On the following day the march was resumed by headquarters and Massy's and Macpherson's Brigades for Zahidabad, a distance of fifteen miles. The road lay along the Logar Valley, past several villages, which formed a pleasant contrast to the inhospitable region about the Shutargardan, and over the Logar River. The movements of the Cabul Field Force were much hampered by the presence in the camp of so many Princes and Sirdars, with their retinue. There were now Yakoob Khan and his father-in-law, Yahya Khan, and his troop of nobles and large escort; Wali Mahomed Khan, and the Barukzye Sirdars, all antagonistic towards each other, and only as one in their distrust and hatred of the foreign invader.

---

* The following is the text of this proclamation issued at Zerghan Shah on the 3rd of October:—

"Be it known to all, that the British Army is advancing on Cabul to take possession of the city. If it be allowed to do so peaceably, well and good, if not, the city will be seized by force. Therefore all well-disposed persons who have taken no part in the dastardly murder of the British Embassy, or in the plunder of the Residency, are warned that if they are unable to prevent resistance being offered to the entrance of the British Army, and to the authority of his Highness the Ameer, they should make immediate arrangements for their own safety, either by coming into the British camp, or by such other measures as may seem fit to them. And as the British Government does not make war on women and children, warning is given that all women and children should be removed from the city beyond the reach of harm. The British Government desires to treat all classes with justice, and to respect their religious feelings and customs, while exacting full retribution from offenders. Every effort will therefore be made to prevent the innocent suffering with the guilty. But it is necessary that the utmost precaution should be taken against useless opposition. Therefore, after the receipt of the proclamation, all persons found armed in or about Cabul will be treated as the enemies of the British Government; and further, it must be clearly understood, that if the entry of the British force is resisted, I cannot hold myself responsible for any accidental mischief which may be done to persons and property, even of well-disposed people who may have neglected this warning."

On the 2nd October, the day Sir Frederick Roberts quitted Zerghan Shah, the Mangals and Ghilzyes made a most determined attack on the entrenched camp at the Shutargardan, where the General had left, as a permanent garrison, 4 guns No. 1 Mountain Battery, the 3rd Sikhs and 21st Punjaub Native Infantry, under Colonel G. N. Money, of the 3rd Sikhs, an officer in whose coolness and judgment he placed a reliance which was justified by subsequent events. The enemy, emboldened by the weakening of the force, and calculating on an easy victory, took up a position on the hills overlooking the crest of the pass at 7 A.M. on the 2nd October. As it was necessary to secure this crest in order to maintain heliographic communication with Sir Frederick Roberts in the Logar Valley, Colonel Money sent Major Griffiths with 100 men of the 3rd Sikhs, together with a party of signallers, to occupy it. But a strong body of the enemy anticipated the movement, and seized the crest, on which Colonel Money sent 100 men of the 3rd Sikhs to reinforce Major Griffiths, who was desired to halt for a short time at the request of Captain Turner, the Political Officer, who expected the arrival in Camp of Alla-ood-deen, brother of Padshah Khan, Chief of the Ghilzyes, who, it was hoped, would exercise a moderating influence and induce the tribesmen to withdraw.

The enemy, some 1,500 men, mistaking this hesitation for pusillanimity, began firing on Major Griffiths's party, on which Colonel Money ordered the advance. Captain Morgan opened fire with his Mountain Battery, and Major Griffiths attacked with 200 men of his regiment, and 50 of the 21st Punjaub Native Infantry, with 150 of the same regiment in reserve, and carried the position at the point of the bayonet, himself receiving a wound. The enemy fled in all directions, and for some time the Shutargardan force received no more molestation.

Owing to the deficiency in the transport animals, which were required to work double tides, General Baker's Brigade halted one day at Zerghan Shah, when they pushed on for Zahidabad. On nearing the bridge over the Logar River, the rear-guard, under the command of Major C. M. Stockwell, 72nd Highlanders (now Colonel Stockwell, C.B., A.D.C.), was attacked by the inhabitants of the neighbouring villages. Captain R. G.

Kennedy, Deputy-Assistant-Quartermaster-General, who was superintending the passage of the river, was wounded. At one time, says the General, the enemy approached so close that it became necessary for the covering companies of the 72nd Highlanders to drive them back at the point of the bayonet. Nothing could exceed the steadiness throughout the campaign of this fine regiment, which repeated in Egypt the lessons they learned in Afghanistan under the leadership of soldiers like Brownlow and Stockwell. As Campbell, the national poet, sings :—

> "Triumphant be the thistle still unfurled,
> Dear symbol wild ! on Freedom's hill it grows,
> Where Fingal stemmed the tyrants of the world,
> And Roman eagles found unconquered foes."

The villagers repeated these hostile acts on the 4th October, and on the following morning, before leaving Zahidabad, Sir Frederick Roberts despatched a force to punish them.*

---

* Sir Frederick Roberts, after perusal of the MS. of this chapter of the Memoir, wrote to us :—" I have just been reading with great interest chapter XII. of the Memoir. It was the part I was most anxious should be carefully written, and I must congratulate you on having done it extremely well."

CHAPTER XIII.

Advance on Cabul—Battle of Charasia—Sir Frederick Roberts arrives before the Capital—His Visit to the Scene of the Massacre of the British Mission—Occupation of the Bala Hissar—Proclamation of the 12th of October—The Punishment Meted out to Cabul.

On the 5th October Sir Frederick Roberts, accompanied by General Baker's Brigade, strengthened by the 92nd Highlanders, marched to Charasia, eleven miles distant from Cabul, and with Baker's and Massy's Brigades he had the honour of adding to the achievements of the British Army, not the least brilliant of the many History records. As the insufficiency of carriage did not permit of both brigades moving together, Brigadier-General Macpherson was left to protect the reserve ammunition and commissariat stores at Zahidabad, with a wing of the 67th Regiment, 28th Punjaub Native Infantry, two guns of No. 2 Mountain Battery, and a squadron of the 5th Punjaub Cavalry.

General Roberts's camp was pitched about a mile from the orchards, south of the village of Charasia, which lies at the foot of the ranges of steep and high hills, extending east and west, the Chardeh Valley lying on the left front over a more gradual slope, and in front a mass of mountains, excluding all view of Cabul.

Charasia is a highly cultivated valley, having a breadth of about two miles. The ranges of hills overlooking the village of the same name rise one behind the other, that in the immediate rear being very precipitous, with four or five peaks standing out in bold relief. Between this range and another lies the Sang-i-Nawishta Pass, through which the Logar River passes into the Cabul valley. The road beside the river, being commanded by the high hills on either side, would be difficult to force if properly defended, and the Afghan Commander, Sirdar Nek Mahomed Khan (son of the great Ameer, Dost Mahomed, and

Sir Frederick Roberts's Plans.

uncle of Yakoob Khan), posted twelve guns on the heights, and three or four others on the plains below. But he counted without his host, for the British General intended to make a feint attack by the Sang-i-Nawishta Pass, and his main attack by the road skirting the hills into the Chardeh valley.

Immediately on arriving at Charasia Sir Frederick Roberts sent reconnoitring parties of cavalry along the three roads leading towards Cabul, but though a few shots were fired at them, there were no traces visible of any large body of the enemy. When night set in the General threw strong pickets all round the camp, and gave directions to the commander of his cavalry brigade to despatch patrols at daybreak to feel for the enemy, of whose intention to attack him, or bar his advance on the capital, he was convinced, though he could obtain no information from the Ameer or his Ministers and Sirdars. But this want of intelligence, and apparent absence of the enemy, did not influence him in his determination to seize as soon as possible after dawn the crest of the Sang-i-Nawishta Pass, by which road to Cabul he had decided to advance, and which was between five and six miles in advance of his camp at Charasia. During the course of the same day the 1,500 baggage animals were sent back to Zahidabad to bring up the stores under escort of Macpherson's Brigade. There was much difficulty in procuring supplies from the neighbouring villages, and Yakoob Khan, who anticipated that the British would meet with a repulse, made no effort to assist them.

Having formed his plans with the rapidity he had displayed on the eve of the memorable capture of Peiwar Kotul, Sir Frederick resolved to attack before the enemy, who were already in great force, had further strengthened their position. He came to this resolution, though he had with him little more than half his infantry; but with the intuition of genius, he divined that no considerations could outweigh those demanding immediate action, although the enemy outnumbered him probably three to one, and held positions along the ridge, which sloped on one side to the Sang-i-Nawishta Pass, and on the other to the road by the Chardeh Valley to Cabul, which would be regarded as impregnable to attack by any but a large force of the best troops. Such were those under Roberts's command, seasoned and highly-disciplined soldiers, for the most part veterans who had learnt to despise the enemy when led by a General in whom they had confidence, and whose eagerness was increased by a strong desire to measure themselves with the recreants who had committed the cowardly massacre of the British Envoy and his escort.

Soon after daybreak on the 6th October, as Benvolio says:—

> " An hour before the worshipp'd sun
> Peer'd forth the golden window of the East,"

Sir Frederick Roberts sent some infantry to work on a difficult place on the road through the Sang-i-Nawishta defile, and was about to follow himself to examine personally the pass and the ground beyond, when, before these arrangements could be carried out, the cavalry patrols were fired upon and compelled to return, and all doubts as to the intentions of the enemy were dispelled. He writes:—" Troops could be seen in large numbers and regular formation, crowning the crest line of the hills which extended from the narrow defile of the Sang-i-Nawishta (both sides of which were held) in their extreme left, to the heights above the Chardeh valley which formed their right. No hurry nor confusion marked their movements; positions were taken up and guns placed with so much deliberation and coolness that it was evident a large number of regular troops were massed against us." Soon afterwards Sir Frederick Roberts received a report that the cavalry patrols had been fired upon, and were retiring slowly.

Meantime General Macpherson's Brigade was making its way from Zahidabad, and a report was received that the road was blocked, and the column, with its endless string of baggage animals, would be attacked. Sir Frederick sent a squadron of cavalry to Macpherson's assistance, and directed him to push on with all despatch to join him.

The condition of affairs at this time was most critical. The enemy occupied in front a position, described to us by a General officer who was present, as "impregnable to a direct attack, but from which it was imperatively necessary that they should be dislodged before dark." Their occupation of the heights intervening between the British advance and Cabul could not be tolerated, while it was evident that they were mustering in strong force on the hills on both sides of the camp, with the object of waiting for nightfall or a favourable opportunity to attack. General Roberts had only two-thirds of his small force at his disposal, and yet he decided on an immediate advance on the enemy's position, for every hour he knew would add to its strength, as behind those hills, and the forces arrayed thereon against him, lay the city of Cabul, with its extensive suburbs of Chardeh and Deh-i-Afghan, and the villages of the Cabul Plain, filled with a teeming population, every male adult of whom was inured to bear arms from his youth, and which, as the events of the following December showed, could turn out over 100,000 fighting men. A reverse, of course, under the circumstances, would mean annihilation, and success could only be achieved by a vigorous offensive movement, such as General Roberts was the officer to conceive and his brave troops the men to execute.

The preparations for capturing the heights above Charasia completed, the General put once more into execution the flanking tactics he had adopted with such success on the 2nd December. "Their position," says the General, "was so strong and could only have been carried with such loss, that I determined the real attack should be made by an outflanking movement upon the right of the enemy, while their left continued to be occupied by a feint from our right." Dividing his force* into two parts, he entrusted to Brigadier-General Baker the difficult task of dislodging the enemy from the heights above the Chardeh valley, which formed their extreme right, and placed at his disposal a force of about 2,000 men, while a second column, under Major White, of the 92nd Highlanders, was directed to proceed towards the Sang-i-Nawishta defile,

---

* General Baker's Column consisted of the 72nd Highlanders, under Colonel Clarke ; 4 guns No. 2 Mountain Battery, Captain Swinley, R.A. ; and 2 Gatling Guns, Captain Broadfoot, R.A.; 7th Company of Sappers and Miners, Lieutenant Nugent, R.E. ; 6 Companies 5th Goorkhas, Major Fitzhugh ; 200 bayonets 5th Punjaub Infantry, Captain Hall ; and 450 of the 23rd Pioneers, Lieutenant-Colonel Currie. Major White took with him 3 guns G Battery, 3rd Brigade, Royal Artillery, Major Parry ; wing of 92nd Highlanders, Major Hay ; 2 squadrons of Cavalry made up of the 9th Lancers, 5th Punjaub Cavalry and 12th Bengal Cavalry, under Major Hammond ; 5th Punjaub Cavalry ; and 100 men of the 23rd Pioneers, Captain Paterson.

where the enemy had concentrated all their guns, in the belief that the main British attack would be on that point.

Owing to his numerical weakness Sir Frederick Roberts could not retain in camp any considerable number of troops from the two attacking columns, and as General Macpherson's Brigade was advancing from the rear, he decided to incur the danger that would have arisen from a determined attack on his camp, which was one of those inseparable from the conduct of warlike operations. He was in constant communication with the operating columns by means of the heliograph, directed by Captain Straton, and indeed without this novel but valuable adjunct to the equipment of an army in the field, he could not have conducted the operations to a successful conclusion with such precision.

General Baker assembled his little force in the wooded enclosures of Charasia, a collection of detached villages, such as are common in the country, in the most convenient of which he placed his reserve ammunition and Field Hospital, and heliographed to General Roberts to increase the strength of the guard he was able to leave in charge. The General, accordingly, sent at once 100 rifles of the 5th Punjaub Infantry, followed by the remainder of the regiment as soon as he could procure sufficient transport for their ammunition. The troops defending the camp were now reduced to between 600 and 700 infantry and 450 cavalry.*

Having secured his base, General Baker advanced over "some bare undulating hills, forming a position easily defensible, and flanked by steep, rocky crags, varying in height from 1,000 to 1,800 feet above the sloping plain which our troops had to cross." The main position of the enemy, which commanded their entire front, and was only accessible in a few places, was about 400 feet higher. Seeing the great natural strength of the position, General Baker directed Major White, who was placed under his orders, "to continue threatening the Sang-i-Nawishta Defile, to prevent the enemy occupying the village of Charasia, and to advance within artillery fire of the

---

* See Sir Frederick Roberts's despatch, dated " Bala Hissar, Cabul, 20th October, 1879," to which we are mainly indebted for the account of the action of Charasia.

Battle of Charasia.

enemy's main position," and finally, as soon as the outflanking movement was fully developed, and the enemy were in full retreat, to pursue through the pass with his cavalry, all which instructions Major White carried out with the soldierly ability anticipated by General Roberts when he selected him to command the supporting column. The first portion of Brigadier-General Baker's force to become engaged was Captain Brooke-Hunt's Company of the 92nd Highlanders, which was extended to crown the heights on the left, the remainder of the regiment, protected by the fire of two mountain guns, making the attack in front. Soon the Highlanders found their advance checked by the extremely difficult nature of the ground on their left flank, where the enemy, ensconced behind "sungas," or stone breastworks, opened a hot fire. General Baker brought forward two companies of the 5th Goorkhas, under Captain Cook, V.C., to strengthen Captain Brooke-Hunt, and two more companies of that regiment, under Major Fitzhugh, and 200 rifles of the 5th Punjaub Infantry, under Captain Hall, were sent to reinforce the direct attack. The Afghan commander now seeing that the real attack was directed against his right, brought his men from the direction of the Sang-i-Nawishta Defile, and his British antagonist strained every nerve to carry the position before it could be reinforced.

After some spirited fighting, in which Lieutenant Martin, of the Goorkhas, specially distinguished himself, about two o'clock the British troops succeeded in seizing the ridge on the left of the position, thus exposing the enemy to a heavy cross-fire, which inflicted great loss. The general advance was now sounded, and soon the British troops were in possession of the first position. The Afghans now took up a position about 600 yards in the rear, but from this they were driven, after some sharp fighting, our troops advancing in rushes, supported by the fire of the mountain guns. In this affair, says the General, the attack made by a company of the 23rd Pioneers, led by Lieutenant Chesney, supported by the 72nd Highlanders, 5th Goorkhas, and two companies of the 92nd Highlanders, "proved irresistible."

By 3.45 the entire ridge was gained, thus exposing the enemy's line of defence to being taken in reverse, which caused them to retire precipitately from their position on the Sang-i-Nawishta, in which quarter the operations were conducted by Major White with a judgment and skill that fully justified the trust reposed in him by Sir Frederick Roberts. When the enemy, perceiving that the real attack was on the right of their position, weakened their left resting on the defile, Major White attacked with spirit, himself leading his men with characteristic gallantry. The Afghans gave way, leaving some guns in his hands, on which he pursued them through the pass and effected a junction with General Baker in the rear of the enemy's position. Their loss was estimated by Sir Frederick Roberts at upwards of 300 men killed, besides a large number wounded. All their guns, 20 in number, brought out from Cabul to assist in the defence of the position, were captured. Sir Frederick Roberts calculated that thirteen regiments of regular infantry were opposed to him, and they were aided by contingents from the city and neighbouring villages. In addition there was a large muster of tribesmen, chiefly Ghilzyes, on the hills which lay to the east and west of the camp, who caused some annoyance, but were dislodged by a detachment of the 92nd Highlanders, and prevented from venturing into the plain by patrols of cavalry. General Macpherson's advance from Zahidabad, with a large convoy of stores and reserve ammunition, was also opposed, but he easily drove off his assailants, and after his arrival at the camp, all anxiety on the score of its safety ceased. The British loss in the action of Charasia was 16 soldiers and 4 camp followers killed, and 3 officers, 59 men and 5 camp followers wounded; of these 38 belonged to the 72nd Highlanders, of whom several died.

Sir Frederick Roberts struck his tents at sunset, as with characteristic promptitude he resolved to follow up the enemy and march through the Sang-i-Nawishta Defile towards Cabul, before they had time to recover themselves and organize further resistance. Events soon proved that had he delayed in attacking the enemy on the 6th October, even to the extent of waiting for the arrival of General Macpherson's Brigade, the resistance to be overcome would have been vastly increased, as the regular regiments of the Afghan Army acted as a nucleus, around which the natives rallied, and every hour brought accessions to the ranks of the opposing force. On this point the Viceroy, writing to the Secretary of State on the 16th October, from Simla, says—"It is now known that the plans for arresting the advance of our troops upon Cabul had been carefully laid, and that the Ghilzyes had been instructed to act against the flanks and rear of our column, while the regular troops and the Cabul people undertook to bar its passage across the hills in front."

It was the receipt of information to this effect that decided the General to attack at once the force on the heights, since delay would have given the enemy time to bring up reinforcements from the city, and to strengthen a position rendered sufficiently formidable by nature.

Early in the morning of the 7th October Sir Frederick moved out of his camp to Beni Hissar (or Ben-i-Shahr, as it is indifferently called) on the Cabul Road, with the cavalry brigade, two guns of F-A, Horse Artillery, two guns of G-3, Royal Artillery, a wing of the 92nd Highlanders, 7th company Sappers and Miners, the 23rd Pioneers, and the Gatling guns, his intention being to gather his whole force at Beni Hissar prior to the final advance on Cabul.* Marching by way of

---

* The following geographical description of the country about Cabul, which was the scene of stirring events during the next three months, is by the correspondent of the *Times* (writing from Cabul on the 19th of June :)—"As Sir Frederick Roberts's force debouched from the Sang-i-Nawishta Pass into the Cabul Valley, it had on its left a range of hills running almost due north and south, which commencing near Char-Asia, is first broken at the Deh-i-Mazung defile, as it has been convenient to call it. The highest point of this range is the Takht-i-Shah, or King's Throne, a little to the south of Cabul. North of the Takht-i-Shah the range makes a dip, and rises again to what is locally known as the Shahr-Dawaza (City Gate) hill, under which to the east nestles the city of Cabul. The Takht-i-Shah is about 7,600 feet, and the Shah-Dawaza, 7,166 feet above the sea level. A long spur, with a tolerably easy slope, is thrown off from the Takht i-Shah due east to the villages of Beni-Hissar, and another from the Shahr-Dawaza, on the lowest extremity of which latter is placed the Upper and Lower Bala Hissar. This last spur encloses the city of Cabul to the south. In very ancient times the safety of the city from attack from the west was provided for by a masonry wall, which starting from where the Bala Hissar wall ends, is continued first up the spur and thence along the whole crest of the Shahr-Dawaza, and down the precipitous northern face of it, into the bed of the Cabul river. The range of hills described above is continued on the northern side of the Cabul river, and here changes its course to north-west. The hill immediately above the Cabul river, and facing the northern slopes of the Shah-Dawaza, is known as Asmai, or Koh-Asmai.

the Sang-i-Nawishta Defile, where some parties of hillmen opened fire upon his troops, but were easily dispersed, he arrived at Beni Hissar, where Brigadier-General Baker joined him with the main portion of his force during the same afternoon.

It must have been with no little eagerness that Sir Frederick Roberts first cast his glance on the towers and ramparts of the Bala Hissar, that famous citadel whose name arouses such painful recollections in the minds of those conversant with the Indian history of 40 years ago. To Roberts the sight must have called up memories of his father, whose services during the Afghan war were so distinguished, and whose warnings were disregarded by a Government who continued to call "Peace, Peace, when there was no Peace." By a strange fatality the son was destined by services that are historical to associate his own name with a fortress which in its blood-stained records has played a part similar to our Tower of London, that palace, prison and fortress in one. Once again, after the lapse of 40 years, the Bala Hissar was to receive a hostile British Army.

History has indeed repeated itself in a remarkable way, and the writer of this memoir,—who, in a work on the first

---

The Koh-Asmai is 6,790 feet above the sea at its highest point, just above the Deh-i-Mazung defile. The wall mentioned as starting from the Bala-Hissar is continued up the Koh-Asmai also, and meets at the culminating point a second wall, also carried up the face of the hill from the village or rather suburb of Cabul called Deh-Afghana. The Koh-Asmai has a length of about a mile, when it sinks into a Kotul or saddle; over it passes one road to Urghundeh and Ghazni, and on the right of the road the hill rises again to a conical point. The whole surface of Koh-Asmai is of the most rugged character, offering numerous peaks and monster rocks most favourable for defence. In conclusion, this range of hills continues a north-westerly course, broken by occasional gaps, until it joins the Pughman range about twenty-two miles from Charasia. It forms the northern limit of the beautiful Chardeh Valley, from whence it alters its direction to north-west, just as during its northern course it had formed the eastern boundary of that valley. It is further the watershed which divides the drainage of the Cabul river from that of the Juibar stream, which runs through the Kohistan country. The Cabul valley itself is a plain only broken by the low flat-topped Siah-Sung hills. The Cabul river approaches the city through the Deh-i-Mazung defile, and is over-hung by the Shahr-Dawaza on one side and Koh-Asmai on the other. After passing through the city it takes a north-westerly course, and crossing the road which connects the Bala Hissar with Sherpur, it flows about midway between Sherpur and the northern part of the Siah Sung Hills."

Afghan war,* (drawn from the papers of the late General Augustus Abbott, who served throughout those protracted operations, and commanded the artillery of Sir Robert Sale's force,) published in 1878, deprecated the outbreak of hostilities, and drew a parallel of the circumstances under which war was declared by the Governments of Lords Auckland and Lytton —could scarcely have supposed that the coincidences would be still further borne out by the murder of a British envoy, followed by the arrival before Cabul of a British Army of retribution, which, moreover, was commanded, as in 1842, by an officer of the old Bengal Artillery.

It was ascertained that the Bala Hissar had been evacuated, and the Ameer assured the General that he would meet with no further opposition. Little reliance, however, could be placed on the statements of a man who confidentially informed the British General that he would meet with no resistance at Charasia, whereas it was afterwards discovered that he was kept informed of the true state of affairs by Afghan emissaries, who visited him in the British Camp during the advance from Kushi, and it was even confidently stated that Nek Mohamed, the Afghan commander at Charasia, was among his visitors, and tried to induce him to place himself at the head of the Army.

On the morning of the 8th October Sir Frederick Roberts, having received information that those of the enemy who had not dispersed to their homes would probably retreat towards Kohistan, directed General Massy to proceed with the cavalry brigade, consisting of 8 squadrons, or 720 sabres, and take up a position across their line of retreat. From General Massy's report it appears that a hostile force, consisting of remnants of the regiments which had fought at Charasia, together with three fresh regiments, which had arrived on the preceding day from Kohistan, supported by the "budmashes," or bad characters, of the city and neighbouring villages, had taken up a strong position, which was further strengthened by

---

* The writer will be pardoned for mentioning that this work found its way into the British Camp before Cabul in 1879–80, and Sir Frederick Roberts informed him that the special correspondent of the *Times* placed it in his hands for perusal.

twelve guns, on a high hill beyond the Bala Hissar, called the Asmai heights, immediately overlooking the city on the north-west side. The enemy were under the leadership of Mahomed Jan, a soldier whose name appears prominently in the succeeding operations; among other chiefs present being Khusdil Khan, who had been deputed by Yakoob Khan to receive and escort to Cabul the Cavagnari mission.

In order to dislodge the enemy and compel them to fall back on the cavalry, Roberts directed Brigadier-General Baker to advance with a column,* consisting of 1,044 infantry, two guns, and one Gatling. Owing, however, to the difficult nature of the ground, much delay ensued, and the day was far advanced before Baker found himself near enough to open fire with his guns on the enemy, who were posted in the angle formed by the two walls running up the Koh Asmai from the Bala Hissar and suburb of Deh Afghan, and on the slopes of the hill to the westward. Reinforcements, consisting of a wing of the 67th Regiment, two companies of the 5th Goorkhas, and the remaining two guns of No. 2 Mountain Battery, were despatched to his aid from camp, but did not reach him until past five o'clock, when there was not sufficient daylight to render an attack advisable. About this time Sir Frederick Roberts received intelligence that three regiments of regular infantry and twelve guns had started from Ghuznee a few days before in order to join Mohamed Jan's troops on the Asmai heights, and helio-graphed to General Baker his intention to strengthen him during the night with four guns of F-A, Royal Horse Artillery, on elephants, the remaining wing of the 67th Regiment, and the 28th Punjaub Native Infantry, under General Macpherson, who, as senior officer, would assume chief command. General Baker was also informed that Brigadier-General Gough had been sent with two Horse Artillery guns, and two squadrons of cavalry to watch the Kohistan road.

Meanwhile General Massy, who had left the camp an hour before noon, had crossed the low Siah-Sung range of hills, and

* The following was the constitution of General Baker's command:—2 guns, No. 2 Mountain Battery, under Lieutenant E. A. Smith, R.A.; 1 Gatling, Captain A. Broadfoot, R.A.; 2 Companies 72nd Highlanders, Captain C. Guinness; Headquarters wing, 92nd Highlanders, Lieutenant-Colonel Parker; 23rd Pioneers, Lieutenant-Colonel Currie.

proceeding northwards, entered and took possession of the fortified camp at Sherpur, which had been abandoned by the enemy, who had left therein seventy-three guns of various calibre, and three howitzers. Thence General Massy marched to the west, and then, making a great *détour* to the north, in order to get in rear of the enemy's position on the Asmai heights, eventually, about sunset, he debouched into the Chardeh plain, thus blocking the line of the enemy's retreat, and took up a position of observation to the westward of the village of Deh Mazung, though when night fell, he drew in his brigade and bivouacked under cover of the walled enclosures near the road running past Aliabad.*

Unfortunately Sir Frederick Roberts's carefully laid plans were foiled by the roughness of the road, which prevented the reinforcements sent to General Baker from reaching the ground in time to deliver an attack before nightfall, a miscalculation which had a disastrous result in prolonging the struggle and rendering possible the combination of the following December, which required such vigorous measures before it could be dispersed. During the night General Baker, fearing that the enemy might abandon their position under cover of the darkness, sent a strong patrol, at 1.30 A.M., to ascertain if any change had taken place, and three hours later it was reported to him that the camp, containing twelve guns, some elephants, and a large supply of camp equipage, was deserted. General Baker immediately communicated this intelligence to General Massy, and informed him that in accordance with instructions received from Sir Frederick Roberts, any movement of the cavalry in pursuit would be supported both by the troops under his command and those under General Macpherson, who joined General Baker about dawn. Accordingly, General Massy went in pursuit with his cavalry, sending, under instructions from Sir Frederick Roberts, two squadrons across country, up to and beyond the Kohistan road, but such an extraordinary faculty have Afghan levies in dispersing and mixing with the peaceful portion of the community that, though the entire country was scoured throughout the day, of the

---

* See despatch of Sir Frederick Roberts.

thousands assembled on the Asmai heights only a small party of fugitives was overtaken on the Ghuznee road by the 5th Punjaub Cavalry, who sabred twenty or thirty of them. General Massy detached two squadrons of the 12th Bengal Cavalry to continue the pursuit, and returned to camp late in the evening with the remainder of his brigade, who had suffered much from fatigue and scanty food. The troops under Generals Macpherson and Baker, and the small force of cavalry and guns, under Brigadier-General Gough, also arrived in camp before nightfall.*

On the 9th General Roberts moved the camp of the whole of the division from Beni Hissar to the Siah-Sung hills, a low flat-topped ridge, the scene of severe fighting during the first Afghan war, which completely dominates the city of Cabul. The only troops not in camp were the 5th Goorkhas and four guns of No. 2 Mountain Battery, which were stationed on the upper Bala Hissar hill. It soon became apparent, as might have been anticipated, that the villagers of the Cabul Valley, and almost the entire people, were hostile to the invaders, and shooting at the sentinels became a nightly practice, while efforts were made to raise the tribesmen for an organized attack on the camp.

On the following day, the 10th October, Sir Frederick Roberts visited the Sherpur cantonment,† and despatched the 5th Punjaub Cavalry thither for the protection of the guns and stores.

---

* See despatch of Sir Frederick Roberts.
† Sherpur is thus described by the *Times* correspondent :—" Shere Ali's great straggling cantonment of Sherpur takes the shape of a huge parallelogram, the long sides of which lie north and south. The length of the long sides is about 2,700 yards, and of the short sides 1,100. When our troops entered it in October the west and south faces only were completed, and even these were much out of repair. The north side was and is still formed by the Behmaru heights, a round-topped ridge of hill, broken in the centre by a broad gorge, and rising, perhaps, 800 feet above the plain. The fourth side, that on the east, was only traced. Shere Ali's original design is believed to have been to carry the walls all round the Behmaru heights, and thus to form a great square, with the heights in the centre, upon which he had already laid the foundation of a citadel. He had also laid the foundation of a palace for himself at the southern foot of the heights. What was the ultimate object of this ambitious design can only be conjectured. It was possibly part of the same idea which led him to devote such pains to the manufacture of guns, of which, when the war broke out, he possessed no less a number than 379, of which 34 were of siege calibre, 145 field, and 150 mountain. It has also been found, from

It was the general belief that Shere Ali contemplated the removal of Cabul to Sherpur, and the demolition of the Bala Hissar, which is commanded from the adjacent heights; but his false move in throwing himself into the arms of Russia put an end to his plans, and resulted in his dying a miserable fugitive at Mazar-i-Sheriff.

On the 11th October Sir Frederick Roberts, with his staff and a small escort, accompanied by the Ameer's ministers and Daoud Shah, paid an informal visit to the Bala Hissar, where crumbling walls and neglected buildings attested the decay which awaits everything in this distracted land. The General, after closely examining the fortress, visited the ruined buildings of the late Residency, where Cavagnari and his gallant band made their desperate stand for life. Very great, albeit painful, was the interest with which the British General, ascending to a point in the shattered walls affording a commanding view, surveyed the scene of desolation in the immediate foreground, with the beautiful Cabul Valley spread out at his feet.

The quarters occupied by the Guides, adjoining the Residency, were also visited, and the gate where Lieutenant Hamilton made his memorable defence, when, sword and revolver in hand, he three times charged out into the thick of the enemy, like the swift-footed son of Peleus :—

> "High o'er the scene of death Achilles stood,
> All grim with dust, all horrible in blood;
> Yet still insatiate, still with rage in flame,
> Such is the lust of never-dying fame."

Leaving this scene of sadness and pride to every Englishman, Sir Frederick Roberts visited the Ameer's Palace, and returned to camp after an inspection not likely ever to be forgotten.

At noon on the day succeeding this visit, the Bala Hissar was formally occupied by a portion of the British troops. The whole division having lined both sides of the road from the camp to the citadel, a distance of over a mile, Sir Frederick

---

examination of the magazine records, that he possessed no less than 50,000 small arms of all sorts, of which all but about 12,000 were either English, or cleverly imitated, like many of his guns, from English models by Native artificers."

Roberts, accompanied by General Hills and his four Brigadier-Generals, Macpherson, Massy, Baker, and Gough, and a large number of the most influential Sirdars of Cabul, rode slowly along the splendid display of the flower of our British and Indian troops to the Bala Hissar, the infantry presenting arms, the cavalry trumpets braying forth a salute, and the bands playing. As the head of the brilliant procession entered the fortress, the British flag was hoisted over the gateway, under a royal salute of thirty-one guns fired on the glacis. From the gateway one company of the 67th Regiment, followed by the band, led the way to the Diwan-i-Aum, or Grand Reception Room, Sir Frederick and his Generals, with their respective Staffs, following, and the procession being closed by the remainder of the 67th Regiment.

The scene in the Diwan-i-Aum was singular and suggestive. Around the British Commander crowded the Afghan Sirdars, ready to make any promises to their conqueror, and equally ready, as the event proved, to break them. At his side stood Moosa Khan, a child six years of age, heir-apparent of the Ameer, who excused himself from attending on the score of indisposition. This was the ostensible cause of his absence, but the real reason, which was kept secret for manifest considerations of state, is set forth in the following account given by Sir Frederick Roberts:—" Early on the morning of this day the Ameer walked to my camp, accompanied by only two attendants, and expressed his determination to resign the Ameership. He said he had intended doing so before going to Kushi, but had allowed himself to be over-persuaded. He was in very low spirits; said his life had been a miserable one; that he would rather be a grass cutter in the English camp than Ruler of Afghanistan, and begged he might live in this camp until he could be sent to India, or London, or wherever the Viceroy might desire to send him. I placed a tent at his disposal; ordered breakfast to be prepared for him, and begged him to think over the matter for two or three hours, and said I would see him at ten o'clock, the time appointed the previous evening for His Highness to come to my camp, and accompany me to the Bala Hissar. The Ameer knew nothing of the proposed proclamation, and was quite ignorant of my intentions towards the Mustaufi, the Wuzeer, Yahya Khan and his brother. At ten I had a second interview with the Ameer, who stated that he had quite decided to give up the throne of Cabul; that he could not possibly accompany me to the Bala Hissar, but that he would send his eldest son, and all his Ministers would be in attendance. I again pointed out the serious step His Highness was taking; but finding his mind was made up, I said I would telegraph to the Viceroy for instructions; that of course he could not be forced to remain on as Ameer against his will; but that I should ask him to retain the title until I could receive a reply to the telegram."

Sir Frederick Roberts addressed the assembled Sirdars, and then read to them a proclamation* indicating the intentions of

---

* The following is the text of the proclamation :—" Bala Hissar, Cabul, 12th October, 1879.—In my proclamation of the 3rd October, dated Zerghun Shah, I informed the people of Cabul that a British Army was advancing to take possession of the city, and I warned them against offering any resistance to the entry of the troops, and the authority of His Highness the Ameer. That warning has been disregarded. The force under my command has now reached Cabul, and occupied the Bala Hissar; but its advance has been pertinaciously opposed, and the inhabitants of the city have taken a conspicuous part in the opposition offered. They have therefore become rebels against His Highness the Ameer, and have added to the guilt already incurred by them, in abetting the murder of the British Envoy and of his companions, a treacherous and cowardly crime, which has brought indelible disgrace on the Afghan people. It would be but a just and fitting reward for such misdeeds if the city of Cabul was totally destroyed and its very name blotted out. But the great British Government is ever desirous to temper justice with mercy, and I now announce to the inhabitants of Cabul that the city will be spared. Nevertheless it is necessary that they should not escape all penalty, and that the punishment inflicted should be such as will be felt and remembered. Therefore such of the buildings as now interfere with the proper military occupation of the Bala Hissar, and the safety and comfort of the British troops quartered in it, will be at once levelled with the ground; and further, a heavy fine, the amount of which will be notified hereafter, will be imposed upon the inhabitants, to be paid according to their several capabilities. This punishment, inflicted upon the whole city, will not, of course, absolve from further penalties those whose individual guilt may be hereafter proved. A full and searching inquiry will be held into all the circumstances of the late outbreak, and all persons convicted of bearing a part in it will be dealt with according to their desert. I further give notice to all, that, in order to provide for the restoration and maintenance of order, the city of Cabul and the surrounding country, to a distance of ten miles, are placed under martial law. With the consent of the Ameer, a Military Governor of Cabul will be appointed to administer justice, and to punish with a strong hand all evil doers. The inhabitants of Cabul and of the neighbouring villages are hereby warned to submit to his authority. For the future the carrying of dangerous weapons, whether swords, knives, or firearms,

the British Government, and the punishment he intended to mete out to the people of Cabul for offering resistance to his advance and the authority of the Ameer, contrary to the warning conveyed in his proclamation of the 3rd October. He said that he would spare the city, though were he to raze it to the ground, for the treacherous murder of the British Mission, and the rebellion against their sovereign the Ameer, he would only be meting out a just retribution. But he could not permit that the Cabulees should escape all punishment, and he intended to destroy certain buildings that interfered with the military occupation of the Bala Hissar, and to inflict a fine on the whole city, while a full and searching inquiry into the circumstances of the massacre would be held, and all persons convicted of participating in it, would be dealt with according to their deserts. He also declared that the city of Cabul and the surrounding country, for a radius of ten miles, was placed under martial law, and a military governor would be appointed to administer justice and inflict punishment on all evil doers. The carrying of arms was prohibited in Cabul, or within a distance of five miles, and after a week from the date of the proclamation, any person found armed within these limits would be liable to the punishment of death. All arms delivered up would be paid for at a stipulated rate, and finally, rewards, graduated from

---

within the streets of Cabul, or within a distance of five miles from the city gates, is forbidden. After a week from the date of this proclamation any person found armed within these limits will be liable to the penalty of death. Persons having in their possession any article whatever which formerly belonged to members of the British Embassy, are required to bring them forthwith to the British Camp. Any one neglecting this warning will, if found hereafter in possession of any such articles, be subjected to the severest penalties. Further, all persons who may have in their possession any firearms or ammunition formerly issued to, or seized by the Afghan troops, are required to produce them. For every country-made rifle, whether breech or muzzle-loading, a sum of three rupees will be given on delivery; and for every rifle of European manufacture, five rupees. Any one found hereafter in possession of such weapons will be severely punished. Finally, I notify that I will give a reward of fifty rupees for the surrender of any person, whether soldier or civilian, concerned in the attack on the British Embassy, or for such information as may lead directly to his capture. A similar sum will be given in case of any person who may have fought against the British troops, since the 3rd September last, and has therefore become a rebel against the Ameer. If any such person so surrendered or captured be a captain or a subaltern officer of the Afghan Army, the reward will be increased to seventy-five rupees; and if a field officer, to 120 rupees."

120 rupees for a field officer, 75 rupees for officers of inferior rank, and 50 rupees for a soldier or civilian, were offered for the surrender of any persons concerned in the attack on the British Residency, or for such information as might lead to their capture ; and similar rewards were offered for the apprehension of any person who had fought against the British Army since the 3rd September, the date of the massacre, as they had placed themselves by this act within the category of rebels against the authority of their sovereign the Ameer, who had issued a proclamation from the British Camp at Kushi, requiring his subjects to abstain from resorting to arms.

Very severe strictures were passed in the House of Commons and by a portion of the English Press on those provisions of this proclamation punishing with death persons found armed within five miles of Cabul, and those who had been engaged in the recent fighting; but the fact was, that they remained a dead letter, never having been acted upon. Sir Frederick Roberts, writing to us of these provisions, says :—" The order must of course be read in connection with my other orders, and with a clear understanding of the position I was placed in, with Yakoob Khan in my camp, ostensibly as my friend, as being rebelled against by his own soldiers." The order referred to by Sir Frederick Roberts is the proclamation to the people of Cabul, issued at Kushi on the 3rd October, warning them against resisting his advance, and the general orders to his troops of the 24th September and 1st October appealing to the officers and men to exercise mercy and forbearance—orders which the gallant General copied out for us with his own hand, so desirous is he that his countrymen should do justice to the feelings of humanity with which he was actuated in his dealings with the Afghan nation. Those who have a personal knowledge of Sir Frederick Roberts needed no such disclaimer as the above, for a more humane officer does not exist, and no detractor, if any there now be, can point to an incident in his career when he displayed harshness towards the weak or vanquished. No officer in India had acquired a better title to be regarded as humane in a calling which tends to sear the heart, and Roberts fulfilled the requirements of Wordsworth's ideal Christian Warrior :—

> "Who, doom'd to go in company with pain,
> And fear, and bloodshed, miserable train!
> Turns his necessity to glorious gain;
> In face of those doth exercise a power
> Which is our human nature's highest dower;
> Controls them, and subdues, transmutes, bereaves
> Of their bad influence, and their good receives;
> By objects, which might force the soul to abate
> Her feeling, rendered more compassionate."

The comments of Admiral Oliver Jones, in an incident at the storm of Meeangunj in the Oude Campaign (given in a preceding chapter) testify that from an early period in his military career the subject of this memoir had earned a character for humanity in times and under circumstances when this virtue was not a distinguishing trait of the British soldier.

When dismissing the Sirdars from his presence after the durbar, Sir Frederick Roberts directed the arrest of the Mustaufi, Habibullah Khan, the Wuzeer, Shah Mahomed, and Yahya Khan, whom he informed of his intention to retain them until the circumstances connected with the attack on the Residency had been inquired into. The 67th Regiment was ordered to encamp in the gardens which lie immediately in front of the Diwan-i-Aum, and six companies of the 5th Goorkhas were moved into the upper Bala Hissar fort.

On the day following the reading of the proclamation of the 3rd October, the inhabitants of Cabul had to submit to the humiliation of seeing a foreign army march through the streets of the capital. "Horse, Foot, and Dragoons," the whole gallant array, the Cavalry Brigade leading, followed by the General with his Staff and escort, five regiments of Infantry bringing up the rear, traversed its principal streets and bazaars, including the famous Char Chonk, one of the finest in Central Asia, which was partially blown up by Sir George Pollock in 1842 as a punishment for the treachery of the Cabulees. In accordance with the terms of the proclamation, Major-General James Hills, C.B., V.C., who had accompanied the army as the guest of the Commander, was appointed Military Governor of Cabul, and under his rule mercy tempered the stern requirements of martial law.

For the investigation of the causes and circumstances of the late outbreak, and the collection of all possible evidence regarding the conduct of individuals since the arrival of the British Embassy in Cabul, Sir Frederick Roberts nominated a commission, consisting of his Chief of the staff, Colonel C. M. Macgregor, C.B., C.S.I., Surgeon-Major Bellew, C.S.I., and Mahammed Hyat Khan, C.S.I. Their duties were comprehensive, and included the submission of recommendations regarding the punishment to be inflicted on all persons whom they found guilty of participation in the attack on the Residency. The actual trial of the prisoners was confided to a second military commission, consisting of a Brigadier-General and two other officers.

Meanwhile, Sir Frederick Roberts made strenuous efforts to collect a reserve of supplies, for winter was approaching, and he was anxious to guard against any eventualities. As the son of an officer whose warning voice was raised, and raised in vain, during the first Afghan War, he knew well the danger of under-estimating the powers of resistance of the Afghan people, even when seemingly beaten to the earth and powerless, so he kept his troops prepared for a sudden crisis, and busied himself in collecting supplies and perfecting his transport.

CHAPTER XIV.

The Cabul District after its Occupation by the British—Events at the Shutargardan Pass—The Explosion in the Bala Hissar—Occupation of the Sherpur Cantonment—Sir Frederick Roberts Reconnoitres the Passes towards Jugdulluck—Abandonment of the Shutargardan—The Expedition to Maidan—Unsettled State of the Country—Deportation of Yakoob Khan to India—A Review of the Situation in Northern Afghanistan before the Events of December 1879.

THE people of Afghanistan, truculent and treacherous though they are, and tainted, like Byron's Corsair, with "a thousand crimes," possess, like him, "one virtue," and that is a sturdy love of independence. This they displayed in the darkest hour of the first Afghan War, and ultimately compelled a British force to evacuate the country under a humiliating Convention. In the present instance they had to deal with a General of a different calibre to General Elphinstone, but they struggled manfully to shake off the yoke of the invader. During the stirring events of the following December it seemed to the outside world that a terrible tragedy was about to be enacted on the very scene of the disasters of 1841-42. Sir Frederick Roberts's countrymen in England watched with bated breath the struggle for mastery under the walls of Cabul, but never for one moment did the gallant upholder of England's cause, who displayed in the crisis the "antique heroism" with which Lord Raglan was credited by Marshal St. Arnaud, lose his calmness and confidence in the success of his plans.

In the middle of October, to which the course of events has brought us, the Afghans, utterly defeated in the field, and with their capital occupied by a foreign foe, did not lose heart, but, within a few days of the public entry of Sir Frederick Roberts into Cabul, reports were current that a strong force was on the march for the city from Afghan Turkistan. On receiving information to this effect, on the 14th October, Sir Frederick

Fighting at the Shutargardan.

Roberts immediately sent some Cavalry to reconnoitre, but nothing definite could be ascertained of their movements.

On the 13th October, the day Sir Frederick Roberts made his triumphal march through Cabul, he received intelligence from Colonel Money, commanding at the Shutargardan, that he expected to be attacked by the Ghilzyes, who were assembling in great strength in his neighbourhood. This information proved correct, and at 8 A.M. on the following morning, some 2,000 of these tribesmen fired upon the party sent to relieve the detachment occupying the blockhouse in the Sirkai Kotul, which had before been strengthened. Colonel Money ordered Major Griffiths to proceed with two companies of the 3rd Sikhs and two of the 21st Punjaub Native Infantry, with one gun, to hold the steep ridge near the camp, and this post he not only defended throughout the day, notwithstanding every effort of the enemy to dislodge him, but carried at the point of the bayonet a position they had taken up on a rocky ridge and pursued them for two miles.

On the 17th, Sir Frederick Roberts sent Brigadier-General Gough to the Shutargardan with a force consisting of 4 guns No. 2 Mountain Battery, 5th Punjaub Cavalry, and 5th Punjaub Infantry, together with a large convoy of transport animals for the three-fold object of opening out his communications, bringing up supplies, and rendering aid to Colonel Money. Brigadier-General Gough arrived at a most opportune moment, for the tribes that had attacked the Shutargardan position, though defeated, were by no means disheartened, and, on the 15th, had received such large accessions from Zurmat, Hazara, and elsewhere, that by nightfall they were calculated to number about 10,000 men. They dismantled the unoccupied post of Karatiga, and were so confident of overwhelming the British garrison that they brought their women to witness their triumph, and actually offered to spare the lives of the garrison if they would lay down their arms. Colonel Money rejected the terms with scorn, and took the wise precaution of concentrating his strength by withdrawing the garrison of the Sirkai Kotul, but adopted no offensive steps. Encouraged by his apparent inactivity, and strengthened by some hundreds of men belonging to the mutinous regiments of the regular army, the enemy's sharp-

s

shooters opened fire on the garrison. But the tables were soon turned.

On the morning of the 19th Colonel Money learnt by heliographic signal of the arrival of Brigadier-General Gough at Kooshi, and immediately took the offensive. Moving out his skirmishers he opened fire with four guns of the Kohat Mountain Battery, and the enemy finding that their opportunity had gone, quitted their positions, and by the evening not a man was to be seen. Alla-ood-deen, brother of the great Ghilzye Chief, Padshah Khan, was severely wounded by a shell while approaching the advance picket on his return from making an attempt to break up the hostile combination of his countrymen, and paid the penalty of his conduct, which was supposed to be treacherous, with his life, as his wound proved mortal.*

On the 16th October, about 1 P.M., the British troops and the inhabitants of Cabul were startled by a loud report from the direction of the upper Bala Hissar, and a vast column of smoke and showers of *débris* showed that an explosion had occurred in the Arsenal, in which were stored over one million pounds of powder, as roughly calculated by Colonel Perkins, Commanding the Royal Engineers. The 67th Regiment were in tents in the Ameer's garden, and the 5th Goorkhas in the upper Bala Hissar fort, and both Corps suffered some loss. One soldier of the 67th and twelve of the latter regiment, were killed; also three Sowars of the 5th Punjaub Cavalry, and five Ordnance Lascars, fell victims to the explosion, and Captain Shafto, R.A., Commissary of Ordnance, who was examining the godowns containing the ammunition, and making an inventory of the contents, shared the same fate. In addition to these, four men were seriously injured.

Sir Frederick Roberts immediately ordered the 5th Goorkhas to leave their camp, and also directed the 67th Regiment to remove from the garden of the Dewan-i-Aum, which was in dangerous proximity to the now burning ruins. He would not even permit them to remove their tents or kit, and with the exception of their regimental ammunition, everything was

---

* See despatch from Lieutenant-Colonel Murray, dated Shutargardan, 19th October, 1879.

left behind. The wisdom of this precipitate evacuation was soon apparent, as exactly two and a half hours after the first explosion, a second occurred of greater violence, by which some natives, upwards of 400 yards distant from the magazine, were killed by falling stones and *débris*. The 67th Regiment was accommodated for the night in the tents of the 72nd and 92nd Highlanders, and an instance of the *camaraderie* (to use an expressive French term) existing between the 72nd and the 5th Goorkhas, brothers-in-arms at the Peiwar Kotul and companions in many a bivouac, was exhibited by a large number of the Highlanders coming forward and insisting upon lending their great coats for the night to the brave little mountaineers of Nepaul. This was no small act of self denial, as the nights were bitterly cold.*

Sir Frederick Roberts's anxiety was not lessened for some days, as a terrible danger threatened the entire city in the possible ignition of the main magazine, in which were stored upwards of 450 tons of gunpowder. Barely ninety yards intervened between this magazine and the flames, and during the night of the 16th, its explosion was momentarily expected; indeed, its walls, which were by no means of substantial construction, were considerably scorched. Providentially, towards morning the wind went down, and with it the flames began to subside, and the explosions, which had never ceased, became less frequent. On the following afternoon, the 17th October, Sir Frederick Roberts deemed the danger so considerably lessened as to allow of working parties endeavouring to extinguish the conflagration. Even then, he says, the work was one of considerable danger, as the main magazine (to prevent the fire spreading to which was the principal task) was fitted with a weak roof, much projecting woodwork, and badly-fitted doors of the same inflammable material. However, the officers and men worked with energy and devotion, and though the fire smouldered for days, all anxiety as to the safety of the main magazine ceased.

---

* A similar instance of soldierly feeling was afforded during the defence of Jellalabad in the last Afghan War, between Her Majesty's 13th Regiment and the 35th Bengal Native Infantry, a regiment which unhappily subsequently disgraced itself by mutinying in the Punjaub in 1857, as already detailed in a preceding chapter.

"The Arsenal," writes Sir Frederick Roberts to us, "was in the form of an oblong, on slightly sloping ground, and the long low buildings in which the ammunition was placed were simply constructed of mud, the doorways being wooden ones. The powder was stored in the upper buildings of the enclosure, and the small arms ammunition and shells below; but between the end of the long shed containing the various loaded shells, and the wooden door of the nearest building containing powder, there was a distance of barely fifteen yards. The first explosion, which proceeded from a large quantity of powder stored underneath the small arms ammunition, not only ignited a large quantity of cartridges and shells, and caused the death of Captain Shafto, R.A., and the men of the Goorkhas, as you have stated, but the concussion alone was sufficient to burst open the doors of the main powder magazines. These magazines were each filled up to the doorway with large jars, or "Kūppas," of hide, each containing some 200lbs of powder, and had any one of these been pierced by the thousands of bullets or fragments of shell that were flying about from the lower buildings, the friction would no doubt have caused an explosion which would have communicated itself to the surrounding powder, and an enormous loss of human life and destruction to property would have been the result.

"Throughout the night the conflagration went on, varied by rushes of flame, and columns of smoke as the fire reached more powder which had hitherto escaped, but still, to the wonder of the watchers on the Siah-Sung heights, the big magazine gave no sign, though at any moment they were prepared for some almost supernatural explosion. Next day the fire had abated, and though it was not entirely extinguished till some time afterwards, an exploring party managed to make their way inside. The place was a heap of smouldering ruins, and they were reminded by the constant explosion of an eight-inch shell or a box of Snider cartridges, that it was anything but a safe mission they were bound on. Leaning against the wooden frame of the door of the end powder magazine was a burning beam, which was removed by Lieutenant Neville Chamberlain. It had already commenced to char the door itself, and there can be no doubt that another half-hour would have sufficed to ignite the powder—800,000 lbs! We have, perhaps, no record of any such amount having exploded at once, and though it was believed by the Engineer Officers with the Cabul Field Force, that the shock would have caused the large town of Cabul to be levelled in one vast ruin, it requires a skilled mathematician, and one learned in the force of explosives, to tell us, after learning the precise configuration of the ground on which the magazine stood, how far, and to what extent, that gigantic mass would have made its power felt.

"Engineer Officers were immediately ordered to destroy the powder in the most expeditious manner, and daily a large quantity was run down a steep slope in a kind of trough, into the water, which flows round the Bala Hissar; but the place being abandoned during the fighting which took place early in December, a considerable amount remained, which fell into the hands of the Afghans." Sir Frederick Roberts has been blamed for not having destroyed the powder at once, but clearly he has been misjudged. Handling powder at any time is necessarily a delicate and dangerous operation, and must be slowly and cautiously carried on; but when one considers that this enormous mass of powder was in skin jars, which could not be moved without tumbling to pieces, and that it was impossible to blow it up without causing a disaster, it would seem clear that General Roberts took the best measures possible for its destruction, and he cannot be blamed if this was not completed before the troubles of December began.

In the Cabul Force there was at first a decided suspicion of treachery. It was believed that the Afghans had hidden in the vaults of the Magazine some infernal machine which was to explode after our troops had filled the Bala Hissar; but in Sir Frederick Roberts's opinion, subsequent inquiries proved that this was scarcely possible. The General, accompanied by his Staff, visited the magazine the day before the explosion, and found everything in a state of the utmost confusion. Instead of the order which ought to reign supreme in any Arsenal, loose powder, percussion caps, cartridges, loaded shells, fuses, and friction tubes were strewed about indiscriminately. Poor Captain Shafto commented on this at the time, and expressed his intention of getting everything safely arranged, each in its proper place, as soon as possible ; and it was probably the case that, on the following day, as he and his men were at work, some one of them trod on a friction tube or a percussion cap, or powder exploded, which communicated the fire to the whole magazine.

The Military Commission, presided over by Brigadier-General Massy, convicted five persons of participating in the attack on the Residency, and on the 20th October, they were executed in the Bala Hissar. One of these men was the Kotwali, or Police Magistrate, of Cabul, who was implicated in the massacre of the Cavagnari Mission and urged the people of Cabul to resist the advance of Sir Frederick Roberts's force. Another of the prisoners was a Mollah, or priest, of great sanctity, who exerted his religious influence over a fanatical people to induce them to wage war against the unbelievers, and who had taken an active part in the attack on the Residency. The other culprits were a Chief of the Barukzye, or reigning clan, and an officer of the Ameer's Army, who fought against the British on the 6th October. The fifth and most culpable of all was a man who had actually imbrued his hands in the blood of the victims of the treacherous and savage deed of the 3rd September. These and others convicted of participation in the Massacre were executed, and met their doom with the stolidity, or fortitude, whichever we may regard it, characteristic of the Oriental, whose fatalistic creed is embodied in the words Hector addressed to his spouse in his final memorable interview :—

> " Fixed is the term of all the race of men ;
> And such the hard condition of our birth,
> No force can then resist, no flight can save,
> All sink alike, the fearful and the brave."

Since the 12th October, when Yakoob Khan resigned the Ameership into the hands of Sir Frederick Roberts, saying he would rather be a grass-cutter in the British Camp than ruler of so turbulent a race as his quondam subjects, the British General, while awaiting the orders of the Government, had been the *de facto* sovereign of North-Eastern Afghanistan, and exercised autocratic power over life and property. On the 27th

October, he received instructions from the Viceroy, and issued the following proclamation to the people of Cabul.—" I, General Roberts, on behalf of the British Government, hereby proclaim that the Ameer having by his own free will abdicated, has left Afghanistan without a government. In consequence of the shameful outrage upon its Envoy and since the British Government has been compelled to occupy by force Cabul, the Capital, and to take military possession of other parts of Afghanistan, the British Government now commands that all Afghan authorities, Chiefs, and Sirdars, do continue their functions in maintaining order, referring to me whenever necessary. The British Government desires that the people should be treated with justice and benevolence, and that their religious feelings and customs be respected. The services of such Sirdars and Chiefs as assist in preserving order will be duly recognized, but all disturbers of the peace and persons concerned in attacks upon the British authority will meet with condign punishment. The British Government, after consultation with the principal Sirdars, tribal Chiefs, and others representing the interests and wishes of the various provinces and cities, will declare its will as to the future permanent arrangements to be made for the good government of the people."

As for the ex-Ameer, he appeared much relieved since he had ceased to wield the sovereignty of the Afghan nation, and it was his habit, occasionally, in the evening to emerge from his tent in the British camp, and walk with the General while the band discoursed sweet music. " The Ameer," writes Sir Frederick Roberts to us, " was treated with the greatest kindness and consideration, and it was not until I was satisfied from the results of the proceedings of the Court of Enquiry, over which Colonel Macgregor presided, that the attack on the Residency, if not actually instigated, might at least have been checked by Yakoob Khan, that the guard which had hitherto been a guard of honour, was made responsible for his safe custody. Even then, all possible courtesy was shown to the Ameer, but this restraint was rendered still more necessary by information I received, from which I was convinced that Yakoob Khan was contemplating flight, which, if he had succeeded in effecting, would have been the signal for a general rising."*

The General reported to the Viceroy that "the Ameer seems much broken in spirits, and wholly unfit to resume his former position and responsibilities." The despotic ruler of a martial nation found himself a close prisoner under the walls of his

---

* Some time before the Ameer's deportation from Cabul, Sir Frederick Roberts had a conversation with him regarding the political events immediately preceding the rupture between his father, Shere Ali, and the British Government. Sir Frederick took notes of the conversation, the substance of which he stated to be as follows :—" In 1869 my father was fully prepared to throw in his lot with you. He had suffered many reverses before making himself secure on the throne of Afghanistan, and he had come to the conclusion that his best chance of holding what he had won, lay in an alliance with the British Government. He did not receive from Lord Mayo as large a supply of arms and ammunition as he had hoped, but, nevertheless, he returned to Cabul fairly satisfied, and so he had remained until the visit of Nur Mahammud Shah to India in 1873. This visit brought matters to a head. The diaries received from Nur Mahammud Shah during his stay in India, and the report which he brought back on his return, convinced my father that he could no longer hope to obtain from the British Government all the aid that he wanted, and from that time he began to turn his attention to the thought of a Russian alliance. You know how that ended. When my father received from the Government of India the letter informing him that a British Mission was about to proceed to Cabul, he read it out in Durbar. The members of the Russian Embassy were present. After the reading was finished, Colonel Stolietoff rose, saluted the Ameer, and asked permission to leave Cabul. If permitted, he would, he said, travel without delay to Tashkend, and report the state of affairs to General Kauffmann, who would inform the Tzar, and thus bring pressure to bear on England. He promised to return in six weeks or two months, and urged the Ameer to do everything in his power meanwhile to prevent the British Mission from reaching Cabul.

" Colonel Stolietoff never returned to Cabul. He lost no time in reaching Tashkend, where he remained for a few weeks, and he then started for Russia. The Afghan official, Mirza Muhammad Hassan Khan, generally known as the Dabir-ul-Mulk, who had travelled with Colonel Stolietoff from the Oxus to Cabul, accompanied him on his return journey to Tashkend. Here the Mirza was detained under pretence that orders would shortly be received from the Emperor, until the news of my father's flight from Cabul reached General Kauffmann. He was then permitted to leave. Two Aides-de-Camp were sent with him, one a European, the other a native of Bokhara. My father was strongly urged by General Kauffmann not to leave Cabul. At the same time the members of the Embassy were ordered to return to Tashkend, the doctor being permitted to remain with my father, if his services were required. Throughout, the Russian Embassy were treated with great honour, and at all stations between Mazar-i-Shariff and Cabul, orders were given for the troops to turn out, and for a salute to be fired on their arrival and departure."

Sir Frederick Roberts in his letter to the Viceroy giving this summary, refers to the prevalence of Russian ware and coins in Cabul, no less than 13,000 gold pieces having been found in the late Ameer's treasury.

Occupation of Sherpur.

Capital, and bitterly must he have rued his timidity, or treachery, in not restraining the mutinous regiments when they first turned upon the Residency on that fatal 3rd September. With the unhappy cause of Ilium's woes he might have exclaimed :—

> " Would heaven, ere all these dreadful deeds were done,
> The day that show'd me to the golden sun,
> Had seen my death."

On the last day of this eventful month of October, the British troops moved into the Sherpur Cantonments, the barracks of which had been cleared and made habitable by an army of artisans and coolies, and further accommodation was in course of construction to quarter the entire force. A variety of reasons influenced Sir Frederick Roberts in adopting this course, the Chief of which were, that the works raised with such care by Shere Ali, and called after him, afforded better shelter, and were more defensible during the winter; also the Commissariat Depôt was there, to protect which required a guard, and as guards were stationed in the Bala Hissar and City, the strength of the troops was not only unduly taxed, but they were more scattered than was judicious. The wisdom of concentration and keeping the supplies within the lines occupied by the troops, were among the chief lessons inculcated by the disastrous teachings of the first Afghan War, and soon again received a striking illustration.

Writing of the reasons that influenced him in his choice of Sherpur Sir Frederick Roberts says :—" The advantage of using all existing roof accommodation at the first glance pointed out the Bala Hissar as the quarter which promised best to meet my requirements; but its dangerous proximity to the large magazine which had escaped destruction, and the fact that it would not accommodate all my force, and that the troops would have to be more or less scattered, eventually led me to decide upon occupying the large, and for the most part fortified, cantonment of Sherpur, which was built by the late Ameer as winter quarters for his regular troops. This Cantonment lies rather less than a mile north-east of the city, and contains long ranges of brick buildings, which will at once enable me to house the entire European portion of my force, and also provide accommodation for the Commissariat Stores. The Native troops are engaged hutting themselves, and, aided by the materials at hand and woodwork brought from the dismantled portion of the Bala Hissar, have already made considerable progress." The Cantonment, though more extensive than was desirable for this small force, was enclosed on three sides by a lofty and massive loop-holed wall, with numerous flanking towers, while the rear was protected by the Behmaroo heights (on which General Roberts proposed erecting certain defensive works), at the base of which lay the Cantonment. The site was close to the old British Cantonment, and actually embraced in its defences the heights which were such a danger in 1841, and for the possession of which many sanguinary struggles took place, as recorded in the pages of Lady Sale and Sir Vincent Eyre. By the end of October Sir Frederick Roberts had laid in sufficient supplies to relieve him of all anxiety regarding the provisioning of the force during the winter.

As regards the fort of the Bala Hissar, the General wrote to the Government proposing to raze it to the ground, as an act of retributive justice, which he considered would have a deeper significance than the destruction of any number of houses belonging to obscure individuals in the city. It was historical, its name was symbolical of Afghan power, and it was intimately connected with the past history of the country. Moreover, the fact that it had been destroyed and levelled with the ground, would spread throughout the length and breadth of Afghanistan, bearing with it a political significance that could not be under-rated. As a further reason for its demolition he urged, that from its walls a heavy fire was kept up on the defenders of the Residency, and he was of opinion that not a vestige of any place which bore a part in that day's doings should be allowed to remain.

Of the preparations made by the Ameer Shere Ali to engage in hostilities with the British, the General wrote: "Before the outbreak of hostilities last year the Ameer had raised and equipped with arms of precision, sixty-eight regiments of Infantry, and sixteen of Cavalry. The Afghan Artillery amounted to near 300 guns. Numbers of skilled artisans were constantly employed in the manufacture of rifled cannon and breach-loading small arms. More than a million pounds of powder, and, I believe, several million rounds of home-made Snider ammunition were in the Arsenal at the time of the late explosion, and swords, helmets, uniforms and other articles of military equipment, were stored in proportionate quantities. Finally, Shere Ali had expended upon the construction of the Sherpur Cantonments, an astonishing amount of labour and money. The extent and cost of these works may be judged of from the fact that the whole of the troops under my command, will find cover during the winter within the Cantonment and its outlying buildings, and the bulk of them in the main line of parapet itself, which extends to a length of nearly two miles under the southern and western slopes of the Behmaroo hills. Shere Ali's original design was apparently to carry the wall entirely round the hills, a distance of five miles, and the foundations were already laid for a considerable portion of this length."

The reasons given by Sir Frederick Roberts for occupying Sherpur Cantonment dispose of certain statements by an historian of the war, which have given rise to inferences that the occupation of Sherpur was done in a hap-hazard sort of way, and that the commanding General, having overcome the Afghans in the field, had grown careless.

But nothing could be more erroneous than such a supposition, which was opposed to the character of the subject of this Memoir, who never left anything to chance, and, from his knowledge of Afghan warfare, derived not only in the field, but from the lessons inculcated by his father, would have been the last man to regard a lull in the active resistance of such a turbulent people as the Afghans, as aught but evidence of the existence of a ground-swell which experienced mariners know is the prelude to a coming storm. Regarding his reasons for placing his force in Sherpur in October, Sir Frederick Roberts writes to us :—" The fact is, that I thought over our position most carefully before I decided on occupying this Sherpur Cantonment. Instead of being deceived by the state of quiet we happened to be then in, I felt very sure we should have trouble once winter set in. I knew that it was essential to keep my force together, and that it would be very difficult in the short time before snow usually fell, to house the troops and followers, and collect a sufficiency of supplies and forage. I examined the Bala Hissar most particularly, for I quite appreciated the advantages it offered. I found that it would not contain one third of my force, and that the remainder, with all the transport animals, would have to go elsewhere. There were no villages or forts near the Bala Hissar that would answer;—in fact, there was but the one place, Sherpur, which could accommodate all the troops and animals, as well as the required amount of supplies,—added to which, shelter already existed in Sherpur for the whole of the British troops, and three-quarters of the native ones. The fault of Sherpur was its size, too large for my forces to defend properly—a fault which would have been far more serious had I diminished my strength by occupying the Bala Hissar as well. Another drawback was that the whole of the City of Cabul intervened between Sherpur and the Bala Hissar, and holding the Bala Hissar would not have prevented the enemy from occupying the city, once we had been beaten off the Asmai heights—which we were by the sheer force of numbers on the 14th December, 1879. I had about 6,000 men, and the enemy were certainly not less than 100,000. In my despatch, I said about 60,000, as I wished to be well within the mark, and it was impossible to get any accurate estimate,—but many influential natives, who had the means of judging, told me that the enemy numbered 100,000 or 120,000. I mention all this as Hensman's book is certainly misleading; he, no doubt, never knew how much thought I had given to our position during the winter. So anxious was I to hold the Bala Hissar, that I consulted the Commanding R.E., as to the possibility of hutting the balance of the troops on the Siah-Sung ridges, where we first encamped, but it was pronounced an impossibility within the time."

On the 26th October, Sir Frederick Roberts visited Bootkak, where he selected a position for an outpost in the direction of the line of advance of the Khyber column, which, under the command of Major-General Bright, had entered Jellalabad two days before. On the 1st November, Brigadier-General Macpherson proceeded to Bootkak to open communications with General Bright's column, the line by the Shutargardan being

Roberts Reconnoitres towards the Khyber.

closed for the winter. Many chiefs of the Tezeen valley and neighbouring country between it and Jellalabad, came into his camp to make their submission and get the best terms procurable from the British Commander.

On the following day Sir Frederick Roberts, accompanied by Colonel Macgregor, Chief of the Staff, and Daoud Shah, the Commander-in-Chief of the late Afghan Army, rode out to Bootkak, and, joining General Macpherson there, proceeded with a strong escort to reconnoitre the Lutterbund Pass. On the following morning the General, who was joined by the headmen of the neighbouring Ghilzyes, reconnoitred to within three or four miles of Tezeen, proceeding thence to the Khoord-Cabul, that terrible defile which bears such an ominous sound in the ears of those who remember the fearful scene of slaughter enacted within its savage and precipitous gorges. Threading the Khoord-Cabul, the General returned to Bootkak, and in the evening rode back a further distance of ten miles to the Sherpur Cantonment by the line of Telegraph just completed, making over forty miles of country covered during the day.

As the result of this examination, General Roberts decided to use the Lutturbund Pass for the future line of communication with General Bright at Jellalabad, the road by the Khoord-Cabul (which General Macpherson was directed to use in forming a junction near Jugdulluck with Brigadier-General Charles Gough* advancing from Jellalabad with a portion of General Bright's division) being considerably longer.

On the 4th November the General rode out towards Beni Hissar to meet Brigadier-General Hugh Gough, who arrived at Sherpur escorting a large convoy, and bringing with him the troops lately stationed at Shutargardan, under Colonel Money. The General warmly congratulated Colonel Money and thanked the 3rd Sikhs and the Mountain Battery for their gallant re-

---

* This officer must not be confounded with his brother, Hugh Gough, though both were at Delhi in Hodson's Horse. Hugh Gough served in Sir Hope Grant's force throughout the mutiny with the subject of this Memoir; Charles Gough was also a cavalry officer, and, like his distinguished brother, earned the Victoria Cross in the mutiny; and during the first phase of the Afghan War, ending with the Treaty of Gundamuck, commanded the cavalry of the Khyber, or Sir Samuel Browne's, Division.

pulse of the attack by an overwhelming force of Mangals and Ghilzyes. And these brave native soldiers received an ovation from their comrades on their arrival in camp. On the way the General was met by Padshah Khan, the intriguing Ghilzye Chief, to whom he gave a cool reception. The British force at Cabul had been seriously weakened by the absence of the troops under Generals Macpherson and Gough, and the return of the latter with the Shutargardan garrison, made a welcome addition to a force of insufficient strength, as later events proved, to cope with a combination of the tribes.

During the next few days Sir Frederick Roberts visited the Chardeh valley, and inspected the scene of the fighting on the 6th and 8th October; and a column proceeded under command of Brigadier-General Baker to the villages in the same valley, and brought away some soldiers of the regiments who had taken part in the attack on the Residency, whose names and addresses were found on the regimental muster rolls. These men were handed over for trial to the Military Commission, under Brigadier-General Massy, and such as were found to be guilty were hanged. The claims of justice being satisfied, on the 12th November Sir Frederick Roberts issued a Proclamation of Amnesty* to all persons who had fought against the British

---

* The following is the text of the proclamation:—" To all whom it may concern. On the 12th October, Shawal, a proclamation was issued in which I offered a reward for the surrender of any person who had fought against the British troops since the 3rd September, fifteenth Ramazan, and had thereby become a rebel against the Ameer Yakoob Khan. I have now received information which tends to show that some at least of those who shared in the opposition encountered by the British troops during their advance on Cabul, were led to do so by the belief that the Ameer was a prisoner in my camp, and had called upon the soldiery and people of Cabul to rise on his behalf. Such persons, although enemies to the British Government, were not rebels against their own sovereign. And the great British Government does not seek for vengeance against enemies who no longer resist. It may be that few only of those who took up arms were thus led away by the statements of evil-minded men; but rather than punish the innocent with the guilty, I am willing to believe that all were alike deceived. On behalf of the British Government, therefore, I proclaim a free and complete amnesty to all persons who have fought against the British troops since the 3rd September, fifteenth Ramazan, provided that they now give up any arms in their possession and return to their homes. The offer of a reward for the surrender of such persons is now withdrawn, and they will not for the future be molested in any way on account of their opposition to the British advance. But it must be clearly understood that the benefits of this amnesty do not extend to any one, whether soldier

troops since the 3rd September, provided that they gave up any arms in their possession and returned to their homes; but those persons who took part in the attack on the Residency, or who might be found in possession of any property belonging to members of the Embassy, were exempted. Up to the 15th November, the executions at Cabul, under the recommendation of the Military Commissioners, were seventy-eight, chiefly soldiers of the regiments which attacked the Residency.

A more pleasing duty to a humane officer like Sir Frederick Roberts was the establishment in Cabul of a Civil Dispensary, of which not only the male inhabitants but the ladies of the Sirdars' families availed themselves.

Sir Frederick Roberts appointed as Governor of Afghan Turkestan, Sirdar Wali Mahomed Barukzye, to whom an advance of two lacs of rupees (£20,000) was made for the pay of levies, and to the charge of Kohistan, always a turbulent district, he commissioned Shahbaz Khan. Besides these Sirdars there were in the British Camp during the month two leading Ghilzye Chiefs, from Hissarak, near Jugdulluck, who agreed to keep open the road, and Mahomed Said, Governor of Ghuznee, where disturbances had already broken out, under the fiery exhortations of the aged Moollah, Mooskh-i-Alum, who now appeared on the stormy sea of Afghan politics. The influence wielded by this turbulent priest was enormous, though we have seen its counterpart in Mediæval Europe, with which Central Asia, at the present time, bears a striking resemblance, both in its religious and political conditions. The monks in the priest-ridden courts and peoples of Europe, a thousand years ago, possessed an influence paralleled by the Moollahs among the ignorant and fanatical clansmen of Afghanistan and our frontier, or in the cabinet of such a bigot as the late Nas-

---

or civilian, who was concerned directly, or indirectly, in the attack upon the Residency, or who may hereafter be found in possession of any property belonging to members of the Embassy. To such persons no mercy will be shown. Further, I hold out no promise of pardon to those who, well knowing the Ameer's position in the British camp, instigated the troops and people of Cabul to take up arms against the British troops. They have been guilty of wilful rebellion against the Ameer's authority, and they will be considered and treated as rebels whenever found." Up to the 13th November the Cabulees surrendered 6,729 rifles and muskets, of which 742 were Enfields, and 560 Sniders.

rullah Khan, Ameer of Bokhara. The ninety years of Mooskhi-Alum (literally " Scent of the Universe ") had not softened his fanatical hatred of the unbeliever. He was zealous in the cause of the faith, and his saintly life gave him great influence over his countrymen, who placed implicit faith in the assurances of one
> "Whose beard the silver hand of peace hath touch'd,
> Whose white investments figure innocence."

But now his utterances breathed not of peace, as became his years and calling, but of slaughter and extermination. The "Jehad" was preached from every minaret and mosque, and the Minister of Peace dedicated the remainder of his days to urging futile resistance in which thousands of his countrymen perished.
> "Turning his books to graves, his ink to blood,
> His pens to lances, and his tongue divine,
> To a loud trumpet and a point of war."

It was the old intolerant spirit of the Israelitish priest who maddened the people to deeds of blood by appeals to "the Sword of the Lord and of Gideon," though in this instance the call was to defend his countrymen's hearths from aggression, and therefore justifiable, if affording a chance of success.

Meanwhile the General took active steps to provide against the contingencies of the coming winter, and busied himself in collecting a reserve of supplies from Maidan, Logar, and Kohistan, advances being made to the Sirdars for its transmission, and all ineffective transport animals were sent back to India, in order to economize forage. To facilitate the transport of supplies from India the road on the Lutterbund was improved by the Pioneers; at this time also the British Camp was put in communication with Jellalabad by means of the telegraph wire.

Sir Frederick Roberts found his hand strengthened against the possibility of the dangers of a divided command by his promotion to the local rank of Lieutenant-General, with the command of all the troops as far as Jamrood at the mouth of the Khyber Pass, so that General Bright's division of 12,000 men was placed in subordination to him. Towards the end of November, on the return of General Macpherson's Brigade to

Sherpur, Sir Frederick Roberts despatched Brigadier-General Baker with a strong force to Maidan, about twenty-five miles from Cabul, in the direction of Ghuznee, to enforce the collection of grain and forage, which is ordinarily due from that district as part of the revenues of the State. On the following day, taking with him a small Cavalry escort, Sir Frederick joined General Baker. A chief of some local importance proved recalcitrant, and refused to send in his quota of supplies; on which Captain Turner, Assistant Political Officer, was sent with two Squadrons of Cavalry, to bring him in; but the troopers were fired upon and compelled to retire.

In order to compel his submission, at daybreak on the 24th November, Sir Frederick moved against the rebel chief's fort, but it was found to be deserted. Having burnt the fort and the neighbouring villages he returned to Maidan, and, on the following day, rode back to Sherpur, leaving General Baker to complete his mission.

On his arrival he was greeted with reports of the disturbed state of Afghan Turkestan and Kohistan, where large bodies of men were collecting, and the Governor recently appointed to the latter district found his position untenable. General Baker returned to Sherpur early in December, having collected the forage demanded from Maidan. He reported that he left all quiet in the district; but it was a deceptive lull, for hardly had he left the valley than the Governor he had installed, a Barukzye Sirdar and a son of the great Ameer Dost Mahommed, was murdered. The Governor appointed to the Logar District was equally an object of suspicion and contempt by the people, who refused to recognize the authority which lacked the support of British bayonets. On every hand there were portents, and the situation resembled that of 1840, when Sir William Macnaghten represented the British power in Afghanistan, and Shah Sojah was his puppet. The catastrophe, doubtless, would have been equally fatal to British interests and prestige had not there been in Sir Frederick Roberts an officer wielding supreme political and military command, who was fully alive to the dangers of the situation, and quite capable of coping with them. Meanwhile, the question of supplies, especially forage for the thousands of troop-horses and transport animals, continued to engross the General's attention, over 100,000 maunds (80 lbs. to the maund) being necessary to complete the supply for the winter. He had also not completed the storage of fuel and provisions for six months, which, with wise prevision he had set himself to collect from the day of his arrival at Cabul.

The winter set in with severity early in December, the thermometer marking 20° of frost, and Sir Frederick Roberts was reluctantly compelled to forego an expedition he had meditated to Ghuznee, the head-quarters of the malcontents on that side of Cabul, as it would expose his soldiers to considerable hardship.

Early in the morning of the 1st December, before the camp was astir, the ex-Ameer Yakoob Khan turned his back on his late Capital and proceeded a prisoner to India, guarded by an escort of Cavalry. The Commission of Inquiry into the circumstances of the massacre of the British Mission at Cabul, consisting of Colonel Macgregor, Dr. Bellew, and Mahomed Hyat Khan, had presented their report to the General on the 18th November, and the Government of India, on learning its conclusions, ordered the deportation of the ex-Ameer. Sir Frederick Roberts and some of his Staff were present to bid him farewell, and so ended the brief and stormy reign of the son of Shere Ali, who shared the vicissitudes which make the history of the family of his grandfather, Dost Mahommed, one of the most interesting and romantic recorded in the annals of any country.

Little more than a twelvemonth before, his father, Shere Ali, had attained a more powerful position than "the Dost" or any of the Ameers of the preceding Suddozye dynasty since the time of Ahmed Shah; but evil advisers and a reliance on Russian promises of support, which he found the broken reed it proved in the hands of his father forty years before, brought him down to the dust. His armies, defeated at Ali Musjid and the Peiwar Kotul, and his southern capital, Candahar, captured, Shere Ali fled to Afghan Turkestan, but in vain sought permission to proceed to the throne of the Czar, there to plead his cause against the Indian Viceroy. After a few weeks' illness, broken-hearted at all his ambitious schemes having so utterly failed, he died at Mazar-i-Sheriff, and, like Wolsey, there were "none so poor to do him reverence."

> "But yesterday, and who had mightier breath?
> A thousand warriors by his word were kept
> In awe; he said, as the Centurion saith,
> 'Go,' and he goeth; 'Come,' and forth he stepp'd.
> The trump and bugle till he spake were dumb,
> And now nought left him but the muffled drum."

Scarcely more fortunate was his son and successor, Yakoob Khan, at one time one of the most fiery and successful warriors in Central Asia. To the sword of Yakoob Khan his father owed his throne, for when quite a youth he wrested Candahar from his enemies, when Shere Ali's fortunes were at their lowest ebb, and inflicted a crushing defeat on his uncle Azim, and his cousin Abdurrahman, now, in the see-saw of Afghan politics, the ruler of a united Afghanistan. The most brilliant anticipations were formed of Yakoob's future. But whether it was that his successes were due to fortune, and not to superior skill, or that his energies and spirit were broken by five years' incarceration in a dungeon, Yakoob Khan displayed none of the royal qualities that distinguished many of the Barukzyes, and specially his father and grandfather. His cowardice on the 3rd September, when a display of personal energy would have saved the life of the man he called his friend, rendered him an object of contempt, and was the measure of his degradation from the Yakoob Khan who was the "King-maker" of Afghanistan. He was still in the prime of youth, not being over thirty years of age, was prepossessing and distinguished in appearance, and his personal valour had been the theme of all tongues.* But he had signally failed to rule his turbulent

---

* Writing of Yakoob Khan before the outbreak of the Afghan war, one well versed in Oriental politics says :—"The character of Yakoob Khan shines out from among that of all his countrymen, not only as the most able and the most intelligent, but also as the most courteous, the most moderate, and the most refined. The life of such a man is a study in itself, and its recital will arouse sympathy in the hearts of all true lovers of brave deeds and noble actions. His life is also conterminous with the most eventful portion of modern Afghan history, and his career is closely intertwined with the fortunes of Shere Ali." The following is a brief sketch of his history :—

Yakoob Khan was born in or about the year 1849 of a noble mother. Arminius Vambéry speaks of him in November, 1863, when the Afghan Prince appeared to the traveller "a good-humoured, inexperienced child."

countrymen, and, while not possessing the courage to strike a blow in defence of his throne, suffered his chiefs and soldiers to engage in a strife from which he would profit in the event of success, while he was careful that failure should compromise only his honour. How fallen he was from the warrior prince whom his countrymen had regarded as the pink of chivalry and the mould of form!

> "Unlike that Arthur, who, with lance in rest,
> From spear to plume a star of tournament,
> Dashed through the lists at Camelot and charged
> Before the eyes of ladies and of knights."

The General political situation, as it developed itself in the early part of December, and the causes which contributed to produce a state of affairs that at one time appeared to be fraught with disaster, may be summarised from a despatch by Sir Frederick Roberts to the Adjutant-General in India.

After the outbreak of September and the massacre of the

His career in the history of his country commenced very shortly after his interview with the Hungarian traveller; for, in 1864, Shere Ali's brother disputed his possession of the crown, and Yakoob Khan was left in command at the recently captured fortress of Herat. While Shere Ali was carrying on the war with varying fortune—victorious at Kujhbaz, routed at Shaikhabad, losing his eldest son in the former fight, and deserted by his best general, Mahomed Refik, on the eve of the latter, but in the end expelled from Candahar and all the eastern country—Yakoob Khan was slowly but surely consolidating his rule over Herat and Ferrah, and propitiating, in so far as he was able, the northern Khan of Maimené. So it happened that when Shere Ali suffered his last overthrow beneath the walls of Khelat-i-Ghilzye and fled to Herat, he had not abandoned all hope of restoring the declining fortunes of his cause. During three years Yakoob Khan had preserved peace in the west, had restrained the Persians, and had sent many a welcome contingent of hardy troops to the scene of battle in Candahar and Cabul. There was yet one chance left; but the degree of success that might be attained no longer rested with Shere Ali. In the field of battle he had been worsted, both by Azim and Abdurrahman, and his own reputation had become dimmed by disaster. The fate of Cabul trembled in the balance when its real arbiter advanced on Candahar in the early days of 1868. That city fell at once after a sharp fight in the outskirts of the town, and then once more Candahar became Shere Ali's base for the reconquest of Cabul. At first the joint army of Shere Ali and Yakoob Khan encountered little opposition. Cabul, after an absence of more than three years, was entered in triumph, and south of the Hindoo Koosh there remained no rebel. Azim in the meanwhile had fled to Balkh to join his nephew, and in face of the great emergency they each agreed to forego their jealousies. With a large force they advanced against Cabul, but their adversary had been more prompt, Yakoob Khan held the Bamian Pass as they came forth from the Sighan Valley, and worsted them in a pitched encounter. But they found their retreat cut off. The Khan of Maimené had declared for Shere Ali, and was operating in their rear. They had no

The Situation at Cabul.

Envoy, the advance of the British force from Ali Kheyl was too rapid to give the Afghans as a nation time to create an effective opposition, and the defeat of Charasia put an end to all organized resistance. The Afghans, judging from antecedent history, believed that, as in 1842, after some signal act of retribution had been inflicted on the city of Cabul, the British Army would withdraw to India. It thus happened that, after the action of Charasia, there followed a period of expectation and doubt. The Afghans were waiting on events, and the time had not yet arrived when any national movement was possible. But this pause was marked by certain occurrences which touched the military pride of this turbulent nation to the quick. The occupation of the fortified cantonment called after their Ameer, the appropriation of the park of artillery and vast munitions of war which he had accumulated with such care and at so great expense, the dismantling of the Bala Hissar, the historic fortress of the nation and the residence of its Kings and principal nobles, and, lastly, the imprisonment and deportation to India of Yakoob Khan and his leading ministers, all conspired to inflame to a high degree the national animosity felt towards a foreign invader.

The temper of the people being in this condition, it was clear that only mutual jealousy and distrust among the chiefs could prevent their making common cause against their con-

---

hope left now, except in making one desperate rush on the capital and surprising Shere Ali. But each of these schemes was frustrated. They crossed the Hindoo Koosh by a pass to the east of Bamian, but Yakoob Khan was close behind, driving them before him. Past Cabul they fled with the young chief hot on their track, until they turned to bay in sheer despair in the neighbourhood of Ghuznee. Routed there they fled for safety to Persia, where Azim died, and Abdurrahman passed on to Khokand and Russian territory. The five years war had at last terminated, but its close brought credit to Yakoob Khan alone. Since then Yakoob was Governor of Cabul (1869), of Candahar (1870), and, after a brief exile, of Herat (1871). In all these posts, says the writer before quoted, he exhibited the same great capacity that he had demonstrated on the field of battle; but Shere Ali feared him, as he recognized his superior, and believed that ties of blood would prove but a slight restraint upon the impulses of ambition. In 1872 Yakoob Khan came to Cabul, trusting to a safe conduct from Shere Ali, and was imprisoned for five years, and his younger brother, Ayoob Khan, threatened in Herat, was glad to find safety in Persia. The invasion of Afghanistan by the British brought the three cousins to the front once again, and in different ways their names are indissolubly associated with the history of the war.

querors, and that, if any sentiment could be found strong enough to dominate such internal dissensions and fuse the discordant elements into one mass, a powerful movement might be evoked, having for its object the expulsion of the foreigners from the country.

Such an impulse was supplied by the fervent addresses to Mahomedan religious feeling made by the aged Mooskh-i-Alum and by the denunciation of the English in the mosques of every city and village. It was further fanned by the ladies of Yakoob Khan's family, who appealed to the popular sympathies, and distributed the concealed treasure which was at their command; and, lastly, a powerful incentive was added by the expectation of sharing in the plunder of the British Camp.

The Moollahs, having once succeeded in subordinating the private jealousies of the chiefs to a desire for revenge on the common foe, the movement rapidly assumed the proportions of a national uprising against the English invaders. The memories of the disaster of 1841–42 were appealed to; it was urged that what had happened once might happen again; and the people were assured that if they would only rise suddenly and simultaneously the small English Army in Sherpur might easily be driven from its position, and, as before, be overwhelmed in its retreat through the difficult passes between Afghanistan and India. Such were the hopes of the chiefs and religious leaders, who for a wonder were, for a brief period, united against the English infidels.

According to information received by Sir Frederick Roberts, their intention was to gain possession of the city and Bala Hissar, and after occupying the numerous forts and villages in the neighbourhood of Sherpur, to surround the cantonments. To attain this object, they arranged that the forces from the south, that is, from Logar, Zurmat, the Mangal and Jadran districts, and intervening Ghilzai country, should seize the range of hills which extend from the city towards Charasia and include the Bala Hissar and the high conical peak called the Takht-i-Shah; that the forces from Kohistan should occupy the Asmai heights and hills to the north of the city; while those from Maidan, Wardak, and the Ghuznee direction moved upon the city from the westward.

As it was evident that if these several bodies once concentrated on Cabul they would be joined by the disaffected portion of the people of the city and adjoining villages, the General formed his plans to break up the combination before it came to a head, and to deal in detail with the forces gathering in Maidan, under Sultan Jan, and in Koh Daman, the southern part of the Kohistan, under Meer Butcha, whose rôle was to march southward and coalesce with Sultan Jan.

CHAPTER XV.

The National Rising of December, 1879—The Plans of Sir Frederick Roberts to Check the Movement—The Cavalry Action of the 11th December—Critical Condition of Affairs at Sherpur and in Cabul—Prompt Action of Sir Frederick Roberts—Movements of Brigadier-Generals Macpherson and Baker—The Attempt to Capture the Takht-i-Shah on the 12th December—Severe fighting on the 13th December—Capture of Koh Asmai—Successful Counter-attack by the Enemy—Heavy Losses Experienced by the British Force—Sir Frederick Roberts Determines to Concentrate in Sherpur—Retirement of the British Troops within the Cantonment.

IN pursuance of his plans, on the 8th December Sir Frederick Roberts despatched Brigadier-General Macpherson with a column* towards the west, via Killa Aushar and Urghundeh, in order to meet and drive the enemy back on Maidan.

On the following day, Brigadier-General Baker also marched with a force,† via Charasia, towards Maidan with the object of placing himself across the line by which the enemy, after being defeated by General Macpherson, would have to retire. To give time for the completion of this movement, and to draw the enemy forward by an appearance of hesitation, Sir Frederick Roberts halted General Macpherson at Killa Aushar on the 9th. By the absence of these two Brigades the troops at Sherpur were reduced to a point of dangerous weakness, but in order to strike a decisive blow against the hostile confederacy, the General decided to incur the risk, which was inseparable from the conduct of military operations with so limited a force as was at his disposal, barely 8,000 men. However, he guarded against any eventualities to the best of his power, by ordering up from Jugdulluck, on the 7th

---

* Four guns F Battery, A Brigade, R.H.A.; 4 guns No. 1 Mountain Battery; 1 squadron 9th Lancers; 2 squadrons 14th Bengal Lancers; 401 men, 67th Regiment; 393 men, 5th Goorkhas; and 509 men, 3rd Sikhs.

† Four guns No. 2 Mountain Battery; 2½ squadrons 5th Punjaub Cavalry; 450 men 92nd Highlanders; 450 of the 5th Punjaub Infantry; and 25 men Sappers and Miners.

December, the whole of the guides, Infantry and Cavalry, under Colonel Jenkins. These troops arrived at Sherpur on the night of the 11th at a most opportune moment.

Meanwhile, on the 9th December, when General Macpherson was halting at Killa Aushar, Sir Frederick discovered from a Cavalry reconnoissance, made by Lieutenant-Colonel Lockhart, Assistant Quartermaster-General, that large numbers of the enemy were moving northwards from Urghundeh and Pughman towards Kohistan; and also that a considerable force of Kohistanees had collected at Karez Meer, about ten miles to the north of Cabul. Impelled by the necessity for dispersing this gathering before it could be joined by the enemy hastening from the west, Sir Frederick directed General Macpherson to change his line of advance and attack the Kohistanees, and as their country was unsuited for the movements of Horse Artillery and Cavalry, he ordered him to leave this portion of his column at Killa Aushar, taking with him only one squadron of the 14th Bengal Lancers.

On reaching the Surkh Kotul, about two miles short of Karez Meer, General Macpherson found that his arrival was well timed, that the enemy from the west was still below him in the Pughman Valley, and that it was in his power to deal with the Kohistanees before a junction could be effected. He, accordingly, attacked them vigorously and promptly, and drove them back with heavy loss.

The enemy, advancing from Maidan, seemed inclined at first to ascend the Surkh Kotul from the Pughman Valley, and assist the Kohistanees; but on seeing that our troops held all the commanding positions, and probably hearing of the defeat of their allies, they retreated towards Urghundeh. Of this, says Sir Frederick Roberts in his despatch of 23rd January, 1880, detailing the events of the preceding month, General Macpherson informed him by heliograph soon after noon on the 10th. In order to try and cut in on the enemy's line of retreat, Sir Frederick immediately ordered the advance of the Horse Artillery and Cavalry from Killa Aushar, strengthened by two additional squadrons from Sherpur, the whole being under the command of Lieutenant Colonel Gordon, R.H.A. The movement, however, was unsuccessful, for as soon as the

Cavalry appeared, the enemy took shelter in the villages, and on the skirts of the high hills which surround Pughman.

General Macpherson encamped on the night of the 10th at Karez Meer, and General Baker, who had steadily pursued his march by a very difficult road, halted a short distance to the west of Maidan.

Sir Frederick Roberts sent orders to General Macpherson to march very early on the 11th, to follow the enemy, who were now retreating south and west by the Pughman Valley, and to endeavour to drive them towards General Baker. Macpherson was informed at the same time that the Horse Artillery and Cavalry, under Brigadier-General Dunham Massy, who was sent from Sherpur to assume command of the force,* would leave Killa Aushar at 9 A.M., and that he was to join them on the Urghundeh road. General Massy's orders, says, Sir Frederick Roberts, were, "to advance from Killa Aushar by the road leading directly from the City of Cabul towards Urghundeh and Ghazni; to proceed cautiously and quietly, feeling for the enemy; to communicate with General Macpherson, and to act in conformity with that officer's movements, but on no account to commit himself to an action until General Macpherson had engaged the enemy."

Instead of gaining the Ghuznee road by the ordinary route, General Massy started across country, intending to strike that road beyond the village of Killa Kazi. He detached one troop of the 9th Lancers, under Captain Chisholme, to communicate with General Macpherson, who was some miles behind in the hills, and the troop did not rejoin him during the day. "Although, on nearing Killa Kazi," says Sir Frederick Roberts, "General Massy's advance guard reported to him that the enemy were in considerable force on the hills on either side of the Ghazni road, some three miles in advance, he still moved on. Shortly afterwards further reports were received by him that the enemy were coming down into the plain, with the evident intention of attacking him."

The caution General Massy had been directed to exercise now disappeared, and he committed himself to engaging the enemy

---

* His force was 4 guns F Battery, A Brigade, R.H.A.; 2 squadrons 9th Lancers; and 1 squadron 14th Bengal Lancers.

without regard to the circumstance that he was directed to subordinate his movements to those of General Macpherson. With the object of checking the enemy until he could communicate with that officer, General Massy opened fire with his guns at 2,900 yards, but as this had not the desired effect, he ordered the Battery of Horse Artillery to advance 400 yards nearer; and finding the enemy continued advancing, he directed the guns again to move forward. They came into action at 2,000 yards, and in this position remained until the opposing forces arrived within 1,700 yards' range. The Afghans still continuing to advance, General Massy dismounted thirty men of the 9th Lancers, who commenced firing as soon as carbine range was reached, but the enemy were in such force—according to General Massy's estimate, 10,000—that, as he reported, the fire of the dismounted Lancers "had no appreciable effect."

At this time Sir Frederick Roberts, accompanied by General Hills and Staff, arrived on the ground, in the expectation of witnessing the execution of his carefully laid plans, and taking command of the united columns of Generals Macpherson and Massy. His disappointment was great on finding the tables turned, and his troops in difficulties. Recognizing the critical state of affairs, and the inutility of continuing an action with Cavalry and Horse Artillery against an enemy in such overwhelming strength, and on ground so unfavourable, he ordered General Massy to retire and watch for an opportunity for a Cavalry charge in order to extricate the guns. He also directed General Massy and Colonel Gordon, who had accompanied the former from Killa Aushar, where he had previously been in command, to find a road by which the guns could be withdrawn in safety. Sir Frederick Roberts writes to us of the situation, and the further steps he took at this juncture:—"From the moment of my arrival on the ground I saw how critical the position was, and at once despatched one of my aides-de-camp, Lieutenant Sherston, of the Rifle Brigade, to General Macpherson, with a written order to wheel to his left, and advance to the assistance of the guns and Cavalry as rapidly as possible. At the same time I directed General Hills to gallop to Sherpur, and warn General Hugh

Gough of what had occurred, to order him to be on the alert, and to send a wing of the 72nd Highlanders, with all possible speed, to the village of Deh Mazung, where they were to hold the gorge of the Cabul river at all hazards. Seeing at a glance the hopelessness of continuing the fight on such difficult ground with a handful of Cavalry, and observing that the extreme flanks of the Afghan Army were rapidly overlapping the small party, I ordered General Massy to retire the guns towards Cabul, and to cover the movement by a Cavalry charge."

The Cavalry charge, gallantly led by Lieutenant-Colonel R. S. Cleland, who was dangerously wounded, and by Captain Bloomfield Gough, on the flank, was well delivered, and did considerable execution, but did not succeed in checking the enemy for more than a few minutes. The gallant Colonel of the 9th Lancers was dangerously wounded,* and many others, officers and men, fell in the vain effort to check the advance of an army. The charge was necessary to save the guns, but it was well-nigh as desperate as that of Balaclava. In its incidents it resembled that made by the 2nd Bengal Cavalry at Purwandurrah, in the Kohistan, in December, 1840, when Dost Mahommed led the opposing horsemen, though it was more creditable, as the native troops disgraced themselves by leaving their officers to bear the brunt of the action. This act of infamy British Lancers were not likely to imitate.

Retiring alternately, two Royal Horse Artillery guns re-opened fire, but the Afghans pressed on them hard, the gunners found their further movements stopped by a deep and narrow nullah, and in order to give them time while searching for a passage across, Sir Frederick Roberts ordered a second Cavalry charge. He writes to us: "Seeing that the guns were stuck in the watercourses, and the enemy still pressing on, I ordered General Massy to try a second charge, but this was not carried out; the 9th Lancers were much broken, and before they could be got together, the guns had to be abandoned and spiked." During the retirement, Lieutenant Hardy, R.H.A., who was last seen endeavouring to help Lieutenant Forbes, 14th Bengal

---

* Colonel Cleland died of his wounds on his return to India, after much and prolonged suffering.

Lancers, whose leg was broken, was killed, but the gunners and drivers succeeded in retreating in safety with the cavalry.

"When the retreat took place my first object," writes Sir Frederick Roberts to us, "was to rally the Cavalry; and together with my own small escort, a sufficient number of the 9th Lancers, 14th Bengal Lancers and gunners were got together, who by their dismounted fire checked in some slight measure the onward rush of the enemy. Slowly this weak party retired in the direction of the Deh Mazung village, the object being to give the Highlanders time to get there from Sherpur before the Afghans could seize the position." During the retirement, the squadron of the 14th Bengal Lancers, under the command of Captain Neville, covering the retreat, behaved with great steadiness and coolness. Many men had lost their horses in the charges, fifty-one having been killed in the small column, and many opportunities were afforded for the display of that devotion which is never absent in a British force, even when most hardly pressed by an enemy.* The situation had become extremely grave, when the 72nd Highlanders, led by the chivalrous Brownlow, were seen advancing at the double through the gorge. Their advent was received with cheers by the troopers of the 9th. "It was literally touch and go as to who should reach the village first, the Highlanders or the Afghans, but our men swept in, and swarming to the tops of the houses the breechloaders soon checked the advancing tide." In vain the Afghans, headed by some Ghazees, surged round

---

* In his despatch Sir Frederick Roberts gives the British loss as twenty-seven killed, of whom eighteen belonged to the 9th Lancers, and twenty-five wounded. The 9th Lancers lost two officers, Lieutenants Ricardo and Hearsey; the Artillery one officer, Lieutenant Hardy; and the 14th Bengal Lancers, one officer, Lieutenant Forbes. He writes :—" Brigadier-General Massy specially mentions Lieutenant and Adjutant E. B. McInnis, and Lieutenant C. J. W. Tower, both of the 9th Lancers, for their gallantry ; whilst I personally witnessed the devoted bravery of the Reverend J. W. Adams, the chaplain attached to my force. Mr. Adams dismounted to assist a wounded man of the 9th Lancers, and, while so occupied, lost his horse ; when making his way back on foot, and although the enemy were but a few yards distance from him, Mr. Adams, regardless of his own safety, was mainly instrumental in saving the lives of two men of the 9th Lancers, who were caught under their horses, which had fallen in a water-course, and who, but for his aid, must have been speedily killed by the advancing enemy." For his gallantry Mr. Adams received the V.C., being the first clergyman who has gained the decoration. Captain Stewart-Macken-

the village, whence a deadly fire decimated their ranks. Foiled at every attempt to capture it by the rush, they abandoned the attempt to enter Cabul by the gorge, and took ground to the right, and occupied the Takht-i-Shah and all the slopes leading up to it, as well as the large walled villages in the Chardeh valley, thereby threatening the Upper Bala Hissar. We will now follow the operations of Brigadier-General Macpherson, as detailed in the despatch.

Marching from the Surkh Kotul at 8 A.M., Macpherson moved in a south-westerly direction towards Urghundeh, but observing large bodies of the enemy crossing his front and proceeding towards Cabul, and hearing the firing of General Massy's guns on his left, he brought his right forward, and at 12.30 P.M., or about an hour after the Cavalry and Artillery had commenced retiring, he found himself very nearly on the ground where General Massy's action had been fought. Here he came across the rear of the enemy, who were speedily dispersed, some making for the hills above Killa Kazi, others for the Chardeh Valley. General Macpherson, not being fully informed of the result of General Massy's action, decided, about 3.30 P.M., to halt for the night at Killa Kazi, but afterwards received an order from Sir Frederick Roberts, directing him to fall back on Deh Mazung, where he arrived at 7 P.M., thus still further securing the approach to the city.

Writing to us of General Macpherson's movements during the day, his Chief says: "His soldierly instinct had told him to wheel to his left on hearing Massy's guns, before my order to that effect reached him, and rapidly advancing, he soon came into collision with a large body of the enemy who were holding the ground over which the 9th Lancers had previously charged. Elated by their recent victory, these seemed disposed to show fight, but the brigade steadily advanced in line, and company volleys soon put them to flight." On his arrival at Deh Mazung, Sir Frederick Roberts, leaving with him the wing of the 72nd

---

zie and Captain Bloomfield Gough, both of the 9th Lancers, distinguished themselves on this occasion, and the former officer brought the regiment out of action, and remained in the field until late in the day, although suffering from a severe contusion. Second-Lieutenant Hunter and some non-commissioned officers and men of the 9th Lancers were also specially commended by Sir Frederick Roberts.

The Crisis in Cabul and Sherpur. 287

Highlanders, returned to Sherpur, where he arrived about 8 P.M., after an exciting day, destined, however, to be followed by others equally full of incident.

The position of affairs at Sherpur at one time had been sufficiently serious. With a vast cantonment, full of the winter supplies of food and forage for the British army, and almost denuded of troops, Brigadier-General Hugh Gough made the best dispositions for defence that lay in his power. His resolute bearing and military experience inspired confidence, until the arrival of Colonel Jenkins,* from Lutterbund, with the Guides, Cavalry and Infantry, tended to lessen the immediate danger somewhat, though reports were current of an intended attack on the Cantonments by the Kohistanees.

The situation in Cabul during the day was also a very anxious one for General Hills, who, after despatching the Highlanders to Deh Mazung, took steps to defend the city committed to his charge against the soldiers of Mahomed Jan, or the malcontents and "budmashes," or swash-bucklers, who, as well as fanatics, swarm in these cities of Central Asia. The resources at General Hills's disposal were but limited, but a braver-hearted soldier does not exist, and he put a bold face on it, which goes a long way with the scum of great cities. At the Kotwallee,† or Magistrate's office, where he administered justice, General Hills placed a guard of forty Kuzzilbashes (literally "red heads," from the colour of their turbans), a tribe descended from the followers of Nadir Shah, who have always been friendly to the British, and he manned the gates with strong armed bodies of the same race. He himself patrolled the city with 100 Sikhs, and there was a company of the 72nd Highlanders posted on the Upper Bala Hissar. Though these were all the troops at his disposal, his arrangements averted a rising. Sir Frederick Roberts, on his way to the Cantonment from Deh Mazung,

---

* Sir Frederick Roberts writes :—"Foreseeing the probability of reinforcements being required, and thinking that troops coming from India would have a good effect politically, I had ordered Colonel Jenkins on the 7th December to march on Cabul from Jugdulluck."

† Had General Hills been attacked, as then anticipated, his fate might have been that of Sir Alexander Burnes in 1841, or Sir Louis Cavagnari in 1879, though what he chiefly feared was being burnt out, for which these buildings offer peculiar facilities.

detached a party of the 72nd Highlanders to reinforce the picket of the 67th, and this force, numbering 213 men, under Captain Jarvis, of the latter regiment, though attacked during the night with great determination, repulsed the enemy with heavy loss.

Meantime the lost guns had been recovered by Colonel Macgregor. When his chief fell back on Deh Mazung, that gallant officer, judging that the infantry ordered from Sherpur might take the road by the Kotul to the north by Killa Aushar, went in that direction to meet them, and observing from this point that the ground where the guns were lying had been partially cleared of the enemy by the advance of General Macpherson's troops, he, with the assistance of some officers, collected a small party of the 9th Lancers, 14th Bengal Lancers, and Artillerymen, who had remained with him, retraced his steps, and picking up, *en route,* a few soldiers belonging to General Macpherson's baggage guard, was enabled to recover the guns and bring them into Cantonments before night. The Afghans had stripped them of all movable parts, and the ammunition boxes had been emptied, but otherwise they were intact, and were ready for use on the following day.

During this eventful day the force detached under Brigadier-General Baker had also been engaged with the enemy. Starting early on the morning of the 11th from his encampment in the neighbourhood of Maidan he found the enemy in considerable force, occupying the hills on either side of the Urghundeh road. The main body of General Baker's force was allowed to proceed unmolested, but his rear-guard and baggage were somewhat hotly attacked; owing, however, to the able manner in which the rear guard was commanded by Captain McCullum, 92nd Highlanders, and to the energy of the officers in charge of the Transport, the whole of the baggage was brought through in safety. Baker's advanced-guard had, in the meantime, reached Urghundeh, and found the Afghans in possession of both sides of the gorge through which the road runs into the Chardeh Valley. Although late in the afternoon it was necessary to dislodge the enemy from their position, commanding, as it did, the road to Cabul. This was effected in a brilliant manner by a portion of the 92nd Highlanders, under the command of Major White, gallantly led by Lieutenant the Hon. J. Scott Napier, son of Lord Napier of Magdala. General Baker encamped that night at Urghundeh, being unaware of the misfortune that had befallen General Massy's force, all efforts to communicate with him on the part of the commanding General having been unsuccessful. Early on the morning of the 12th a heliographic signal from Sherpur put Baker in possession of the changed situation. He was informed that the enemy were threatening the city in very considerable numbers, that Sir Frederick Roberts had found it necessary to withdraw General Macpherson's brigade to Deh Mazung, and that it was his wish he should return forthwith, as it was important that the whole force should be concentrated in the neighbourhood of the city and cantonment. Accordingly General Baker marched on Sherpur, where he arrived during the day.

It has been said that Sir Frederick Roberts underrated the strength of the forces from Wardak, Logar, and Maidan, controlled by Mahomed Jan, and that he committed an error in denuding Sherpur and despatching two brigades by the Chardeh and Logar Valleys, and thus separating them by a mountain range so that no communication could be maintained between them ; but even if this is so, the responsibility of failure in his arrangements does not rest with him, and all would have gone well had his plans been carried out as he intended. Sir Frederick, from his lengthened experience of the warlike capabilities of the Afghan levies, such as constituted the bulk of the forces arrayed against him under Meer Butcha and Mahomed Jan, was of opinion that either Macpherson's or Baker's brigades could have dealt with them singly, while they were on the march and not entrenched in strong positions ; but once they acquired the prestige of success by the capture of British guns they became infinitely more powerful, both morally and numerically, as our experience of the events round Cabul in 1841 amply testified would be the case. Had Sir Frederick kept Brigadier-General Baker back, and sent him by the Indikee route, that officer would have been in a position to attack Mahomed Jan as he slipped past Brigadier-General Macpherson, but the Afghan Commander, who displayed considerable astuteness and military capacity, hearing that Baker was in his

U

rear, made for the Cabul Valley, and at one time the position of the Sherpur Cantonment was most critical.

At no juncture in his remarkable career did Sir Frederick Roberts display the genius of the great commander in a more striking manner than when, with the intuition of genius, he occupied the gorge leading to the city with the 72nd Highlanders. That move, perhaps, saved the Cantonment from capture, for though the dispositions of Brigadier-General Gough were all that skill could devise and calm courage carry out, yet what would his small force of about 1,000 men, distributed over the vast *enceinte* of Sherpur, have effected against an infuriated horde of soldiers, villagers, and Ghazis, bent on revenge and rapine? In a letter detailing the critical events by which the Camp at Sherpur was saved Sir Frederick Roberts says:—" I reached Deh Mazung with the Cavalry which had been rallied, and which retired very steadily, squadron by squadron, keeping the enemy in check. We came as slowly as possible, as I knew that unless the 72nd Wing, sent for from Sherpur, could reach Deh Mazung before we did, it would be scarcely possible for us to prevent the enemy from occupying that village and the neighbouring heights. The 72nd arrived just in time, and I remained until the arrival of General Macpherson's brigade, which I had ordered to fall back from Kila Kazi." It would be ungenerous to bear hard on General Massy, who suffered much for his rashness, as not only did Sir Frederick Haines, the Commander-in-Chief, animadvert severely on his conduct, but he was recalled to India. There was an error of judgment on his part, but mistakes have been made by the greatest commanders, and General Massy was a very gallant officer.*

---

* A distinguished officer, who was an eye-witness of these events, places the blame of the disaster of the 11th December unreservedly on Brigadier-General Massy, who, he maintains, did not carry out Sir Frederick's instructions. He said to us:—"Sir Frederick Roberts thought each column, unassisted, quite able to drive off any force. Baker was to have caught Mahomed Jan's troops, but they, hearing he was in the rear, gave him the slip and made for the city. The enemy halted about six miles from Cabul, when Massy attacked them without orders. He took it upon himself to do so, as he had distinct orders to wait for Macpherson to attack with the infantry. The cavalry ought to have retired by the Ghuznee main road, which protected the city, or by the way by which they came, which was practicable for guns; had they done so the guns would have been saved. But instead of that Massy moved them through the fields and watercourses,

On the following day, Friday the 12th December, Sir Frederick Roberts resumed operations against the enemy, who, on finding that they were unable to enter the city, took up a strong position on a lofty peak known as the Takht-i-Shah (or King's throne), which is connected with the hill above the Bala Hissar by a long neck, or saddle, of very rough and difficult ground. Sir Frederick Roberts felt that unless he was to play the part of a second Elphinstone, an effort must be made to dislodge the enemy, and directed General Macpherson to make the attempt. Accordingly, Colonel Money, 3rd Sikhs, who had gained such distinction by his defence of the Shutargardan, was directed to make the attempt with two guns and 560 men.*

The position held by the enemy was of great natural strength. The slopes of the Takht-i-Shah are very steep, strewn with jagged masses of rock and intercepted with scarps, and the natural impediments with which the assaulting party had to contend were still further increased by "sungars," or breastworks, which the enemy had thrown up at different points on the ascent to the peak. Behind these defences the Afghans, like Easterns, might be credited with fighting with resolution.

In spite of the gallantry of the troops and the accuracy of the fire of Captain Morgan's guns, it was speedily manifest that a much larger force than Sir Frederick Roberts could spare from the defence of Sherpur, with Baker's Brigade absent, would be necessary to carry the heights. "The position," writes the

between these two roads, and so got into difficulties and lost his guns. Sir Frederick Roberts at once grasped the situation, and sent General Hills to Sherpur with orders to turn out a wing of the 72nd Highlanders under Colonel Brownlow, to seize the gorge leading to the city. Hills did so, and just got there in time to save the retreating column and check the rebels from getting into the city. Meanwhile Macpherson was doubling up at the rear. It is, therefore, nonsense to declare that Massy threw himself into the gap as there were no British troops, and saved Sherpur. Had he waited for Macpherson there would have been no difficulty at all. Sir Frederick Roberts was driven back to the gorge, the guns being lost, and there were the 72nd Highlanders." The highest authority on the events of the 11th December writes to us with characteristic generosity of the part played by Brigadier-General Massy : "He was taken by surprise, and failed to appreciate the part which his cavalry was intended to play, as a portion of General Macpherson's brigade, upon the movements of which he should have waited."

* The following was the constitution of the small column :—2 guns No. 1 Mountain Battery ; 215 men from 67th and 72nd Regiments ; 150 of the 3rd Sikhs ; and 195 men of the 5th Goorkhas.

General, "was an exceedingly formidable one, and after gallant attempts to carry it, which lasted during the greater part of the day, I ordered the assault to be deferred. I saw that to ensure success without very serious loss, and to prevent the enemy relieving and reinforcing the party holding the peak, as I had observed them to be doing during the day, it was necessary not only to attack in front, but to operate also on the enemy's line of retreat."*

General Macpherson was, accordingly, directed to hold the ground of which he had already gained possession, and informed that, on the following morning, General Baker, who only arrived at Sherpur in the evening, after a long and fatiguing march, would co-operate with him from the Beni Hissar side.

Early on the morning of the 13th December, Sir Frederick Roberts commenced operations with vigour. Brigadier-General Baker was despatched with a column† with orders to proceed by the Bala Hissar road in the direction of Beni Hissar, to seize the heights above that village, and to operate on the enemy's position on the Takht-i-Shah from the south-east. At the same time Brigadier-General Macpherson was instructed to act in conjunction with General Baker from the direction of the north of the Bala Hissar.

Soon after passing the Bala Hissar General Baker observed the enemy streaming out of the villages immediately below the Beni Hissar ridge, and resolved to cut their line in two. Covering his advance with the fire of his two batteries, the infantry advanced on the villages, the centre of which was seized by a movement described by the General as "bold and rapid." The 92nd Highlanders led the advance, under Major

---

* The losses during the day were four killed and twelve wounded, including three officers, Lieutenant Faskin, 3rd Sikhs, Lieutenant Fergusson, 72nd Highlanders, and Major Cook, V.C., 5th Goorkhas, who died on 29th December, mortification of the leg having ensued from his wound. Sir Frederick Roberts issued a graceful order to his troops, recounting the services of this gallant officer, whose loss was deplored by the entire force and was indeed of national concern. "He was one," says the General, "who would, had he been spared, have risen to the highest honours of his profession."

† Four guns G Battery, 3rd Brigade, R.A.; 4 guns No. 2 Mountain Battery; 1 squadron 9th Lancers; 5th Punjaub Cavalry; 6 Companies 92nd Highlanders; 7 Companies Guides Infantry; 300 rifles 3rd Sikhs; afterwards reinforced by 150 rifles 5th Punjaub Infantry.

White, who had so greatly distinguished himself at Charasia and elsewhere during the present campaign, and the attack on the enemy's first position was gallantly headed by Lieutenant Forbes, who, together with his Colour-Sergeant, James Drummond, was killed in a hand-to-hand fight. On seeing them fall there was a momentary waver among the Highlanders, when Lieutenant Dick Cunyngham rushed forward, and rallied the men by his example and cheering words.* As a national poet sings :—

> " Joy to the chiefs that lead old Scotia's ranks,
> Of Roman garb and more than Roman fire."

The Afghans on this occasion displayed unwonted daring, but the position was won after a brief struggle, and a large portion of the enemy were thus prevented from uniting themselves with those occupying the Takht-i-Shah. The 92nd Highlanders and Guides, covered by the fire of Major Swinley's guns, which had by this time gained the summit of the lower ridge, and aided by that of Major Craster from the plain below, continued the advance on the conical hill, though every foot of the way was contested. At length, shortly before noon, the 92nd Highlanders and Guides had reached the summit, where they were met by a party from the Bala Hissar side, consisting of the 72nd Highlanders, 3rd Sikhs and 5th Goorkhas, under the command of Major Sym, 5th Goorkhas, who had arrived there a few minutes before.†

Large bodies of men were about this time seen issuing from the lower Bala Hissar and city, part of whom made for the heights of Siah-Sung, whilst the rest, advancing towards Beni Hissar, occupied two strongly fortified villages situated on either side of the road. One of these was captured by General Baker's troops on their return from the Takht-i-Shah; the other, later in the day by a detachment of the 5th Punjaub Infantry, under Major Pratt, which Sir Frederick Roberts had sent from Sherpur to keep open the communication with General Baker. Observing the collection of men on the Siah-Sung, and thinking that Brigadier-General Baker might have some

---

* This officer was awarded the V.C. for his gallantry on this occasion, and never was that much-coveted distinction more worthily gained.

† Colour-Sergeant John Yule, 72nd Highlanders, was the first man up, and captured two standards. This gallant non-commissioned officer was killed on the following day.

difficulty in dealing with so many detached parties of the enemy, Sir Frederick despatched Brigadier-General Massy with the Cavalry brigade* to his assistance. During the operation the Guides Cavalry, under Lieutenant-Colonel G. Stewart, made a brilliant charge, as did the 9th Lancers, under Captain Butson, who was killed, together with Sergeant-Major Spittle and three men; Captain Chisholme and Lieutenant Tower with eight men of the same regiment being wounded. Notwithstanding the severity of his wound, Captain Chisholme remained in the saddle, and brought his regiment out of action. The 5th Punjaub Cavalry, under Lieutenant-Colonel Williams, also distinguished themselves, Majors Hammond and Stewart both leading successful charges, so that the Cavalry had an ample revenge in the loss they inflicted on the enemy for the misadventure of the 11th December.

The result of the day's operations was regarded by Sir Frederick Roberts as very satisfactory. The enemy had been driven from the southern range, and their advance in that direction had been stopped; they had suffered greatly from the British Artillery and infantry fire when on the hill sides; and on the plain below they had been severely dealt with by the Cavalry. In the evening Sir Frederick recalled General Baker to cantonments, and directed General Macpherson to move from Deh Mazung and occupy the Bala Hissar heights, leaving the 5th Goorkhas to retain possession of the Takht-i-Shah.† But stern work was before the Cabul Field Force, and before nightfall on the succeeding day, the aspect of affairs changed, and the aggressors became the defenders.

Every one in Sherpur, including Sir Frederick Roberts, was of opinion that the marked success that had attended the operations of the day, and the heavy losses inflicted on the enemy, would result in their dispersion, but the light of morning

---

* General Massy took with him from Sherpur:—1 squadron 9th Lancers, and 2 squadrons 14th Bengal Lancers; and was joined on Siah-Sung by 2 squadrons 5th Punjaub Cavalry, and 1 squadron 9th Lancers. The Guides Cavalry were an independent command.

† The losses during the day were:—Killed, two officers, Lieutenant Forbes, 92nd Highlanders, and Captain Butson, 9th Lancers, and twelve men, half British. Wounded—two officers, Captain Chisholme and Lieutenant Tower, 9th Lancers, and twenty-seven British soldiers and sixteen natives. Twenty horses were also killed and thirty-two wounded.

quickly dispelled the illusion. Fortunately the British Commander was prepared for any fortune, and reverses found him as calm and collected, and his resources as well in hand as after such successes as the Peiwar Kotul and Charasia.

When daylight broke on the 14th December, large masses of men, with many standards, were observed in occupation of a high hill on the Kohistan road, about a mile north of the heights of the Koh Asmai; and as the day advanced, they passed in great numbers from this hill, and also along the Kohistan road, to the crest of the heights, where they were joined by other bodies from the direction of Chardeh and the city. It now became apparent, adds Sir Frederick Roberts, that, "foiled in their western and southern operations, the enemy had concentrated to the north-west, and were about to deliver an attack in great strength from that quarter." The General was not the man to sit tamely by while the enemy took the initiative, but resolved to drive them off the Asmai heights, and to cut their communications with the north. The Koh Asmai, it should be noted, flank Sherpur in the west, at a distance of about a mile, and as their occupation in force was a menace to the security of the cantonment, the expulsion of the enemy was a paramount necessity.

Accordingly, at 9 A.M. on the 14th, Sir Frederick Roberts despatched Brigadier-General Baker with a force* to the eastern slope of the Asmai, to drive the enemy off the range. Under cover of the fire of his field and mountain guns, which came into action close to the ruined village of Biland Kheyl, General Baker seized the small conical hill which forms the northern shoulder of the Aliabad Kotul, thus placing himself on the enemy's line of communication, and preventing the force on Asmai receiving support either from the large bodies on the hill to the north or on the Kohistan road. Having gained this preliminary advantage, General Baker sent Colonel Jenkins to attack the conical hill with a small force.† Having effected

---

* Four guns G Battery, 3rd Brigade, R.A., under Major Craster; 4 guns No. 2 Mountain Battery, under Major Swinley; 14th Bengal Lancers; 72nd Highlanders, 192 men; 92nd Highlanders, 100; Guides Infantry, 460; 5th Punjaub Infantry, 470 men.

† One hundred and ninety-four men, 72nd Highlanders; 70 of 92nd Highlanders; and 422 Guides Infantry.

this with small resistance on the part of the enemy, Colonel Jenkins left a party of sixty-four men of the 72nd Highlanders and sixty of the Guides Infantry, commanded by Lieutenant-Colonel Clarke, of the former regiment, who had led the successful attack upon this point, to hold the conical hill, and with the remainder pushed on to dislodge the enemy from the position on Asmai, from the western side. The 5th Punjaub Infantry was held in reserve with the guns, while the Cavalry, following the attacking force, descended into the Chardeh Valley. The advance on the enemy's position at Asmai was led by Lieutenant-Colonel Brownlow with his Highlanders, the Guides Infantry on the right affording assistance by operating on the enemy's flank, and it was conducted with the gallantry that had distinguished those regiments on the previous day.

As soon as the eastern point of the main position had been carried, General Baker directed four guns of No. 2 Mountain Battery, escorted by 100 rifles of the 5th Punjaub Infantry, to reinforce the party which had been left on the conical hill, with a view of supporting the advance by engaging the enemy in the Chardeh and Kohistan directions. He also covered the advance by the four guns of G Battery, 3rd Brigade, under Major Craster, R.A., and Sir Frederick Roberts rendered assistance by bringing into action four guns of F Battery, A Brigade R.H.A., commanded by Captain H. Pipon, which was posted near the south-west corner of the Sherpur cantonment. The attack was further assisted by the fire of four guns of No. 1 Mountain Battery, under Captain Morgan, R.A., attached to Brigadier-General Macpherson's Column, from the Bala Hissar hill, and by two companies of the 67th Regiment, under Major G. Baker, which, crossing the Cabul river and acting on the enemy's left rear, contributed to render their position on the Asmai heights untenable.

The ground was most difficult, and the enemy fought with the greatest obstinacy; the Highlanders and Guides were, however, not to be denied, and eventually reached the highest peak, where stood a number of Ghazis in their white robes, as typical of their resolution to die for the faith. Here a severe struggle took place, and many acts of gallantry were performed, but at 12.30 the British troops were in possession of the

Asmai heights. It seemed as if complete success had rewarded the combinations of Sir Frederick Roberts and the gallantry of his troops; but a change suddenly came over the scene, and victory was turned into very like defeat, due to the overwhelming forces of the enemy.

The first intimation to cause anxiety was a heliographic message from Brigadier-General Macpherson, informing Sir Frederick Roberts that very large bodies of the enemy were moving northwards from Indikee, with the apparent intention of effecting a junction with the hostile force that still held the hills towards Kohistan, and of endeavouring to re-take the original position. Similar information was about this time communicated to Brigadier-General Baker by Colonel Ross, commanding the cavalry, which he had sent over the low western spurs of the conical hill to ascertain the numbers and movements of the enemy, and suddenly a large body of the Afghans, creeping up the hill-side from the Chardeh villages, made an attack on the small party left on the conical hill, and before a reinforcement of 100 men of the 5th Punjaub Infantry, sent by General Baker, could arrive to their assistance, the enemy stormed the position. In seeking to rally his men and re-take the hill, Captain Spens, 72nd Highlanders, was killed, and two guns of the Mountain Battery were lost, though no blame whatever attached to the officers and men, who displayed conspicuous gallantry. "The mountain guns," writes Sir Frederick Roberts to us, "had already limbered up, and were retiring down the hill in good order, when the Afghans gained the crest—two of the gun mules were shot, and though the gunners rolled the two 7-pounders down the hill, it was found impossible to carry either of them away, and they fell into the hands of the enemy. Though Captain Hall's reinforcement of the 5th Punjaubees was at first carried away by the panic, yet they and the remainder of the party re-formed again at the foot of the slope, and with their fire covered the retreat of the other two guns of Swinley's battery."

Sir Frederick Roberts witnessed these events with great chagrin, but he had done all that lay in his power to prevent the loss of the hill, by despatching to General Baker's assistance from Sherpur 200 men of the 3rd Sikhs, who had been escorting Captain Pipon's guns. Meanwhile, as on the previous day, heavy masses of the enemy were observed collecting on Siah-Sung, and proceeding round the eastern flank of cantonments in the direction of Kohistan. Sir Frederick accordingly despatched a small force of cavalry and two guns of F Battery, A Brigade, R.H.A., under the command of Brigadier-General Hugh Gough, to disperse them, but owing to the ground in that direction being much intercepted by deep watercourses, the advance of the guns was necessarily slow, and by the time the obstacles had been overcome, the enemy had got so far on the road towards Kohistan and so close to the hills that pursuit was impossible.

A party of the 5th Punjaub Cavalry, under Captain Vousden, who had done good service in the Kurram campaign, met with better success. This regiment was quartered in the Shah Bagh (King's garden)—which played so prominent a part in the siege of General Elphinstone's army in 1841—situated about a third of the way between Sherpur and the city, and Sir Frederick had in the morning sent orders to the commanding officer, Lieutenant-Colonel Williams, to be on the look-out for any enemy that might pass in that direction. About 1 P.M. some 300 or 400 were observed moving along the left bank of the river, and Captain Vousden, who, with one troop, was out on reconnoissance, most gallantly charged into the midst of them. Though only twelve of his men were able to follow him, he succeeded in dispersing the enemy, and in inflicting severe loss upon them, killing five men with his own hand. Half of his gallant little band were placed *hors de combat.*

" My object throughout these operations," writes Sir Frederick, "had been either to break up the combination against us by dealing with the enemy in detail, or at least to prevent their getting command of the hills to the north and west of Cabul, and thus gain possession of the city and Bala Hissar. Up to this time I had no reason to apprehend that the Afghans were in sufficient force to successfully cope with disciplined troops, but the resolute and determined manner in which the conical hill had been re-captured, and the information sent to me by Brigadier-General Macpherson from the signal station on the Bala Hissar, that large masses of the enemy were still advancing from the north, south, and west, made it evident that the numbers combined against us were too overwhelming to admit of my comparatively small force meeting them, especially on ground which still further increased the advantages they possessed from their vast numerical superiority. I, therefore, determined to withdraw from all isolated positions, and to concentrate the whole force at Sherpur, thus securing the safety of our large cantonments, and avoiding what had now become a useless sacrifice of life." It was with great reluctance that General Roberts adopted this measure, as it involved the temporary abandonment of the city and the Bala Hissar, a loss serious in itself, and likely to produce a bad effect on the country at large. Under the circumstances, however, no other course was left to him but to remain on the defensive, and wait until the arrival of reinforcements, or the growing confidence of the enemy should afford him a favourable opportunity for inflicting a defeat on them. Time, under any circumstances, would work in his favour, as the enemy did not possess supplies sufficient to enable them to keep the field in such vast numbers in the depth of winter.

Orders to retire within Sherpur were accordingly issued to Brigadier-Generals Macpherson and Baker, and the withdrawal from the Bala Hissar and Asmai heights was accomplished without loss, and in a manner highly creditable to the discipline of the troops. General Macpherson, whose brigade had to pass through a portion of the city and the suburb of Deh Afghan, had before him a critical task, but he performed it with the coolness and ability that had distinguished him throughout the past few days. His rear-guard was harassed, and his troops were subjected to a heavy fire as they moved along the narrow streets and through the numerous gardens and orchards, but the Brigadier-General brought off his men and baggage in perfect order, and with comparatively little loss. General Macpherson was well seconded by the officers commanding corps, especially Colonel Knowles, commanding the 67th Regiment.

The retirement of Brigadier-General Baker's troops down the eastern face of Asmai, under a heavy fire, was also well conducted by Colonel Jenkins, who spoke in high terms of the gallantry of Colonel Brownlow and Major Stockwell, 72nd Highlanders, and also of Colonel R. Campbell, of the Guides. During the retreat an officer of the Guides displayed great devotion. Captain Hammond had been very forward during the storming of the Asmai heights, and now, when the enemy were crowding up the western slopes, he remained with a few men on the ridge until the Afghans were within thirty yards of them, and when one of the Guides was shot, he stopped and assisted in carrying him away, though the enemy were at the time close by and firing heavily.*

By the evening of the 14th all troops and baggage were within the cantonments, and that night the Afghan army occupied the city and Bala Hissar.

Sir Frederick Roberts directed the operations of the 12th, 13th, and 14th, from the roof of the quarters he occupied in Sherpur, whence he could see very fairly all the surrounding country. Except when riding out to meet the troops returning from fighting, in order to encourage the men and speak to the wounded, he did not quit the Cantonment during those days.

As the British General mustered his soldiers behind the sheltering ramparts of Sherpur he had reason to deplore the loss of many gallant men† during the past eventful week. Eighty-three had fallen, including 8 officers, and 192 were wounded, among whom were 12 officers, some of whom died, including Colonel Cleland and Major Cook, V.C. Like Hector, after his warriors had been chased within the sheltering walls of Troy—

"Round the battlement and round the plain
For many a chief he look'd, but look'd in vain."

Considering the vast numerical superiority of the enemy and

---

* Captain (now Major) Hammond received the Victoria Cross for his gallantry on this occasion, as did likewise Captain (now Major) Vousden of the 5th Punjaub Cavalry.

† The losses on the 14th December were:—General Baker's brigade— Killed, 2 officers, Captain Spens and Lieutenant Gaisford, 72nd Highlanders, and twenty-seven men; wounded, three officers, Captain Gordon, 92nd Highlanders; Captain Battye, Guides; and Lieutenant Egerton, 72nd Highlanders, and eighty-six men. General Macpherson's brigade had five killed and eleven wounded. Cavalry brigade, eight wounded. Grand total, thirty-four of all ranks killed, and one hundred and sixty-six wounded.

the nature of the positions from which they were dislodged during the operations, this loss is very moderate, though heavy in comparison with that suffered in previous encounters with the Afghans.

It has been sought in some quarters to convey the impression that Sir Frederick Roberts was taken by surprise during the month of December, but this is not so. Though the Commanding general had no reason to expect the rapid gathering of such enormous numbers as beleagured Sherpur, computed by the Afghan leaders themselves at between 100,000 and 120,000 men—and certain Sirdars in camp, notably Daoud Shah, the late Commander-in-Chief of the ex-Ameer, who was placed under arrest for his treachery, gave false information—he anticipated being closely pressed during the winter, and it was to guard against this probability that he made strenuous preparations to provide for a siege or blockade by laying in supplies for men and animals in such vast quantities. He says :—" Though my information for some weeks previous to the disturbances made me aware of the increasing hostile feeling with which we were regarded, and of the fact that the tribes were assembling in considerable strength, yet it was impossible to form any estimate as to what numbers we should have to contend with at Cabul." At the same time, he was too well versed in Asiatic warfare and too familiar with the Afghan character to act on the defensive, and leave the gatherings in Logar and Kohistan to develop into a national rising without seeking to suppress them by vigorous action, which was only ineffectual from the circumstance, as he writes to us, " that 6,000 men were numerically incapable of, at the same time, leaving a sufficient garrison in Sherpur, and taking the offensive against armies numbering twenty times their strength."

CHAPTER XVI.

The Situation at Sherpur and in Cabul—The City and Bala Hissar Seized by the Enemy—Their Movements against Sherpur—Sir Frederick Roberts places the Cantonment in a Condition of Defence—Colonel Hudson and the Garrison at Lutterbund—Desultory Fighting with the Enemy between the 14th and 21st December—The Attack of the 23rd December—The Final Rout of the Afghans by Sir Frederick Roberts—Arrival of Brigadier-General Charles Gough with Reinforcements—The future Government of Afghanistan—The Rival Pretenders to the Ameership—Sir Donald Stewart Succeeds to the Chief Command in North-Eastern Afghanistan.

To some in the Camp unaccustomed to the vicissitudes of war, and to most of their countrymen in England, who received the intelligence by telegraph, the situation of affairs on the evening of the 14th December was alarming; but it was not so in the eyes of the general officer commanding the Cabul Field Force, who had gone through the leaguer of Delhi, and at the Peiwar Kotul and Charasia showed the world what military genius and indomitable resolution could effect against enormous odds. He was much stronger now than when achieving either of these memorable feats of war, and though he was placed under the disadvantage of temporarily assuming the defensive, an uncongenial rôle to one of his ardent temperament, yet he had in his favour an easily defensible position, with ample supplies of stores and ammunition, thanks to his own prescience. Time also would work in his favour, as the elements of coherence were wanting in the ranks of the enemy, and an assault of his works would only end in their own discomfiture, while reinforcements would be despatched to his aid as soon as practicable. Nevertheless, these were anxious days, but the cheerful and confident bearing of Sir Frederick Roberts instilled a like feeling into the officers and men, who were quite content to trust their lives and the honour of the flag to the tried commander who had weathered so many of the storms of war. There was also a bracing effect in—

"the stern joy which warriors feel
In foemen worthy of their steel."

There were not wanting critics in India who condemned the abandonment of the Bala Hissar, and the concentration of the force at Sherpur, pointing to the disastrous effects of the former step in the first Afghan War. But the conditions of the problem were altered, and concentration in an easily defensible position was widely different from concentration in a cantonment commanded on all sides and with the supplies stored without its walls. Sir Frederick Roberts set forth the causes that induced him to place his force at Sherpur in preference to occupying the Bala Hissar and the Siah Sung heights in a despatch to the Commander-in-Chief, written at this time. His chief reason was the inadequacy of the Bala Hissar to contain and afford shelter to the entire force, with its camp followers and numerous transport animals. Hence it would have been obligatory to have divided his troops—a measure to which he was very averse—by locating a portion of them elsewhere, possibly upon Siah Sung, a bare and bleak plateau, nearly a mile distant from the remainder of the force, where water would have been procurable with difficulty, and where no single facility for carrying on the necessary hutting operations existed. On the other hand, there was an abundant supply of running water at Sherpur, and wells could be readily sunk, water being procurable within seven feet of the surface. Again, the disastrous explosions of the 16th October led Sir Frederick Roberts to regard as a grave risk the permanent settlement of the greater portion of the force close to and around a vast magazine, which, there was a strong presumption to suppose, was mined. These facts, added to the existence of accommodation sufficient to at once house the Commissariat stores, the entire European portion of the force, and a large part of the native troops, and the rapid approach of the Afghan winter, induced him, after carefully weighing the matter, to decide upon the occupation of Sherpur, and, he added, in writing after the critical events of December, "I see no reason, in the light of recent occurrences, to alter that opinion."

On the other hand, there were drawbacks to placing the force in Sherpur, the chief of which were, the vast extent of the Cantonment, and the impossibilty of at all reducing its line of defences.

Sherpur was in the form of a parallelogram, whose northern side was formed by the Behmaroo ridge,* a range of low but steep, isolated hills, rising some 300 feet above the surrounding plain, and running almost due east and west for a distance (including the slopes at either end) of 2,500 yards. A large lake, or "jheel," whose breadth varies from a quarter to half a mile, lies between the northern slope of the ridge and the steep hills which form the southern boundary of the Kohistan country. As this lake is not more than a mile and a half distant from, and is parallel to, the Behmaroo heights for quite three miles, it formed a barrier, round whose flanks and between which and the heights, no troops would dare advance against an enemy well provided with artillery.

The southern face of the cantonment, which had a length of 2,650 yards, was a continuous and massive mud wall, sixteen feet high, pierced at intervals of about 700 yards by three gateways, which again were protected by lofty circular bastions. Between these gates, and also at the angles, were a series of lower bastions, which gave an admirable flanking fire. The western flank, about 1,000 yards in length, was constructed on a precisely similar plan, save that the northern portion was much damaged by an explosion which occurred the day before the cantonment was first entered by General Massy. The eastern face was the weakest, as the original design was never completed; the wall, which was intended to resemble that of the other faces, did not exceed seven feet in height, and even this was incomplete for a considerable distance. From this point the line of defence tended to the north-west, and, skirting the village of Behmaroo, ran into the eastern slope of the Behmaroo ridge.

The first step that recommended itself to the judgment of Sir Frederick Roberts on occupying Sherpur, in order to

---

* This ridge, which commanded the old cantonment in 1841, played a chief part in rendering it untenable, and much fighting occurred on its slope and base.

prevent annoyance in the event of a strong combination, was to destroy the villages and walled enclosures surrounding it, so as to create an esplanade round the Cantonments; but the pressure of even more important work, the collection of supplies and the provision of shelter for such of the troops as had not already been housed, combined with the scarcity of labour, compelled him in a great measure to defer this precautionary step. He was, also, unwilling to arouse ill-feeling on the part of the people of Cabul, by what might have appeared an unnecessary act of harshness. As he said :—" It was his constant endeavour, from the first, to make the occupation of the country as little irksome to its inhabitants as the safety and welfare of the troops permitted." But he paid the penalty of his humanity, for several of the villages, which were described as " small fortresses protected by massive mud walls, impervious to all but heavy artillery, and guarded by strong, loopholed, flanking towers," gave considerable trouble during the events which occurred between the 15th and 23rd of December, and eventually had to be razed to the ground.

As soon as it became apparent that the events of the 11th December were the forerunners of a serious movement, Sir Frederick took all the necessary steps for strengthening the defences of Sherpur, and made every preparation to meet the large force known to be assembling. As regards food and ammunition he had no anxiety at this period. Sufficient supplies were actually stored in Sherpur to last the entire force for nearly four months, with the exception of "bhoosa" (chopped straw), of which there was only enough for six weeks. There was ample firewood for all purposes; medicines and hospital comforts were sufficient for all possible requirements for a similar time; and there was enough ammunition, both for guns and rifles, to have carried on an obstinate defence for three, or even four, months.

To facilitate the strengthening of the defences, Sir Frederick Roberts divided them into five sections, which were placed under the following officers:—Brigadier-General Macpherson, C.B.,V.C., to command the section from the 2nd Brigade gate, on the southern face, to the Behmaroo village on the east. Colonel Jenkins, C.B., Corps of Guides, the section from the

Behmaroo village up the eastern slope of Behmaroo ridge. Brigadier-General Hugh Gough, C.B., V.C., that from the eastern extremity of the Behmaroo village to the gorge which divides the ridge. Major-General J. Hills, C.B., V.C., the section from the gorge to the head-quarters gate. Lieutenant-Colonel Brownlow, C.B., that from the head-quarters gate to the 2nd Brigade gate. Brigadier-General Massy was placed in the centre with the Cavalry, whilst Brigadier-General Baker, C.B., commanded the reserve, which was formed up at the southern entrance to the gorge leading through the Behmaroo ridge.*

Telegraphic communication was established between Sir Frederick Roberts's head-quarters on the west face, and the temporary head-quarters of Generals Macpherson, Gough, Hills and Baker, and the Native field hospital. All the five sections and the Behmaroo heights were also brought into communication with each other and head-quarters by means of visual signalling.

The defences adopted to strengthen the works were the following:—A "laager," made out of captured Afghan gun-carriages and limbers, was constructed at the north-western corner of Cantonments, closing the open ground which lay between the front of the Behmaroo heights and the north-west circular bastion, and the ground in its immediate front was strengthened by means of abatis and wire entanglements, whilst a village, which formed an excellent flank defence along the western and northern face, was held as an independent post. Six towers had been previously constructed on the Behmaroo heights,

---

* The troops were allotted for the defence, says the *Times* correspondent, as follows:—The 3rd Sikhs, the 5th Goorkhas, and a wing of the 23rd Pioneers held the Behmaroo heights, each that portion near its own lines; the Guides held Behmaroo village; a detachment of the 28th Punjaub Infantry the field hospital and adjoining defences. On the east face the 67th Foot had a company in the redoubt near the south-east angle; and the remainder of the regiment and a wing of the 72nd Highlanders held the parapet and three gateways on the south face. The west face and the General's gateway were held by the Sappers, some marksmen from the British regiments, and the 5th Punjaub Infantry, the latter regiment being also answerable for the defence of the gap at the north-west angle. The reserve consisted of the 92nd Highlanders and a wing each of the 67th and 72nd, one mountain battery, and six squadrons of dismounted cavalry at night.

The Defences of Sherpur. 307

and the shelter-trenches which existed there were deepened and so prolonged as to form one continuous line of defence throughout its entire length. An abatis protected the front of the shelter-trench, and gun-pits were constructed at those points where artillery fire could be most advantageously used. The works in the gorge were strengthened and so arranged as to bring a galling flanking fire to bear upon an enemy advancing from the north. In order to strengthen the north-east corner a two-gun battery was thrown up on the eastern slope of the heights, and connected with the tower above it and the village below. Behmaroo village was loopholed, the outlying buildings to the front made defensible, and the open space to the north-east obstructed with abatis and wire entanglements. The same steps were taken at the Native field hospital, and sand-bag parapets built upon the roof, which was somewhat exposed. The low wall of the eastern face of the Cantonments was raised by logs of wood being placed along the top in several tiers, thus affording good shelter—the front here, as elsewhere, being faced with abatis, for which purpose the wood cut down in clearing the nearest gardens and enclosures supplied the material.*
The construction of all these defences was conducted under the superintendence of Lieutenant-Colonel Perkins, C.B., Commanding Royal Engineers.

In order to supplement the field guns,† and leave them free to move out as opportunity offered, several of the captured Afghan guns were utilized, and, under the superintendence of Colonel Gordon, R.A., mounted on the defences, whence they subsequently played with good effect. A number of marksmen were provided with Enfield rifles and cartridges found in the Bala Hissar, by which means ammunition was economised.

Early in the morning of the 15th December the telegraph wire was cut, but not before Sir Frederick had communicated the situation of affairs to the Commander-in-Chief and the

---

* See despatch of Sir Frederick Roberts.
† The field guns of the British force consisted of twelve 9-pounders and four 7-pounders. Among the ordnance captured was a complete battery of siege guns, four smooth bore 18-pounders, and two 8-inch howitzers, presented to Shere Ali by the Indian Government, which were mounted on the southern face.

Government of India, and urged the advisability of sending reinforcements as speedily as possible to enable him to assume the offensive. At the same time he sent orders to General Bright at Jellalabad, to move Brigadier-General Charles Gough's brigade from Gundamuck to Cabul without loss of time, and to send Brigadier-General Arbuthnot's brigade towards Cabul as soon as fresh troops should reach Jellalabad from India. He decided upon recalling to Sherpur the small garrison of Bootkak, which was in an exposed and isolated position, and considered the expediency of withdrawing the force under Colonel Hudson, 28th Punjaub Native Infantry, at Lutturbund, which consisted of two mountain guns, the 28th Punjaub Native Infantry, and a wing of the 23rd Pioneers, regarding whose safety he was very anxious. But as the position was a strong one, ammunition plentiful, and it was in direct heliographic communication with Cabul, he decided to maintain the post. He had every confidence in Colonel Hudson, and felt satisfied that, so long as Lutturbund was held, no serious opposition could be offered to General Gough's advance; and the result justified this decision, for but slight resistance was offered to General Gough at Jugdulluck, and none whatever after that point was passed. This post of Lutturbund was, in fact, the chief link in the line of communications, but there was some hazard in holding it with a weak garrison, who, moreover, were known to be short of provisions, and as the troops at Bootkak had been withdrawn to Sherpur the only assistance they could receive was from Brigadier-General Charles Gough, against whom the tribesmen, under Asmatullah Khan, were gathering.

The General heliographed an order through Colonel Hudson for Gough to advance with all speed, and directed him to hold his own as best he could until the arrival of that officer, which he anticipated would be in two days, though it was delayed until the 23rd, owing, says a General officer present at Cabul, to the order not appearing of a peremptory character. Colonel Hudson flashed a reply to the General that the Lutturbund garrison were on half rations, but after the 20th would have nothing, upon which Sir Frederick Roberts got some Hazara men, with sixty mules, to carry provisions to

The Investment of Sherpur. 309

Colonel Hudson, under the promise of a large reward if they reached Lutturbund that night. On leaving Sherpur these faithful mercenaries made a great *detour*, passing round Bootkak, then held by the enemy, and reached Lutturbund on the following morning with the loss of only a few animals. This timely assistance saved the Lutturbund garrison from retiring, with the probability of suffering heavily, as the tribesmen were all in arms in the passes. On the 16th, a body of about 1,000 men threatened Colonel Hudson, who, however, attacked and dispersed them, inflicting considerable loss in both killed and wounded.

The Afghans, as is usual with Asiatics, showed an extraordinary incapacity to take advantage of their recent good fortune, and allowed the fever-heat produced by [the intoxication of success to pass away without making an effort to assault the works of Sherpur. They appeared on the heights above Deh Afghan in great force, but beyond shouting and carrying standards took no active measures to profit by their success. On the other hand, Sir Frederick Roberts, with the assistance of his Engineers, pushed the construction of the defences of the Cantonment where they were defective or incomplete, and the respite of the few days succeeding the 14th December was put to such excellent use that the works soon became practically impregnable to the assaults of any army Afghanistan could bring against them. The Infantry and a portion of the dismounted Cavalry were stationed along the extensive *enceinte*, and slept at their posts, being provided with extra blankets to guard against the cold. The reserve, under General Baker, was kept in readiness to turn out at a moment's notice and proceed to any threatened point.

But the enemy were seemingly busy sacking the Hindoo and Kuzzilbash quarters in Cabul, and the houses of all those citizens and Sirdars who had shown favour to the British, and no reliable estimate could be formed, from the reports of spies, of the intentions of Mahomed Jan and the other leaders of the movement. It was known, however, that Moosa Khan, Yakoob Khan's heir, had been proclaimed Ameer, but, from his tender years, he was of course a mere puppet to give the pretence of legality to the proceedings of Mahomed

Jan, whose low extraction made him obnoxious to the Sirdars, though the boy's mother, a woman of remarkable energy, threw herself heart and soul into the movement, and the assistance and countenance afforded by Mooskh-i-Alum gave an air of religious respectability that tended to rally to the national standard all the Ghazis and fanatics of the country. The excitement, as was to be expected, extended to the passes between Bootkak and Gundamuck, and the Tezeen valley, which a fortnight before was the scene of a junction between the brigades of Generals Macpherson and Charles Gough, was in a disturbed state, and the Jugdulluck Pass—through which Sir Michael Kennedy had ridden to Cabul shortly before, escorted by a few Sowars, and Yakoob Khan had passed, guarded by a single troop—was held in such strength that Brigadier-General Charles Gough, who was advancing to the relief of the beleaguered garrison of Sherpur at the head of 5,000 men, reported that it was impracticable without reinforcements. Not only did the Ghilzyes and Khugianis oppose Gough's advance, but further to the eastward, on the line of advance from the Khyber, the Mohmunds were actively hostile to the British, who had deported to India their chief, father-in-law of the ex-Ameer Yakoob.

During the next few days the enemy confined their active efforts against the garrison of Sherpur to a distant fusillade from old walls and dismantled forts, and the King's garden, or Shah Bagh, which figured in the former investment of 1841–42. On the 17th they assembled in crowds on the Siah Sung hill and the heights over Deh Afghan, but all the fervid promptings of the Moollahs could not bring them to advance, and they dispersed after receiving a few shots amidst their ranks.

The Afghan strength brought together at this time round Sherpur in the hope of plunder, united with hatred of the unbeliever, was placed by Sir Frederick Roberts in his despatches at 60,000; but this, he informs us, was an under-estimate, and he afterwards heard from reliable native sources, that between 100,000 and 120,000 men had gathered at Cabul in response to the fiery exhortations of the Moollahs.

Again, on the 18th, the enemy came out of Cabul in great strength, the Ghazis, as usual, exposing themselves, but they were met by such a hot and well-directed fire from the walls, that they could not be brought to encounter the perils involved in leaving the cover of the gardens and buildings, and risking assault across the open. Nothing could exceed the excellent spirit animating the troops, both European and Native, though the intense cold and the night bivouac in the snow must have severely taxed the latter especially. Nevertheless cheerfulness reigned throughout the camp, the men looking forward with eagerness to the time when their trusted commander would lead them from behind the rampart of Sherpur against the enemy who insulted them by voice and gesture, but abstained from making the long-threatened attack.

Sir Frederick Roberts was very desirous of keeping open his communications with India, and as cavalry would be of great service to General Charles Gough in the advance from Lutturbund, he despatched the 12th Bengal Cavalry at 3 A.M., on the morning of the 22nd, to effect a junction with him. Major Green, their commanding officer, acting under instructions, finding that Bootkak was occupied by the enemy, passed on to Lutturbund and joined Colonel Hudson, after a skirmish, in which he lost some men. Major Green conducted this duty in a manner that elicited the commendations of his chief.

Each day, between the 14th and 21st December, Cavalry reconnoissances were made from Sherpur, and some portion of the force turned out to dislodge the Afghans from points in vicinity to the walls. Some of the forts and other cover in the immediate neighbourhood of Sherpur were also destroyed. In one of these affairs, an attack on the fort of Meer Akhor ("Master of the Horse"), a gallant young officer, Lieutenant Montanaro, R.A., received a mortal wound. Sir Frederick, however, confined himself to minor operations of this description, and did not undertake any sortie in force with the object of gaining possession of portions of the enemy's position. His force was not sufficiently large to admit of his holding them, and he, therefore, wisely determined to wait until he could act decisively.

Mahomed Jan and his coadjutors thinking that, as they had compelled the British to retire within their own cantonments, as in the dismal days of 1841, they had only to complete the parallel and destroy the army in the passes on the return march to India, had the audacity to offer terms almost identical with those wrung from the timid and incompetent General Elphinstone nearly forty years before. Mahomed Jan, playing the part of Mahomed Akbar Khan, offered to permit the Army to retire from Afghanistan without molestation—too well history has taught us what reliance could be placed on such a promise from an Afghan—while the British General was to place two officers of rank in his hands—as was done in the case of Major Pottinger, and Captains Lawrence and Colin Mackenzie—and was, further, to engage to restore Yakoob Khan to the throne— one of the conditions proposed by Akbar Khan, who required the return to Cabul of his father, Dost Mahommed, then a prisoner at Calcutta. But these insolent demands were received with the scorn they merited. Roberts was no Elphinstone, and, save that the combination against him was numerically more powerful than that which besieged the British Cantonment* in 1841, all the conditions were in his favour. He possessed a far greater proportion of European troops; his Sepoys were not effeminate Bengalees; all his soldiers were armed with weapons superior to those of the enemy; he possessed ample supplies of ammunition, and reinforcements were coming up to his assistance, some 17,000 men being assembled between Rawul Pindee and Jugdulluck. At no time was Sir Frederick Roberts anxious as to the safety of his force, and having taken every precaution to guard against an assault by overpowering numbers operating on all sides of Sherpur, the only real danger, he was content to bide his time, and abstain from throwing away his soldiers' lives in attempts to expel the enemy from Cabul, which could be effected on the arrival of reinforcements, or after Mahomed Jan had delivered his long-promised assault on the Cantonments.

Every night, he says, information reached him that an attack was contemplated, but it was not until the 21st December that the enemy showed signs of special activity. On that day and the following, large numbers of them moved from the city, and,

---

* The site of Sherpur was close to that of General Elphinstone's entrenched camp, portions of the walls of which could yet be traced near the Shah Bagh.

Assault by the Enemy.

passing round to the eastward of Sherpur, occupied the numerous forts in that direction in great force. It became apparent that this movement was preparatory to an attack from that quarter. At the same time information was received that the enemy was preparing a number of ladders, with the intention of scaling the southern and western walls. Sir Frederick Roberts made all his dispositions, which, indeed, were complete already, and awaited in confidence the signal for the assault, which he and every man in the force under his command felt would also be the signal for the discomfiture of the combination that had enjoyed the unwonted triumph of beleaguering a British force.

The night of the 22nd passed quietly, but the songs and cries of the enemy, as they sought to encourage each other to deeds of valour, resounded in the night air. From his spies the British General learned that the 23rd of December, being the last day of the "Muhurram," was selected for the great effort; and, further, in order to encourage the Ghazis and religious devotees, it was announced in the Afghan ranks that Mooskh-i-Alum would, with his own hand, light the beacon fire at dawn on the Asmai heights, which was to be the signal for the commencement of the attack.

The appearance of the signal fire on the Asmai heights, shortly before daybreak, showed at once that the information was correct, and announced the beginning of the assault. But it found the British General calm and confident of success, and every soldier at his post and rejoicing that the hour for action had struck. General Roberts took up his station at the western gateway, and throughout the succeeding operations was in constant communication with the officers commanding the different posts. Heavy firing almost immediately commenced against the southern and eastern faces, and by 7 o'clock A.M. an attack in force against the eastern side was fully developed, whilst a large number of the enemy, provided with scaling ladders, were drawn up under cover of the walls to the south. The intelligence telegraphed him from General Hugh Gough and Colonel Jenkins of the determined attack by the enemy in dense masses, found self-possessed and confident one who had long been impatiently waiting for it, and whose preparations for meeting the crisis were complete. It was welcome news that

> "The enemy comes on in gallant show,
> Their bloody sign of battle is hung out."

For three hours repeated attempts were made to carry the low eastern wall by escalade, but though the enemy on several occasions reached the abattis, they were each time repulsed, and many dead marked the spots where the assault had been most resolutely pressed home. This part of the defences was held by the Guides, under Brigadier-General Hugh Gough, who was struck full in the breast by a spent ball, which buried itself in his "posteen," or sheepskin cloak.

About 9 A.M. it was reported to General Roberts that the Ghazis had taken possession of a small village outside the defences, and just under the eastern end of the Behmaroo heights, and that the fire of the field guns which could be brought to bear was ineffectual to dislodge them. To this point General Baker had already directed a considerable portion of his reserve, both infantry and guns, and a wing of the 3rd Sikhs had been also withdrawn to the neighbourhood of Behmaroo from the western end of the heights. As the General saw that the fire of the 18-pounders and howitzers on the walls was sufficient to deal with the attack on the south and south-west faces, and that the danger of anything serious in this quarter might be disregarded, he determined to deal at once with the Behmaroo attack. Finding, he says, that it was impossible to dislodge the enemy by any fire that could be brought to bear on them from our defences, he determined to attack them in flank, and for this purpose directed four guns of G Battery, 3rd Brigade, Royal Artillery, under Major Craster, and the 5th Punjaub Cavalry, under the command of Lieutenant-Colonel Williams, to move out through the gorge in the Behmaroo heights. This counter-attack was delivered with energy, and the effect was immediate and decisive. The Afghans wavered and shortly afterwards broke. And now, says the General, the time for the action of Cavalry having arrived, Brigadier-General Massy was directed to ride out with every available man and horse, and do his utmost against the enemy.

Sir Frederick Roberts proceeded to the heights above Behmaroo, and made arrangements for reaping the fruits of his success. A party of Infantry and Sappers moved out to destroy some villages to the south, which had caused considerable annoyance, and from which it was necessary the enemy should be driven to facilitate the arrival of Brigadier-General Charles Gough's brigade. This work was successfully accomplished, but two gallant English officers, Captain J. Dundas, V.C., and Lieutenant C. Nugent, commanding the 7th Company Sappers and Miners, were killed by the premature explosion of a mine.

The Cavalry, meanwhile, made a wide circuit round the east side of Sherpur, and succeeded in intercepting the rear of the Kohistanee fugitives, who were sabred by the 5th Punjaub Cavalry. This movement of the Cavalry caused the enemy in all the villages on the east and south-east to abandon them to prevent their retreat being cut off. Continuing their victorious advance round the eastern face of Sherpur, the Cavalry ascended the Siah Sung hills, and there the 9th Lancers and 5th Punjaub Cavalry did further execution among the fugitives, numbers of whom fell beneath their sabres, the remainder fleeing in utter rout towards the city. The scene afforded a counterpart to that so graphically drawn in the "Iliad," when the Trojans fled before the face of the conquering Greeks to the shelter of their works.

> "Tumultuous clamour fills the fields and skies,
> Thick drifts of dust involve their rapid flight,
> Clouds rise in clouds, and heaven is snatch'd from sight,
> Th' affrighted steeds, their dying lords cast down,
> Scour o'er the fields, and stretch to reach the town."

It was the impression of those who watched General Massy's progress, says a General officer, that the Cavalry were well handled this day, and the 5th Punjaub Cavalry, which was in front, rendered excellent service. In the course of the afternoon clouds of dust in the direction of Bootkak gave intimation of the approach of Brigadier-General Charles Gough's brigade, and his camp was afterwards descried pitched within easy distance of the bridge over the Logar river, about six miles from Cabul.

By evening all resistance had ceased, and daylight on the following morning showed that the enemy, abandoning all hope of success, had dispersed, not a man being found in the adjacent villages or visible on the surrounding hills. The city was clear of them, and so precipitate was their flight that they left their dead unburied where they fell. On the morning of the 24th, a party of the 72nd Highlanders occupied without opposition the fort of Mahomed Shereef—the capture of which, on the 6th November, 1841, had been one of the few successes achieved by the British troops during the siege; this fort, with the adjoining Shah Bagh, played an important part in both investments. During the day the force under General Charles Gough joined Sir Frederick Roberts.

The Cavalry, divided into two parties, commanded respectively by Brigadier-Generals Massy and Hugh Gough, proceeded by Beni Hissar and the Chardeh Valley in pursuit, but their movements were impeded by a snowstorm, and so rapid had been the enemy's flight that they were compelled to return to Sherpur after nightfall, without meeting with any armed men.

The casualties between the 5th and 24th December were 2 officers and 16 men killed, and 4 officers—Brigadier-General Hugh Gough, Lieutenant C. A. Montanaro, R.A. (died), Lieutenant J. Burn-Murdoch, R.E.,* and Lieutenant C. F. Gambier, 5th Punjaub Cavalry—and 66 men wounded.

The religious and military chiefs of the movement having fled from Cabul, Sir Frederick Roberts, on the following day, directed the occupation of the city and Bala Hissar. Cabul presented the appearance of having been sacked by an enemy. The Mahomedans had wrecked the houses of the Hindoo and Kuzzilbash quarters, the bazaars were deserted and all business suspended. Captain Hall, with one company of the 5th Punjaub Infantry, took post for the night in the Kotwallee, which up to the previous evening had been the head-quarters of the Ghazis, who had shown their spite before leaving by doing as much damage as possible to the building, and by defiling all the adjoining houses and shops. General Hills, the Military Governor of the city, now resumed his functions, and was heartily welcomed by all the peaceable and well-disposed inhabitants.

---

* This young officer, who was specially mentioned in despatches by Sir Frederick Roberts for his gallantry, gained equal credit during the recent Egyptian campaign, when serving with the Indian Contingent at Tel-el-Kebir and Zagazig.

Collapse of the Hostile Combination. 317

The collapse of the combination was complete, although it included all the fighting elements of North-Eastern Afghanistan, from Kohistan to the Ghilzye country, whose chief, Padshah Khan, a former ally, and Asmatullah Khan, the principal Lughman chief, had thrown in their lot with Mahomed Jan. The arrangements of Sir Frederick Roberts had met with complete success, and the wisdom of his plan of permitting the enemy to select their own time of attack, and not wasting valuable lives by quitting the sheltering walls of the Cantonment in desultory attacks on them and the strong forts in the neighbourhood, was amply justified by the result. But though he is entitled to full credit for his sagacity, and acted throughout on his own opinions without seeking advice from subordinates, he was singularly fortunate in the superior officers under his command. Brigadier-Generals Macpherson, Baker, and Hugh Gough were unsurpassed by any officers in the army in the possession of the qualities that command the confidence of all ranks under their orders; and Colonel Macgregor, though young in years, was a veteran in experience. Three of those four officers, like the commander of the Cabul Field Force, bore on their breasts that cross "for valour" which it is the most eager aspiration of every soldier to win. Then among the corps commanders were such excellent officers as Colonels Perkins, R.E., Gordon, R.A., Hudson, Brownlow, Money, Parker, White, and Jenkins; also heroes like Cook, Vousden, Hammond, Cunyngham, and others in the ranks.

In such warfare as that in which the Cabul Field Force had been engaged, military capacity and personal prowess had many opportunities for display. As in the defence of Jellalabad, in the first Afghan War, men like Havelock, Abbott, Backhouse, and Broadfoot made their reputations, so in the somewhat analogous circumstances of the investment of Sherpur, and the events of December, brave spirits like those mentioned above showed to the front, though they had not the same opportunities for distinction, for the leader of the Cabul Field Force was of a different calibre from the gallant but irresolute commander of the Jellalabad garrison, who owed his most memorable achievement, the victory over Akbar Khan on the 7th April, to the promptings of some of the officers mentioned above.

A General officer, before quoted, described to us the bearing of Sir Frederick Roberts during the anxious time now brought to a close. "Throughout the investment of Sherpur, Roberts was the most cheerful man in camp. His bright face and cheery smile instilled confidence among his soldiers, and one felt there could be no doubt of success as long as he was with them." Indeed, Sir Frederick Roberts never entertained any anxiety as to the result, though his countrymen at home, who exaggerated the power of the Afghan nation, failed to recognize the fact that it was the hope of plunder that kept these undisciplined Asiatics together, and gratified, as they were, by the sack of Cabul, it was impossible for any commander not possessed of military genius, such as no Afghan has displayed since the days of Ahmed Khan, to keep together the heterogeneous assemblage of tribesmen which constitutes the nation in arms.

The total loss during the operations commencing with the 10th December, and ending in the dispersal of the Afghans, was 103 killed, including 10 officers; and 263 wounded, including 15 officers, of whom 3 died.

Notwithstanding the want of ammunition and the hindrance to rapid progress caused by the heavy fall of snow, Sir Frederick Roberts determined to punish the Kohistanees, and Brigadier-General Baker left with a strong column for the district in the Koh Daman belonging to Meer Butcha, and returned on the last day of the old year, having destroyed the villages and the strong fort under whose protection they nestled. This act of severity showed the Afghans that the British troops were quite in a condition to resume the offensive, though owing to the inclemency of the weather, the General determined to postpone his visits to the other tribesmen till the spring. Brigadier-General Charles Gough's brigade, which included the 9th Regiment, now occupied the Bala Hissar, and Colonel Hudson's small force was moved from Lutturbund to Sherpur, giving a welcome increase to the strength of the garrison, seriously decimated by the losses during the recent fighting and the large number of sick.

At this time Daoud Shah, the Commander-in-Chief of the ex-Ameer's Army, who was found to have been in communication with the leaders of the recent rising, was sent to join his master in exile in India, and the Military Commission, whose functions were revived for the trial of certain offenders—a few of whom were hanged—completed its labours and was dissolved. Political capital was sought to be made out of the acts of retributive justice of Sir Frederick Roberts by the opponents, in the Press and Parliament, of the Conservative Government, whose agent he was, but the attempt was futile. On this point he writes to us:—" I gave full explanation of my acts while supreme at Cabul to the Government to whom I was responsible, and furnished them with a list of all executions, with the reasons given in each case. I stated at the time that no soldiers had been executed for fighting against us. These papers are published in the Blue-book, and can be read by every one. Had any other troops but British been at Cabul in October, 1879, the city would have been razed to the ground. The Afghans quite expected this, and never ceased to wonder at our leniency."

Sir Frederick Roberts now issued a proclamation of amnesty, exempting only a few leaders, on condition of the tribesmen sending delegates to Sherpur, to whom should be made known his will as to the future permanent arrangements to be made for the good government of the people. The Kohistanee chiefs generally responded to this invitation, as well as some from Lughman, Logar, and the Ghilzye country, and, on the 9th January, Sir Frederick Roberts held a grand durbar at Sherpur, to present gifts to those who had proved faithful to the English in their hour of trial. This durbar was attended by a large number of these nobles, including Padshah Khan, the great Ghilzye chief, who had borne arms against the British, and also many powerful Barukzye Sirdars, among them Wali Mahomed Khan, and other near relatives of the late Ameer Shere Ali.

The scene presented was very picturesque, and suggestive of British clemency and magnanimity, when it is remembered that not many days since most of these chiefs were leading vast masses of their countrymen against the small army that so gallantly rallied round the British General, before whom they now *salaamed*, and cringed with true Oriental subserviency, wondering, no doubt, at the generosity, or weakness, which ever way they construed it, of the Government that could hold out the hand of forgiveness to those who so recently bore arms against them. It was a study to watch the expressions on the countenances of these Afghan chiefs. Curiosity, mingled with respect, as they gazed on the man who scattered to the winds their combinations and well-laid plans—for your Oriental can only understand the logic of the sword; and, doubtless, they were puzzled at the issue of the Amnesty so soon after the crushing defeat, which left them, their property and families, at the mercy of the conqueror—for an Afghan victor would have ruthlessly executed every malik that fell into his hands, and destroyed their villages and forts.

During the durbar Sir Frederick Roberts addressed* the

---

* The following is the address made by Sir Frederick Roberts:—" Sirdars and Maliks,—I am very glad to see that so many of the Kohistan maliks have taken advantage of the Amnesty published on the 26th of December last, and have come to Cabul to pay their respects to the British Government, and to express their regrets for having taken a part in the recent disturbances. I trust that those maliks who are still holding aloof will follow the good example that has thus been set them, and will soon make their appearance at Cabul. I told you, when you visited me in my camp at Siah Sung, after the arrival of the British troops at Cabul, that the British Government had nothing but goodwill towards the people of Afghanistan; that it is their desire to respect your lives, your property, and your religion, and to molest no one who would live at peace with them. You have had ample proof of the truth of what I told you. At the instigation of ill-advised men you came from your homes in Kohistan to attack the British troops at Sherpur. All that you succeeded in doing was to plunder from your own countrymen who live in the City of Cabul. You did the British troops but little injury, and in a few days you were beaten off, and had to return to your homes with the loss of several hundred killed and wounded. You brought this punishment upon yourselves, and must not blame the British Government. What that Government did was to offer a pardon to all who would come in—except the malik who, it is believed, was the main cause of your being led astray. It was necessary he should be punished; but, in doing so, every care was taken that no one else should suffer injury. The British troops marched through your country as far as Bala Kuch Kar, treating you all as friends, and paying liberally for everything in the shape of food and forage you were able or willing to provide. I hope the lesson will not be lost upon you, and that you will not misunderstand the generosity and forbearance with which you have been treated. It is a great pleasure to me to find that so many of the more intelligent and well-informed of the people of Afghanistan took no part in the recent disturbances. First and foremost, I would name Sirdars Wali Mahomed Khan, Ibrahim Khan, Hashim Khan, Abdulla Khan, Mahomed Yusuf Khan, Mahomed Karim Khan, Shahbaz Khan, Ahmed Ali Jan, Mahomed Sirwar Khan, Ataullah Khan, Anitoollah Khan, Habibulla Khan (the Mustaufi), Malik Hamid Khan, and Khan Mahomed Khan. Then several of your own chiefs remained with me throughout. General Faiz Mahomed Khan, the son of Naik

assembly, especially directing his remarks to the Kohistan Chiefs, on the recent events, and having expressed his intention of sending Shahbaz Khan as Governor of Kohistan, invited them to select some of their number to remain at Sherpur as representatives. But the malcontent faction, headed by Mahomed Jan, who had borne off Moosa Khan to Ghuznee, refused to give in their adhesion, and sent a demand for the restoration of Yakoob Khan, which was treated with silent contempt.

Meanwhile the Engineers were employed in strengthening the works for the defence of Cabul, according to the plan approved by Sir Frederick Roberts before the recent events, so that the city could be held against any army Afghanistan could furnish. Towers were commenced on commanding positions on Koh Asmai and the heights above the Bala Hissar, military roads were cut round the city, and the weak points about the cantonment were strengthened, and all buildings affording cover within 1,000 yards of the walls levelled with the ground. Sir Frederick Roberts appointed the Wali Mahomed Governor of Cabul in place of General Hills, in order to conciliate native opinion, and as a testimony that annexation had no place in our plans for the future government of the country. This Sirdar was a consistent adherent of the British—" faithful 'mid the faithless found;" though, unfortunately, he did not possess the strength of character necessary to rule over such a turbulent race as his countrymen.

But this was only a temporary measure, as the Indian Government, yielding to pressure from home, and alive to

---

Aminulla Khan, of Logar; the family of the Mustafi, Sirdar Habibulla Khan, of Wardak; the Kuzzilbashes, and many other influential men in the city of Cabul, refrained from joining the disturbers of peace and order; and I am glad to have this opportunity of thanking them on the part of the British Government for the good service they thereby performed. I am now about to give Khilluts to those Kohistanis who remained at Sherpur with me, after which you are at liberty to return to your homes. I am sending back with you to Kohistan Sirdar Shahbaz Khan, whom you have yourselves asked for as your Governor. He will settle your disputes and preserve order in the country. Also that I may be fully informed by yourselves of all that passes, and of all that you may wish to represent hereafter, I invite you to select certain of your number, who will remain here and act as a medium of communication between us. They will be treated with consideration and will have free access to me. The rest of you may return to your homes, and for your own sake remember all that has passed."

the strain on the resources of the great dependency committed to their charge from the continued occupation of Afghanistan, began seriously to consider the question of the future administration of the country. Lord Lytton and his Council addressed a despatch, on the 7th January, 1880, to Lord Cranbrook, the Secretary of State for India, expressing their view that "the question of the resuscitation of the fallen kingdom of the Barukzyes cannot now be entertained, and that we must accept the separation of its constituent provinces as our basis for the political reconstitution of Afghanistan." In order to carry out this policy the Viceroy proposed, in accordance with a decision already adopted by the Home Government, that "Persia should be provisionally permitted to occupy Herat, under sufficient guarantees for her good administration of it, and for her adequate protection of British and Indian interests, and with a special reservation of our right to occupy the place with British forces on certain eventualities." The districts of Pisheen, Sibi, and Kurram, being assigned to England under the treaty of Gundamuck, were to be retained, but Cabul and Candahar were to be separated; the proposal being "to establish the province of Candahar as an independent and separate state, under an hereditary ruler selected from the representatives of the old ruling families;" but while contemplating "no interference in the internal administration of the province," they proposed "to retain a British garrison at or near Candahar."

In order to assist Sir Frederick Roberts in political affairs in North-Eastern Afghanistan, which Lord Lytton proposed should "remain in military occupation until all resistance has ceased," Mr. Lepel Griffin, an experienced political official, was despatched to Cabul, where he arrived on the 20th March. Meanwhile the Wali Shere Ali was appointed "hereditary ruler" of Candahar, but the task of finding a ruler for Cabul proved a difficult one, owing to the number of candidates, each with his adherents, and the choice at first lay between Wali Mahomed Khan, Hashim Khan, Moosa Khan, and Ayoob Khan, all members of the ruling Barukzye family.

On reference to the Viceroy's despatches, the first mention

Abdul Rahman Khan.

we have of Abdul Rahman, the present ruler of Afghanistan, as a candidate for the Ameership, is in a telegram,* dated the 14th March, addressed to the Secretary of State, in which his lordship advocates the "early public recognition of Abdul Rahman as legitimate heir of Dost Mahomed, and open deputation of Sirdars with British concurrence to offer him the throne of Afghanistan, as sole means of saving country from anarchy." The reply, on the following day, from the India Office, authorized the nomination of Abdul Rahman, if he was "acceptable to the country and would be contented with Northern Afghanistan." This resolve, as proved by subsequent events, was a wise one, though it encountered much opposition, owing to Abdul Rahman having been for ten years a resident in Russian Turkestan, and in receipt of a pension of 25,000 roubles a year from the Czar. Yakoob Khan was impossible, Moosa Khan was a child, Ayoob Khan, Yakoob's brother, was not considered acceptable, and events seemed to point to Abdul Rahman, son of Afzul Khan, elder brother of Shere Ali, as the most desirable personage to ascend the *musnud*.

Abdul Rahman, who was now about fifty, accompanied his father when he crossed the Indus to aid the Sikhs in their final struggle against us in 1848–49, and after the death of Dost Mahomed fled to Bokhara when Afzul, who was appointed Governor of Balkh by his brother, Shere Ali, was removed to Cabul by that Prince for intriguing against his authority. When Shere Ali was at Candahar, Abdul Rahman crossed the Oxus, and having established his authority at Balkh, marched with his uncle, Azim, on Cabul, which surrendered to him on the 2nd March, 1866; this success was followed up by a victory at Sheikhabad and the capture of Ghuznee, when Afzul became Ameer, and his son consolidated his rule by his victory over Shere Ali at Khelat-i-Ghilzye early in the following year. But soon a change came over the political scene with the frequency and rapidity characteristic of Afghan affairs. Afzul died of his excesses, Azim was equally incapable and more tyrannical, and Abdul Rahman retired in disgust to Afghan Turkestan. Now

---

* See Blue Book, "Afghanistan (1881), No. 1."

Yakoob Khan came forward to champion his father's rights, and, advancing from Herat, followed up a victory on the Helmund, which resulted in the flight of Azim's son from Candahar, by defeating Abdul Rahman at Bameean, and finally restored his father to the throne by the crushing defeat inflicted in the winter of 1868 at Tinah Khan. Abdul Rahman and Azim fled from Balkh, and thence to Meshed, in Persia, where the latter died in October, 1869, while his nephew proceeded to Khiva and Bokhara, and arrived in May, 1870, at Tashkend, where he received permission from General Kaufmann to reside on Russian territory as a pensioner of the Czar.

It seemed as though the possibility of Abdul Rahman obtaining another favourable opportunity to strike a blow for the throne of Cabul was remote indeed, for Shere Ali had firmly established himself in power; but his ill-advised intrigue with Russia gave the desired chance, and involved that unhappy prince and his country in a period of prolonged anarchy, disaster, and bloodshed, from which it has only now apparently emerged. The words of Hector to Paris might be applied to the ill-fated Shere Ali:—

> "Bleak fate hangs o'er thee from th' avenging gods,
> Imperial Troy from her foundations nods:
> Whelm'd in thy country's ruins shalt thou fall,
> And one devouring vengeance swallow all."

After the deportation to India of Yakoob Khan, the people of Afghan Turkestan, remembering the moderation with which he formerly ruled them, rallied to the cause of Abdul Rahman, and on the 17th March, 1880, Lord Lytton telegraphed to the Secretary of State, that he had received "authentic intelligence that the Sirdar is in Afghan Turkestan, having lately arrived there from Badakshan, where he defeated the Meer Shahzada Hassan." Such was the new aspirant for the perilous honour of ruling the race whom his former conqueror declared were so turbulent that he would rather be a grass-cutter in the British camp than their sovereign.

By the middle of March, Sir Frederick Roberts had under his command at Cabul about 11,500 men and twenty-six guns. The Cabul Field Force was divided into two divisions, the first being under the immediate command of Sir Frederick, and the second under Major-General Ross, C.B., while the command of the line of communications was held by Major-General Bright. Brigadier-General Massy had been ordered to proceed to India, and was succeeded in the command of the Cavalry by Brigadier-General Hugh Gough. Sherpur had been made impregnable against the attack of any Asiatic army, and forts were built on both sides of the Cabul gorge and on the Siah Sung hill.

In response to an invitation to discuss the question of the future of their country, addressed by Sir Frederick Roberts to the Chiefs of Mydan, Logar, and the neighbouring districts, through Habibullah Khan, whom he had found trustworthy, a large number of Chiefs and Sirdars assembled at Sherpur to learn the intentions of Government.

Sir Frederick Roberts, attended by his Staff, and accompanied by Mr. Griffin and his general officers, entered the Durbar tent, and took his place amid the respectful salutations of the assembly. Sir Frederick opened the proceedings by a short speech,* and Mr. Griffin delivered a lengthy address in Persian, in which he explained to the Sirdars and people of Cabul generally, and to the delegates who presented the demands of the Maliks and Chiefs of Logar, Ghuznee, Mydan, Wardak, and the southern Ghilzye country, the general instructions of the Indian Government regarding the future government of Cabul. The restoration of Yakoob Khan was

---

* "Sirdars and Maliks,—I am very glad to meet you here to-day, especially those who through the good offices of the Mustaufi have been induced to come into Cabul to make their wishes known to me. I trust this Durbar is the beginning of the end, and that it will now be possible for us to enter into such an arrangement with the people of Afghanistan as will ensure an honourable peace and lasting friendship between them and the British. Some of you, I understand, hesitated to accompany the Mustaufi, fearing your treatment and reception by us might not be such as we have promised you, and that some evil might befall you. You need never have any such fear when your safety has been assured on the word of a British officer. The British do not say one thing and do another. You who have come in have been honourably treated, and after this Durbar you are all at liberty to depart. I trust, when you leave Cabul, you will carry away with you a more friendly feeling towards us than some of you have hitherto entertained ; and that those of your party who are still holding aloof will be wise enough to follow the good example you have set them, and will accept our invitation to come to Cabul. Mr. Lepel Griffin, Chief Political Officer in North and Eastern Afghanistan, with whom you have already become acquainted, will now, on the part of the Government of India, answer the request you have made."

declared impossible, and their choice of rulers was restricted to the other members of the ruling family, Wali Mahomed, brother of Shere Ali, Hashim Khan, who had married a daughter of the ex-Ameer, and possessed his money, or Moosa Khan and Ayoob Khan, his son and brother. The British troops, it was haughtily notified, would be withdrawn from Afghanistan "when the Government considers the proper time has come; as they did not enter Afghanistan with your permission, so they will not withdraw at your request."

Chief mention should here be made of a hardly contested action fought, on the 26th April, on the old battle ground of Charasia, by a portion of Sir Frederick Roberts's force, under Colonel Jenkins, who had left Sherpur a few days before with a small column. Sir Frederick Roberts, learning by heliographic signal that Colonel Jenkins was hard pressed, sent some reinforcements to his aid, under General Macpherson, and the enemy were defeated with heavy loss. Sir Frederick ordered the column to return to Sherpur, and rode out to meet them and congratulate the successful leaders. The excitement in Camp during the 26th April brought back recollections of the days of December. All the forts were manned and the whole of the Cabul Field Force was on the *qui vive*, as an attack of Kohistanees was expected.

A few days later Sir Frederick Roberts was relieved of the chief political and military command in North-Eastern Afghanistan by the arrival of his senior officer, Sir Donald Stewart, who had marched from Candahar to break up any hostile combination at Ghuznee, and open communications with Cabul, leaving a division of troops from the Bombay Presidency, under Lieutenant-General Primrose, to hold the city and province, which he had administered so successfully, and the civil government of which was now handed over to the Wali Shere Ali.

In order to act in co-operation with Sir Donald Stewart, Sir Frederick Roberts, on the 16th April, sent a strong column from Sherpur under command of Major-General Ross. Little actual resistance was met by Ross's column, though the Mydan people were sulky and ill-disposed. General Ross was accompanied by General Hills, who had served at Candahar in the first phase of the Afghan War, as Assistant Adjutant-General to Sir Donald Stewart's Division; and that officer related to us how at the moment when he and General Ross had topped the watershed between Wardak and Mydan, a heliographic signal was flashed to them by General Stewart, a distance of about forty miles, giving news of his arrival at Ghuznee and his victory at Ahmed Khel on the 19th April. General Hills, when he left Sir Donald Stewart at Candahar, told him that he would meet him at Ghuznee, and on the previous day had been anxious to redeem his promise, but General Ross would not give him leave, as Sir Frederick Roberts had ordered that the Cavalry should not advance beyond the pass. Having got half a troop of Cavalry as escort, General Hills now rode on and found his old chief two miles on the Cabul side of the Dahan pass. Sir Donald Stewart's troops turned off into the Logar country, and, accompanied by General Hills, he joined General Ross's column and proceeded to Sherpur, where he arrived on the 1st May, and making over his own division to Brigadier-General Hughes, 63rd Regiment, who held the command until relieved by General Hills,—on the 2nd May he assumed command of the troops in North-Eastern Afghanistan, also relieving Sir Frederick Roberts of the charge of political affairs. Our hero looked forward to shortly quitting the country in whose eventful history he had played so important a *rôle*, and, like Richard, his

"Bruised arms hang up for monuments."

But, again, for the third time within two years, he was to be called upon to encounter the responsibilities of command in an emergency; for the time had not yet come when he could exclaim with Gloucester:—

"Our stern alarums chang'd to merry meetings,
Our dreadful marches to delightful measures."

CHAPTER XVII.

Sir Frederick Roberts and the Negotiations with Abdul Rahman—Appointment of the Sirdar to the Ameership—Restless State of the Sirdars and People of Afghanistan—Arrival of Abdul Rahman at Cabul and Assumption of the Ameership—Sir Frederick Roberts's Views on the Kurram Valley Question—The Maiwand Disaster—Sir Frederick Roberts appointed to the Command of the Relieving Column—The Dramatic Aspects of the Afghan War—His Preparations for the March on Candahar.

SOME notice is necessary in a biographical work of the personal share taken by Sir Frederick Roberts in the political proceedings which ended in the acceptance by the British Government of Abdul Rahman as Ameer of North-Eastern Afghanistan. Lord Lytton having authorized him and Mr. Griffin to open negotiations with the Ameer, on the 2nd April a Kohistan Chief, Surwar Khan, an active adherent of the Pretender, was despatched from Sherpur to Koondooz, in Afghan Turkestan, where he arrived on the 10th. At an interview with Abdul Rahman, Surwar Khan expressed the friendliness entertained towards him by the British General, and advised him to repair to Cabul, where he would be honourably received. Surwar Khan received a letter from the Sirdar, couched in guarded and general terms, expressive of his gratitude to the British Government, and his desire to live at amity with both England as well as Russia, whose hospitality he had enjoyed for twelve years,* and, leaving Koondooz, arrived at Sherpur on the 21st April. He was also the bearer of a message from Abdul Rahman, offering to go to Charikar, in Kohistan, with an escort of 500 men, and there discuss matters with the British Political Officers in person.

Sir Frederick Roberts and Mr. Griffin, after consideration of the letter and message, decided to accede to the Sirdar's request, proposing Cabul as an alternative place of meeting, and to

---

* For letter see p. 22 of Blue Book on Afghanistan.

offer him the Ameership on his agreeing to accept the conditions regarding Candahar, the frontier between the two countries, and the foreign relations of Afghanistan conceded to the British by the treaty of Gundamuck. On communicating the steps they had taken to the Viceregal Government, Sir Frederick Roberts and Mr. Griffin received a lengthy despatch, dated the 27th April, communicating the intentions of Lord Lytton, which briefly were to the effect that Cabul was to be evacuated by the British troops "not later than October next," and impressing on their attention "the importance of avoiding any expression which might appear to suggest or admit matter for negotiation or discussion in reference to the relative positions of the Sirdar and the Government of India." They proposed "unconditionally transferring the government of the country" to Abdul Rahman, who would receive, if he required it, assistance from the Viceroy, and in the event of his proving "able and disposed to conciliate the confidence of his countrymen, without forfeiting the good understanding he seeks with us, will assuredly find his best support in our political appreciation of that fact."

Further, the Government of India declared that their "only reasons for not immediately withdrawing their forces from Northern Afghanistan have hitherto been, first, the excited and unsettled condition of the country round Cabul, with the attitude of hostility assumed by some leaders of armed gatherings near Ghuznee; and secondly, the inability of the Cabul Sirdars to agree among themselves on the selection of a ruler strong enough to maintain order after the evacuation of the country." The first-named of these reasons no longer existed after the victory at Ahmed Kheyl achieved by Sir Donald Stewart during his advance from Candahar, and on the arrival of that officer at Cabul on the 2nd May, Sir Frederick Roberts, being junior in rank, ceased to be supreme political no less than military chief in Northern Afghanistan, and the negotiations with Abdul Rahman were conducted in the name of Sir Donald Stewart, acting in conjunction with Mr. Griffin.

To the subject of this Memoir it seemed as if no further chance of increasing the renown he had earned by his conduct of military affairs, could offer itself in Afghanistan. By his victories at Peiwar Kotul and Charasia, and generally by the masterly and daring advance on Cabul, no less than by the complete success of the operations in December, he had earned for himself a high place among England's most trusted soldiers. Nothing more brilliant had been achieved for many years than this series of successes, which were gained not by fortune or any adventitious aid, but by boldness and able strategy. "Nothing succeeds like success," and Sir Frederick Roberts possessed the complete confidence of every officer and man under his command, whose only regret was that no further chances of earning distinction under his orders could accrue, since the Liberal Government, following up the policy of their predecessors in office, had decreed that the evacuation of North-Eastern Afghanistan was to take place as soon as Abdul Rahman had been accepted as the future Ameer by a sufficient portion of his countrymen, or, in any case, not later than October. But in these calculations of the late Cabul Field Force, sufficient allowance was not made for the unforeseen, always a potent factor in Oriental politics. The vicissitudes of political and military affairs in Afghanistan had extended their influences to British interests, and the reputations of two general officers in South-Western Afghanistan suffered as sudden and disastrous an eclipse as the character for military prowess of Yakoob Khan, Ayoob Khan, and Abdul Rahman had experienced during their chequered careers. On the other hand, the military fame of Sir Frederick Roberts shone out with increased lustre during the hour of trial still in store for the arms of England, and when he emerged at Candahar after his famous march through Afghanistan, he added to the reputation already achieved, a European renown as one of the greatest soldiers of the age, a claim conceded to him by the illustrious Skobeleff, the hero of Plevna and Geok Tepe.

Notwithstanding the overwhelming force of 18,000 seasoned soldiers, the flower of the Indian army, assembled at Cabul, under the command of Sir Donald Stewart and Sir Frederick Roberts, the Afghans were as truculent as ever, and it was manifest that they would never submit to the foreign yoke; and in the latter part of June, General Hills marched into the Logar district with the late Candahar division, in order to procure supplies and put down a gathering of Zoormuttees and

Wardakees. In his account to us of his proceedings in the Logar Valley, he describes all the hill-sides as covered with the watch-fires of the villagers, who thought he was going into Zoormut. Soon after, he moved temporarily to Cabul with his division, on which the tribesmen, under Hassan Khan, an adherent of Yakoob Khan, came down into the Logar Valley, and tried to induce the Logarees to join them for another rising similar to that in December. On General Hills returning to the Logar Valley, most of the tribesmen retired, but about 1,500 Zoormuttees took up a position at the village of Padkao Shana, where they were attacked and dispersed by the cavalry of Hills's division, under Brigadier-General Palliser.

These were the men of whom Sir George Campbell, M.P., asked in the House of Commons whether it was true that "inoffensive ryots" had been attacked. With his Indian experience and knowledge of the character of the officers of the Indian Army and the reputation of General Hills, the member for the Kirkaldy boroughs ought to have known better than to have inferred that an officer whose character for humanity stood as high as his own, would have been capable of attacking inoffensive ryots. These tribesmen, whose leader, Mahomed Hassan Khan, had run away from Jellalabad with treasure, thought that Mahomed Jan had come down from Wardak to assist them, and took advantage of General Hills's absence to work up the Logarees to fight; but these latter declined to join them, saying that the General and Major Ewan Smith, Political Officer with the division, had treated them well and paid for all supplies.

The only other noteworthy incident was the deportation to India of the Mustaufi, Habibullah Khan, who was accused of conspiring against the English, and was sent to join his master and Daoud Shah.

During May and June negotiations were carried on with Abdul Rahman at Khanabad, near Koondooz, in Afghan Turkestan, the British Agents being Sirdar Ibrahim Khan, Sher Mahomed Khan, and Afzul Khan, a ressaldar of the 11th Bengal Lancers. The Mission left Sherpur on the 3rd May, and was received with honour by the Sirdar, who hesitated before giving a final answer, as his acceptance involved the surrender of Candahar and the Kurram Valley, which would make him unpopular with his countrymen.

Sir Frederick Roberts quite agreed with the Liberal Government that an end should be put to the occupation of North-Eastern Afghanistan by our army during the autumn, whether terms were made with Abdul Rahman or not. On this point he writes in his despatch, dated 29th May:—" If the present negotiations with Abdul Rahman succeed, I should hamper him with the fewest possible conditions; if they fail, I would be inclined to let the tribes of Eastern Afghanistan please themselves about an Ameer. In course of time some strong man would win his way to power, and meanwhile it would be wiser not to force a ruler upon them. Any nominee of ours would certainly not be acceptable, and, in all probability, would not be able to hold his own after our departure. Under any circumstances, I am strongly in favour of not remaining at Cabul after the great heat of the Indian summer has passed and travelling through the Khyber is possible. If we cannot settle matters with the Afghans at this season of the year, when everything is in our favour, we shall certainly not be able to do so in the winter, when the difficulties of an occupation are immeasurably increased." On the Afghan question, so far as Russia is concerned, he says:—" We have learnt by experience what a considerable force is required to occupy Cabul and to maintain our communications with India by the Khyber route. There is no denying the fact that, if the ruler of Cabul should at any future time be assisted by Russian officers, the army of 25,000 men which we now find it necessary to employ on the Khyber line alone would have to be very considerably increased. Nor do I think that, even if the Afghans themselves were on our side, we could deal as effectually with Russia in Eastern as in Western Afghanistan. To what extent those offensive measures might be pressed in Southern or Western Afghanistan scarcely comes within the scope of this paper, depending, as they assuredly would, on numerous and complicated eventualities, such as the attitude of Persia, the object and strength of Russia, and the state of Afghanistan generally. It might be found necessary to make a rapid advance on Herat and mass a considerable army there, or it might, on the other hand, be deemed desirable to confine operations to Candahar itself, or to Seistan, and the valley of the Helmund. It will be sufficient for our present purpose if we can come to the conclusion that the Candahar line will be the one by which all offensive movements against Russia would be carried on. If this point be admitted, it only remains for us to consider to what extent communication should be maintained between the north-west frontier of India and Cabul. My own opinion, which I offer with considerable diffidence, is that the Kurram line should be given up altogether, and that the responsibilities which we ought to incur on the Khyber route should be limited to such as would ensure the execution and integrity of any guarantees we have given to the rulers of Lalpura and Kuner. Viewing Cabul in the altered and powerless condition in which we shall leave it, with a ruler quite unable to cause us trouble or even anxiety in India, and knowing (as we now do) with what ease and quickness we can again at any time make ourselves masters of Cabul by either of the two roads under consideration, I can see no reason why regular troops should be kept either in the Kurram or the Khyber. Moreover, I cannot too strongly urge upon the consideration of the Government of India the desirability of not leaving the Native portion of the army in the field after the ensuing autumn. Many of the regiments will then have been on service since October, 1878; they have done admirably,—indeed I doubt if at any former period the Native Army has ever behaved more loyally or gallantly; all ranks are in good heart, and will cheerfully carry out any work they may be called upon to perform. There is, however, a limit beyond which it would be impolitic to require them to remain away from India. This limit I place at two years. It would be found difficult, if not impracticable, to relieve the troops now on service. All the Goorkhas, and nearly all the Punjaub Corps, are in the first line. This is another strong argument in favour of an early withdrawal."

Abdul Rahman and his advisers hesitated to give a definite answer to the British demands, or to come to Cabul, because, as Mr. Lepel Griffin wrote on the 4th August, they "feared greatly that our intention was to rid ourselves of a formidable opponent, and that, had he come straight into Cabul, he would have been arrested, and deported to British India."

So critical did the negotiations appear towards the end of June that Sir Donald Stewart, with whom the Viceregal Government left considerable discretionary powers, advised no further dealings with Abdul Rahman. In the despatch of the 27th July, giving in detail the negotiations with that Sirdar, Lord Ripon, the newly-arrived Viceroy, and his Council wrote: " Sir D. Stewart and Mr. Griffin represented to the Government of India, for the second time, their conviction of the danger of trusting Abdul Rahman, the imprudence of delaying immediate action, and the necessity, in this critical situation, of breaking off with Abdul Rahman, and adopting other means of establishing a government in Cabul before our evacuation." But Lord Ripon fortunately decided otherwise, as he considered that, " as matters stood then, an arrangement with Abdul Rahman offered the most advisable solution, while he doubted whether it would not be found very difficult to enter into any alternative arrangement."

The subsequent course of events fully justified the statesmanlike course adopted by the Indian Viceroy, and Abdul Rahman, having made up his mind to accept the terms offered him by the British Government, left Khanabad on the 28th June, with 2,000 men and 12 guns, and, crossing the Hindoo Koosh, reached Tootumdurrah, near Charikar, at the entrance of the Ghorebund Valley—the forts of which were successfully attacked by Sir Robert Sale in 1840. The Sirdar arrived on the 20th July at Charikar, and a large number of leading Chiefs and other influential personages, including Mooshk-i-Alum, and some of the principal Ghilzye and Wardak Chiefs, signified their acquiescence in his recognition, and many went to meet him at Charikar. The faithless Asmatullah Khan, Ghilzye,[*] Abdul Guffoor, Logaree, and thirty-five others of less note, who wrote from Maidan that all there assembled were ready to accept as Ameer whomever the British Government

---

[*] True to his character, Asmatullah has recently intrigued against the Ameer Abdul Rahman, who put a letter of his to Ayoob Khan in his hand in open Durbar and threw him into prison. Mahomed Jan and Abdul Guffoor have also been executed, and Meer Butcha is a fugitive.

might select, whether Yakoob Khan, or Abdul Rahman, or Ayoob Khan; but that in the interests of the country and the Government, it was essential to at once declare the choice of the authorities, as there was no other way of bringing to an end the period of uncertainty, and of re-assuring the people.

Abdul Rahman was acknowledged by the British military and political authorities as Ameer of Afghanistan, and received a promise of support so long as he remained friendly to England. The ceremony took place at a grand Durbar, held on the 22nd July, at Sherpur, at which Sir Donald Stewart, accompanied by Sir Frederick Roberts and Mr. Lepel Griffin, received the representatives of Abdul Rahman.* The new Ameer left Charikar, and was met on 3rd August at Zimma, about 16 miles from Cabul, by Mr. Lepel Griffin, who proceeded with an escort from General Charles Gough's camp in the Kohistan road, and arrangements were made for his taking over Cabul, the governorship of which had been resigned by the Wali Mahomed Khan, who himself had been a candidate for the throne.

Abdul Rahman's chance of election was supposed to be remote indeed, a few months before, the taint of Russian support being regarded as an absolute bar to his selection by the British Government, who preferred the claims of the Barukzye Sirdars, Wali Mahomed, Hashim Khan, and Ayoob. But by a turn of the wheel of fortune all this was changed, and Abdul Rahman came to power under the ægis of British protection and with subsidies in money and arms, which have enabled him to gain over by force of arms and the power of the purse the whole of Afghanistan. But all Afghan history shows that the fickle nobles and people of Cabul may soon tire of him, and should fortune declare against him in the field, like the Roman

---

* Mr. Lepel Griffin thus describes him :—" Amir Abdul Rahman Khan is a man of about forty, of middle height, and rather stout. He has an exceedingly intelligent face, brown eyes, a pleasant smile, and a frank courteous manner. The impression that he left on me and the officers who were present was most favourable. He is by far the most prepossessing of all the Barukzai Sirdars whom I have met in Afghanistan, and in conversation showed both good sense and sound political judgment. He kept thoroughly to the point under discussion, and his remarks were characterized by shrewdness and ability. He appeared animated by a sincere desire to be on cordial terms with the English Government."

people upbraided by Marullus, they would hail his successful rival :—

> "Many a time and oft
> Have you climb'd up to walls and battlements,
> To towers and windows, yea, to chimney-tops,
> Your infants in your arms, and there have sat
> The livelong day, with patient expectation,
> To see great Pompey pass the streets of Rome."

Popularity among the Sirdars and people of Afghanistan is very much a question of bribes and license to the former, and a liberal dispensation of the *panem et circenses* to the latter.

Meanwhile important military events had occurred, which removed Sir Frederick Roberts from the scene of these protracted negotiations, and gave him employment in the field, a more congenial sphere to one of his temperament than the fetid atmosphere of Afghan intrigue.

On the 29th July the startling news arrived at Cabul that General Burrows' brigade had been "annihilated" at Maiwand; and though subsequent details placed the disaster in not quite so bad a light, the utter rout of a British force, followed by the investment of Candahar, and the virtual supremacy of Ayoob Khan over the province, formed a sufficiently grave conjuncture of affairs to demand prompt and energetic action. All eyes in England and India were instinctively turned to Sir Frederick Roberts as the man for the crisis that had so suddenly arisen, and the British Army in Afghanistan felt no one was equally fitted to cope with the new peril that had arisen, and lead them to wipe away the stain from their arms.

Sir Donald Stewart and Sir Frederick Roberts both agreed that it would be necessary to send a strong division from Cabul, and not to leave the retrieval of our position in South-Western Afghanistan to General Phayre, who commanded the Bombay troops in reserve on the Scinde frontier and at Pisheen, whose want of transport would, they felt certain, delay his arrival at Candahar. With soldierly alacrity, and pending orders from the Supreme Government, steps were taken to prepare a force of about 10,000 men to march upon Candahar. Sir Frederick Roberts's offer to assume command was at once accepted by Sir Donald Stewart, and the appointment was hailed by the army with satisfaction, for all felt that success was already almost assured.

The Maiwand disaster came at an unfortunate time, and was near imperilling the negotiations in progress between Abdul Rahman and Mr. Griffin, acting on behalf of the Indian Government; but these difficulties were tided over at an interview, and the new Ameer, who was glad to be quit of the British army from Cabul, raised but slight objection to a division marching through the country to Candahar. The Indian Government, on the urgent representations of Sir Donald Stewart, who telegraphed on the 5th August, and wrote a lengthy despatch in the same sense five days later, directed the immediate withdrawal of the remainder of the British troops from Afghanistan, the posts at Lundi Kotul and in the Khyber Pass being held in temporary occupation. Accordingly, on the 11th August, Sir Donald Stewart quitted Sherpur, having that morning had an interview with the new Ameer, at which Mr. Lepel Griffin and General Hills, commanding the Cabul Division, were present.

Before the news of the defeat of Burrows's Brigade at Maiwand, the military authorities at head-quarters had ordered the evacuation of Afghanistan by the army of 18,000 men assembled at Cabul. The withdrawal was to be effected in two bodies. One portion was to retire by the Khyber Pass, under Sir Donald Stewart, and the other, under the orders of Sir Frederick Roberts, by the Kurram Valley, where a division, under the command of Major-General Watson, C.B., V.C., had remained since Sir Frederick quitted Ali Kheyl to commence his march on Cabul in the preceding autumn. These troops were for the present directed to remain in the Kurram Valley; but, on the 3rd of September, the Viceroy and his Council came to the resolution, in accordance with the wishes of the inhabitants, to place the Jajis of the Upper Kurram, and the tribes of the Hurriab district beyond the Peiwar Kotul, under the new Ameer; though the Turis, in the Kurram Valley, whose independence had been solemnly promised to them by Sir Frederick Roberts, were not included in this arrangement. Accordingly, the Kurram Valley was evacuated by General Watson on the 16th October, and the Turis were placed under their leaders,

Badshah Gul and Meer Mahomed Khan. While noting this termination to our occupation of districts conquered by Sir Frederick Roberts, it should be borne in mind that, as a soldier thoroughly conversant with the strategical and political value of the Kurram Valley, he agreed with the almost unanimous consensus of opinion against the occupation of this territory, though in his elaborate and well-reasoned Memorandum on the situation in Afghanistan, as it affected our position in India, penned at Cabul on the 29th May, Sir Frederick Roberts based his opinion on the hypothesis of the retention of Candahar.* But his main argument was directed towards proving the inutility of holding positions on the Kurram line by showing that, in any future war in Afghanistan, we ought to remain on the defensive on our North-West frontier, and that our most effective line of advance against an enemy in the interior of the country would be from the southward; while, apart from strategical considerations of this general nature, the special weight of his reasoning on military, political, and financial grounds, bears decidedly against our maintaining garrisons on the Kurram highlands.

Sir Frederick Roberts's connection with Cabul and North-Eastern Afghanistan was now to cease, and he turned his face westwards to reap fresh honours, and add a glorious page to the military annals of his country. Upon receipt at Cabul of the telegram from the Viceregal Government announcing the Maiwand disaster, both the British Commanders concluded

---

* The following paragraphs from this Memorandum are of especial value, and no notice of the views in this important question, held by Sir Frederick Roberts, would be complete without them:—"The state of affairs which brought about the Treaty of Gundamuck has completely changed. In place of our being obliged to occupy the advanced strategic positions secured to us by that treaty, and which the safety of our Indian Empire forced us to hold as long as Cabul was the centre of a great political and military power, we can now afford to withdraw our troops within our original frontier. We have nothing to fear from Afghanistan, and the best thing to do is to leave it as much as possible to itself. It may not be very flattering to our *amour propre*, but I feel sure I am right when I say that the less the Afghans see of us the less they will dislike us. Should Russia in future years attempt to conquer Afghanistan or invade India through it, we should have a better chance of attaching the Afghans to our interests, if we avoid all interference with them in the meantime. The military occupation of Candahar is, as I have before stated, of vital importance; but even there we should make our presence but little felt, merely controlling the foreign policy of the ruler of that province."

that a division should march from Cabul, in addition to any troops despatched from Scinde, which could only reach Candahar at this season of the year with great difficulty and delay. The Cabul *corps d'armée* of 18,000 seasoned troops, accustomed to act together, and commanded by some of the best generals in the British army, was fit to go anywhere and do anything at a moment's notice.

The following were the circumstances under which Sir Frederick Roberts assumed command of the force ordered to avenge the disaster at Maiwand. As it had been arranged that he should return to India by the Kurram route with a portion of the troops, he rode to Jellalabad to visit scenes so interesting to every soldier. "While there," he writes to us, "I instinctively felt anxious in case any disturbance, owing to the near approach of Abdul Rahman, should take place at Cabul; so I hurried back, riding from Gundamuck to Cabul on the 28th July. Sir Donald Stewart met me a few miles out, and told me what had happened at Maiwand. Feeling it was most important that troops should be sent from Cabul to Candahar, and believing that the authorities at Simla would hesitate to send troops who were under orders to return to India, I telegraphed to the Adjutant-General, urging that a force should be sent without delay, and guaranteeing that none of the soldiers at Cabul would demur at going, provided I could assure them that they would not be kept to garrison Candahar after the work in the field there was over. I begged the Adjutant-General to show the telegram to the Foreign Secretary, by whom it was given to Lord Ripon, who then decided to send me with a force. Before despatching the telegram I showed it to Sir Donald Stewart."

The reply of the Viceroy sanctioning the despatch of an expedition from Cabul to Candahar, in conformity with the suggestion of Sir Frederick Roberts, was received on the 3rd August, and the equipment and constitution of the force were left to the two Generals, who were required to state the earliest date on which the relieving column could march, and when it was expected to arrive at Candahar. After consultation they returned an answer that Sir Frederick Roberts would leave Cabul on the 8th August, and that he expected to reach the capital of Southern Afghanistan on the 2nd September.

With the public spirit and friendly feeling that always characterized Sir Donald Stewart in his dealings with his brother-in-arms, that officer gave *carte blanche* to Sir Frederick Roberts as to men and equipment. Colonel Chapman, R.A.,* Chief of the Staff to Sir Donald Stewart, who now took up the same appointment in the force about to march on Candahar, only does justice to his former chief when, in a lecture on this famous march, delivered at the Royal United Service Institution on the 9th March, 1881, he observed : " No record of the work thus undertaken would be complete which did not set forward very prominently the self-abnegation and high military capacity evinced by Lieutenant-General Sir Donald Stewart, who was in supreme command at Cabul, and who, without reference to the difficult task of withdrawal by the Khyber, which was to be his share of the programme, placed unreservedly at Sir Frederick Roberts's disposal the entire resources of the North Afghanistan Field Force in transport and equipment ; nor would it be possible to pass by without respectful recognition the singleness of purpose and true genius with which the two Commanders devoted themselves to perfect the machinery which it was intended to employ in the execution of a difficult enterprise. The spirit they evinced became the leading principle that guided all ranks in the task of preparation."

During the succeeding few days Sir Frederick Roberts busied himself in selecting the troops he intended to take with him in his march, which, for the adventurous spirits in camp, had all the charm, and much more than the hazard, of a knight-errant's expedition in mediæval times, so great was the element of uncertainty attaching to its progress from the moment the troops, without base and cut off from all communication with the outer world, plunged into the heart of Afghanistan with, at the other extremity, a triumphant enemy and a defeated and beleagured body of fellow-countrymen awaiting their arrival.

The present Afghan war has been not less full of romantic incidents and sudden melodramatic changes than the war we had waged forty years before in the same country, and this last

---

* This officer, like Sir Frederick Roberts and Colonel Perkins, Chief Engineer in the Kurram and Cabul campaigns, had received his professional training at Addiscombe, whence he entered the old Bengal Artillery.

scene formed a fitting climax to the play in which human lives and a kingdom had been the stakes. Not only India and England, but the whole civilized world watched with breathless interest the *dénouement* of the drama about to be played out, which may be said to have divided itself, with strict regard to the unities, into five acts. The first unfolded the gathering of the three armies, the insult offered to the British Envoy at Ali Musjid, the swift and victorious advance into Afghan territory, and the signing of the Treaty of Gundamuck, the curtain descending amid a shower of honours on the victors, and the banquet given by Lord Lytton at Simla to "the hero of the Peiwar Kotul." The second act dealt with the brief record of the Cavagnari Mission, received with such honour at Cabul, and expiring in a scene of fire and blood, in which British valour and devotion to duty shone out proudly and shed an undying lustre on its victims.

But a change now came over the spirit of the play. With the rising of the curtain the third act deals with the revenge justly inflicted by a British army on the cowardly crew who dishonoured the flag of England, and dragged through the mire of the Afghan capital the headless body of her representative. The brilliant advance of Sir Frederick Roberts from Ali Kheyl, the victory of Charasia and occupation of the Bala Hissar, with his visit to the still smoking and reeking ruins of the Residency, brought to a conclusion one of the most exciting episodes of this drama amid the plaudits of the auditory. But again the storm of war, long foreseen, and its contingencies thoughtfully provided for by the British General, burst on the scene. After a chequered struggle against vast odds, the British army was driven within its entrenched camp, whence, after the enemy had in vain attempted to overwhelm it by force of numbers, it issued to inflict severe chastisement on its enemies. Again sunshine succeeds storm, and with the junction of the armies of Sir Donald Stewart and Sir Frederick Roberts, and the conclusion of terms with the new Ameer for peacefully evacuating the country, it seemed as though the sword might be returned to its sheath, and an era of peace and goodwill inaugurated between Briton and Afghan. But this was not yet to be, and the ambition of one man and the incompetence of another, resulted in a disaster transcending Isandhlwana, and only surpassed by that experienced by General Elphinstone in the passes between Cabul and Gundamuck. But like those reverses, only more speedily, if not more decisively, Maiwand was wiped out by the victory of the 1st September, on which followed the withdrawal of our troops from the scene of so much glory and disaster. For the last time the curtain descends, and the Afghan War of 1878-80 was " as a tale that is told."

CHAPTER XVIII.

English Public Opinion on the Projected March through Afghanistan—Sir Frederick Roberts quits Cabul for Beni Hissar—Incidents of the Forced March to Ghuznee—Arrival at Ghuznee and Surrender of the Town and Citadel—The Forced March to Khelat-i-Ghilzye—Relief and Removal of the Garrison—Sir Frederick Roberts on the Line of March—The Advance on Candahar—Preparations for the Attack on Ayoob Khan's Position.

WHEN it was announced by telegraph in England that Sir Frederick Roberts proposed to march through Afghanistan without a base of operations or communications of any kind, as is usual, a host of military critics in Parliament, and the Club-gentlemen who are more familiar with "the shady side of Pall Mall" than with the deserts and mountain ranges of Afghanistan, and the conditions attaching to waging war with Oriental races, adduced numberless reasons, drawn from precedent and theoretical treatises, satisfactorily demonstrating that, by the rules of war, Sir Frederick Roberts was courting disaster, and insisting that the step he was taking must be contrary to the better judgment of both himself and General Stewart, and was doubtless due to a determination on the part of the Government to carry out the evacuation of the country as previously arranged, without consideration for the safety of Roberts's force. But these military critics were at fault alike in their judgment of the prudence of the march under existing conditions, as was proved by the inexorable logic of events, and in their opinion as to the views held by the two experienced Generals in Afghanistan, who never had any doubt that a division of 10,000 properly equipped and commanded British troops could traverse Afghanistan in safety.

As it had been determined to evacuate the Bala Hissar and the Sherpur Cantonment by the 11th August, when Sir Donald Stewart intended to commence the retrograde movement on India, Sir Frederick Roberts had expressed his intention to march three days before that date. The time at his disposal in which to select his force, and survey and complete its equipment was brief; but it was sufficient for the purpose. In this instance the selection of the troops, especially the Native corps, that were to accompany him, was an exceptionally difficult task. As pointed out by him in his Memorandum of 29th May, two years was, in his opinion, the limit at which the latter could be kept away from their homes; but this had now been exceeded in the case of some of the Goorkha and Punjaubee regiments, and it would have been an ungracious task to disappoint these gallant soldiers, who were looking forward to return to their families after an unexampled absence from them, and call on them to undergo the chances of a forced march of over 300 miles, and, perhaps, of an arduous campaign. They had suffered heavily in action and through sickness, and naturally longed for a period of rest, so when it was understood that the usual proportion of Native regiments would accompany the column, the intelligence was not received with enthusiasm, and the selection was anxiously awaited. The Chief of the Staff, Colonel Chapman, says on this point:—"It was not with eager desire that the honour of marching to Candahar was sought for, and some commanding officers of experience judged rightly the tempers of their men when they represented for the General's consideration the claims of the regiments they commanded to be relieved as soon as possible from field service. I lay stress on this fact, and claim for those officers, who subordinated their own wishes in the interest of the soldiers they commanded, as also for the Generals who acted on their representations, an insight into the character of our Native troops, the result of long experience. It was not easy to estimate the confidence created by such knowledge as was thus brought to bear on the question of selection, nor rightly to describe the sense of duty, and of absolute trust in their commanders, which marked the behaviour of the troops at this time. The enthusiasm which carried Sir Frederick Roberts's force with exceptional rapidity to Candahar, was an after-growth evolved by the enterprise itself, and came as a response to the unfailing spirit which animated the leader himself."

The constitution of the force was published in General Orders on the 3rd August. It was to consist of 3 Brigades, each of one British and three Native Battalions, with a Battery of guns attached. The Cavalry Brigade worked independently, its commander reporting direct to Head-quarters.* The guns, 7-pounders, were carried on mules, no wheeled artillery being taken, and one of the batteries consisted of screw-guns, which had a reputation for accuracy exceeding the 9-pounders, which they did not belie in action. On this question of artillery, opinions differed in the camp; but both the Generals were of one mind, and the result proved that they were correct in their judgment. The object was to reach Candahar in the shortest possible time; and it was not improbable that should Ayoob Khan endeavour to march on Ghuznee and Cabul, he would

---

* The following was the strength of the regiments and batteries taken from Colonel Chapman's lecture:—

	Officers.	British Soldiers.	Native Drivers and Muleteers.
Staff	79		
Royal Artillery—			
6-8 Royal Artillery	6	95	139
11-9 ,,	6	95	139
			Sepoys.
No. 2 Mountain Battery	5	...	140
Cavalry Brigade—			
9th Lancers	19	318	...
3rd Bengal Cavalry	7	...	394
3rd Punjaub Cavalry	9	...	408
Central India Horse	11	...	495
First Brigade—			
92nd Highlanders	19	651	...
23rd Pioneers	8	...	701
24th Punjaub Infantry	7	...	575
2nd Goorkhas	7	...	501
Second Brigade—			
72nd Highlanders	23	787	...
2nd Sikhs	7	...	612
3rd Sikhs	7	...	570
5th Goorkhas	8	...	561
Third Brigade—			
2-60th Rifles	21	616	...
15th Sikhs	10	...	650
4th Goorkhas	8	...	629
25th Punjaub Infantry	7	...	637
Total	274	2,562	7,151

This total of 9,987 was increased to 10,148 by the discharge of sick from hospital.

avoid the ordinary road and move by the valleys of the Urgundab or the Urgustan. The nature of the ground throughout Afghanistan is such that Artillery can never be safely employed with Cavalry alone unsupported by Infantry, as was shown on the 11th December in General Massy's action. Nor is the rapidity of movement of this arm so much required in countries like Afghanistan, as the power of being able to operate over the most difficult ground without causing delay to the rest of the troops. It was not forgotten, moreover, that on arrival at Candahar the column would be augmented by a battery of 40-pounders, a battery of field artillery, and four guns of Horse Artillery. "It is unquestionable," says Sir Frederick Roberts, "that had either horse or field artillery accompanied the force the march could not have been performed with the same rapidity."

Before leaving Cabul everything that was possible was done to lighten baggage. Ten British soldiers were told off to each mountain battery tent, usually intended to hold six, and fifty to a sepoy's tent of two pâls, 34lbs. of kit only being allowed for each man. The allowance to each Native soldier was 20lbs. of baggage, inclusive of camp equipage. Each officer was allowed one mule, and an additional mule to every eight officers for mess. The amount of supplies taken with the force was for Europeans, thirty days' tea, sugar, rum, and salt, and five days' flour, and five days' rations for Native troops. One day's grain was carried by Cavalry horses and transport animals in addition to the ordinary load. The exact strength of the Cabul-Candahar Field Force, as it was officially designated, was 10,148 combatants, 223 Medical Staff, and 8,134 Native followers, including 2,192 doolie bearers.*

So admirable were the arrangements elaborated by Sir Frederick Roberts, whose genius for organization received a fresh

---

* The number of animals that left Cabul on the 8th August was 1,779 Cavalry chargers and 450 Artillery mules; for the service of the transport, 1,589 yaboos (Afghan ponies), 4,510 mules, 1,244 Indian ponies, and 912 donkeys; and for sick transport 286 ponies, 43 donkeys, and 6 camels. The grand total of animals was 10,819, exclusive of 415 purchased on the line of march. A formidable number to feed while making forced marches over 300 miles of country! The casualties were 733, due to the hard work.

illustration during this famous march, and so excellent was the service rendered by Lieutenant-Colonel Low and Major Badcock, the officers in charge of the Commissariat and Transport Departments,* and their assistants, that no instance was brought to notice in which either a soldier or camp-follower failed to receive his daily ration. Sir Frederick, we were told by a General officer, not only personally organized every detail of his force, but examined every man and beast, excluding those that were weakly. Flour and sheep were procurable throughout the country to be traversed, with the exception of some thirty miles before reaching Khelat-i-Ghilzye ; and the crops were in season for the cattle, so that forage was obtainable to any amount.

The Division of Infantry was under the command of Major-General J. Ross, C.B., the 1st, 2nd, and 3rd Brigades being commanded respectively by Brigadier-Generals H. T. Macpherson, T. D. Baker, and C. M. Macgregor. Brigadier-General Hugh H. Gough commanded the Cavalry ; Colonel Alured C. Johnson the Artillery ; Colonel Æ. Perkins was commanding Royal Engineer ; Colonel Chapman, R.A., Chief of the Staff, and Deputy-Surgeon General J. Hanbury, Principal Medical Officer.

The head of the Political Department was Major Hastings, who had held the office at Cabul before Mr. Lepel Griffin's arrival, his principal assistant being Major Ewan Smith, who had been Chief Political Officer under Sir Donald Stewart at Candahar and during the advance on Cabul, and was therefore familiar with the country. These officers, with their assistants, were of great service during the march in assisting the Quarter-

---

* Sir Frederick Roberts writes of these officers and their assistants:—
"Sufficient praise cannot be bestowed upon all these officers (enumerating the names of twelve officers). They never spared themselves ; and often, after the longest march, and with the prospect of having to start off again at a very early hour the following morning, had to work on until a late hour in the night. In the collection of supplies the Commissariat and Transport Departments were materially aided by Major E. G. G. Hastings and his staff of Political Officers. Fortunately for the welfare of the Cavalry horses and transport animals, a fair amount of green Indian corn was almost everywhere procurable. Barley was very scarce, but the Indian corn proved to be so nutritious that the large majority of the horses, ponies, and mules reached Candahar in excellent health and condition. The reserve of flour had on several occasions to be indented upon ; but by replenishing whenever supplies were to be obtained, the force arrived at Candahar with still about three days' flour in hand."

master-General's Department to procure intelligence and the Commissariat to collect supplies. They were selected for their knowledge of Persian or Pushtoo, the Afghan dialect of that language, or on account of their special experience in dealing with frontier tribes, and commanded the services of Native officers and soldiers of tried ability.

Last, but not least for the value of services rendered, mention should be made of the Army Signalling Department, under the direction of Captain Straton, who, by the judicious use of the heliograph, spared the troops much fatigue, the brigades being in constant communication.

Before Sir Frederick Roberts quitted the scene of his triumphs Mr. Lepel Griffin and the Political Officers returning to India with Sir Donald Stewart gave a farewell banquet in his honour, at which Sir Donald and the principal officers of the army were present. In responding to the toast of his health, the guest of the evening, after eulogizing the Cabul force, from the brigade commanders and staff to the troops under his command, " with whom," he said, " success is a certainty," made a graceful allusion to the services of his hosts, who, he declared, "had borne as important, if not as active, work as the soldier."*

---

* The following was the interesting speech delivered by Sir Frederick Roberts at the banquet on the 5th August :—

"Mr. Griffin, Sir Donald Stewart, and Gentlemen,—I scarcely know how to thank you all for the kind way in which you have drunk my health and that of the column under orders for Candahar. To the very flattering terms in which Mr. Griffin has spoken of me I should have considerable difficulty in replying, were it not that I can honestly say, that any successes which I may have attained hitherto, have been due entirely to the experienced commanders I have had with me, the most capable staff that ever accompanied a general officer in the field, and the gallantry and discipline of the troops under me. I do not think there ever have been, and I doubt if there ever will be, more efficient troops sent from India than those which General Stewart and I have had the honour to command for the last two years. With such troops success is a certainty. Without wishing to underrate the dangers and difficulties of the task before us, I feel quite confident that the efficient force which Sir Donald Stewart has placed at my disposal will succeed in reaching Candahar as quickly as possible, and in effectually disposing of any Afghan army that may be brought against us. As Mr. Griffin has said, we must all deplore the cause which requires Cabul troops to be now sent to Candahar. A few days ago we were all congratulating ourselves upon the prospect of a speedy return to India. Some of us had laid in a store of Nipal pepper for use at home; others, I have heard, had actually named an early date for leaving Bombay for Eng-

The several brigades of Sir Frederick Roberts's force moved out of Sherpur into camp at Beni Hissar, Charasia, and Indikee on the 8th August, and in the evening Sir Frederick Roberts, accompanied by Sir Donald Stewart and other friends and well-wishers, rode out of Sherpur for the last time and joined his troops at Beni Hissar. He anticipated that the march would not be a military promenade, and the night before leaving the Cantonment issued the following characteristic General Order to his troops:—"It has been decided by the Government of India that a force shall proceed with all possible despatch from Cabul towards Khelat-i-Ghilzai and Candahar for the relief of the British garrisons in those places, now threatened by a large Afghan army under the leadership of Sirdar Mahomed Ayoob Khan. Sir Frederick Roberts feels sure that the troops placed under his command for this important duty will cheerfully respond to the call made upon them, notwithstanding the privations and hardships inseparable

---

land. Well, Sir Donald Stewart is willing to guarantee—and were it not an indecorous thing for an officer so high in rank, would even bet—that we shall reach India again, viâ Candahar, in November next. Gentlemen, this is a country of great uncertainties. We have been living in a state of uncertainty for many months; but, thanks to the political skill of our kind host, affairs have during the last few weeks progressed so rapidly and favourably, that we have reason to hope the country may now have comparative rest and quiet, and that some settled form of government will be established. However, we must not be too sanguine; and I trust that our fellow-countrymen, who have not had the same opportunity that we have had of knowing Afghanistan and the Afghans will not be disappointed if matters do not go altogether smoothly after the British troops leave Cabul. No Ameer has ever yet occupied the throne for any time until he has proved himself capable of governing the country, and it is not likely that Ameer Abdul Rahman will be an exception. We all know what difficulties Mr. Griffin has had to contend with, and we all rejoice at the great success which has attended his efforts—efforts so ably assisted by the Political Officers now with him. It now remains for Abdul Rahman to show that he is capable of filling the great position in which he has been placed. From the commencement of this campaign, the Political Officers have borne as important, if not as active, work as the soldiers. First and foremost, the gallant Cavagnari, known to and mourned by us all, and more than liked by many of us; with him many brave men fell, and it was to avenge their base and treacherous murder that this force came to Cabul. It is a great satisfaction to me to think that at present, at any rate, no officers will be required to remain at Cabul, and that all the Political Officers I see around me will return to India with the troops. But I feel quite sure, if the decision had been otherwise, officers would have been found to accept the dangerous post, either officers of the Civil Service, or among those military politicals who have gained for themselves a reputation on the frontier and other parts of India."

from a long march through a hostile country. The Lieutenant-General wishes to impress on both officers and men the necessity of preserving the same strict discipline which has been so successfully and uniformly maintained since the commencement of the war, and to treat all the people who may be well disposed towards the British with justice and forbearance. Sir Frederick Roberts looks confidently forward to the successful accomplishment of the object of the expedition, convinced as he is that all ranks are animated with the proud feeling that to them is entrusted the duty and privilege of relieving their fellow-soldiers and restoring the prestige of the British Army."

On the 9th August the Cabul-Candahar force set their faces towards Ghuznee, distant $97\frac{1}{2}$ miles, marching by the Logar Valley, where supplies were more abundant, instead of by Mydan, which was ten miles shorter. The former route had also the incidental advantage of keeping the Afghans in doubt as to the ultimate destination of the force, for the first three stages from Beni Hissar led directly towards the Shutargardan Pass and the Kurram Valley, and were those by which Sir Frederick Roberts had advanced on Cabul in September of the preceding year. The latest news received from Candahar previous to the departure of the force was of the 3rd August, on which day Ayoob Khan was reported to be still twenty miles to the west of Candahar. The troops under Lieutenant-General Primrose's command were, however, shut up within the walls of the citadel and city by a rising of the people of the district. "It was known," says Colonel Chapman, "that the walls could scarcely be surmounted by assault, and that they could not be breached by field artillery, and it was therefore assumed that the large garrison which held Candahar could with ten light field guns and a heavy battery resist any attack which the Afghan army might make, and would be secure for so long a time as provisions held out."

The camp at Beni Hissar was struck at 2.45 A.M., as was the practice throughout the greater part of this memorable march, and the 1st and 2nd Brigades halted for the night at Zahidabad, distant sixteen miles, the route from Indikee taken by General Baker's Brigade being slightly longer. The troops,

The March to Ghuznee.

after the long halt at Sherpur, were not yet in good marching order, and the difficult nature of the ground, with the heat, probably made this march more distressing than the longer ones they made later on.

While at Zahidabad Sir Frederick Roberts issued an order on the necessity for treating with care and properly feeding the transport animals, on the efficiency of which the success of the expedition largely depended. This matter claimed his attention in the Kurram campaign, as during the first phase of the war the carelessness of transport officers, who had had no experience of the treatment of animals, had caused so great a mortality among them that when hostilities again broke out, sufficient transport could with difficulty be scraped together to ensure the mobility of 6,000 men. On the 10th August the Cabul Field Force marched to Zurgunshahr, a distance of thirteen miles. Here supplies were had in abundance, as many old enemies of the Logar Valley were working in the British interest, and the agents of the new Ameer accompanied the army. At Zurgunshahr, Sir Frederick Roberts issued instructions on the order of march, the brigades and regiments being directed to lead by rotation. In such movements, says Colonel Chapman, although halts were ordered at regular intervals, it was found impossible to assimilate the pace, and preserve a regular rate of marching. When the Highlanders led the column the Goorkhas were worn out by their efforts to keep up, and when the Goorkhas were in front the pace became generally so slow as to fatigue the Europeans and the Sikhs; yet it was very important for brigade commanders to strive at a uniform rate of marching, and to adhere to the halts of ten minutes ordered at the end of each hour of march, as well as the breakfast halt of twenty minutes, fixed for eight o'clock.

The march of the 11th August was to Padkao Rogani, sixteen and a half miles. The orders directed that the "rouse" was to be at 2.45, the brigades to march at four. The Cavalry and 2nd Infantry Brigades crossed the river Logar at Hissarak, and marched to Baraki-Barak, where they encamped on the sloping ground overlooking, and to the west of, the village. The 1st and 3rd Infantry Brigades marched in columns of brigades, the 3rd Brigade crossing the small Kotul to the west of the camp and marching through Dadu Kheyl towards Hissarak. These brigades then marched in parallel lines to the rising ground situated to the left of Padkao Rogani, distance fifteen miles.

From their respective camping grounds the four brigades of the army marched the following day a distance of ten and a half miles to Ashrak, or Ameer Killa, at the entrance of the pass known as the Tang-i-Wardak, by which the united waters of the Logar and Shineez rivers find their way from the Wardak to the Logar valley. The passage of the defile was effected with some difficulty, and the passage of the Zamburak Pass, 7,000 feet high, was laborious for the troops; though owing to the absence of wheeled artillery and to the equipment of the entire force with mule and pony transport, no halt was made until the encamping ground was reached. It had been anticipated, says a Staff officer, that the passage of the Zamburak would be disputed; but neither here nor at the Sher-i-Dahan Pass was any opposition offered; the road over the latter is open and easy, and had been made practicable for heavy field-guns by Sir Donald Stewart on his advance from Candahar.

The march of the 13th August was from Ashrak to Takia, in the valley of the Shineez, a distance of twelve miles, and on the following day thence to Shahgao, seventeen miles. The supplies during the last three days did not come in with the plentifulness experienced in the Logar Valley, as the people were not so friendly, but they were astute enough to raise no opposition, and hoped that this would be the last they would see of their unwelcome visitors.

On the 14th the Division was concentrated within three miles of the Sher-i-Dahan (Lion's Mouth) pass, having an elevation of 9,000 feet above sea level. The road over the pass was easy, having been made practicable for Artillery by Sir Donald Stewart. The chief inconvenience experienced by the troops, besides the heat and sand storms, and the suffocating dust raised by the column on the march, was the want of water. The daily camping ground was selected with due regard to the presence of this necessary, but, says an officer, long stretches of desert had often to be traversed without meeting with a drop of water, causing great inconvenience to man and beast marching under a burning sun. The variations of climate were also very trying, there being at times as much as 80° difference between the temperature by day and by night. This caused great hardship to the men, who had to march in the same clothes when the heat was tropical or the thermometer marked freezing point.

A march of twelve and a-half miles, on the 15th August, brought the Division over the Sher-i-Dahan pass to Ghuznee, thus completing the first stage of this memorable march, the distance traversed in seven days being ninety-seven and a half miles, over difficult country, without the loss of a mule-load of baggage.

Every precaution was taken in the advance through the Sher-i-Dahan pass to guard against an attack by marauders on the baggage, but there was no opposition of any kind. The tribal gatherings, whose patriotism had been fanned to fever heat by the old Moollah, Mooskh-i-Alum, during the early period of the campaign, and which had resisted Sir Donald Stewart's march, had long since dispersed; while the faction which acknowledged Mahomed Jan as chief had accepted temporarily the Ameership of Abdul Rahman, and such of the chiefs as professed themselves adherents of the Yakoob Khan party had left to join Ayoob Khan at Candahar.

Close to the spot where Sir Frederick Roberts halted, at the village of Roza, lies buried the great conqueror Mahmoud, the founder of Ghuznee, and of the dynasty called after that city. It was the gates of this handsome mausoleum taken by Mahmoud from the temple of Somnauth, in Guzerat, during one of his invasions of India, that were removed by General Nott in 1842, under instructions from Lord Ellenborough, who issued one of his magniloquent orders on the occasion.

Sir Frederick Roberts sent for the acting Governor of Ghuznee, and having received from him the keys of the gates, proceeded in his company to inspect the town and citadel, the scene of one of the most brilliant feats of arms in the first Afghan war, with which the names of Thomson, Durand, Sale, and Dennie are inseparably connected, and which conferred a cheaply-earned peerage, with a pension of £2,000, on Sir John Keane. The General placed guards and sentries in and around Ghuznee to preserve order; while parties of officers and men took advantage of the permission accorded them to visit the citadel, bazaars, and other places of interest.

The question of supplies was the only one causing anxiety to Sir Frederick Roberts, and foraging parties were sent out, the people being loth even to sell what was required, though afraid to do more than show a sullen demeanour, for the chastisement inflicted at Ahmed Khel was too recent to require a repetition. Before the break of the following day the force was many miles on its way towards Khelat-i-Ghilzye, and the ground traversed on this march was twenty miles, being the longest but one made by the Cabul-Candahar Force. The "rouse" was sounded at 2.45 A.M., and the troops marched at 4.15, the Cavalry covering the movement at a distance of five miles in advance of the 2nd and 3rd Brigades, which were followed by the baggage, ordnance, and commissariat reserve, the 1st Brigade, with one troop of cavalry, bringing up the rear of the column. The Chief of the Staff says of the order of march issued by Sir Frederick Roberts before leaving Ghuznee:—" The method of such marching as was now put in practice is not easy to describe; it combined the extreme of freedom in movement with carefully regulated halts, and the closest control in every portion of the column; it employed the individual intelligence of each man composing the masses in motion, and called on all for exertion in overcoming the difficulties of the march, in bearing its extraordinary toil, and in aiding the accomplishment of the object in view. Once movement had commenced the animals of the baggage column, moving at different paces, were checked as little as possible; the large number of officers detailed for baggage duty reduced confusion to a minimum, and secured a pace in marching that could not have been anticipated, the baggage animals reaching camp for the most part very soon after the arrival of the troops." But it was weary work for the rear-guard, who were engaged in assisting the camp-followers, pressing forward the feeble among the cattle, and shifting loads and rendering such assistance as was required. Assuming that the march commenced daily at 4 A.M., the rear-guard seldom left camp before 7 A.M., and only reached the next encampment shortly before sundown. The actual length of the column of march, by the shortest computation, says the same authority, amounted to from six to seven miles. But, nevertheless, there was an absence of confusion, and every person and animal fell into his or its place with order and regularity. Though the collection and distribution of food, fuel, and forage, together with the establishment of markets within each brigade, where the villagers might find a sale for articles of supply, necessitated an elaborate system, seldom during the entire march to Candahar had the British troops to substitute flour-cakes ("chupatties") for the regular bread ration, and no instance was brought to notice in which either a soldier or a follower failed to receive his rations. The first day's march from Ghuznee brought the column to Yerghalta, the route passing the battle-field of Ahmed Khel, where a "zizarat" to the memory of 1,100 martyrs to the faith indicated the terrible losses suffered by the gallant Ghazis when 3,000 of them, sword in hand, charged down on the British line and braved the storm of bullets and canister that swept over the open plain, destitute of any cover. Those who witnessed this grand display of heroism were not likely again to jeer at these fanatics, who were spoken of with respect also by the old Cabul Force after the events of December.

This day caused the severest strain of any throughout the march on the officers and men of the Division. Daily the number of those footsore or unable to proceed through weariness or debility increased, until the General, who each day had careful reports presented to him of the health and condition of the combatants and camp-followers, had serious thoughts of reducing the length of the day's march. But the limit of the strain seemed to have been reached on this first march out of Ghuznee, and afterwards daily many footsore men rejoined the ranks, and the army gained in marching powers until it attained a high degree of excellence, though the doolie-bearers continued to suffer greatly. To appreciate the endurance of the troops, or to understand the very high order of discipline they attained, it was necessary to have seen them at work. While history records many instances of a regiment or small column making marches similar to those accomplished by the

Cabul-Candahar Force, the merit in this case lay in the numerical strength of the column, 10,148 troops, 8,143 native followers, and 11,224 animals, including cavalry horses—the daily supply for which was drawn from the country after arrival in camp. The food daily distributed to every individual was cooked with fuel brought in from a distance; bread was issued almost daily, and ample forage provided. When we consider these facts, it will be readily conceded, as Colonel Chapman urges, that the march from Ghuznee to Khelat-i-Ghilzye, executed in eight days, ranks high in the annals of similar achievements.

On the 17th August the march was to Chardeh, a group of villages, some deserted, the distance covered being thirteen miles. On the following day the column marched to Kareez-i-Oba,* sixteen miles, and on the 19th to Mukur, fourteen miles, a great portion of the route on both days being over a sandy stretch of desert without a drop of water to relieve the parching thirst of man or beast. The country being here very open, the army marched with the three brigades of Infantry abreast, a formation which enabled the baggage to be brought into camp at an earlier hour.

On the 20th the Field Force marched to Killa-i-Tuman, a distance of twenty-one miles, being the longest day's march made. Owing to the excessive heat and want of shade the sufferings of the troops were great, but there was no choice in the halting-ground, as water could not be procured in sufficient quantity for so large a column short of it.

Soon after arriving here Sir Frederick Roberts received a letter from Colonel (now Sir Oriel) Tanner, 29th Bengal Native Infantry, commanding at Khelat-i-Ghilzye, in which he said :—
" All was well with the garrison, and the neighbouring country was still quiet. A letter had been received from Major-General Phayre, C.B., dated Quetta, 12th August, in which he states that he is marching with a large force of Cavalry, Artillery, and Infantry, British and Native, and expects to reach Candahar

---

* A kareez is an underground gallery, which is a common method of conducting water from a subterranean spring in Persia and Afghanistan. These aqueducts often convey water some miles, wells being opened at every twenty-five or thirty yards of the course, by which means extensive tracts of country are brought under cultivation.

The March on Khelat-i-Ghilzye.

not later than the 2nd of September." In publishing this gratifying intelligence for the information of the column, Sir Frederick Roberts expressed his thanks "for the admirable manner in which they had executed the march from Cabul hitherto;" and he added:—" If the present rate of marching be continued Khelat-i-Ghilzye should be reached not later than the 23rd, and Candahar not later than the 29th. By the latest accounts the Afghan army under Ayoob Khan is still at Candahar. The Lieutenant-General hopes it may remain there, and that the honour of relieving the British garrison may fall to the lot of the magnificent troops now with him." It may here be mentioned that though the General frequently despatched messengers while on the road between Beni Hissar and Khelat-i-Ghilzye, reporting progress, none of these men reached their destination, and it was not until after his arrival at this place that success attended his efforts to communicate with the outer world.

On the 21st August the force marched to Gajai, eighteen miles, and during the day, Captain Straton heliographed to Khelat-i-Ghilzye, thirty-three miles distant, and received a response from Colonel Tanner, announcing the disastrous sortie at Candahar of the 16th August, resulting in the death of General Brooke and many other gallant officers and men, and conveying the reassuring news as to the condition of the garrison and their power to hold out. During the day the agents of the local Governor, under instructions from Colonel Tanner, met the force and assisted in obtaining supplies, and when the division arrived at Baba Kazai, on the 22nd, seventeen and a half miles from Gajai, they found there food, forage, and other supplies sent from the fort, under an escort furnished by the 2nd Belooch Regiment.

The march of the 23rd August of sixteen and a half miles, brought the column to Khelat-i-Ghilzye, the total distance of 136 miles from Ghuznee having been traversed in eight days, or a daily average of sixteen and three-quarters miles.*

During the march the loss had been surprisingly small. Although a hostile population hovered on all sides ready to attack stragglers, but three Native soldiers were cut off from the

---

* The average daily march from Beni Hissar to Khelat-i-Ghilzye, a distance of 232 miles, accomplished in fifteen days, had been $15\frac{1}{3}$ miles,

column between Cabul and Khelat-i-Ghilzye, there were two suicides among the troops, and the number of followers missing at the end of the march was less than forty, and many of these, being Afghans or Hazaras, had deserted. The troops had been thoroughly seasoned by the hardships they had undergone, and were, probably, unsurpassed as a marching body by any recorded in modern history. After a march of eight hours in the burning sun the men had to take their turn of duty at fetching fuel and forage, providing guards and doing sentry at night. But all was done without a murmur.

On his arrival at Khelat-i-Ghilzye Sir Frederick Roberts received a letter from General Primrose, giving particulars of the sortie of the 16th August, and sent messengers to Chaman, at the foot of the hills between Candahar and Pisheen, with letters to General Phayre, giving details of his march, and the probable time of arrival at Robat—at which point it was hoped that communication with the column marching from Quetta might be established with a view to a combined movement on Candahar.

The division halted at Khelat-i-Ghilzye on the 24th August, and on the following day continued the march, accompanied by the garrison of that fortress. Sir Frederick Roberts before leaving Cabul had received no instructions regarding the disposal of this outpost, but he considered it unadvisable to leave a garrison behind in this isolated position, with which for some time to come it would be difficult to keep open communications or furnish supplies. Further, the numerical weakness of the garrison did not permit of offensive action, while its safety might be a source of embarrassment in the forthcoming operations against the enemy. The fortress was accordingly evacuated and entrusted to Mahomed Sadik Khan, a Jokee Ghilzye chief, who had had possession of it when Sir Donald Stewart arrived there in January 1879. On the 25th August the column—now strengthened by the addition of the garrison of Khelat-i-Ghilzye, who were equipped with their own transport, and had supplies for ten days, besides reserves of meat, soup and vegetables—set its face towards Candahar, eighty-six miles distant, by the route which follows the valley of the Turnuk.

From ignorance of the intentions of Ayoob Khan and of

Illness of Sir Frederick Roberts.

the events which had happened at Candahar since the disastrous sortie of the 16th August, Sir Frederick Roberts was placed in a position of some perplexity. Besides the road to Candahar by the Turnuk valley, there are the parallel roads to the north and south of it, by the Urgundab and Urgustan Valleys; but these were impracticable for wheeled artillery, though it was possible that Ayoob—who had the assistance of a skilful soldier in Hafizoolah Khan, a trusted officer of Shere Ali's—in his anxiety to avoid an encounter with his renowned adversary, and gain possession of Ghuznee, might take one of these alternative routes. But unless Ayoob determined to abandon his Artillery—an unlikely contingency—it was certain he would adopt the route by the Turnuk Valley; and as apart from the relief of Candahar it was imperative that a crushing defeat should be inflicted on the vanquisher of a British force, so that the superiority of our arms might be acknowledged, Sir Frederick Roberts resolved to make a rapid march with his whole force by the Turnuk Valley to a point where heliographic communication might be established with Candahar and the movements of Ayoob ascertained.

At this time Sir Frederick Roberts was suffering from an attack of fever. At no period of his life possessing robust health, this depressing malady, induced by the fatigues of the daily march and the tropical rays of the sun, acting upon a frame debilitated by two years of arduous service, and further affected by the trying daily changes of temperature, it is not surprising that the attack assumed a somewhat severe form, and for some time his medical advisers entertained no slight anxiety on his account—an anxiety equally shared by every officer and man of the force, who felt that none even of the distinguished generals present with them could fill the place of their commander in the critical operations now imminent.

The march of the 25th August was to Jaldak, $15\frac{3}{4}$ miles, and, on the 26th, to Tirandaz, 16 miles. Here the General received a letter from Lieutenant-General Primrose, dated the previous day, which conveyed the intelligence that the rumour of the arrival of the Cabul-Candahar Force at Khelat-i-Ghilzye had caused Ayoob Khan to change his position. On the night of the 23rd that Sirdar had abandoned the villages to the east and west of Candahar, and, on the following day, he had struck his camp and moved to a position in the Urgundab Valley between Baba Wali and Mazra, due north of the city, thus practically abandoning the investment.

Sir Frederick Roberts resolved to send forward two regiments of Cavalry, under Brigadier-General Hugh Gough, to Robat, a distance of 34 miles, for the purpose of opening heliographic communication with General Primrose, and, if possible, with General Phayre, the remainder of his force being directed to move to a point about half-way to Robat.

At one o'clock in the afternoon of the 27th, on the arrival of the Cavalry at Robat, heliographic communication was established with Candahar, and flashed to Sir Frederick Roberts at the Infantry camp at Tirandaz, 39 miles from that city. During the afternoon General Gough, who was accompanied by Colonel Chapman, was met by Colonel St. John, Chief Political Officer at Candahar, and Major Adam, Assistant Quartermaster-General, escorted by two squadrons of Cavalry, and from the information supplied by these officers General Roberts was led to believe that Ayoob Khan was strengthening his position and intended to make a stand.

On the 27th August the infantry encamped at a point 39 miles from Candahar, whence the Urgundab Valley could be reached in two marches of seventeen miles each, by a road passing through the Bori Valley and emerging in the district of Dallah, above Candahar, upon the Urgundab river. Seven thousand men of all arms were held in readiness to proceed on the 28th August by this line, it being intended that if the movement was undertaken the two regiments of Cavalry thrown forward to Robat should cover the advance and strike the Urgundab some miles nearer to Candahar than the point where the Infantry would debouch. The baggage, field-hospitals, and non-effectives would, at the same time, have been advanced slowly towards Candahar, under an escort of 2,500 Infantry, two field-guns, and a regiment of Cavalry, with the view of occupying an entrenched position at or near Robat during the ensuing operations.*

---

* See lecture by Colonel Chapman.

On the morning of the 28th August the entire force was concentrated at Robat, where the General determined to halt for one day and divide the remaining distance to Candahar, 19 miles, into two short marches. Throughout the trying march now concluded, and the goal of which was almost within sight, the utmost good feeling and alacrity had been exhibited by the troops European and Native. Cheered by the example of their indefatigable leader, who, though suffering from an exhausting malady, never spared himself, but considered first their well-being and comfort, they responded heartily to the exacting calls on their powers of endurance. What these were may be gathered from the fact that this march was made under an August sun, from which the troops often had no shelter until 3 or 4 P.M., and the rear-guard at times were not in camp until evening, though the "rouse" during the latter part of the march was sounded at 1 A.M., and the march began at 2.30, when the cutting wind and low temperature scarcely gave promise of the burning sun that would a few hours later tax the energies and endurance of the hardiest.

CHAPTER XIX.

Arrival of the Cabul-Candahar Force at Robat—Letter from General Phayre—Sir Frederick Roberts's State of Health—Arrival before Candahar—Reconnoissance of the 31st August—Preparations for the Attack—Dispositions of the Army—The Advance on the Pir Paimal Position—Storming the Village of Gundi Mulla Sahibdad—Death of Colonel Brownlow—Capture of Pir Paimal—Brilliant Advance of Macpherson's and Baker's Brigades—Gallant Conduct of Major White—Incidents of the Fight—Capture of the Enemy's Camp at Mazra—Losses of the British—Results of the Victory—Sir Frederick Roberts Resigns his Command in Afghanistan.

It was satisfactory to Sir Frederick Roberts, no less than to the officers and men under his command, to know that though Ayoob Khan had abandoned the investment of the city, he had apparently no intention of retreating; for it would have been a source of bitter disappointment to these gallant men who had come so far and undergone so much had they been denied the compensation of a brilliant victory, to which they had looked forward. Little, however, could be gathered of the position and dispositions of the Afghan General, but as he evinced no intention to deprive his British antagonist of the opportunity of winning fresh laurels at his expense, Sir Frederick Roberts resolved to halt at Robat for a day in order to rest the men and animals, who were much fagged by their long and continuous forced marching.

During the halt on the 29th, the General received a letter from General Phayre, dated Killa Abdullah, the 24th August, stating that he hoped his division would be assembled there by the 28th, and that he would be able to march for Candahar on the 30th. The difficulties of moving troops in the usual state of unpreparedness, though forming a reserve division, through Scinde and the country between Sibi and Pisheen in the month of July, were not easily surmounted, though Sir Frederick Roberts in his advance from Ali Kheyl on Cabul showed what could be done by the exercise of boundless energy and an iron will. Feeling that General Phayre's answer precluded all hope of co-operation for many days, on the 30th August Sir Frederick Roberts moved to Momand, and on the following morning advanced a distance of twelve miles, two brigades of Infantry leading the advance, while the Cavalry covered the baggage on either flank, and the remaining infantry brigade formed a rear-guard to a point near the Shikarpore, or south, gate of the city. Thus was accomplished the march from Khelat-i-Ghilzye to Candahar, a distance of eighty-eight miles, in seven days, including the halt at Robat.

After the troops had breakfasted, at 10 A.M. on the 31st August, the 1st and 3rd Brigades of Infantry, under Brigadier-Generals Macpherson and Macgregor, moved off from under the city walls, and occupied a position stretching from the range of hills immediately above the old city of Candahar, through Kareez hill to Picket hill, an eminence commanding the former cantonment, whence the enemy could be observed in occupation of the Baba Wali Pass. The day was intensely hot, and the trees and gardens afforded little shelter from the rays of a tropical sun, while Ayoob Khan had cut off the water which is brought from the Urgundab. Sir Frederick Roberts, who had not recovered from his attack of fever, was carried in a doolie, but mounted his horse on approaching the city.*

---

* The *Times* correspondent, an Indian soldier of high reputation and great military experience, writing from Robat, says of Sir Frederick Roberts :—" Let me once more place upon record my belief that in General Roberts the British army has a general of whom it may well be proud, and on whom it may confidently rely, come what may. While full of enterprise and adventure, he is prudent and calculating, and when once his mind is made up his resolution is carried almost to the verge of obstinacy. More than this, he possesses the affection and full confidence of all officers and soldiers serving under him. How he has made himself master of the former will be readily understood by those who know his constant thought for the soldiers' comfort and welfare, and have marked the patience and self-denial with which at the end of the longest and hottest march, and with a thousand matters pressing on his attention, he will ride back for miles to meet and cheer, by the announcement that camp is near, the weary and struggling soldiers. The troops retained their full confidence in General Roberts during the somewhat depressing events of last December, and they have now the conviction that he is about to lead them to victory, and to compensate them for all the sacrifices he is at present calling upon them to make. In this conviction I fully share, and only trust that Ayoob will, as he is now reported to mean to do, meet this splendid force in fair fight."

A brief survey of the ground resolved him to take up a position west of Candahar, with his right on the cantonments and his left touching Old Candahar, as such a position covered the city, and not only placed him within striking distance of Ayoob Khan's camp, but afforded an ample supply of good water to his troops. The movement was effected without opposition, the 2nd Brigade, under Brigadier-General Baker, and the Cavalry, under Brigadier-General Hugh Gough, remaining for the present on baggage and rear-guards. Sir Frederick Roberts says he came to the conclusion, from a cursory examination of the ground made on his arrival in the morning, that any attempt to carry the Baba Wali Kotul by a direct attack would be attended with very serious loss. He therefore determined to turn it; but in order to decide how this operation could best be effected, it was necessary to ascertain the strength and precise extent of the positions occupied by Ayoob Khan, who had posted his troops to the north-west of the city, between it and the river Urgundab. Sir Frederick, accordingly, ordered a small column, consisting of two guns No. 11 Battery, 9th Brigade, R.A., 3rd Bengal Cavalry, and 15th Sikhs, to proceed to reconnoitre, under the command of Brigadier-General Hugh Gough, accompanied by Colonel Chapman, Chief of the Staff, who possessed complete knowledge of the locality, acquired when acting in the same capacity under Sir Donald Stewart.

The reconnoitring column started at 1 P.M. from the British left, near Old Candahar, and General Gough, halting the guns and infantry on some high ground above the village of Gundigan, moved forward with the cavalry for about a mile and a half, avoiding the numerous orchards and enclosures, and came out within a mile of Pir Paimal, where the enemy were found strongly entrenched. Having drawn the fire of their guns along this line, the 3rd Bengal Cavalry fell back, admirably handled by Lieutenant-Colonel Mackenzie, and two companies of infantry, thrown forward to cover this withdrawal, became engaged with the enemy's skirmishers, while the mountain guns were brought into action at a range of about 1,800 yards from the enemy's artillery in front of Pir Paimal. The Afghans advanced rapidly into the orchards in front of Gundigan, and as soon as the cavalry had passed in rear of the line, the guns were withdrawn towards the line of pickets under escort of the two companies, while the remaining six companies of the 15th Sikhs, under Lieutenant-Colonel Hennessy, held the Gundigan Hill. The enemy in large numbers occupied the ground just vacated, and took possession of the village itself, and endeavoured so persistently to follow up the reconnoitring column that the 3rd Brigade and part of the 1st were placed under arms, and about sunset firing was taken up along the whole line. Fortunately, says Colonel Chapman, the shooting of the Afghans was very bad, only ten casualties being reported.

It was evident that a hot day's work was in store for the Cabul-Candahar Field Force, as the enemy, unused to European methods of warfare, regarded the retirement as an indication of timidity or defeat. As a matter of fact, the object of the reconnoissance was attained in unmasking the Afghan position, which was so close to that occupied by the British force that Sir Frederick Roberts resolved upon action on the morrow. Having matured his plan of attack* on the Afghan position during the afternoon, at 8 P.M. he ordered his Divisional and Brigade Commanders, with their staffs, and the officers next in rank in the Brigades, to assemble at his head-quarters in camp at 6 A.M. on the following morning; and by means of a field telegraph line laid down between this point and the city, he requested the presence of Lieutenant-General Primrose, commanding the Candahar garrison, who had been directed by the Indian Government to act in subordination to him. At the same time orders were issued for the troops to breakfast at 7 A.M., and for one day's cooked rations to be carried by all

---

* The orders for the attack next morning were as follows:—The troops to be formed up as under at 8 A.M.—"First Brigade behind Picket Hill; second Brigade behind Khareez Hill; third Brigade in front of its own camp; Cavalry Brigade, together with E Battery, R.H.A., two companies of British and four of Native Infantry, to assemble in rear of Gundigan at 9 A.M. C Battery, 2nd Brigade, R.A., No. 5 Battery, 4th Brigade, R.A. (heavy battery), four companies British, and two regiments Native Infantry, all to be detailed from the Candahar garrison, together with the Bombay Cavalry Brigade, to assemble at the old cavalry lines north-east of the cantonments by 8 A.M., to threaten the Baba Wali Pass and watch the Murcha Pass. The heavy battery to open fire on the former pass at 9 A.M. The second reserve of infantry ammunition to take post near the house occupied as head-quarters."

ranks. Tents were to be struck and, with the kits, to be stored in a walled enclosure, and the troops were to be under arms by 8 A.M. on the morning of the 1st September.

The Lieutenant-General personally explained to the officers commanding divisions and brigades his plan of attack, which was, briefly, to threaten the enemy's left on the Baba Wali Kotul and attack in force by the village of Pir Paimal. The following was the distribution of the troops. The Infantry Division Cabul Field Force, on whom devolved the duty of carrying the enemy's position, was formed up in rear of Picket and Kareez Hills, and in prolongation to the left as far as Chilzina, immediately below the range which covers Old Candahar. The 1st and 2nd Brigades—the former with C Battery, 2nd Brigade, R.A., of the Candahar Force attached, in addition to No. 6 Battery, 8th Brigade, armed with the new pattern jointed guns—forming the column of attack, were massed, the former behind Picket Hill and the latter behind Kareez Hill. The 3rd Brigade, forming the reserve, was assembled in front of its camp and extended to the left of the main column. The Cavalry Brigade, with E Battery, B Brigade, R.H.A. (four guns), two companies 7th Fusiliers, and four companies of the 28th Bombay Native Infantry, carrying two days' cooked rations from the Candahar force, was formed at 9 A.M. in rear of Gundigan, under Brigadier-General Hugh Gough, who was directed, in the event of his finding his front clear, to push forward the infantry and guns to occupy the position above Gundigan, the Cavalry being advanced to the bed of the Urgundab, in order to cut off the enemy's line of retreat to Girishk, and threaten that which led to Kakreez.

The Candahar garrison, under the orders of Lieutenant-General Primrose, C.S.I., were directed to provide sufficient guards for the city gates, and Brigadier-General Daubeny's Brigade was to hold the ground from which the Cabul force would advance to the attack, while the remainder of Brigadier-General Burrows's Brigade, with four 40-pounders attached, took up a position to the north of the old Cantonment, under shelter of some high ground actually in the enemy's possession, from which point the guns were to shell the Baba Wali Pass, and cover the main design in the attack. The Bombay Cavalry,

Dispositions for Attack.

under Brigadier-General Nuttall, were ordered to move to the right and cover the approach to the city from the Murcha Pass, the extreme left of the enemy's position.*

The enemy displayed such confidence, generated by their assumed success of the previous day, that very early in the morning of the 1st September, they took the offensive by occupying the village of Gundigan, and, consequently, the movement of General Gough's Cavalry was delayed until the main attack by the Infantry on the right should be developed. The enemy also held in strength the village of Gundi Mulla Sahibdad, some 1,500 yards in advance of the British line, forming a very strong defensive position, and their skirmishers along the front through the orchards and gardens connecting this village with Gundigan, covered the movement of the main body advancing from Pir Paimal to the front. On the left of this position, the Baba Wali Pass, where they expected the chief attack, was crowded with Ghazis, the Cavalry occupying the low ground in advance. The battle about to be waged was full of momentous consequences alike to the Afghans and to the conquerors of Hindostan, but there was no doubt in the minds of the latter as to the result of the day. As Byron writes of Suwarrow's Army before the assault of Ismail:—

> "All was prepared—the fire, the sword, the men
> To wield them in their terrible array.
> The army, like a lion from his den,
> March'd forth with nerve and sinews bent to slay."

Ayoob Khan commenced the operations of the day by a desultory fire from the orchards in front of the villages in his occupation, but no reply was made until about 9.30, when the 40-pounders opened against the Baba Wali Pass, which was the signal for the advance on the enemy's position at Pir Paimal. Accordingly, the 1st Brigade,† led by Brigadier-General Macpherson, moved to attack the village of Gundi Mulla Sahibdad, under cover of the two batteries of Royal Artillery, while the 2nd Brigade,‡ under Brigadier-General

---

* See lecture at Royal United Service Institution by Colonel Chapman, R.A.

† 92nd Highlanders, 2nd Goorkhas, 23rd Pioneers, 24th Punjaub Native Infantry, 6-8 R.A. (attached), C-2 R.A. (attached).

‡ 72nd Highlanders, 2nd Sikhs, 3rd Sikhs, 5th Goorkhas.

Baker, extended in support to the left, keeping touch with the 1st Brigade, and clearing the orchards and gardens in their immediate front. The 3rd Brigade was at the same time formed in support in advance of the village of Abasabad, with the double object of being a reserve to the other brigades of the division, and meeting a possible counter-attack by the enemy from the Baba Wali Pass. To the 2nd Goorkhas, Lieutenant-Colonel Battye,* and 92nd Highlanders, Lieutenant-Colonel Parker, forming the leading regiments of the 1st Brigade, was entrusted the honour of the advance, and gallantly they performed their duty.

The village of Gundi Mulla Sahibdad was carried in dashing style at the point of the bayonet, the Goorkhas and Highlanders, who entered at opposite sides, vieing in honourable rivalry. The enemy withdrew leisurely, though a considerable number remained within the buildings and stone walls of the village, where they met their fate at the point of the bayonet. The Ghazis here, as throughout the war, proved themselves the backbone of the defence, and offered a desperate but unavailing resistance.

Meanwhile General Baker, with the 2nd Brigade, was hotly engaged, the 72nd Highlanders, under Lieutenant-Colonel Brownlow—whose hours on earth were almost numbered—and the 2nd Sikhs, under Lieutenant-Colonel Boswell, being in the front line. Threading their way through the lanes and walled enclosures which lay in the line of attack these gallant regiments pushed on in spite of a most determined resistance from the enemy, who were sheltered behind high loopholed walls.

It was in clearing these enclosures that Colonel Brownlow and Captain Frome met their deaths. In Colonel Brownlow the Army and country sustained a severe loss, as his professional attainments promised a distinguished career. By no one of the Cabul Field Force was he more sincerely mourned than by Sir Frederick Roberts, who had learned to appreciate his high military qualities from the day he assisted at the capture of the

---

* This officer was one of nine brothers who served in the Indian Army, one of whom fell at Delhi and a second in a cavalry charge during this Afghan war at Futtehabad, near Jellalabad. His father also was one of six soldier brothers.

Peiwar Kotul. But "to every man upon this earth death cometh soon or late," and to a soldier of the temperament and impetuous valour of Colonel Brownlow, the last enemy could not have presented himself in more welcome guise, for in the words Tacitus applied to Agricola, "he was happy in the occasion of his death."

Sir Frederick Roberts wrote of Colonel Brownlow :—"In him the Army has experienced a great loss. He had on many occasions highly distinguished himself as a leader,—at the Peiwar Kotul, during the operations around Cabul at the latter end of 1879, and, notably on the 14th December, when he won the admiration of the whole force by his brilliant conduct in the attack and capture of the Asmai Heights."

Equally with the Highlanders, the 2nd Sikhs distinguished themselves, and on one occasion they repulsed with fixed bayonets the charge of the enemy.

The Highlanders, now led by Major Stockwell, an officer who has recently added to his reputation by his services in Egypt, after a severe struggle dislodged the enemy; and a portion of the regiment, with the 5th Goorkhas, the latter led by Lieutenant-Colonel Fitzhugh, finally compelled the enemy to withdraw his right at Gundigan towards Pir Paimal, and the 1st and 2nd Brigades pushed on rapidly, almost without a pause. Turning the shoulder of the hill above Pir Paimal, the 1st Brigade came under a heavy fire, and a stout resistance was offered in the village itself; but the 92nd and 2nd Goorkhas were not to be denied, and the village was carried at 12.15 P.M., the 2nd Brigade being at this time clear of the village and so far advanced as to be obliged to delay until Pir Paimal was captured.

Meanwhile Sir Frederick Roberts—fearing an attack by Ayoob Khan on the rear of the British position, large numbers of his troops having descended the Baba Wali Pass and occupied some low hills to the right front of General Burrows's Brigade—before moving up the 3rd Brigade to the support of the others, sent to General Burrows to ask if he was prepared, after the success that had been achieved, to hold his own unsupported. The answer received was in the affirmative, on which he issued orders to Brigadier-General Macgregor to advance towards Pir Paimal. General Roberts himself proceeded to join General Ross at Paimal, and found that his leading brigades had pushed on without halt, and were then at least one mile beyond that point. A message from the front explained that after the village of Paimal had been taken, the enemy was still so active and menacing, and kept up such a heavy fire upon the troops, that General Macpherson had obtained General Ross's permission to continue the advance without pause, the 2nd Brigade assisting, in order to drive the enemy, before he had time to rally, out of the enclosed gardens, with which the ground beyond Paimal was covered.

The same order of attack was preserved, the 92nd Highlanders and Goorkhas leading on the right, close under the hill, the 2nd Brigade being a little behind on the left. On reaching the open ground beyond the village, the troops found themselves exposed to a heavy fire from some guns and a large body of the enemy, who had taken up a position in an entrenchment to the south-west of the Baba Wali Kotul, commanding an open piece of ground. This entrenchment they were evidently prepared to hold with their usual determination; reinforcements were being rapidly pushed up from their reserves, while the guns on the Baba Wali Kotul were turned round so as to increase the heavy fire of artillery which was brought to bear upon our troops. It became necessary to take this position at once by storm, and recognizing this with true soldierly instinct, Major G. S. White, who was leading the advance companies of 92nd Highlanders, called upon his men for just one charge more "to close the business." The battery of screw-guns, under Brevet-Major J. C. Robinson, had been shelling the enemy with a well-directed fire, under cover of which, and supported by a portion of the 2nd Goorkhas and the 23rd Pioneers, the Highlanders responded with alacrity to their leader's call, and, dashing forward, drove the enemy from their entrenchments at the point of the bayonet. "The gallant and ever foremost Major White," as Sir Frederick Roberts calls him, was the first man to reach the enemy's guns, being closely followed by a soldier of the Goorkhas, who, placing his rifle

Complete Defeat of the Enemy.

upon one of the guns, exclaimed that it was captured in the name of the 2nd (Prince of Wales's Own) Goorkhas.*

After passing the village of Pir Paimal, Brigadier-General Baker had directed a detachment of the 3rd Sikhs, under Lieutenant-Colonel Money, of Shutargardan fame, to take possession of the point of the detached hill in rear of the enemy's right. Finding himself commanded by a further spur, Colonel Money pushed on by the northern side of this hill and made himself master of four guns, obtaining a full view of the enemy's camp, then full of men, and with a line of cavalry drawn up in rear. Before the Mountain Battery attached to this brigade could be brought up, the advance of the troops from the other side of the hill put all these men into motion, and, in the absence of Cavalry, their retreat could not be intercepted.

The enemy was now completely routed; but this, owing to the nature of the ground, it was impossible for General Ross to realize. Expecting, therefore, that they would take up a fresh position further on, he ordered the 1st and 2nd Brigades to halt and replenish their ammunition. When this had been done, the troops continued their advance about one mile, the 2nd Brigade leading, and at 1 P.M. they entered the enemy's camp, which was found to be deserted, with tents standing apparently as it had been left in the morning, when the Afghans moved to the attack. Ayoob Khan lost during the day all his Artillery, numbering thirty-two pieces, including five in position at the Baba Wali Kotul, and the two guns of E Battery, Royal Horse Artillery, which he had captured at Maiwand on the 27th July. The body of Lieutenant Maclaine, of this battery, who had been carried off a prisoner from Maiwand, was found lying outside his tent, which was close to that of Ayoob, his guard having murdered him before retreating.

Sir Frederick Roberts, when he found how complete had been the success of his Infantry, ordered Brigadier-General Nuttall to proceed with the Bombay Cavalry Brigade, which had formed part of General Burrows's command opposite the Baba Wali Pass, in pursuit through the village of Mazra up the Urgundáb

---

* See Sir Frederick Roberts's despatch.

Valley; the result, however, was disappointing. The cavalry of the Cabul-Candahar Force continued the pursuit throughout the day, the brigade crossing the Urgundâb and pushing beyond the line of the enemy's retreat towards Kakreez. None of the Afghan regular troops were encountered, but some 350 of the fugitive Ghazis and Irregulars were killed.

Scarcely less to be mourned than the loss of Colonel Brownlow was the death of another officer who had rendered great service throughout the campaign. Shortly before the final advance, Major-General Ross, wishing to heliograph to Sir Frederick Roberts his success in turning the enemy's position, directed Captain Straton,* Superintendent of Army Signalling, to proceed with a company of the 24th Punjaub Native Infantry to the Baba Wali Kotul. This gallant officer had only gone a short distance when a Ghazi, springing out of a ravine close to him, shot him dead.

It was a proud moment for Sir Frederick Roberts when he entered the camp of Ayoob Khan. He was still suffering from fever induced by the fatigues and anxieties of the march, but his high spirit had kept him up throughout a day, memorable in his career and in the history of the British Army, as that on which the cloud hanging over the military fame of England was dispersed by the sun of victory. After a brief rest in Ayoob's camp, the General rode to the different assembled regiments in succession, beginning with the 92nd Highlanders, and thanked and praised them for the great success they had achieved. "The cheers," says an officer who was present, "with which he was received by each regiment, British and Native, in succession, will never be forgotten by those who heard them, and show the respect and confidence in which he is held. The resolution he showed in accomplishing the weary march from Cabul to Candahar in twenty days, with an army so large and so completely equipped, was fitly crowned by a

---

* "In Captain Straton," says Sir Frederick Roberts, "Her Majesty's Service has lost a most accomplished, intelligent officer, under whose management army signalling, as applied to field service, reached a pitch of perfection probably never before attained. His energy knew no difficulties, and his enthusiasm was beyond praise. He had won the highest opinions from all with whom his duties had brought him in contact, and his death was very deeply felt throughout the whole force."

victory so complete as to leave scarcely anything to be desired, and which completely effaced, so far as a victory can, the disasters which preceded it. His feelings on the evening of the 1st of September must, indeed, have been truly enviable, and his good fortune gratifies every one."

The defeat inflicted on Sirdar Ayoob Khan was crushing and decisive, and he fled towards Herat with only a handful of horsemen and a small party of infantry, the remains of a force of 4,000 regular infantry, 5,000 Ghazis, 800 regular and 3,000 irregular cavalry. His horses were estimated at over 1,000 in killed alone. The British loss during the action and the reconnoissance of the 31st August, was 40 killed, including 3 officers,* and 228 wounded, including 11 officers. Of this total the greatest sufferers were the 92nd Highlanders, with 84 casualties. The 72nd Highlanders had 33; the 2nd Goorkhas 33; and the 2nd Sikhs 29 casualties.

By this brilliant victory Sir Frederick Roberts completely restored the prestige of British arms; and so great was the effect produced that no further military operations were necessary, and not a shot was fired during the remainder of the British occupation of Candahar.†

Sir Frederick Roberts was not less fortunate in the soldiers he commanded than they were in their leader. The native troops were the *élite* of the Indian Army, and the three regiments of British Infantry worthily represented their country:—

> "Types of a race who shall the invader scorn,
> As rocks resist the billows round their shore."

To the quality of the officers and men of the Cabul-Candahar Field Force he only does justice when he says:—" The rapidity with which the march was accomplished—taking into consideration the strength of the force, the variations of climate, and the difficult nature of the country traversed—is the best testimony I

---

* During the Afghan War the total loss of British officers killed, or died of wounds, was seventy-four.

† Ayoob Khan displayed all the tenacity of purpose of his race, and after the departure of the British army, contested the sovereignty with the Ameer Abdul Rahman. He defeated his generals near Candahar on the 27th July, 1881, but himself suffered a crushing reverse on the 22nd September following.

can produce to the efficiency, discipline, and spirit of the troops. Their conduct, under circumstances often of the most testing nature, cannot be expressed in terms too strong or too full. They all seemed to be animated with but one desire—that, cost what it might in personal risk, fatigue, or discomfort, they would effect the speedy release of their beleagured fellow-soldiers in the city of Candahar. The unflagging energy and perseverance of the troops seemed to reach the full height when they knew they were about to put forth their irresistible strength against a hitherto successful enemy. Notwithstanding the provocation caused by the cruel murder of any stragglers (soldiers as well as followers) who fell into the hands of the Afghans following in the wake of our column, not one act infringing the rules of civilized warfare was committed by our troops. The persons and property of the natives were respected, and full compensation for supplies was everywhere given. In short, the inhabitants of the districts we passed through could not have been treated with greater consideration nor with a lighter hand, and the conduct of the troops will ever remain as memorable as the results which they achieved."

The most enthusiastic admirers of the march of Sir Frederick Roberts's "Ten Thousand" are the phlegmatic German strategists, who aver that it is the finest performance of any British General since Waterloo. Be this as it may, it bears some analogy to the celebrated "Retreat of the Ten Thousand" under Xenophon, due not alone to the similarity in numbers. The defeat at Cunaxa led to the latter, and the disaster at Maiwand brought about Roberts's advance through an enemy's country. Both commanders displayed some of the highest attributes of generalship on the line of march as on the field of battle, and the high state of discipline and valour of the troops was certainly no less in the British than in the Greek "ten thousand." Both marches alike afford a valuable lesson to the student of the art of war, and to complete the parallel, it only remains for the modern General to give to the world a narrative equal in soldierly conciseness to the celebrated treatise of the classic commander.

Sir Frederick Roberts had suffered considerably in health by his recent exertions and the long service in Afghanistan, of which country and its inhabitants his experience is unequalled by that of any British General. No event of importance occurred during his stay at Candahar, and he was glad to resign the command into the hands of General Phayre, and, in October, quitted Afghanistan on sick leave,* having been the central figure in a series of events possessing surpassing interest to the patriotic Englishman.

The names of some of the greatest conquerors of the world are associated with that country of mountain and desert. Alexander marched from end to end of it; and his mighty name, after the lapse of twenty centuries, is as well known in Afghanistan as that of its present ruler. The country gave to the world the only less famous Mahmoud of Ghuznee, who many times poured his armies upon Hindostan and showed future conquerors how its plains might be overrun. During the eight centuries succeeding the time of Mahmoud the unwarlike people and rich cities of India have been the prey of the warriors of Central Asia; and in comparatively recent times, Nadir Shah and Ahmed Khan have penetrated through the passes traversed by Alexander and Mahmoud—the one to Delhi and the other to Lahore. Even so late as the time of Lord Wellesley's rule, a tremor of apprehension at the Afghan name was felt in Calcutta, and Shah Zemaun, who died a blind pensioner of the British at Loodiana, might have boasted with the Roman General, "I fluttered your Volsces in Corioli."

Our experience of Afghanistan has been of a varied character; and, indeed, the country may be said to be the grave of many military reputations. The names of Elphinstone and Shelton call up memories other than glorious to British arms, and the only consolatory feature in a retrospect of the disasters associated with their names is, that every Englishman displayed personal gallantry under trying circumstances. Equally has the name, Afghanistan, been associated in our annals with glorious memories of honour retrieved and defeat wiped out by victory. Nott, Sale, and Pollock—the last, a brother officer of Roberts,

---

* In the official notification of leave Sir Frederick Roberts is described as proceeding to the port of embarkation for thirty days from date of availing himself of it, and thence to England for twelve months from date of embarkation on medical certificate.

reposes in Westminster Abbey—are names which Englishmen must ever hold in respect as those of soldiers who restored our prestige—that impalpable, but essential, attribute of our sovereignty in the East, without which our tenure of India would be quickly challenged by our subject races. To these great names those of Roberts and Stewart must hereafter be added—the march of the latter being in the footsteps of Nott, and his victory at Ahmed Khel one of which any soldier might be proud. Roberts's victory at Charasia and dispersal of Mahomed Jan's forces at Sherpur, may likewise be likened to Pollock's action at Tezeen and Sale's defeat of Akbar Khan at Jellalabad; though the achievements of the subject of this Memoir were more remarkable, as, at Charasia, he was opposed by regular troops, and not tribesmen alone, and, at Cabul, 100,000 men beleagured the British cantonments, while Akbar Khan led only 8,000 followers against Sale's compact brigade of 1,800 men. But the forced march from Cabul to Candahar, with the swiftly following reconnoissance and victory of the 1st September, remain without parallel in the record of our relations with Afghanistan, and place the name of Roberts first among the soldiers who have led the British armies in that region.

CHAPTER XX.

Sir Frederick Roberts quits Afghanistan—The Question of the Retention of Candahar—Sir Frederick Roberts Arrives in England—His Reception by his Countrymen—Rewards conferred on Sir Frederick Roberts— Precedents in the Case of Rewards for Military Services—His Speech at the Mansion House—Changes in Army Reform due to Sir Frederick Roberts's Criticisms—He is appointed to the Command of the Army sent to Coerce the Boers—Departure for and Return from South Africa —Sir Frederick Roberts attends the German Autumn Manœuvres—His Comments on the German Army and Military System—Sir Frederick Roberts is appointed Commander-in-Chief of the Madras Army—He leaves England for India—Conclusion.

SIR FREDERICK ROBERTS left Candahar on the 9th September, with a portion of his division, and marched to Quetta, where he remained until the 12th October. Thence he proceeded to Sibi, the terminus of the railway projected to Candahar, where he resigned his command on the 15th October and went to Simla. Here he spent a few days as the guest of the Marquis of Ripon,* and journeying thence to Bombay, embarked on the 30th October for England.

---

* The Viceroy wrote of Sir Frederick Roberts's services in the following terms:—" Sir Frederick Roberts has achieved what the Commander-in-Chief in India justly describes as one of the most complete and successful operations of recent times. The Government of India appreciates the foresight which governed the preparation of the force at Cabul, the energy which conducted it to Candahar, and the skill through which its operations were fitly crowned by the total defeat of the enemy against whom its movements had from the first been directed. These operations, in their inception and their execution, will remain an enduring record, no less of the courage and devotion of the troops than of the skill of the officers on whose services the Queen-Empress can rely for the security and honour of her Indian Empire. The high, soldierly spirit which animated this force throughout its ranks, had been conspicuous in every arm of the Service during all the operations of the war in Northern Afghanistan and on Sir Donald Stewart's march from Candahar, and formed the ample justification of the Government of India in sanctioning an enterprise that could not have been prudently entrusted to a leader less able or to troops less efficient than Sir Frederick Roberts and the soldiers so worthy of his leading. Even had the march thus undertaken and carried out served merely to raise the investment of Candahar, it would have been a military achievement of which any country

The two years' war with Afghanistan, in which Sir Frederick Roberts played so conspicuous a part, and in which twenty millions of treasure were expended and many valuable lives were lost, has been absolutely destitute of material results. At its conclusion the British Government surrendered the "scientific frontier," the possession of which Lord Beaconsfield vaunted in his memorable speech at the Mansion House on the 5th August, 1879, as having been "achieved with a rapidity and a precision of execution which cannot easily be paralleled in the annals of war;" though a painful commentary was supplied to this description by the massacre of the Cavagnari Mission on the 3rd of the following month. In this retirement within our former frontier, as regards the Khyber and Kurram lines, not only Sir Edward Hamley, who possesses too profound a knowledge of the principles of strategy to be under any delusion as to the true value of the "scientific frontier," but Sir Frederick Roberts and Sir Donald Stewart, also, assented. The former says in his exhaustive and masterly memorandum,* dated Cabul, 29th May, 1880:—"My own opinion is that the Kurram should be given up altogether, and that the responsibilities which we ought to incur in the Khyber route should be limited to such as would ensure the execution and integrity of any guarantees we have given to the rulers of Lalpura and Kuner." If political necessity required that we should control the Khyber, he recommended the employment of Hazara or Afreedee levies, and strongly deprecated the employment of any regular troops beyond Peshawur; and speaking from five years' experience of the unhealthiness of that station, he advocated the withdrawal of the greater portion of its garrison to the left bank of the Indus, somewhere near Campbellpore. Sir Donald Stewart expressed his agreement with Sir Frederick Roberts, both as regards the abandonment of the Khyber and Kurram lines and the removal of the garrison of Peshawur to a

---

might be proud. All the more, therefore, is Lieutenant-General Sir Frederick Roberts to be congratulated on the opportunity afforded him of showing, in the defeat of Ayoob Khan, that the enterprise and endurance of himself and his troops were perfected by a consummate skill and devoted gallantry, adequate not merely to the battle of Candahar, but to any eventuality of war which they might be called on to meet."

* See also *ante*, pp. 332-333, and 338.

healthier position on the eastern side of the Indus, with the exception of a small force established in an entrenched position to cover the railway terminus.

But Sir Frederick Roberts—while proposing to make over Kurram and Khost to native chiefs, and withdraw from the Khyber, except in so far as our presence was necessary to fulfil our engagement to the Mohmund Chief of Lalpura, and Syud Badshah of Kuner, thus, as he expresses it, "refusing our right," and "remaining merely on the defensive on our north-west frontier"—strongly advocated the military occupation of Candahar. "We have," he says, "neither sufficient men nor material to warrant our operating on more than one line," and his experience taught him that the army of 25,000 men found necessary, in May, 1880, to maintain on the Khyber line alone, would have to be considerably increased if the ruler of Cabul should be assisted by Russian officers. As a result of the shattering of the military power of the Ameer Shere Ali, he adds, "We have nothing to fear from Afghanistan, and the best thing to do is to leave it as much as possible to itself. It may not be very flattering to our *amour propre*, but I feel sure I am right when I say that the less the Afghans see of us the less they will dislike us. Should Russia in future years attempt to conquer Afghanistan or invade India through it, we should have a better chance of attaching the Afghans to our interest if we avoid all interference with them in the meantime. The military occupation of Candahar is, as I have before stated, of vital importance; even there we should make our presence but little felt, merely controlling the foreign policy of the rulers of that province."

But on entering Afghanistan we had expressed our intention of refraining from annexing Candahar, and a departure from our word, even to the limited extent of a military occupation, would have inflicted far greater injury on our prestige than was involved in the evacuation of that city. Moreover, holding Candahar demanded as a military necessity the garrisoning of Khelat-i-Ghilzye to the east, and Giriskh, on the Helmund, to the west, if not of Herat itself; while by concentrating at Pisheen, the passes to Chaman and the open country thence to Candahar, only a distance of eighty miles, lay at our mercy.

This, indeed, was conceded by Lord Lytton,* who wrote before entering on hostilities:—"It is true that the recent occupation of Quetta has materially improved our position. The command of the southern passes is now in our hands; and from Multan to the sea, a distance of 500 miles, our frontier is well guarded. While we, securely established at Quetta, can at any moment descend on the plains of Candahar, or advance to meet our adversary in the open field, no enemy can debouch on our plains without first besieging and taking Quetta—a task of no slight difficulty, and involving much loss of precious time—and then forcing a long and difficult pass held by us. But on the northern, or more directly exposed, portions of our frontier, our line is as fatally defective as ever." But regarding this northern frontier military opinion is now almost unanimous against occupying the Khyber and Kurram passes, and only on the retention of Candahar is there a serious divergence. This question—though decided contrary to the views held by the majority of professional opinion, including Lord Napier of Magdala, Sir Henry Rawlinson, Sir Frederick Roberts, Sir Edward Hamley (who lectured on the subject at the Royal United Service Institution), and Sir Donald Stewart, though in his minute, dated "Candahar, April 18th, 1879," that officer strongly combated the retention of the capital of Western Afghanistan—has more than an academic interest, for any movement of Russia on Herat, or the precipitation of a conflict with that power in Central Asia, would immediately bring it into prominence, and renew the clamour for its adop-

---

* See Lord Lytton's minute, dated Simla, 9th September, 1878, which appears in the Afghan Blue Book No. 2 of 1881. In this minute, Lord Lytton sketched a magnificent scheme of Imperial extension, from the Pamir to Herat, 360 miles from our present frontier. He says, "As a purely military line, the strongest frontier we could take up would be along the Hindu Kush from the Pamir to Bamian, holding the northern debouches of the principal passes; and thence southward by the Helmund, Giriskh, and Candahar to the Arabian Sea. Though political considerations of the moment may compel and justify an extension of our line to the Northern frontier of Afghanistan, this would weaken rather than strengthen our general position. But the political and strategical importance of Herat is so great that, though it lies beyond our natural frontier, it cannot be excluded from our line of defence. This line, therefore, should ultimately run from the Hindu Kush along the Paropamisus to Herat, and thence down the western frontier   Afghanistan and Beloochistan to the Arabian Sea."

tion. Lord Napier, in his able memorandum, advocating the annexation of Candahar, and the adjacent territory, considers the question of expense an immaterial one, though in point of fact it is of prime importance to a poor country like India. With an ignorance of the English people that would be astonishing were it not remembered that his lordship has passed his distinguished career exclusively in the East, he proposed that the taxpayers of this country should be called upon to pay half the cost of the military occupation of Candahar, which Sir Henry Norman places at £1,400,000, though other authorities estimate it at not less than two millions annually. As regards the dislike of the Native soldiery to serve in Afghanistan, regarding which Sir Frederick Roberts said that it had " affected recruiting," his lordship, with characteristic disregard for financial considerations, says, " Let the soldiers be sufficiently paid for the hardships and dangers of exile in Afghanistan, and there will be no danger of filling the ranks." Sir Henry Rawlinson's proposal that we should " continue our military occupation, but leave the civil administration in the hands of any governor whom Abdul Rahman may appoint," though an attempt to solve the political difficulty, would leave the financial problem untouched.

Authorities of no less weight than the preceding are opposed to the occupation of Candahar on political, military, and financial grounds. Among these are Lord Wolseley, Sir Henry Norman, Sir John Adye, Sir Archibald Alison, and General Charles Gordon* (" Chinese Gordon "); also statesmen of

---

* General Gordon's opinion, as that of a soldier of original genius and practical experience, is of special value. He writes to the *Times:* —" From a military point of view, by the retention we should increase the line we have to defend by twice the distance of Candahar to the present frontier, and place an objective point to be attacked. Naturally, we should make good roads to Candahar, which on the loss of a battle there—and such things must be always calculated as within possibility—would aid the advance of the enemy to the Indus. The debouches of the defiles, with good lateral communications between them, is the proper line of defence for India, not the entry into these defiles, which cannot have lateral communications. If the entries of the defiles are held, good roads are made through them; and these aid the enemy, if you lose the entries or have them turned. This does not prevent the passage of the defiles being disputed. The retention of Candahar would tend to foment rebellion in India, and not prevent it, for thereby we should obtain an additional number of fanatical malcontents,

frontier experience such as Sir Robert Montgomery and the late Lord Lawrence; while statesmen * and soldiers of a past age, as Sir Charles Napier and Sir James Outram, who knew Afghanistan and the Afghans well, were opposed to our going beyond the passes to encounter a Russian advance.

Sir James Outram's opinion of the unwisdom of advancing into Afghanistan to meet a Russian army, instead of waiting behind the mountain barriers given by nature to India as its strongest defence, though written in 1854, is still applicable. From Merv to the Indus is a distance of about 1,000 miles, throughout which, except in the vicinity of Herat and Candahar, supplies are limited. If Russia advanced with an army of only 50,000 men, she would eat up the supplies of Afghanistan and exasperate the people; "and no efforts of their chiefs," says Sir James Outram, "could then restrain them from acting as hostilely towards their *quondam* friends as heretofore they did against the British army. Ere Russian or Persian troops could reach Candahar or Cabul, we certainly should have authentic knowledge of their approach. It would then be time enough to enter upon defensive preparations. It is scarcely possible that less than one season would be required

---

who, as British subjects, would have the greatest facility for passing to and fro in India, which they would not have if we did not hold it. That our prestige would suffer in India by the evacuation, I doubt; it certainly would suffer if we kept it and forsook our word—*i.e.*, that we made war against Shere Ali, and not against his people. India should be able, by a proper defence of her present frontier, and by the proper government of her peoples, to look after herself. If the latter is wanting, no advance of frontier will aid her. I am not anxious about Russia, but were I so, I would care much more to see precautions taken for the defence of our Eastern colonies, now that Russia has moved her Black Sea Naval establishment to the China Sea, than to push forward an outstretched arm to Candahar. The interests of the Empire claim as much attention as India, and one cannot help seeing that they are much more imperilled by this last move of Russia than by anything she can do in Central Asia. Politically, militarily, and morally, Candahar ought not to be retained. It would oblige us to keep up an interference with the internal affairs of Afghanistan, and would increase the expenditure of impoverished India."

* Lord Wellesley wrote on 4th July, 1842, to Lord Ellenborough :— "Your Lordship, I'm satisfied, would reject Afghanistan and Cabul with the rocks, sand, deserts, ice, and snow, even if Shah Soojah had bequeathed them as a peace offering to England;" and his brother, the Duke of Wellington, with the strong common sense that distinguished him, wrote, on the 3rd September following, to the same correspondent, objecting to "discuss national disgrace, unburied bones, &c."

by the enemy to recruit in Afghanistan ere descending the passes; but allowing that a shorter halt would suffice, there still would be ample time to concentrate sufficient forces at Shikarpore and Peshawur to meet the enemy when he debouches from the Bolan or Khyber." If we were involved in hostilities with Russia or any other power, it would be impossible for this country, with its vast colonial possessions, to send any considerable force to India beyond that already maintained in that dependency. As Sir Henry Norman, arguing against the retention of Candahar, observes:—" Any great forward movement on our part would necessitate large European reinforcements, which England might not be able to send, while, if the defence was in the main confined to our old frontiers, large reinforcements might not be necessary."*

Lord Wolseley, whose opinions must carry great weight, in his memorandum dated 20th November, 1880, after invoking the lessons taught by the great Indian mutiny, when we were so hardly pressed that Lord Lawrence seriously considered the propriety of retiring from Peshawur, observes: " To occupy a point so far removed beyond our frontier would be a serious financial burden, even in times of profound peace, and in time of any great trial, its possession would indeed be a white elephant, capable of ruining our Indian Empire by the cost which the necessity of supporting it would entail upon us. In my humble opinion, the question of the retention of Candahar is not a military one, for I can see no possible strategical advantage in its present occupation. Its retention will certainly cripple our military resources, and it would seriously hamper our strategical operations in the event of any great internal disturbance in India. My opinions on this point are somewhat influenced by the conviction that if we determine to keep

---

* Colonel East, of the Intelligence Department of the War Office (see his Memorandum of August 16th, 1880, which was generally approved by Sir Archibald Alison), while arguing against the retention of Candahar, proposed the occupation of Kooshi, on the further side of the Shutargardan Pass, but no military authority of weight agreed with this recommendation. Sir Edward Hamley and his school, while advocating an advance for strategic reasons beyond the mountains, prefer the country towards Candahar, and, indeed, as the Shutargardan is impassable during the winter months, a force holding Kooshi would be cut off from assistance.

a garrison at Candahar, the annexation of the surrounding district and of the country between it and our frontier, would sooner or later be forced on us, and I feel that any such extension would be an increasing source of weakness to us. Our recent operations in Afghanistan have taught us the true value of Afghan military power. We can now afford to smile at the superstitious horror with which we have hitherto contemplated all idea of military operations in that country—a horror which has come down to us from the disasters of 1840. We have now learnt to appreciate the Afghan troops at their proper value, and to realise the fact that any well-appointed column of our troops, if ably commanded, can march from one end of the land to the other. The English people have begun to see that our military disaster in 1840, as, indeed, all the disasters that have ever befallen us, are the result of the incompetence of the commanders employed. There is no Afghan army that could prevent an English division from marching from Quetta to Candahar whenever it might become advisable to do so. If, therefore, we can at all times occupy Candahar when we wish, why go there until the necessity for doing so has arisen? Whenever the Russians march upon Herat we must certainly occupy Candahar, unless we intend to give up India or allow it to be taken from us; but the longer we can postpone that occupation the better we shall be able to incur the vast expenditure it will necessarily entail upon us. As we can always get there with the greatest ease, I would deprecate in the strongest terms our going there until the necessity for doing so actually arises, and I am therefore of opinion that the sooner the troops now there can be withdrawn from it with safety and honour, the better it will be for the true interests of our Indian Empire." A popular fallacy is involved in the assertion we hear so confidently made at political meetings by Conservative speakers, that the Liberal Government reversed the policy of their predecessors in withdrawing from Candahar. On this point the evidence of Sir Lepel Griffin, the agent selected by Lord Lytton to carry out Lord Beaconsfield's policy, is conclusive. He says—"While the Conservative Government were in power I was directed by the Viceroy to declare at Cabul, and repeatedly did so declare, that the British Government had no intention of occupying permanently or annexing Candahar, and our withdrawal was in direct accordance with the reiterated and solemn professions which I had been instructed to make, and the assurances of the Government of India to the chiefs and people of Cabul. We could not have remained without a breach of public faith. The Liberal Viceroy was quite prepared to support the man who had been proclaimed hereditary ruler of Candahar, and, in fact, did support him until he refused to hold the office any longer. The wisdom of the policy of retiring from Candahar may be a fair matter for argument, but it was one on which both Governments were agreed. I am convinced that withdrawal, after our public assurances, was the only practicable policy."

As that sagacious and cool-headed soldier-diplomatist, Sir Henry Durand, who served in Afghanistan, foretold in 1867, the Afghans were unable to offer effective resistance to a British invading force, while Russian action in 1878 proves that the apprehended interference of that power, under present conditions, with Afghan affairs, is a delusion, at least until the authority of the Czar is consolidated in Turkestan, and the enormous drain on his resources occasioned by the military occupation of the territories in Central Asia under his flag, calculated at not less than two millions annually, has ceased. The Russian frontier, from the Caspian to the Pamir, is about 1,200 miles long, 200 miles longer than our north-west frontier; of this, however, less than half is open to attack, as from the Caspian to Samarcand it is covered by the great Khivan desert. On the other hand the great defect in this line is its want of intercommunication, and its distance from support. While every part of our frontier is within 200 miles of railway communication, and most of it much nearer, Tashkend, the centre of Russian power in Turkestan, is more than 1,000 miles from the nearest railway; and many of the frontier posts are 1,500 miles distant from such support. The difficulties attending a military occupation under such conditions are necessarily great, and the entire force that Russia, with her vast military resources, can maintain in Turkestan does not exceed that which we maintain in the Punjaub alone. Lord Lytton, in his lengthy and ably written minute of the 4th September, 1878, referring to the defencelessness of the Russian possessions, expresses an opinion that it would be easier for us to collect 100,000 men at any point on our frontier than for Russia to collect 25,000 on hers. Skobeleff, that remarkable soldier whose premature death was a crushing blow to the Slavonic cause, declared that the difficulties of camel transport rendered an invasion of India impracticable, and the conqueror of Geok Tepe spoke from actual experience of Central Asiatic warfare. And yet we are periodically oppressed with a Russian scare, and called upon to believe in the imminence of a Russian invasion, to obviate the dangers of which we are required to occupy Candahar at an enormous cost. It is within the boundaries of India that exist the dangers against which we must guard—her vast feudatory armies, and the possible combination of her diverse nationalities welded, for the nonce, under the leadership of a great soldier, such as the East has produced, who has received a military training in some European army. The true policy that, in our opinion, should guide our councils in India, was stated in eloquent and forcible terms by Lord Lawrence, on the 4th January, 1879 :—" We foresee no limits to the expenditure which such a move (*i.e.*, a permanent advance of the frontier) might require, and we protest against the necessity of having to impose additional taxation on the people of India, who are unwilling as it is to bear such pressure for measures which they can both understand and appreciate. And we think that the objects which we have at heart, in common with all interested in India, may be attained by an attitude of readiness and firmness on our frontiers, and by giving all our care and expending all our resources for the attainment of practical and sound ends over which we can exercise an effective and immediate control. Should a foreign power, such as Russia, ever seriously think of invading India from without, or what is more probable of stirring up the elements of disaffection or anarchy within it, our true policy, or strongest security, would then, we conceive, be found to lie in previous abstinence from entanglements at either Cabul, Candahar, or any similar outpost, in full reliance on a compact, highly-equipped, and disciplined army stationed within our own territories, or on our own border; in the contentment, if not in the attachment of the masses, in the sense of security of title and possession with which our whole policy is gradually imbuing the minds of the principal chiefs and the native aristocracy, in the construction of material works within British India, which enhance the comfort of the people, while they add to our political and military strength, in husbanding our finances and consolidating and multiplying our resources, in quiet preparation for all contingencies, which no Indian statesman should disregard, and in a trust in the rectitude and honesty of our intentions, coupled with the avoidance of all sources of complaint which either invite foreign aggression or stir up restless spirits to domestic revolt." As Mr. Gladstone said in the House of Commons on the 12th June, 1878, "We are too apt to fall back on the abstract and theoretical splendour of the Indian Empire, and we do not sufficiently recollect that the administration of that Empire, in the final judgment of history, will bring no advantage or glory to us, except in the exact and precise proportions that that administration confers benefit upon that Empire, and renders India prosperous and happy." The chances of prosperity and happiness among the natives of India would be greatly lessened by the increased expenditure required for the annexation or occupation of Candahar, and hence for financial no less than military and political reasons this step appears to us undesirable.

As we have seen, intelligent military opinion—Roberts, Stewart, and Hamley, equally with Wolseley, Gordon, Adye, and Norman— is against the much vaunted scientific frontier, now discovered to be no scientific frontier at all, though as regards the retention of Candahar, professional opinion is divided. But both have been abandoned, and with them have disappeared all the results of the extensive operations extending over two years, and involving an expenditure of twenty millions of money and thousands of lives. When our troops are withdrawn from Pisheen,* if that measure is adopted, the sole result for this

---

* If we conformed strictly to our treaty obligations, the occupation of Quetta itself is to be regarded not as a permanent measure, but as one for the protection of the Khan and his subjects with whom we have entered into engagements. This is manifest by the terms of the despatch of Lord

direful waste, beyond the solution of the military problem as to the feasibility of our overrunning Afghanistan at any time we may desire to do so, will be the freeing the Turis of the Kurram valley from the yoke of the Ameer of Afghanistan. From time immemorial this miserable people have been subject to the exactions of the Sirdars and tax gatherers placed over them by the Ameer, and their condition may be aptly described in the words applied by Wordsworth to Roy Roy and the Highland caterans, who lived and moved and had their being in a state of society entirely analogous to that still existent on the north-west frontier of India

> "——the good old rule
> Sufficeth them; the simple plan
> That they should take who have the power,
> And they should keep who can."

The obscure tribe of Turis, of whom the British public never heard, have alone benefited from the vast expenditure of blood and treasure resulting from the invasion of Afghanistan. But this abortive result in no way detracts from the merits of the commander whose reputation was made by the Afghan War, but is due solely to political causes with which he, as a soldier, had no concern.

On the 18th November, accompanied by Major-General Hills, Brigadier-Generals Macpherson and Baker, and Major Pretyman, A.D.C., Sir Frederick Roberts waited on the Duke of Cambridge, who received him with the utmost cordiality; and he was summoned to Windsor, where Her Majesty treated her distinguished subject with special honour. It was generally anticipated that a peerage would have been conferred on the victor of the Peiwar Kotul and Charasia, the commander of the brilliant march from Cabul to Candahar, and of the battle of the 1st September, but the Government were not so liberal as in the days when the capture of Ghuznee was rewarded with

---

Salisbury to the Government of India, dated December 13th, 1877. "The existing force has been placed there for the purpose of preserving the peace of the Khan's dominions, the security of commerce in the Bolan Pass and the plain below it, and the safety of your agent." By Article 3 of the Supplementary Treaty of December 8th, 1876, we bind ourselves to "respect the independence of Khelat;" and Article 6 expressly declares that the location of British troops at Quetta was in response to the expressed desire of the Khan and his Sirdars.

a coronet and a pension of £2,000 a-year. Certainly, if services of doubtful value rendered before Sebastopol were thus acknowledged, or even more recently, when the late Lord Airey, who had never commanded an army in the field, received a coronet for long and faithful service, Sir Frederick Roberts would not have been over-rewarded by the bestowal of a similar honour for the brilliant services he rendered his country at a crisis.

It may be pleaded that this niggardliness in conferring a peerage for military services is according to precedent, and that it has been the practice of all Governments to reserve a seat in the House of Lords, with few exceptions, for their political supporters. But this plea, though according to modern practice, is far from affording a satisfactory reason, and it would be well (as long as decorations and titles have any value in the eyes of the world) if not only the peerage, but the Garter and the other Irish and Scotch National orders of Knighthood, now reserved for great nobles, were conferred, as in the time of their institution, on soldiers who have bled for their country and done good service in maintaining her vast empire.

Sir Frederick Roberts, in common with Sir Donald Stewart, received only a baronetcy, and even the local rank of Lieutenant-General, which he had held in Afghanistan, was not confirmed. He also received a "Distinguished Service pension" of £100, like many of his less-known contemporaries; and Parliament, on the recommendation of the Marquis of Hartington, Secretary of State for India, voted him (and also Sir Donald Stewart) a capital sum of £12,500—which cannot be considered an excessive pecuniary reward for services such as he had rendered to the State.* We are such sticklers for precedent, that it is

---

* This will be allowed on comparing the above grants with the pensions conferred for special military service to other officers of the Royal and Indian Armies since 1835. The following were chargeable on the revenue of India:—Major-General Sir William Nott, G.C.B., £1,000; Field-Marshal Viscount Hardinge, G.C.B., Governor-General of India, £5,000; Field-Marshal Viscount Gough, G.C.B., Commander-in-Chief in India, £2,000; Field-Marshal Sir George Pollock, G.C.B., £1,000; General Sir Archdale Wilson, G.C.B., £1,000; Field-Marshal Lord Clyde, G.C.B., Commander-in-Chief in India, £2,000; Lieutenant-General Sir James Outram, G.C.B., £1,000 (with continuance to his eldest son). The following pensions were paid from the Consolidated Fund or Civil Service Votes:—Lord Seaton, £2,000 (for three lives); Lord Keane, £2,000 (for three lives); Lord Gough, £2,000 (for three lives); Lord Hardinge, £3,000 (for three lives); Lord Raglan,

somewhat strange that the course followed in the analogous instances of Sir Colin Campbell and Sir Hugh Rose (and since in that of Lord Wolseley), who were confirmed in their local rank, was not adopted in the case of Sir Frederick Roberts, and the rank of Lieutenant-General was not made substantive.

But there is a clue to the reasons that guided the "authorities" in making a breach in the continuity of their cherished principle of precedent. Probably the denial of a simple act of justice did not arise from a disinclination on the part of the Horse Guards, who were favourable to the claims of Sir Frederick Roberts, but to the circumstance that their refusal to confer a similar honour upon Sir Garnet Wolseley on his return from South Africa, where he had completed the pacification of Zululand, and subdued the Basuto chief, Secocoeni, precluded them from adequately rewarding a deserving public servant, and following the precedent which confirms in his rank a General who has achieved a striking military success.

Sir Frederick was advanced to the G.C.B.* on the 21st September, and was invested by the Queen with the insignia of the Order at Windsor Castle on the 25th November; and never had a knight of the olden time more worthily earned his spurs. During his career he had been wounded, had gained the V.C., and the Mutiny Medal, with three clasps for Delhi and the Relief and Siege of Lucknow, also the India Medal for Looshai, the North-West Frontier Medal, with clasp for Umbeyla, the Abyssinian Medal, the Afghan War Medal, with four clasps, and the bronze decoration for his famous march. He had been twenty-three times mentioned in despatches before the Afghan War, during which he was eight times thanked by the Viceroy and Commander-in-Chief in India, and also twice received the thanks of Parliament.

£2,000 (for two lives); Sir William F. Williams, £1,000; Sir H. M. Havelock, £1,000; Lord Napier of Magdala, £2,000 (for two lives); Lord Wolseley, a gratuity of £25,000 for the Ashantee campaign, and £30,000 for the Egyptian war. The annuities to Lord Raglan and Sir Henry Havelock were granted in respect of the services of their fathers, who died before the date of the grant.

* Sir Frederick received the C.B. on 6th September, 1872, for his services in the Looshai campaign, and was promoted to K.C.B. on the 19th July, 1879. He was also appointed a Companion of the Indian Empire, a newly-created Order, on the 1st January, 1880.

Sir Frederick Roberts was entertained at a banquet by the United Service Club, at which the Duke of Cambridge presided and the Prince of Wales attended; and other public dinners were given in his honour, including one by the East India United Service Club. After this initiation he fell into the hands of the City Companies and "lion-hunters" of the Metropolis, and like Lord Napier, with whom he had gone through the ordeal on the conclusion of the Abyssinian War, and Sir Garnet Wolseley on his return from Ashantee, was compelled to undergo a severe course of public dinners, with the concomitant speech-making. The "Worshipful" Companies of Grocers, Merchant Taylors, and Fishmongers feasted him, and conferred on him their freedom; and in the following February he was entertained, with many of his principal officers, at a grand banquet by the Corporation of London, who, later, presented him with a sword of honour of the value of 100 guineas.

Sir Frederick Roberts's speech on this occasion was, perhaps, the most remarkable and outspoken oration addressed to any English audience by an officer of the Army. Sir Frederick's oratorical utterances—save to the Chiefs and Maliks of the Kurram Valley and Afghanistan—had been few; but we were informed by a general officer who had attended at many Guildhall dinners, that the speech referred to was delivered without break or hesitation, and with an ease of manner and command of language that astonished his audience. And yet the speaker, like Mark Antony, a plain, blunt man, professed to have neither

"Action, nor utterance, nor the power of speech
To stir men's blood."

Though most military men disapproved of the changes introduced by the new system of Army organization, identified with the names of Lord Cardwell and Mr. Childers, and of which Lord Wolseley and Sir John Adye have been the powerful and consistent supporters in the Service, no officer out of Parliament had hitherto displayed the courage, or possessed sufficient prestige, to lodge a protest, with any chance of its being efficacious, against the proposals of a Minister of War representing an Administration that had just come into power with an enormous Parliamentary majority at its back. The advocates of the new system replied to those who pointed to certain features in which it did not come up to expectation, that the system was still incomplete, and, further, that it did not receive that intelligent and whole-hearted execution which could alone ensure success. Time will show whether this criticism is well founded. The problem to be solved—to maintain, in face of the vast Continental armies, an efficient and adequate force for the defence of the country and her vast colonies, under our voluntary system of enlistment—appears almost to be insoluble without conscription, or a larger expenditure than the representatives of the people will sanction.

Sir Frederick Roberts's speech was mainly an appeal, supported by irrefragable arguments, for a longer period of service with the colours. He also gave vent to a spirited defence of the regimental system of the British army; and strongly deprecated the practice of arbitrarily removing men from regiments to which they had become attached: "Every soldier," he said, "experienced in war will tell you that we should do all in our power to uphold the regimental system, and to foster and encourage that sensitive plant, *esprit de corps*, which, like other sentiments having their roots in our coarse nature, play as large and influential a part in life as the dictates of reason itself." He specially dwelt on the necessity of having old soldiers in the ranks, and adduced his own experience in the Kurram Campaign, when he represented to the Commander-in-Chief that he could not take the field without some seasoned soldiers, as the 2nd Battalion 8th Regiment, his only European corps, contained "a number of untrained boys," and was "not in a fit state for a campaign," having dwindled down at Kurram, only seventy miles from our own territory, "to a weak half battalion." He was reinforced, he said, with a wing of the 72nd Highlanders, which had been eight years in India, and "was composed of seasoned soldiers." At the capture of the Peiwar Kotul, his European Infantry fit for service numbered 366 men of the 8th Regiment, and 330 of the 72nd Highlanders, and he added, that "without the latter I have no hesitation in stating my firm belief the force would have been annihilated," as there was no reserve nearer than Kohat, 150 miles distant, and " on the first check, all the tribes occupying this intervening distance would have risen against us."

But a change took place in the marching powers of the 72nd when they formed part of the column which he took with him in his famous march from Cabul to Candahar. Early in the spring the regiment had received a draft of 170 men, and Sir Frederick said :—" While on the march to Candahar I made it my business to find out every day how many men of each corps had fallen out on the way. This information was necessary to enable me to judge whether the troops were being taxed beyond their powers. I discovered that the 72nd Highlanders had more casualties in proportion to their numbers than either the 60th Rifles or 92nd Highlanders; and, on further inquiry, I ascertained that the majority of cases occurred amongst the men of the last draft—in fact, among the young soldiers. The average service of the 72nd Highlanders on our leaving Cabul was : Serjeants, thirteen and a-half years ; Corporals, twelve and a-half years ; Privates, seven years. And of the 92nd Highlanders : Serjeants, fifteen years ; Corporals, eleven years ; Privates, nine years. I have not the return of the 2nd Battalion of the 60th Rifles, but feel satisfied that the men were not of less service than those of the 72nd Highlanders. Such a return as this it will be quite impossible ever to prepare again if our system of short service is persisted in ; and, my lords and gentlemen, let me add something more, it will be as impossible for a British force ever again to perform such a march as those magnificent troops I had the honour and pride to command made from Cabul to Candahar. No commander would venture to undertake such a service except with soldiers on whose discipline, spirit, and endurance he could thoroughly rely. I never, for a moment, had a doubt as to the result, but then I had tried men, not untried and untrained boys, to depend upon."

Sir Frederick denied that he was opposed to reform ; on the contrary, he said, he was regarded in India by some of the older officers, "as the representative of the Army Reform Party." He expressed a hope that his object in speaking plainly would be appreciated by the nation :—" If I speak somewhat more candidly and decidedly to-night than is perhaps customary on an occasion such as this, it is because I cannot resist giving my country the benefit of the experience I have gained, in return for the high distinctions which have been conferred upon me; and because I hope that what I am now saying may cause those in power to pause before they change altogether a system under which England has become the great and powerful nation that she is at present."

His peroration was not unworthy a more practised orator:— " These are trying times—times in which it behoves every Englishman to think of what is best for the country and the State. We have enemies without and within, and we must not hope to maintain the place we hold in the world, unless we are prepared to maintain it alike by the wisdom of our counsels and by the strength and valour of our arms. At such a time it were little less than treason to know, or to believe, that there was a flaw in our armour, and not to call attention clearly and earnestly to the fact. This must be my apology. I have spoken warmly and strongly, because, had I not seized this great opportunity to do so, I feel that I should have failed in my duty, not only to the noble service to which I have the great privilege to belong, but also to my country and my Queen."

Mr. Childers was patriotic enough to rise to the appeal of the guest of the evening, and, with a frankness that did him infinite credit, admitted that he had "struck the right key-note," and expressed a determination that "his words will be well weighed by all who are responsible for the government of the Army."

In a recent article in the *Nineteenth Century*, Sir Frederick Roberts explained more fully the views on Army Reform he propounded at the Mansion House on the 14th July, 1881, and justly laid claim to the merit of having, by his strictures, caused certain important changes in the scheme of Army organization as it then existed; but with the candour and moderation that distinguishes him, he recognized the good work that has been done by Army reformers, among whom he classes himself. And, indeed, he has no slight claim to this distinction, for as he says:—" In India I am considered a reformer of a very advanced type. Many of the older officers, both civil and military, look upon me as something like a revolutionist for persistingly advocating changes which I believe to be essential to the well-being of the Indian Army, but which they regard as unnecessary, if not dangerous."

While accepting the new Short Service System as irreversible —for though initiated by Lord Cardwell, it had been cordially adopted by a Conservative War Minister, Colonel Stanley, of whom Lord Wolseley has said, that of all the Secretaries for War under whom he had served, not excluding Lord Cardwell and Mr. Childers, he considered Colonel Stanley the most ardent reformer—Sir Frederick Roberts took exception to what he considered, in common with most military men, five important blots in the original Short Service System, and changes were instituted tending to remedy these defects.* He gave expres-

---

* The defects pointed out by Sir Frederick Roberts were: "(1.) That men intended for service abroad did not remain for a sufficiently long period with the colours. (2.) That non-commissioned officers were discharged just at the time they were becoming most useful; and that the best men for this rank were disinclined to enlist, from the fact that little or no prospect of serving on for a pension was held out to them. (3.) That absolute boys were often accepted by the recruiting authorities, and sent abroad before their constitutions were matured. (4.) That battalions, when ordered on service or to India, were hastily made up by drafts of the youngest soldiers from other regiments, with which they had no local ties or connections. (5.) That the Army was being sacrificed to obtain a Reserve, which was one only in name." With regard to the first and second points, whereas, previous to July, 1881, enlistment in the Infantry was for six years' Army service and six years' Reserve service, with the option of joining the Reserve, under certain conditions, after three years' Army service—after that date it was changed to seven years' Army and five years' Reserve service, to be converted into eight and four years' service respectively, if the period of Army service expired whilst the soldier was abroad. Further, in the event of war, provision is made to extend the Army service for one year, or to nine years, thus reducing Reserve service to three years. So with non-commissioned officers. Before July, 1881, they could, under certain conditions, and if specially recommended, receive *permission* to extend their Army service to twelve years, and subsequently to re-engage up to twenty-one years. Since that date all non-commissioned officers of the rank of corporal and upwards have the *right* to extend their Army service to twelve years; while sergeants have the right, subject only to the veto of the Secretary of State, to re-engage up to twenty-one years. As to Sir Frederick Roberts's third point, it will suffice to say that, since July, 1881, the minimum age for enlistment has been extended from eighteen to nineteen years. With regard to his fourth point, it has lately been ruled that men are not eligible for embarkation to India with less than one year's service, unless over twenty years of age. On all these points, then, Sir Frederick Roberts certainly scored a success.

sion to an opinion, which is generally shared by military men, that "the Army was being sacrificed to secure a Reserve."

On the question of young *versus* old soldiers, so much and hotly debated, Sir Frederick Roberts, who is an advocate for the veteran, invokes in his article the high authority of the Duke of Wellington, and also that of Von Moltke, who thinks from twenty-one to twenty-seven years of age the best age. Lord Wolseley, on the other hand, is the consistent and powerful advocate, not only for young soldiers, but for young officers and young non-commissioned officers. As he said, in an article in the same magazine, in March, 1881 :—"I believe it is as essential to have young sergeants as it is to have young officers." But youth and age are comparatively relative terms, and his lordship would probably not object to the limits of the famous German strategist, though Sir Frederick Roberts defines the term old soldier as a man of between five and twelve years' service. With comparatively young soldiers Lord Wolseley stormed Secocoeni's stronghold and the lines of Tel-el-Kebir, and thus has sincere grounds for the faith that is in him. Again, with old soldiers Sir George Colley failed to hold his own on the Majuba Hill. Statistics prove that the average service of the men who overthrew Arabi's army, entrenched behind formidable earthworks, was five years; and that of the soldiers who fled panic-stricken before the attack of the Boers was seven years, the average age being twenty-seven; and among the battalions was a portion of the famous 92nd Highlanders, who formed the *élite* of the army that marched and fought under Sir Frederick Roberts in Afghanistan. The argument as to age, *within certain limits*, affecting efficiency, therefore fails to prove much, as good leading outweighs everything. Most officers will, however, endorse Sir Frederick Roberts's description of the characteristics of the old and young soldier, the man under and over five years' service, in the following powerful passage :—" The characteristics of young soldiers are to play a winning game ; to attack with dash where success seems probable ; or even to stand up to superior forces when courage has not been damped by previous reverses, and faith in their leader remains unimpaired. Under such conditions they may even surpass their older comrades. But in times of danger and panic, when the bugle sounds the retire, when everything seems to be going against us, and when total rout can only be avoided by order and presence of mind, then it is that the old soldier element becomes of incalculable value. Without it a commander would indeed be badly off."*

In conversation with us on our military system, Sir Frederick Roberts expressed his opinion that the active Army is practically sacrificed to the Reserve, which, as now constituted, is too small to be of any great value; and he would prefer regarding the Militia and Volunteers forming the auxiliary forces as the Reserve, which would then be a tangible and numerically powerful second line. Something like this will, in his opinion, be the end of the changes through which our military forces are passing. We now, he says, adopt portions of the Prussian system, such as short service and territoriality—both desirable features in a military system founded on conscription or universal service, but of doubtful benefit in a small army raised by voluntary enlistment, and subject to service in India and the Colonies. As, therefore, we cannot adopt the Prussian system, we might at

---

* Since the above was written, Sir Frederick Roberts's warnings as to the present system resulting in the sacrifice of the army to the formation of a reserve, would appear to have received confirmation by the alarming extent to which recruiting has fallen off. It was admitted by Lord Hartington, Secretary of State for War, in his speech in the House of Commons on the 1st June, and by Lord Morley, in the Upper House, that on the preceding 1st May, the deficiency on the English establishment was 8,554 men, and on the Indian establishment 321, while on that date no less than 4,971 soldiers were on their way from India to claim their discharge. The Army Reserve at that date stood at 28,700 men, and the Militia Reserve at 25,000, being 5,000 below the establishment. This deficiency was, in part, artificial, as the army was increased by 3,700 men, and it was also due to the fact, that in 1882, an abnormally large number of men, enlisted for twelve and six years, in 1870 and 1876 respectively, were discharged. The following are the changes proposed to remedy this state of affairs. Those soldiers in the ranks who are eligible to pass into the Reserve will be offered a bounty as an inducement to serve on till they have completed in effect five years' more service, or twelve years in all. They will then have the option of re-engaging so as to complete twenty-one years' service, on the recommendation of their commanding officers. Men belonging to regiments in India are to be offered a bounty of £2 for the purpose of extending their service in that country. These regulations, together with the reduction of height and chest measurement, and the practical lowering of the minimum age to eighteen years, will no doubt increase the flow of recruits, but the Reserve must suffer proportionately as men re-engage for a pension. "The length of time," said Lord Hartington, "during which these measures will continue, will depend upon the state of recruiting and upon the number of men who appear inclined to avail themselves of our proposals."

any rate copy its perfection of organization, which constitutes it simply the most finished and easily-worked fighting machine the world has known.

It seemed at one time as though Sir Frederick Roberts would have a new field for the exercise of his military talents, when telegraphic intelligence was received of the defeat at Majuba Hill and death of Sir George Colley on the 27th February. On the following day he was called upon by the Government, with the unanimous approval of the nation, to forego the remainder of his sick leave and sail for the Transvaal, in order to assume command of the troops, some 10,000 men, assembled at Newcastle under the command of Sir Evelyn Wood. Though little glory could be reaped from a victory over the Boers, and the task of coercing a small nationality who had been clearly wronged by the policy pursued towards them, was not a congenial one to an officer of his sense of justice and humanity, yet at the call of duty Sir Frederick Roberts cheerfully waived his own predilections, and, accepting the command at such short notice, sailed from England on the 6th March in the *Balmoral Castle*, accompanied by Major-General Newdigate and some Staff officers.

Two days before quitting this country he repaired to Eton, where his old school presented him with a sword—bringing to the memory that saying of Wellington, that "Waterloo was won on the playing-fields of Eton"—and thence proceeded to Windsor Castle, where he had an audience of the Queen. On the 23rd March peace was concluded with the Boers,* and Mr. Childers telegraphed to Sir Frederick Roberts to proceed no further than Cape Town. Accordingly he left South Africa the day following his arrival, and on the 19th April—the same day that Lord Beaconsfield died—arrived in England, *re infecta*, it is true, but having proved that his services were at the disposal of his country for any task, without regard to personal convenience or his state of health.

Sir Frederick Roberts was present at the Review held by the Queen at Windsor Great Park, when 52,000 Volunteers marched

---

* The convention between the British and Boer Commissioners was not signed until the 3rd August, and it was not until the 25th October that it received the ratification of the Volksraad.

past the Sovereign, in the presence of the Royal Family and the Crown Prince of Germany. He also attended, as a private spectator, for such are "the rules of the Service," at the Review of Scottish Volunteers held at Edinburgh on the 25th August, when over 40,000 men marched past the Queen, so that he had the advantage of seeing over 90,000 of our citizen soldiers under arms.

Among honours paid to Sir Frederick Roberts by his countrymen should be mentioned the degrees of D.C.L., conferred at Oxford, and of LL.D. at Dublin. He was also feasted by the citizens of the Irish capital, of Liverpool, and Bristol, where a service of plate was presented to him by his numerous friends, who remembered him when residing there as a boy with his father.

Sir Frederick Roberts was despatched by the War Office to attend the autumn manœuvres of the German Army in 1881, and brought away with him the pleasantest reminiscences of his visit to Germany as military representative of his country at the manœuvres of the Hanover and Schleswig-Holstein Army Corps, held for the fortnight between the 5th and 17th of August. In the preceding year Sir Garnet Wolseley had been despatched by the War Office to the head-quarters of the German Emperor, who, as well as his Army, appreciated the compliment paid by this country in accrediting her most eminent generals to this mimic "sport of Kings."

The Emperor William received Sir Frederick Roberts with the utmost cordiality, and congratulated him on his successful campaigns in Afghanistan, the fortunes of which, he assured him, the German Army had followed with great interest. Again, when taking leave of his English guest, the fine old monarch, who so worthily represents the armed might of Germany, said that, perhaps, after the exciting scenes of real war in which he had been the central figure, the manœuvres he had witnessed might appear tame, but he trusted they had interested him. Von Moltke, the organizer of victory, also expressed himself to Sir Frederick Roberts in complimentary terms as to the military qualities he had displayed in his conduct of the Afghan campaigns; and praise from that great soldier must have sounded sweet even in the ears of one who, like our hero, has been satiated with compliments from people of every degree, and with very varying qualifications to appreciate his achievements. Of the German generals, who received him with consideration and treated him with the utmost hospitality, Sir Frederick Roberts was very favourably impressed, especially with Count Von Waldersee, Chief of the Staff to the 10th, or Hanoverian, Army Corps, who has been recently promoted to the office of Quartermaster-General at Army Head-quarters, an appointment held in abeyance since the Franco-German War of 1870. Count Waldersee is now the assistant, or *adlatus*, of Count Von Moltke, and is designated as the successor of that great soldier.

But it was the German Army as a military machine, that filled Sir Frederick Roberts with wonder. To such perfection has its organization been brought, that in one night any Army Corps can be mobilized. He was told that in the bureau of the General Staff, letters were ready stamped and addressed to every department and commanding officer of the several Army Corps, only requiring the date to be filled in for despatch in ten minutes. He was assured that all the horses belonging to private people throughout the country were marked off for the regiments and batteries to which they would be attached in war time, and also the hour and the train by which each horse would be despatched to its destination. The whole country was organized for war, and every individual capable of bearing arms knew where to go and what to do in the event of a call being made for his services. All the railway officials, telegraphists, and other public bodies—in England consisting of civilians—in Germany are soldiers, and the heads of these departments are general officers, who organize them chiefly to meet the exigencies of war. Even the private servants of the Emperor are old soldiers, always in uniform, with their breasts covered with medals; and while the talk everywhere is military, every one appeared as though on the alert for immediate service. Of course such a state of affairs, though desirable from a military point of view, and perhaps necessary to a country placed like Germany between three powerful military monarchies, any two or all of which might coalesce against her, is utterly destructive of national progress, the accumulation of wealth (a doubtful advantage), or the enjoyment of freedom as we understand it in this happy island; and few who have witnessed the condition of feverish expectation characterising the country, now transformed into a vast camp, would change for it our freedom from anxiety, coupled though it be with a military system which, in comparison with that in force on the Spree, may be considered a happy-go-lucky one.

Sir Frederick Roberts was much surprised at the favourable condition of the German officer, which he was always led to believe was far from being an enviable one. On the contrary, he found the German officer better dressed and horsed than his British brother-in-arms, and though their private incomes are small—every officer is expected to possess between £25 and £180 a-year—and the pay not handsome; yet there are many attendant advantages; and, above all, the officers are attached to regiments which are never moved out of the province in which the *corps d'armée* is raised. The State allows each officer of Cavalry and Artillery one horse, which, at the end of five years, becomes his own property, and the Cavalry spend much money in mounting themselves. Sir Frederick Roberts declares he never saw officers, both Regimental and Staff, so well mounted as in the German Army.

The German officer personally knows every man under his command, and having drilled them, has the assurance that when the country requires their services after they have returned to Civil life, they will come back to him. Not only do the officers drill their men, but they teach them riding and shooting; for the riding master and instructor of musketry are unknown in the German Army. Every Captain is responsible to the Colonel that every man in his company is efficient by a certain date, the subalterns being responsible again to their immediate superior. This system, which is practically in force in the Indian Army, Sir Frederick Roberts thinks should partially be adopted in the British Army, and he would make the officers responsible for the fitness of their men. Our officers would doubtless hail this change if the men they have trained could remain under their command. By the present system officers train men who are drafted off to other corps or the "linked battalion," when the pressure to fill gaps in regiments on active service arises ; and General Roberts, in speaking of this reform, referred to the expressions of disappointment with which some officers of his acquaintance spoke of their unending and resultless labours, reminding one of the classic legend of Sisyphus and his stone.

During his residence in England the late commander of the Army operating in Afghanistan has been inundated with letters from soldiers who have served under him, stating their hard case, and asking for his advice or assistance with the War Office. In this country the claims of old soldiers are almost totally ignored ; but in Germany long and honourable service is the stepping-stone to remunerative employment, and to " have done the State some service " is rightly regarded as a claim for provision in old age. When we consider the cruel neglect meted out to the wives and families of our soldiers who have died on active service, or succumbed to disease in the unhealthy climates to which they are exposed, one may hope that short service will have the redeeming feature of limiting military marriages, which in too many instances have brought untold misery on innocent women and children ; and this absence of domestic ties, if one may believe Lord Byron, has a further incidental advantage, if it is true that :—

> "Nought so bothers
> The hearts of the heroic in a charge
> As leaving a small family at large."

Sir Frederick Roberts was offered, and accepted, the Command-in-Chief of the Madras Army, with the local rank of Lieutenant-General, and, on the 26th October, in company with Lady Roberts, left London for India, on his way visiting Paris and Venice. Already his energetic spirit has shown itself in the institution of much-needed reforms, including the formation of three camps of exercise in one cold season, an innovation in the history of the old " coast army."

There is complete unanimity among military men as to the deserts of General Roberts. Though his latest achievements astonished the world by their brilliance, his career was not of that meteoric character which owes its celebrity to some exceptional combination of good fortune with a spasmodic display of military talent. Those who knew him best and had watched his career through the long years of uphill work, from the lowest rung of the ladder of the Quartermaster-General's Department to the head of the office, predicted great things of him, should he ever be placed in a position of responsibility. To them his success was no surprise. But it was otherwise to the world, which, it is said, "knows not its greatest men." When the Kurram campaign brought to the front the young General, exceptionally fortunate in attaining rank and a command at the age of forty-six—an unusual circumstance in our seniority-ridden service, though Wellington and Napoleon fought their last field at that age, and Nelson closed his wonderful career at forty-seven—much interest was excited in General Roberts, and the bald enumeration of his services showed that Lord Lytton had exercised sound discrimination in his choice. We have within recent years seen the phenomenon in our military history of a youthful General repeated in the case of Lord Wolseley, who, even more fortunate, was a Major-General commanding an army in the field at the age of forty, and achieved his last and most striking success in Egypt at the age of forty-nine, Roberts's age at the battle of Candahar.

The career of these two distinguished soldiers have other singular points of resemblance. Both were Irishmen, and passed the greater portion of their service in the Quartermaster-General's Department of the Staff. Both, moreover, served as Assistant-Quartermaster-General during the Mutiny on Sir Hope Grant's Staff, one succeeding the other, and on one occasion they were brought into connection with one another. There are also many points of resemblance in the attainments and military method of these successful soldiers, whose names have been so much in the mouths of their countrymen during recent events, and whose services and relative merits have been contrasted with more freedom than good manners. Small and spare of body, they are remarkable for their skill in horsemanship and powers of enduring fatigue. Both are gifted with the bright geniality of expression, soldierly frankness, and that charm of manner which conciliates all with whom they come into contact; and equally they possess the confidence of all ranks and the affection of their immediate subordinates. Again, alike they have that exhaustless energy, that ardent love of their profession, that boundless resource in difficulty, and that indomitable spirit which rises in the hour of danger, and instils a like lofty spirit in all around. One advantage Wolseley has had over Roberts, the want of which still further increases the claims of the latter to our admiration. The victor of Arabi Pasha possesses an iron constitution, which has been denied to the conqueror of Ayoob Khan, who has found in Indian fever the hardest enemy he has had to battle against—an enemy to combat whom has only brought into greater relief the heroism of the man, whose military genius, as at Candahar, shone with a brighter light amid the deadening vapours of earth.

To the annals of our Indian Empire the subject of this Memoir has added achievements which will form one of its brightest pages. In the history of Afghanistan—that highway by which the conquering races in Central Asia have descended upon the fertile plains and rich cities of India, and which has formed the battle-ground of some of the mightiest conquerors of antiquity, through which Semiramis and Alexander marched on their way to Hindostan, the former to be vanquished and the latter to triumph, which was traversed by Genghiz Khan, Tamerlane, and Nadir, and ruled by Mahmoud and Ahmed Shah—in that historic country, with its memories lost in the haze of antiquity, the name of Sir Frederick Roberts will be remembered as one who, at Peiwar Kotul, Charasia, and Candahar, achieved some of the most striking successes recorded in history. But there is no memorial of his victories, either political, owing to our abandonment of the country, or material, such as a fortress or monument; and indeed, there is none of any of the conquerors of this "land of stones and men," as Dost Mahomed bitterly called it when surveying the palaces of Calcutta, for they passed through it as a ship passes through the sea, leaving no trace in its wake. The only exception is Alexander, the Sekunder of the East, whose name and fame have survived more than 2,000 years, unlike the Assyrian monarchy of Nimrod and Semiramis, with its—

"thirteen hundred years
Of empire ending like a shepherd's tale."

Not only in India, on the banks of the Sutlej and at Mooltan,

Conclusion.

but in Afghanistan, at Bamian and near Candahar, are memorials of the "Macedonian madman," of whom it may be said, in the words put by Byron, in his play of "Sardanapalus," into the mouth of the effeminate grandson of the great Assyrian Queen, when speaking of Bacchus, the legendary Conqueror of India:—

> "Of all his conquests a few columns
> Which may be his, and might be mine, if I
> Thought them worth purchase and conveyance, are
> The landmarks of the seas of gore he shed,
> The realms he wasted, and the hearts he broke."

Unlike these great soldiers and sovereigns, who were animated solely by ambition and the greed of power, Roberts invaded Afghanistan at the bidding of his Government, who deemed that the security of the vast dependency committed to their charge was menaced by the military preparations of the Afghan Ameer, whose claim of neutrality, as between the gigantic neighbours on his northern and southern boundaries, was belied by the welcome he accorded to the Ambassador of the Czar, and his refusal to receive the Envoy of the Empress of India. Whether our Government was justified in drawing the sword or wise in precipitating the quarrel, is a question for politicians, with which Sir Frederick Roberts, as a soldier, had no concern. Much bloodshed and suffering ensued, and many homes in Afghanistan and England were made desolate, yet for these inevitable results of war our hero was not responsible. He was guiltless of shedding "seas of gore" or of "wasting realms;" but, on the contrary, strove to soften the asperities incidental to the conduct of warlike operations. He spared the vanquished when often he lay at his mercy, and, when enforcing the behests of a code which demands blood for blood, tempered the claims of justice with clemency.

THE END.

www.ingramcontent.com/pod-product-compliance
Lightning Source LLC
Chambersburg PA
CBHW031130160426
43193CB00008B/93